D1507827

Principles of
Database
Systems

COMPUTER SOFTWARE ENGINEERING SERIES

ELLIS HOROWITZ, Editor
University of Southern California

CALINGAERT
Assemblers, Compilers, and Program Translation

CARBERRY, KHALIL, LEATHRUM, and LEVY
Foundations of Computer Science

EVEN
Graph Algorithms

FINDLAY and WATT
PASCAL: An Introduction to Methodical Programming

HOROWITZ and SAHNI
Fundamentals of Computer Algorithms

HOROWITZ and SAHNI
Fundamentals of Data Structures

ULLMAN
Principles of Database Systems

Principles of
Database Systems

Jeffrey D. Ullman
Stanford University

COMPUTER SCIENCE PRESS

Computer Science Press, Inc.
9125 Fall River Lane
Potomac, Maryland 20854

1   2   3   4   5   6   85   84   83   82   81   80

Library of Congress Cataloging in Publication Data

Ullman, Jeffrey D   1942-
   Principles of database systems.

   Bibliography: p.
   Includes index.
   1.   Data base management.   I.   Title.
QA76.9.D3U44   001.6′4   79-20071
US ISBN 0-914894-13-7
UK ISBN 0-273-08476-3

Preface

It is evident that a course in database systems now plays a central role in the undergraduate and graduate programs in computer science. However, unlike the more traditional and better established systems areas, like compilers and operating systems, where a good mix of principles and practice was established many years ago, the subject matter in database systems has been largely descriptive.

This book is developed from notes I used in a course at Princeton that attempted to bring database systems into the mainstream of computer science. The course was taught to a mix of seniors and first-year graduate students. In it, I tried to relate database ideas to concepts from other areas, such as programming languages, algorithms, and data structures. A substantial amount of descriptive material was included, since students, being used to conventional programming languages, may find query languages rather unusual. The data structures relevant to databases are also somewhat different from the kinds of structures used in conventional programming, since the large scale of a database makes practical many structures that would be only of theoretical interest otherwise.

However, I added to the mix of topics the relevant theory that is now available. The principal concepts that have been found useful are concerned with relations and with concurrency. I have devoted a large portion of the book to a description of relations, their algebra and calculus, and to the query languages that have been designed using these concepts. Also included is an explanation of how the theory of relational databases can be used to design good systems, and a description of the optimization of queries in relation-based query languages. A chapter is also devoted to the recently developed protocols for guaranteeing consistency in databases that are operated on by many processes concurrently.

Exercises

Each chapter includes exercises to test basic concepts and, in some cases, to extend the ideas of the chapter. The most difficult exercises are marked with a double star, while problems of intermediate difficulty have a single star.

Acknowledgments

I am grateful for the comments and suggestions I received from Al Aho, Brenda Baker, Peter deJong, Ron Fagin, Vassos Hadzilacos, Zvi Kedem, Hank Korth, and Joseph Spinden. The initial draft of this manuscript was ably typed by Gerree Pecht. Her efforts and the support facilities at Princeton University are appreciated.

J. D. U.

Table of Contents

Chapter 1: An Overview of a Database System 1
   1.1: A database System 1
   1.2: Levels of Abstraction in a DBMS 2
   1.3: Differing Perceptions of the Database 6
   1.4: A Model of the Real World 10
      Exercises 17
      Bibliographic Notes 18

Chapter 2: Physical Data Organization 20
   2.1: A Model for External Storage Organization 20
   2.2: Hashed Files 24
   2.3: Indexed Files 30
   2.4: B-trees 42
   2.5: Files with a Dense Index 49
   2.6: Files with Variable Length records 52
   2.7: Data Structures for Lookup on Nonkey Fields 58
   2.8: Partial Match Retrieval 60
      Exercises 69
      Bibliographic Notes 71

Chapter 3: The Three Great Data Models 73
   3.1: The Relational Data Model 73
   3.2: The Network Data Model 83
   3.3: The Hierarchical Data Model 91
   3.4: Comparison of the Models 98
      Exercises 100
      Bibliographic Notes 103

Chapter 4: Data Manipulation Languages for the Relational Model 104
   4.1: Relational Algebra 105
   4.2: Relational Calculus 110
   4.3: General Comments Regarding Query Languages 122
   4.4: ISBL: A "Pure" Relational Algebra Language 125
   4.5: SQUARE and SEQUEL: Evolutionary Steps Between
      Algebraic and Calculus Languages 131

4.6: QUEL: A Tuple Relational Calculus Language 141
4.7: Query-by-Example: A Domain Calculus Language 149
  Exercises 162
  Bibliographic Notes 164

Chapter 5: Design Theory for Relational Databases 166
5.1: What Constitutes a Bad Database Design? 166
5.2: Functional Dependencies 167
5.3: Decomposition of Relation Schemes 180
5.4: Normal Forms for Relation Schemes 187
5.5: Multivalued Dependencies 196
5.6: Fourth Normal Form 203
  Exercises 206
  Bibliographic Notes 208

Chapter 6: Query Optimization 211
6.1: General remarks About Optimization 211
6.2: Algebraic Manipulation 214
6.3: The QUEL Decomposition Algorithm 223
6.4: Exact Optimization for a Subset of Relational Queries 232
  Exercises 239
  Bibliographic Notes 240

Chapter 7: The DBTG Proposal 241
7.1: Basic DBTG Concepts 241
7.2: The Program Environment 248
7.3: Navigation Within the Database 250
7.4: Other Database Commands 258
7.5: Some Other Features of the DBTG Proposal 264
  Exercises 269
  Bibliographic Notes 270

Chapter 8: IMS: A Hierarchical System 271
8.1: An Overview of IMS 271
8.2: The IMS Data Manipulation Language 277
8.3: Logical Databases 285
8.4: Storage Organizations 292
  Exercises 301
  Bibliographic Notes 304

Chapter 9: Protecting the Database Against Misuse 305
   9.1: Integrity 306
   9.2: Integrity Constraints in Query-by-Example 307
   9.3: Security 310
   9.4: Security in Query-by-Example 312
   9.5: Security in Statistical Databases 314
      Exercises 320
      Bibliographic Notes 322

Chapter 10: Concurrent Operations on the Database 324
   10.1: Basic Concepts 325
   10.2: A Simple Transacton Model 331
   10.3: A Model with Read- and Write-Locks 337
   10.4: A Read-Only, Write-Only Model 340
   10.5: Concurrency for Hierarchically Structured Items 347
   10.6: Protecting Against Crashes 351
      Exercises 356
      Bibliographic Notes 358

Bibliography 360

Index 372

1

An Overview of a Database System

In this chapter we consider the different levels of abstraction present in a typical database management system and look at the principal functions of such a system. We then discuss a "real world" model against which to measure the capability of database systems to represent and manipulate real data. This model, called the "entity-relationship" model, is discussed in Section 1.4.

1.1 A Database System

Let us consider an enterprise, such as an airline, that has a large amount of data kept for long periods of time in a computer. This data might include infomation about passengers, flights, aircraft, and personnel, for example. Typical relationships that might be represented include bookings (which passengers have seats on which flights?) flight crews (who is to be the pilot, copilot, etc., on which flights?), and service records (when and by whom was each aircraft last serviced?).

Data, such as the above, that is stored more-or-less permanently in a computer we term a *database*. The software that allows one or many persons to use and/or modify this data is a *database management system* (DBMS). A major role of the DBMS is to allow the user to deal with the data in abstract terms, rather than as the computer stores the data. In this sense, the DBMS acts as an interpreter for a (very) high-level language such as APL, ideally allowing the user to specify what must be done, with little or no attention on the user's part to the detailed algorithms or data representation used by the system. However, in the case of a DBMS, there may be even less relationship between the data as seen by the user and as stored in the computer, than between APL arrays and the representation of these arrays in memory.

There are many other functions that can and should be carried out by the DBMS, including the following.

1. *Security.* Not every user should have access to all the data. For example, if personnel records are kept, only key personnel with the right and need to know salaries should be able to access this data. We shall discuss this aspect of a DBMS in Chapter 9.

2. *Integrity.* Certain kinds of *consistency constraints,* (i.e., required properties of the data) can be checked by the DBMS, if it is told to do so. Easiest to check are properties of values, such as the requirement that the number of passengers booked on a flight does not exceed the capacity of the aircraft. Somewhat harder to check are requirements involving equalities and inequalities of values, without reference to the values themselves (e.g., two aircraft may not be assigned to the same flight). Chapter 5 covers some aspects of structural integrity; Chapter 9 discusses integrity in general.

3. *Synchronization.* Often many users are running programs that access the database at the same time. The DBMS should provide protection against inconsistencies that result from two approximately simultaneous operations on a data item. For example, suppose that at about the same time, two reservation clerks issue requests to reserve a seat on flight 999. Each request results in the execution of a program that might examine the number of seats available (say one seat is left), subtracts one, and stores the resulting number of seats in the database. If the DBMS does not sequence these two transactions (the two invocations of the reservation program) properly, two passengers might wind up sitting in the same seat. We shall investigate measures for assuring proper synchronization in Chapter 10.

4. *Crash protection and recovery.* There should be facilities to make regular backup copies of the database and to reconstruct the database after a hardware or software error. This subject is also considered in Chapter 10.

1.2 Levels of Abstraction in a DBMS

It should be obvious that between the computer, dealing with bits, and the ultimate user dealing with abstractions such as flights or assignment of personnel to aircraft, there will be many levels of abstraction. A fairly standard viewpoint regarding levels of abstraction is shown in Fig. 1.1. There we see a single database, which may be one of many databases using the same DBMS software, at three different levels of abstraction. It should be emphasized that only the physical database actually exists. We prefer to think of the physical database not at the level of bits, but at a somewhat higher level, as a collection of files and perhaps simple data structures.

The conceptual database is an abstract representation of the physical database (or, equivalently, we may say the physical database is an implementation of the conceptual database), and the views are each abstractions

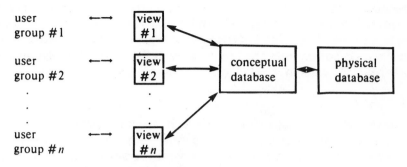

Fig. 1.1. Levels of abstraction in a database system.

of portions of the conceptual database. The difference in the level of abstraction between views and the conceptual database is generally not great. Both deal with abstractions such as "passenger" and abstract relationships such as "booked on."

Schemes and Instances

In addition to the gradations in levels of abstraction implied by Fig. 1.1, there is another, orthogonal dimension to our perception of databases. When the database is designed, we are interested in plans for the database. When it is used, we are concerned with the actual data present in the database. The current contents of a database we term an *instance of the database.* Note that the data in a database changes frequently, while the plans remain the same over long periods of time (although not necessarily forever).

Plans consist of an enumeration of the types of entities that the database deals with, the relationships among these types of entities, and the ways in which the entities and relationships at one level of abstraction are expressed at the next lower (more concrete) level. The term *scheme* is used to refer to plans, so we talk of a *conceptual scheme* as the plan for the conceptual database, and we call the physical database plan a *physical scheme.* The plan for a view is often referred to simply as a *subscheme.*

Example 1.1: To illustrate the difference between schemes and instances, suppose we have a database of flowers. The conceptual scheme could include the entity types FLOWER and HABITAT, as well as other types of entities, and it might include the relationship GROWS_IN between FLOWER and HABITAT, along with other relationships. The conceptual database might include the entities **rose** and **tulip** of the type FLOWER, with the information that **tulip** GROWS_IN **Holland**, while **rose** GROWS_IN **Texas** and **rose** GROWS_IN **Tralee**, the entities **Holland**, **Texas**, and **Tralee** being instances of HABITAT.

Turning to the next lower level, the scheme for the physical database might declare that entities of type FLOWER and HABITAT are each character strings of length 10, and GROWS_IN is represented by linked lists of habitats for each flower, with the header of each list obtained by applying a particular hashing function to the name of a flower. □

The Physical Database

At the lowest level of abstraction with which we deal, there is a physical database. The physical database resides permanently on secondary storage devices, such as disks and tapes. We may view the physical database itself at several levels of abstraction, ranging from that of records and files in a programming language such as PL/I, perhaps through the level of logical records, as supported by the operating system underlying the DBMS, down to the level of bits and physical addresses on storage devices. Chapter 2 will discuss the principal data structures used to implement a physical database, while Chapters 4, 7, and 8 point out the salient implementation features of some important existing database systems.

The Conceptual Scheme and its Data Model

As we have said, the conceptual scheme is an abstraction of the real world pertinent to an enterprise. It is roughly at the level of passengers, flights, and so on, which we have discussed in connection with the enterprise of an airline. A DBMS provides a *data definition language* to specify the conceptual scheme and. most likely, some of the details regarding the implementation of the conceptual scheme by the physical scheme. The data definition language is a high-level language, enabling one to describe the conceptual scheme in terms of a "data model." An example of a suitable data model is the directed graph (the *network model* in the jargon), where nodes represent sets of similar entities (e.g., all passengers, or all flights) and arcs represent associations (e.g., the assignment of aircraft to flights).

The choice of a data model is a difficult one, since it must be rich enough in structure to describe significant aspects of the real world, yet it must be possible to determine fairly automatically an efficient implementation of the conceptual scheme by a physical scheme. It should be emphasized that while a DBMS might be used to build small databases, many databases involve millions of bytes, and an inefficient implementation can be disastrous. If we have no clue where a particular piece of information is to be found in the physical database, it could take hours to search the entire database to find it.

There are at least three major data models that have been used in database systems.

1.   *Hierarchical.* This data model is a tree, where nodes might represent entity sets, such as flights, and the children of a node are associated with their parent in some particular relationship. For example, all passengers booked on a flight could be children of the node for that flight.

2.   *Network.* This is the directed graph model mentioned above.

3.   *Relational.* This model is based on the set theoretic notion of a *relation,* that is, a set of k-tuples for some fixed k. For example, bookings could be represented by a set BOOKINGS of triples

   FLIGHT_NO DATE PASSENGER

so BOOKINGS = $\{(n, d, p) \mid$ passenger p has a reservation on flight n on date $d\}$.

   The three data models will be introduced in Chapter 3, and the theory and techniques surrounding each will be discussed in turn. Chapters 4-6 discuss the relational model. Chapter 7 covers the DBTG proposal, a significant influence regarding the network model, and Chapter 8 covers IMS, a major system using the hierarchical model. In Section 1.4 we discuss a slightly more general model, called the entity-relationship model, that in a sense generalizes the other three mentioned.

Views

A *view* or *subscheme* is an abstract model of a portion of the conceptual database or conceptual scheme. For example, an airline may provide a computerized reservation service, consisting of data and a collection of programs that deal with flights and passengers. These programs, and the people who use tham, do not need to know about personnel files or the assignment of pilots to flights. The dispatcher may need to know about flights, aircraft, and aspects of the personnel files (e.g., which pilots are qualified to fly a 747), but does not need to know about personnel salaries or the passengers booked on a flight.

   In a sense, a view is just a small conceptual database, and it is at the same level of abstraction as the conceptual database. However, there are senses in which a view can be "more abstract" than a conceptual database, as the data dealt with by a view may be constructable from the conceptual database but not actually present in that database.

   For a canonical example, the personnel department may have a view that includes each employee's age. However, it is unlikely that ages would be found in the conceptual database, as ages would have to be changed each day for some of the employees. Rather, it is more likely that the conceptual database would include the employee's date of birth. When a user program, which believed it was dealing with a view that held age information, requested from the database a value for an employee's age, the DBMS would translate this request into "date of birth minus current date," which makes sense to the conceptual database, and the calculation would be performed on the corresponding data taken from the physical database.

A second, more important way in which views are abstractions of a conceptual database is that the associations may be different in a subscheme and its underlying conceptual scheme. For example, in the conceptual database, flights may be sets of passengers, while in the view for reservations, a passenger may be a set of flights he is booked on. This distinction may or may not be significant, depending on the data model used to define the conceptual database and view. In fact, the view need not be defined using the same data model as the conceptual database, although most database systems that support both views and conceptual schemes use the same data model for both.

1.3 Differing Perceptions of the Database

To design, implement, and use a large database requires the effort of many people. Regarding our example of an airline database again, the end user of the database is generally a nonprogrammer, such as a reservations clerk. The clerk might sit at a terminal and type a simple command, such as BOOK. This command invokes a program that might, for example, initiate a dialogue with the clerk, asking him for information in a fixed order, e.g. "enter name of passenger" and "enter desired flight number." Obtaining the requisite information, the program interrogates the database to determine if space is available and if so, modifies the database to reflect the reservation of a seat. If not available, it so informs the clerk.

That operation looks simple; but how did the program get written in such a way that it could communicate with the database? After all, Fig. 1.1 implies that users communicate only with views, which are two levels removed from the physical database. The answer lies in the existence of several specialized languages used for defining databases on the abstract levels and for manipulating the database.

Designing the Conceptual Scheme

As we have mentioned, the conceptual scheme is specified in a language, provided as part of a DBMS, called the *data definition language*. This language is not a procedural language, but rather a notation for describing the types of entities, and relationships among types of entities, in terms of a particular data model. The data definition language is used when the database is designed, and it is used when that design is modified. It is not used for obtaining or modifying the data itself. The data definition language almost invariably has statements that describe, in somewhat abstract terms, what the physical layout of the database should be. Detailed design of the physical database is done by DBMS routines that process statements in the data definition language.

For the implementation of a large database, design of the conceptual scheme will be done by a person generally called a *database administrator,* often in conjunction with a staff of programmers and in consultation with the persons under whose aegis the database is created, e.g., the management of a company. The database administrator and his staff write the specifications for the conceptual scheme and its implementation as a physical database, using the data definition language. As the database is put into use, the database administrator is responsible for all operations that affect the database as a whole. These functions include:

1. The creation of subschemes for views.

2. The granting of authorization to use the database or certain parts of it.

3. Modification of the conceptual scheme should the original design prove faulty or the requirements of the enterprise change.

4. Modification of the implementation of the conceptual scheme by the physical scheme, should evidence regarding usage of the database indicate that another organization would be more efficient.

5. Making backup copies of the database and repairing damage to the database.

The description of subschemes and their correspondence to the conceptual scheme requires a *subscheme data definition language,* which is often quite similar to the data definition language itself, although in some cases the subscheme language could use a data model different from that of the data definition language. There could, in fact, be several different subscheme languages, each using a different data model. Function (2), the authorization of access to the database, requires a specialized language describing the intended privileges and their recipients. This language may be part of the data definition language or part of a language for manipulating data. Functions (3) and (4) are accomplished using the data definition language, while function (5), ensuring reliability of the system will be done using specialized tools that are part of the DBMS.

Application Programs

Suppose that the conceptual scheme for an airline has been designed, and it is decided that there is to be an automated reservation system built. The subscheme for the reservation system and its meaning in terms of the conceptual scheme is designed by a staff of application programmers, and authorization to access the portions of the conceptual database corresponding to this view is granted by the database administrator. The chain of abstractions is as illustrated in Fig. 1.2.

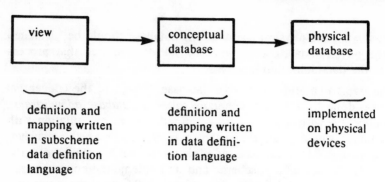

Fig. 1.2. Chain of abstractions.

Now the application programmers are ready to write the programs, such as BOOK mentioned above, that interrogate and manipulate the view, and through it, the conceptual and physical database. Manipulation of the database requires a specialized language, called a *data manipulation language,* or *query language,* in which to express commands such as:

1.   Retrieve from the database the number of seats available on flight 999 on July 20.

2.   Set to 27 the number of seats available on flight 123 on August 31.

3.   Find some flight from ORD (O'Hare airport in Chicago) to JFK (Kennedy airport in New York) on August 24.

4.   Retrieve all flights from ORD to JFK on August 24. Not all data manipulation languages are capable of obtaining unspecified quantities of data in one step, as typified by command (4). In many such languages, one issues a command like (3), to obtain the first such flight and then a command like "get next flight from ORD to JFK on August 24" repeatedly until the response "no more" is received.

It is usually necessary for an application program to do more than manipulate the database; it must perform a variety of ordinary computational tasks. For example, the program BOOK must print on and read from a terminal, make decisions (is seat_count = 0?), and do arithmetic (seat_count = seat_count − 1). For these reasons, an application program is normally written in a conventional programming language, such as PL/I or COBOL, called the *host language.* The commands of the data manipulation language are invoked by the program in one of two ways, depending on the characteristics of the DBMS.

1.   The commands of the data manipulation language are invoked by calls to procedures provided by the DBMS. These procedures are given access to the definition of the subscheme and the conceptual scheme. Necessary linkage may be provided by the operating system underlying the DBMS.

2. The commands are statements in a language that is an extension of the host language. In this case, the application program is written in the extended language. The commands of the data manipulation language will result in calls to procedures provided by the DBMS, so the distinction between approaches (1) and (2) is not a great one.

The view of the data seen by the application program is illustrated in Fig. 1.3. The solid lines represent transfer and manipulation of data, and dashed lines represent causation. Thus data transfers beteen the program's work area and the data base are caused by data manipulation commands, which are in turn invoked by the application program. Data transfer and calculation within the workspace is caused by the statements of the application program as in any ordinary programming situation.

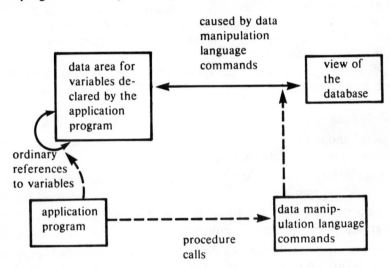

Fig. 1.3. The data seen by an application program.

Data Independence

The chain of abstractions of Fig. 1.2, from view to conceptual to physical database, provides two levels of "data independence." Most obviously, the physical scheme can be changed by the database administrator without altering the conceptual scheme or requiring a redefinition of subschemes. This independence is referred to as *physical data independence*. It should be realized that modifications to the physical database organization can affect the efficiency of application programs, but it will never be required that we rewrite those programs just because the implementation of the conceptual scheme by the physical scheme has changed. The advantage to physical data independence is that it allows "tuning" of the physical database for efficiency while permitting application programs to run as if no change had occurred.

The relationship between views and the conceptual database also provides a type of independence called *logical data independence*. As the database is used, it may become necessary to modify the conceptual scheme, for example, by adding information about different types of entities or extra information about existing entities. Thus, an airline may one day discover it has to provide to the Environmental Protection Agency data about the pollution and noise levels of its flights, while the relevant information about its aircraft is not now in the database and must be added. Many modifications to the conceptual scheme can be made without affecting existing subschemes, and other modifications to the conceptual scheme can be made if we redefine the mapping from the subscheme to the conceptual scheme. Again, no change to the application programs is necessary. The only kind of change in the conceptual scheme that could not be reflected in a redefinition of a subscheme's correspondence to the conceptual scheme is the deletion of information that corresponds to information present in the subscheme. Such changes would naturally require rewriting or discarding some application programs.

1.4 A Model of the Real World

The preceding synopsis of a DBMS raises a number of important questions, which we shall consider in following chapters. Among these questions are:

1. What are appropriate data structures with which to implement a typical physical database?

2. What are the properties of useful data models, and how should they be represented by physical structures?

In order to attack these two questions, we should have a firm grasp of the kinds of information a database system would likely be required to store. Let us introduce an informal model called the *entity-relationship model* of data. This model is not a data model that has been used in data definition languages, although it is closely related to some of these models. Rather, the entity-relationship model will serve to justify the kinds of data structures and data models we introduce later, since the ability of these structures and models to represent entity-relationship structures will be apparent. It will also be intuitively clear that the entity-relationship model does an adequate, albeit imperfect, job of modeling real-world situations, such as business enterprises or the records kept by schools, hospitals, governments, and so on, where database systems are likely to be used. However, if we view the structures defined in the entity-relationship model as conceptual schemes, we shall not be grossly deceived.

Entities

The term "entity" defies an all-inclusive definition. Suffice it to say an *entity* is a thing that exists and is distinguishable; that is, we can tell one entity from another. For example, each chair is an entity. So is each person and each automobile. We could regard each ant as an entity if we had a way to distinguish one from another; otherwise we would not regard an ant as an entity. Higher-level concepts can be entities too. For example, in a biological database, terms like Arachnid, Rodent, Baboon, and Plant would be entities. If we stretch a point, concepts like love and hate are entities.

A group of all similar entities forms an *entity set.* Examples of entity sets are

1. all persons

2. all living persons

3. all automobiles

4. all emotions

Notice from examples (1) and (2), persons and living persons, that the term "similar entities" is not precisely defined, and one can establish an infinite number of different properties by which to define an entity set. One of the key steps in selecting a model for the real world, as it pertains to a particular database, is choosing the entity sets.

Attributes and Keys

Entities have properties, called *attributes,* which associate a value from a *domain* of values for that attribute with each entity in an entity set. Usually, the domain for an attribute will be a set of integers, real numbers, or character strings, but we do not rule out other types of values. For example, the entities in the entity set of persons may be said to have attributes such as name (a character string), height (a real number), and so on.

The selection of relevant attributes for entity sets is another critical step in the design of a real-world model. An attribute or set of attributes whose values uniquely identify each entity in an entity set is called a *key* for that entity set. In principle, each entity set has a key, since we hypothesized that each entity is distinguishable from all others. But if we do not choose, for an entity set, a collection of attributes that include a key, then we shall not be able to distinguish one entity in the set from another. Often an arbitrary serial number is supplied as an attribute to serve as a key. For example, an entity set that included only U.S. nationals could use the single attribute "Social Security number" as a key.

There will be occasional cases in which the entities of an entity set are not distinguished by their attributes, but rather by their relationship to entities of another type. A most important kind of "built-in" relationship (user-defined relationships will be described subsequently) is **isa**. We say A **isa** B, read "A is a B," if entity set B is a generalization of entity set A, or equivalently, A is a special kind of B.

Example 1.2: Suppose we had a database of automobiles with entity set BRANDS having attributes MAKE and MODEL. An entity in set BRANDS would be "Datsun, 280Z." We might have an entity set AUTOS with attribute SERIAL_NO. We might suppose SERIAL_NO is a key for AUTO, but it is conceivable that two makes of cars use the same serial numbers. To make the entities in set AUTOS unique, we need a relationship between AUTOS and BRANDS representing the fact that an auto is of a particular brand. Then we could consider each instance of entity set AUTOS to be defined uniquely by its SERIAL_NO and the attribute MAKE of the related entity of set BRANDS. □

Example 1.3: An example of an **isa** relationship concerns the airline database mentioned before. We may have an entity set EMPLOYEES, with attributes including EMP_NO, a unique employee number for each employee. Another entity set PILOTS might be used. Obviously PILOTS **isa** EMPLOYEES. The entity set PILOTS might have no attributes, but only a relationship with another entity set PLANES, indicating which pilots were capable of flying 747's, DC-10's, and so on. However, because each pilot is an employee, the **isa** relationship from PILOTS to EMPLOYEES provides a unique identifier for each pilot, the EMP_NO. □

Relationships

A *relationship* among entity sets is simply an ordered list of entity sets. A particular entity set may appear more than once on the list. If there is a relationship REL among entity sets $E_1, E_2, \ldots, E_k$, then it is presumed that a set of k-tuples named REL exists. We call such a set a *relationship set.* Each k-tuple $(e_1, e_2, \ldots, e_k)$ in set REL implies that entities $e_1, e_2, \ldots, e_k$, where e_1 is in set E_1, e_2 is in set E_2, and so on, stand in relationship REL to each other as a group. The most common case, by far, is where $k=2$, but lists of three or more entity sets are sometimes related.

Example 1.4: Suppose we have an entity set PERSONS and relationship MOTHER_OF, whose list of entity sets is PERSONS, PERSONS. We presume that the relationship set MOTHER_OF includes all pairs (p_1, p_2) such that person p_2 is the mother of person p_1.

An alternative way of representing this information is to postulate the existence of entity set MOTHERS and relationship MOTHERS **isa** PERSONS. This arrangement would be more appropriate if the database stored values for attributes of mothers that it did not store for persons in general. Then the relationship MOTHER_OF would be a list of entity sets PERSONS, MOTHERS, and to get information about a person's mother as a person, we would compose (in the sense of ordinary set-theoretic relations) the relationships MOTHER_OF and **isa**. □

Functionality

To implement a database efficiently, it is often necessary to classify relationships according to how many entities from one entity set can be associated with how many entities of another entity set. The simplest and rarest form of relationship on two sets is *one-to-one*, meaning that for each entity in either set there is at most one associated member of the other set. An example of such a situation might occur in the database of a business, where two entity sets EMPLOYEES and DEPARTMENTS exist. The relationship HEAD_OF between these two entity sets, indicating the department head of each department, might be assumed to be a one-to-one relationship. Note that the one-to-oneness of this relationship is an assumption about the real world that the database designer could choose to make or not to make. It is just as possible, in fact more plausible, to assume that the same person could head two departments, or even that a department could have two heads. However, if one head for one department is the rule in this organization, then it may be possible to take advantage of the fact that HEAD_OF is one-to-one, when designing the physical database. Also observe that a one-to-one relationship does not imply that for evey entity of one set there actually exists a related entity of the other set. For example, certainly most employees are not head of any department, and there may be departments that at a given time have no head.

More common is the *many-one* relationship, where one entity in set E_2 is associated with zero or more entities in set E_1, but each entity in E_1 is associated with at most one entity in E_2. This relationship is said to be many-one *from E_1 to E_2*. That is, the relationship is a (partial) function from E_1 to E_2. For example, if each course is taught by one teacher, there is a many-one relationship TAUGHT_BY from entity set COURSES to entity set TEACHERS.

As a generalization of the many-one concept, if there is a relationship among entity sets $E_1, E_2, \ldots, E_k$, and given entities for all sets but E_i, there is at most one related entity of set E_i, then we say the relationship is many-one from $E_1, \ldots, E_{i-1}, E_{i+1}, \ldots, E_k$ to E_i.

Also common is the *many-many* relationship, where there are no restrictions on the sets of pairs of entities that may appear in a relationship set. This form of relationship is supported only with difficulty in two of the principal data models, network and hierarchical. An example of a many-many relationship is EXPORTS between entity sets COUNTRIES and PRODUCTS, since a country usually exports more than one product, and few products are exported by only one country.

Example 1.5: Let us undertake the design of a (somewhat) complete database for an airline using the entity-relationship model. Below we list the entity sets and their attributes. The domain of each attribute is declared as in a typical programming language; CHAR(n) means character string of length n, and INT(n) means integer of up to n digits. Comments are set off by /* $\cdots$ */.

1. entity set PASSENGERS with attributes:

> NAME   CHAR(30)
> ADDRESS CHAR(30)
> PHONE   INT(10)

NAME and ADDRESS together form a key for this entity set.

2. entity set FLIGHTS with attributes

> NUMBER   INT(3)
> SOURCE   CHAR(3) /* the source is an airport; all
>   commercial aiports have three-letter codes,
>   e.g. LAX, SFO, ORD, JFK */
> DEST   CHAR(3) /* the destination airport */
> DEP_TIME INT(4) /* the departure time is given as in
>   military form, e.g. 2330 for 11:30 PM */
> ARR_TIME INT(4) /* the arrival time */

For simplicity, we have assumed that flights never make intermediate stops, though in practice, airlines often use the same flight number for a sequence of legs of a flight. The attribute NUMBER is a key here. So is the pair of attributes SOURCE and DEP_TIME. In practice, one key, probably NUMBER because it is a singleton set, would be chosen and referred to as "the key."

3. entity set DEPARTURES with attribute

> DATE INT(3) /* we assume dates are numbered from the
>   beginning of the year, and information about flights
>   is kept no more than a year in advance.
>   For example, date 33 is Feb. 2 */

Each entity of this set is a particular flight on a particular date. The attribute DATE by itself does not define an entity of this set. We shall later introduce the relationship INSTANCE_OF between DEPARTURES and FLIGHTS to define entities of set DEPARTURES completely.

4. entity set PLANES with attributes

> MANUFACTURER CHAR(10)
> MODEL_NO CHAR(10)

The two attributes together form a key.

5.   entity set AIRCRAFT with attribute

> SERIAL_NO INT(5)

We presume serial numbers are assigned by the airline and serve as a key for each aircraft owned by the airline. Note that the entity set PLANES consists of generic designations such as Boeing 747, rather than individual aircraft as are in the set AIRCRAFT.

6.   entity set PERSONNEL with attributes

> EMP_NO   INT(6) /* the employee number */
> NAME   CHAR(30)
> ADDRESS   CHAR(30)
> SALARY   INT(6)

EMP_NO is a key for PERSONNEL. The fact that PERSONNEL and PASSENGERS both have attributes NAME and ADDRESS is of no significance.

7.   entity set PILOTS with no attributes.
We have the relationship PILOTS **isa** PERSONNEL to identify individual pilots. The reason for singling out PILOTS as a separate entity set is so that PILOTS can be related to PLANES by the relationship CAN_FLY, while it might waste space in the database to retain this information about nonflying personnel.

The relationships, in addition to the **isa** relationship between PILOTS and PERSONNEL, are listed below.

1.   relationship BOOKED_ON between PASSENGERS and DEPARTURES, indicating reservations. This is a many-many relationship.

2.   relationship INSTANCE_OF between DEPARTURES and FLIGHTS. This relationship is many-one from DEPARTURES to FLIGHTS, since each departure has a unique flight number, although the same flight number is used from day to day.

3.   relationship ASSIGNED_TO between PERSONNEL and DEPARTURES, indicating the flight crew for each departure. This relationship is many-many.

4.   relationship CAN_FLY between PILOTS and PLANES. Here is another many-many relationship.

5.   relationship TYPE between AIRCRAFT and PLANES, indicating the generic type of each aircraft. The relationship is many-one from AIR-CRAFT to PLANES, since each aircraft is of one generic type, but the airline may own many DC-10's, for example.

Entity-Relationship Diagrams

It is useful to summarize the information in a design using *entity-relationship diagrams,* where

1.   Rectangles represent entity sets.

2.   Circles represent attributes. They are linked to their entity sets by (undirected) edges.

3.   Diamonds represent relationships. They are linked to their constituent entity sets by undirected edges. Order of entity sets in the list for the relationship can be indicated by numbering edges, although the order is irrelevant unless the same entity set appears more than once on a list. However, in the case of a many-one relationship from *A* to *B* we draw an arc (directed edge) to *B*. More generally, if the relationship involves three or more entity sets and is many-one to some entity set *A*, we draw an arc to *A* and undirected edges to the other sets. More complicated mappings that are many-one to two or more entity sets will not be represented by an edge convention. In case of a one-one relationship, an edge with arrows at both ends is shown. As an exception, if *A* **isa** *B*, we draw an arc only to *B*.

Example 1.6: The diagram for the entity set PERSONS with relationship MOTHER_OF (from Example 1.4) is shown in Fig. 1.4.

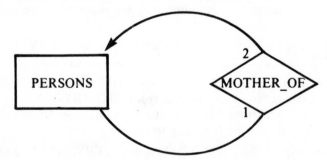

Fig. 1.4. Entity-relationship diagram of motherhood.

Figure 1.5 shows the diagram for the database scheme of Example 1.4. □

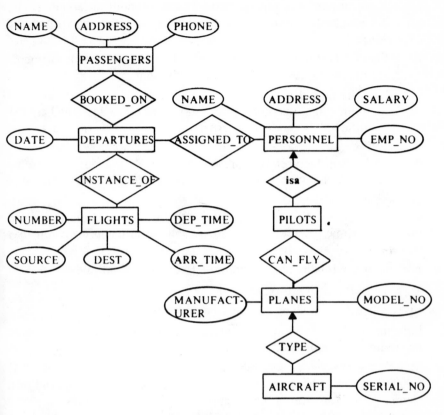

Fig. 1.5. Entity-relationship diagram of the airline database.

Exercises

1.1: Many ordinary programming languages can be viewed as based on a particular data model. For example SNOBOL can be said to use a character string model of data. Can you think of any other programming languages that use a particular data model? What data models do they use? Are any of them well suited to database implementation?

1.2: Suppose that in the conceptual scheme of some enterprise, the attribute DATE, which is an integer from 1 to 366, appears. Suppose also that we wish to design a view in which the attributes MONTH and DAY appear. How can we define these attributes in terms of the DATE attribute in the conceptual scheme?

1.3: Suppose we informally define the data in the database of a department store as follows.

i)   Each employee is represented. The data about an employee are his employee number, name, address, and the department he works for.

ii) Each department is represented. The data about departments are its employees, manager, and items sold.

iii) Each item sold is represented. The data about ~~departments~~ *items sold* are its name, manufacturer, price, model number (assigned by the manufacturer), and an internal item number (assigned by the store).

iv) Each manufacturer is represented. The data about a manufacturer are its name, address, items supplied to the store, and their prices.

Give an entity-relationship diagram for this database. Note that some information may be represented by attributes; other information may be represented by relationships.

1.4:   For the entity-relationship diagram of Exercise 1.3 indicate

a)   a key for each entity set, and

b)   which relationships are one-one and which are many-one.

Indicate any assumptions you make that might or might not hold depending on factors not stated in Exercise 1.3.

*1.5:   Modify the conceptual scheme for the airline database (Example 1.5) to allow flights consisting of more than one leg. That is, instead of a source and destination, a flight has an associated list of cities.

1.6:   Give an entity-relationship diagram for a genealogical database showing fatherhood, motherhood and spouse relationships.

1.7:   Use the entity-relationship model to describe the data connected with an organization with which you are familiar, such as a school or business.

Bibliographic Notes

The three levels of abstraction, physical-conceptual-view, appear in the "DBTG Report" (CODASYL [1971]); they are also a feature of the "ANSI/SPARC report" (ANSI [1975]), where they are called internal, conceptual, and external, respectively. Tsichritzis and Klug [1978] is an informal introduction to a revised version of that report. The three levels are present in a large number of existing database systems; we shall describe some of these systems in Chapters 4, 7, and 8. The entity-relationship model is from Chen [1976].

A variety of other models have been proposed. Bachman [1969] was one of the earliest. The reader may wish to consult the books by Nijssen

[1976], Douque and Nijssen [1976], or Tsichritzis and Lochovsky [1979], or consult the papers by Nijssen [1977] or Kerschberg, Klug, and Tsichritzis [1977] for more information.

2
Physical Data Organization

Before discussing the various abstractions of databases used in database design, let us develop a good understanding of what is easy and what is hard to do on the physical level. The basic problem in physical database representation is to store a *file* consisting of *records,* each record having an identical format. A *record format* consists of a list of field names, with each field possessing a fixed number of bytes and having a fixed data type. A *record* consists of values for each field. The typical operations we desire to perform on a file are:

1. insert a record.

2. delete a record.

3. modify a record.

4. find a record with a particular value in a particular field or a combination of values in a combination of fields.

The complexity of organizing a file for storage depends on the particular combination of these operations we intend to perform on the file. If operation (4), called *lookup,* is permitted, as it usually is, we also need to consider whether desired records are specified by value, by location, or a combination of both, and whether only one or several different fields may be involved in different lookups. We shall discuss the principal file organization methods in Sections 2.2–2.5. Then in Section 2.6 we consider storage of files whose records may contain more than one value for a field; we call such records *variable length records.* Finally, Sections 2.7 and 2.8 discuss file organizations for handling some more general kinds of lookup.

2.1 A Model for External Storage Organization

When we refer to "external" or "secondary" storage, we usually mean disk storage, although what we say applies to drums and, to a lesser extent, to magnetic tape or the newer kinds of circulating storage devices such as magnetic bubble and charge coupled memories. A file system using disk storage usually divides the disk into equal sized *physical blocks.* A typical size for a physical block is in the range 2^9 to 2^{12} bytes, but we shall not assume any particular size, except in examples. Each physical block (or just *block*) has an *address,* which is an absolute address on a disk or another storage device.

A file is stored in one or more blocks, with one or more records stored in each block. A block may have within it bytes that are not used for any record. We assume there is a file system that translates between file names and the absolute addresses of its blocks.

Records have an address, which may be viewed either as the absolute address of the first byte of the record, or as the address of the block in which it is held, together with an *offset,* the number of bytes in the block preceding the beginning of the record.

Pointers

We shall often speak of pointers to records or blocks. A pointer to a block can be its absolute address. Sometimes, secondary storage is organized as a virtual memory, and blocks or records can be pointed to by giving their offset from the beginning of an imaginary area of virtual memory,† with the file system used to translate between offsets in the area and absolute addresses. Another possible way to point to a record is to point to its block. If we choose this representation for pointers, we must be able to find the desired record within the block, once we have found the block. To do so, we must know enough about the record to identify it, a situation which comes up sufficiently frequently that we should be aware of the possibility. The advantage of pointing to blocks is that records can be moved within blocks without causing pointers to *dangle* (i.e., point to the wrong place).

Estimating the Speed of Database Operations

The basic external storage operation is the transfer of a block from secondary to main memory or vice versa; we call either operation a *block access.* It is important to note that in most present day systems, a data transfer involving secondary storage usually takes as long, or longer than searching the block for desired data once it is in main memory. Also, it is necessary in all but some hypothetical or experimental systems, to have the data in main memory before it can be used in any way. Thus when we talk about the speed of various algorithms for accessing data we shall count the number of blocks that must be read into or written from main memory, and this number will represent our estimate of the speed of the algorithm.

---

† Such an area can be viewed as a large random access memory, where bytes are numbered 0, 1, . . . , up to some maximum number.

Interpreting Raw Data

In the simplest organization, we assume that each file has a fixed record format, although we shall later study more complex files. In each stored record of the file the fields appear in the same order, and for each field there is an associated number of bytes, which does not vary from record to record. There is also an associated data type for each field, such as character string, real, or integer, which allows us to interpret the bits of the field. As a consequence of these assumptions, if records are packed from the beginning of blocks (or from a fixed point near the beginning of blocks, if some bytes of each block are set aside for other information) we can uniquely decode the records of the block.

The only problem is distinguishing records from empty space, since we do not assume a block is packed with as many records as it can hold. One solution is to place a count of the number of records in a *block header,* a fixed number of bytes at the beginning of each block used for this information and perhaps other information as well. It is then sufficient that whatever records are in the block be packed as far forward as possible. We shall discuss some alternative schemes later.

Keys

If we recall the entity-relationship model discussed in Section 1.4, we observe that files will be used to store information of two types.

1. There are files representing entity sets. Here each record represents one entity and the fields correspond to the attributes of the entity.

2. There are files representing relationships. If the relationship is many-many, we might represent the relationship by a file of records with two fields (or k fields if we had a relationship among k entity sets). Each field is of pointer type. Assuming a relationship on two entity sets, each record consists of a pair of pointers (p1, p2), where p1 points to the record for an entity of the first entity set, and p2 points to a related entity of the second entity set. If the relationship is one-to-one or many-to-one, other representations are possible and will be discussed later.

An important difference between these two types of files is that the first has a nontrivial *key,* one or more fields that together uniquely identify the record, while the second type of file is not guaranteed to have a key other than the set of all the fields. There are many cases where all interrogations of a file are of the form: given the value of the field or fields in the key, find the record.† Such queries are generally easier to handle than more

---

† Much of what we say in this chapter is not predicated on the key uniquely defining a record. We could just as well ask for all records matching a "key" value and retrieve them all with little additional effort.

general queries, and it is with these sorts of files that we shall begin our examination of file implementation.

Pinned and Unpinned Records

Another issue of importance in determining a file implementation strategy is whether or not records of a file are "pinned down" to a fixed location. Records become pinned because there may exist pointers to them somewhere in the database. For example, we mentioned a possible implementation of mappings in which associated entities were represented by pairs of pointers to their records. We also mentioned in Section 1.4 the possibility of an entity being uniquely identified only by a link to some other entity, in which case the former entity's record needs a pointer to the record of the latter. In such cases, we can never move the records for these entities, or the pointers will "dangle," that is, they will no longer point to the data they pointed to at the time they were created.

In the most general case, we cannot use a file organization in which records move around (say in response to insertions of other records), as we may have no idea of where in the entire database a pointer or several pointers to a record may be. The deletion of records is also dangerous, since any pointers to them must be found or allowed to dangle. Fortunately we may be able to determine that there are no pointers to records of a particular file by studying the overall database organization. In that case we have available some more flexible organizations than if we must assume that records are pinned down to their original location.

The Heap File Organization

The most obvious approach to storing a file of records is simply to list them in as many blocks as they require, although one does not generally allow records to overlap block boundaries. This organization is sometimes called a *heap* when it is necessary to dignify it with a name. The blocks used for a heap may be linked by pointers, or a table of their addresses may be stored elsewhere, perhaps on one or more additional blocks. To insert a record, we place the record in the last block if there is space, or get a new block if there is no more space. Deletions can be performed by setting a *deletion bit* in the deleted record. Reusing the space of deleted records by storing newly inserted records in their space is dangerous if pointers to records exist. However, if we are sure the file is unpinned, one of a number of "garbage collection" strategies (see Knuth [1968], e.g.) can be used to keep track of the reusable space.

Given a key value, record lookup requires a scan of the entire heap-organized file, or at least half the file on the average, until the desired record is found. It is this operation whose cost is prohibitive if the file in question is spread over more than a few blocks. Much of the rest of this chapter is devoted to the consideration of alternative file organizations that allow arbitrary lookups without scanning more than a small fraction of the file. In designing a better file organization we must try to avoid using too much extra space, and we must refrain from making insertions and deletions too complicated. In the next four sections we describe some of the ideas that have been used.

2.2 Hashed Files

The basic idea behind a *hashed access* file organization is that we divide the records of a file among *buckets,* which each consist of one or more blocks of storage. For each file stored in this manner there is a *hash function h* that takes as argument a value for the key of the file and produces an integer from 0 up to some maximum value. If v is a key value, $h(v)$ indicates the number of the bucket in which the record with key value v is to be found, if it is present at all.

It is desirable that h "hashes" v, that is, $h(v)$ takes on all its possible values with roughly equal probability as v ranges over likely collections of values for the key. A great deal has been said about suitable hash functions, and we do not intend to go into the subject deeply here. The following strategy is useful in many situations.

1.   Treat the key value as a sequence of bits, formed by concatenating together the value for each field of the key. This bit sequence is of fixed length, since each field is of fixed length.

2.   Divide the bit sequence into groups of a fixed number of bits, say 16 bits, padding the last group with 0's if necessary.

3.   Add the groups of bits as integers.

4.   Divide the sum by the number of buckets, and use the remainder as the bucket number.

In Fig. 2.1 we see a hashed file organization with B buckets. There is a bucket directory consisting of B pointers, one for each bucket. Each pointer is the address of the first block for that bucket.

A bucket consisting of only one block, such as bucket number 1 in Fig. 2.1, has in that block a header with a *null pointer,* a value that cannot be the address of a block. A bucket consisting of more than one block has in the header of the first block a pointer to the second block, in the header of the second block a pointer to the third, and so on. The header of the last block has a null pointer. For example, bucket $B-1$ in Fig. 2.1 consists of blocks b_4, b_5, and b_6.

If B is small, the bucket directory could reside in main memory; otherwise it will be stored on as many blocks as necessary, and the block of the bucket directory containing the pointer to the first block of bucket i will be

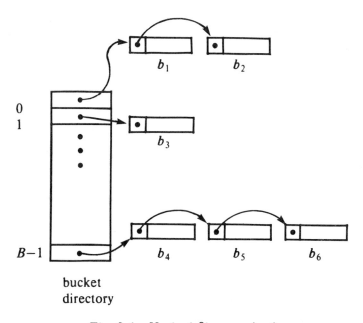

Fig. 2.1. Hashed file organization.

called into main memory when a hash value *i* is computed.

The blocks each have room for a fixed number of records; If a record requires *r* bytes, then we assume each record begins at a multiple of *r* bytes from the first byte following the header. The space used to hold a single record will be called a *subblock*. In certain circumstances the first *r* bytes could be empty while a subsequent subblock of *r* bytes holds a record. We assume there is some way of distinguishing full and empty subblocks of *r* bytes. In some circumstances, a possible but dangerous method is to place in an empty subblock a sequence of bits that could not be a real record. This is feasible if we know a bit sequence that now and forever after could not be the value of a record. A safer method, and the one we shall assume from here on, is to place in the header one bit for each subblock, with 0 indicating that the subblock is empty and 1 indicating that it holds a record. It is sometimes useful to place in the record itself a *deletion bit*, which indicates whether the record has been deleted. It then becomes possible to avoid reusing subblocks that may have dangling pointers to them.

Lookup

Suppose we are given value *v*, which, if there is one field in the key, is the value of that field, or, if the key consists of more than one field, is the list of values for the fields of the key, in a fixed order. We compute $h(v)$, which gives us a bucket number, say *i*. We consult the bucket directory to find the first block for bucket *i*. Next, search each nonempty subblock in the block to see if it holds a record with key value v. If so we have found the record. If the record is not found, and the header of the block has a pointer to further blocks in bucket i, search each of these blocks in turn until either the record with key value v is found, or the last block on the chain of blocks for bucket i has been searched.

Modification

Suppose we must modify one or more fields of the record with key value v. If some field to be modified is part of the key, treat this modification as a deletion followed by an insertion (insertion will be described subsequently), since the modified record probably belongs in a different bucket.[†] If the key value is not to be modified, search for the record with key value v as described under "lookup." If found, modify the fields of the record as desired. If the record is not found we have an error, as it makes no sense to modify a nonexistent record.

Insertion

Apply the previously described lookup procedure. If a record with the given key value v is found, there is an error, as it does not make sense to insert a record if it or a record with the same key value is present. (Perhaps the programmer intended to modify rather than insert.) Having determined that there is no existing record with key value v, we find the first empty subblock in the blocks for bucket $h(v)$. The location of this subblock can be remembered as we search the bucket in the lookup procedure.[‡] Place the record to be inserted in this subblock. If no empty subblocks exist in all the blocks of the bucket $h(v)$, call upon the file system to provide a new block. Place in the header of the last block for the bucket a pointer to this new block, and in the header of the new block put the null pointer. Place the inserted record in the first subblock of the new block.

Deletion

To delete the record with key value v, use the lookup procedure to find the record. We may simply make the subblock for this record empty by setting to 0 its full/empty bit in the header. So doing makes the subblock available for reuse. However, if there may be pointers to records, we don't want to allow the subblock to be refilled, as a dangling pointer may then erroneously point to the new record. In this case, we leave the full/empty bit for the deleted record at 1, so its subblock cannot be refilled, and we set a

---

† If records are pinned, it is not possible to make such a modification.

‡ A subblock can only become empty in the middle of a bucket if deletions actually result in dissapearance of a record, rather than the setting of a deletion bit. The former strategy is safe only if no pointers to records in the file exist.

deletion bit in the record itself to 1, indicating the record has been deleted. Then if we ever follow a pointer to the deleted record, we know the pointer is dangling, and the pointer itself may be deleted or set to null.

If records are not pinned down, we have the option of designing the deletion routine so that when a record other than the last in the bucket is deleted, we find the last record and move it to the subblock of the deleted record. By so doing we shall free the last block of the bucket if it contained only one record. This block may be returned to the file system for use later.

Example 2.1. Our file consists of information about dinosaurs, with the following fields comprising a record.

NAME	CHAR(20)
PERIOD	CHAR(10)
HABITAT	CHAR(5)
DIET	CHAR(5)
LENGTH	INT(4) /* in feet */
WEIGHT	INT(4) /* in tons */

The field NAME by itself forms a key for this file. On the assumption that two bytes hold an integer, a record takes 44 bytes. Let us assume blocks are 100 bytes long (a number too low to be realistic), so each block consists of two subblocks for records preceded by a header with a pointer (say 4 bytes) and two full/empty bits for the two subblocks. The two bits may as well occupy a full byte, which leaves 7 bytes of wasted space in each block.

Let us choose the simple hashing function $h(v)$ equal to the length of string v modulo 5, that is, the remainder when the length is divided by 5.† Consequently there are five buckets. In Fig. 2.2 we see the file with ten dinosaur genuses.‡ Notice that bucket 4 is empty, and there is a null pointer for that bucket in the directory.

Suppose we wish to insert the record

(Elasmosaurus, Cretaceous, sea, carn., 40, 5)

We hash "Elasmosaurus" and get the value 2, since the name has 12 characters. We follow the pointer in the entry numbered 2 in the bucket directory to find the first (and only, it turns out) block in bucket 2. We consult byte 5 of the block to discover that both subblocks hold records. The key value for the first record is found in bytes 6—25, which hold

---

† This is a particularly bad function for names of dinosaurs, since these names tend to cluster around 11-13 chracters in length, and therefore the buckets will tend not to be approximately equally full.

‡ Actually some of these creatures are members of extinct orders of reptiles not usually classified as "dinosaurs."

"Plateosaurus," not what we want. The key value for the second record is found in bytes 50—69, and these hold "Brontosaurus," not "Elasmosaurus." We consult bytes 1—4 of the block to find the next block in the bucket. As there is a null pointer in these bytes, we have scanned the entire bucket. We find that "Elasmosaurus" is not present and can be inserted. We also note that no empty subblocks were found, so we must get a new block and insert the record for Elasmosaurus there. The pointer in the fourth block in Fig. 2.2 is made to point to the new block, bytes 1—4 of the new block are given the null pointers and the fifth byte is made to hold the bits 10.

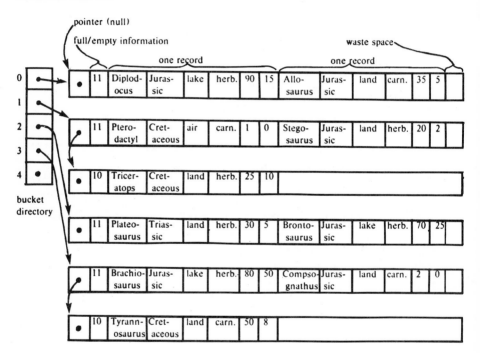

Fig. 2.2. A hashed file.

Now suppose it is recalled that the true scientific name of Bronto- saurus (thunder lizard) is really Apatosaurus (unbelievable lizard). We must modify the Brontosaurus record, and since a key is involved, we delete the record for Brontosaurus, first copying the nonkey field values, and insert a record for Apatosaurus with the same information. To execute these steps, we hash "Brontosaurus" and obtain value 2. Following the pointer for bucket 2, we find a block whose second subblock has key value "Brontosaurus." We copy this record and delete it by setting byte 5 of the block to 10. It is assumed that records are pinned down, so the record for Elasmosaurus cannot replace that for Brontosaurus. We then assemble the record

(Apatosaurus, Jurassic, lake, herb., 70, 25)

and insert it. As the hash value for "Apatosaurus" is 1, we place the
record in the second subblock of the second block for bucket 1. The file at
this time is shown in Fig. 2.3. □

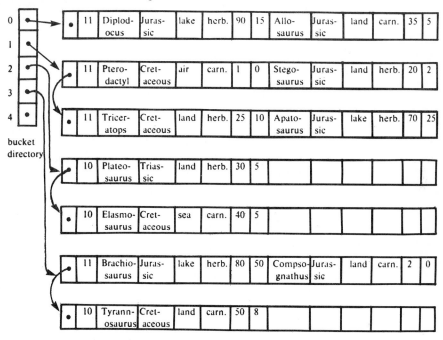

Fig. 2.3. Revised file of dinosaurs.

Time Analysis of Hashing

Each of the operations lookup, modify, insert, and delete require one
access to secondary storage to get the relevant block of the bucket directory
(assuming that directory is not kept in main memory) and no more
accesses to secondary storage to examine the bucket than there are blocks
in the bucket. If the searched for record is present we shall look at half the
blocks on the average. For any operation other than a lookup, we must
write the modified block back into secondary storage.

The best we could hope for is that each bucket consists of one block,
on the average, in which case operations take two (for lookup) or three (for
the other operations) accesses independent of the size of the file. In order
that buckets consist of a small number of blocks, the number of buckets
must be approximately the number of records in the file divided by the
number of records that can fit in one block. If the file is constantly grow-
ing, as many do, it will be necessary on occasion to reorganize the file by

changing the hash function and increasing the size of the bucket directory. This reorganization need not be as chaotic as it seems, if we make two restrictions.

1.   We assume the hash function is computed by taking a key value v, computing from it a very large integer (much larger than the maximum number of buckets that could ever be needed), dividing this number by the number of buckets, and taking the remainder.

2.   We assume that when we reorganize, the number of buckets is multiplied by a fixed integer c (usually $c=2$ is selected).

If we decide to double the number of buckets from n to $2n$, by assumption (1) the records in bucket i will all go into bucket i or $i+n$, and no records in other buckets will go into i or $i+n$. Thus we can split one bucket at a time. The same idea applies if we multiply the number of buckets by some integer $c>2$. Then each old bucket can be divided into c new buckets, independent of the other buckets.

2.3 Indexed Files

We now consider a second representation for files that are to be accessed via a key. In this representation, we begin by sorting the records of a file by their key values. We should first observe that no matter what the domain of values for a field, we can in principle compare values from the domain and therefore can sort these values. The justification is that to be stored in a file, the values must be representable as fixed length bit strings, which can be ordered if we treat them as integers and use numerical order. The usual domains of values, such as character strings, integers and reals have conventional orders placed on them. For integers and reals we have numerical order. For character strings we have *lexicographic,* or *dictionary* order defined by $X_1 X_2 \cdots X_k < Y_1 Y_2 \cdots Y_m$, where the X's and Y's represent characters, if and only if either

1. $k < m$ and $X_1 \cdots X_k = Y_1 \cdots Y_k$, or

2.   For some $i \leqslant \min(k, m)$, we have $X_1 = Y_1$, $X_2 = Y_2, \ldots, X_{i-1} = Y_{i-1}$, and the binary code for X_i is numerically less than the binary code for Y_i.

Whatever code for characters is used by a machine, we have a right to expect that the order of the codes for letters of the same case is alphabetical order and the order of the codes for digits is the numerical order of the digits. Thus, for example, 'AN' < 'AND' by rule (1), and 'BANANA' < 'BANDANA' by rule (2) with $i=4$.

If we have a key of more than one field, we can sort key values by first arbitrarily picking an order for the key fields. Records are sorted by the first field, which will result in clusters of records with the same value in the first field. Each cluster is sorted by the value of the second field, which will result in clusters of records with the same value in the first two fields. These clusters are sorted on the third field, and so on. Note that this ordering is a generalization of lexicographic ordering for character strings where, instead of ordering lists of characters we order lists of values from arbitrary domains.

Example 2.2. Suppose we have a key with two fields, both with integer values, and we are given the list of key values $(2,3)$, $(1,2)$, $(2,2)$, $(3,1)$, $(1,3)$. We sort these on the value of the first field to get $(1,2)$, $(1,3)$, $(2,3)$, $(2,2)$, $(3,1)$. The first cluster, with 1 in the first field, is already sorted by the second field. The second cluster, consisting of $(2,3)$ and $(2,2)$, needs to be interchanged to sort on the second field. The third cluster, consisting of one record, naturally is sorted already. The sorted order is $(1,2)$, $(1,3)$, $(2,2)$, $(2,3)$, $(3,1)$. □

If we are willing to maintain a file of records sorted by key values, we can take advantage of the known order to find a record quickly given its key value. We are probably familiar with at least two examples of searching for key values in a sorted list: using the dictionary and using the phone book. In both cases each page has in the upper left corner the first word or name on the page.† By scanning these first words we can determine the one page on which our word (if a dictionary) or name (if a phone book) could be found.‡ This strategy is far better than looking at every entry on every page. Except for one page, which we must scan completely, we need only look at one entry per page.

Turning now to the representation of a sorted file, (which we call the *main* file), we could create a second file called a *(sparse) index,* consisting of pairs (key value, block address). In the index file the pair (v, b) appears if the first record in the block with address b has key value v. The first field is a key for the index file, and the index file is kept sorted by its key value. In a sense, an index file is like any other file with a key, and in fact, we may take advantage of the fact that in an index file, records are never pinned down by pointers from elsewhere.

However, there is an important difference between index files and the general files we have been discussing. In addition to (possibly) wishing to do insertions, deletions, and modifications on index files, we wish to obtain the answer to questions of the form: given a key value v_1 for the file being indexed, find that record (v_2, b) in the index such that $v_2 \leqslant v_1$§ and either

---

† The upper right contains the last word/name, but this information is redundant, since the first word/name of the next page provides equivalent information. It is inconvenient for a human to flip pages, but the analogous task for the computer presents no difficulty.

‡ In practice we use our intuitive feeling about the distribution of words/names to take an educated guess as to where our goal lies, and we do not search stolidly starting at page 1. We shall have more to say about adapting this idea to computer search later.

§ $\leqslant$ is whatever order on key values is being used, e.g., lexicographic order if key values are character strings.

(v_2, b) is the last record in the index, or the next record (v_3, b') has $v_1 < v_3$. (Say that v_2 *covers* v_1 in this situation.) This is how we find the block b of the main file that contains a record with key value v_1, since the index file is guaranteed to be sorted.

Queries of the above type rule out certain organizations for index files. For example, it would not be convenient to use the hashed file organization of Section 2.2 for index files, since there is no way to find the value v_2 that covers v_1 in a hashed file without searching the entire file.

Searching an Index

Let us assume the index file is stored over a known collection of blocks, and we must find that record (v_2, b) such that v_2 covers a given key value v_1. One strategy is to use *linear search*. Scan the index from the beginning, looking at each record until the one that covers v_1 is found. This method is undesirable for all but the smallest indices, as the entire index must be called into main memory. Yet even linear search of an index is superior to linear search of the main file; if the main file has c records per block, then the index has only $1/c^{th}$ as many records as the main file, and index records may be shorter than records of the main file, allowing more to be packed on one block.

A better strategy is to use *binary search*. Given key value v_1, and an index on blocks $B_1, B_2, \ldots, B_n$, look at the middle block, $B_{\lceil n/2 \rceil}$† and compare v_1 with the key value v_2 in the first record on that block.‡ If $v_1 < v_2$, repeat the process as if the index were on blocks $B_1 \cdots B_{\lceil n/2 \rceil - 1}$. If $v_1 \geq v_2$, repeat the process as if the index were on $B_{\lceil n/2 \rceil} \cdots B_n$. Eventually, only one block will remain to be considered. At this time, use linear search on the remaining block to find the key value in the index thaat covers v_1.

As we divide the number of blocks by two at each step, in $\lceil \log_2(n+1) \rceil$ steps at the most we narrow our search to one block. Thus the binary search of an index file requires that about $\log_2 n$ blocks be brought into main memory. Once we have searched the index, we know exactly which block of the main file must be examined and perhaps must be rewritten to perform an operation on that file. The total number of block accesses, $3 + \log_2 n$, is not prohibitive, as an example will show.

Example 2.3. Suppose we have a main file of a million records, and ten records fit on a block. The index for this file thus has 100,000 records;

---

† $\lceil x \rceil$ is the ceiling of x, the least integer equal to or greater than x.

‡ Note that we need a table of block addresses, which could be resident in main memory or called into main memory when needed, so we can translate from integer i to the location of block B_i.

since the index records are short, perhaps 100 will fit on a block. Hence 1,000 blocks are needed for the index, that is $n=1000$ in the above calculation. Therefore, accessing and rewriting a record of the main file requires $3+\log_2 1000$, or about 13 block accesses. This figure compares with 3 for the hashed organization. However, there are some advantages to the sorted organization. For example, with the hashed organization it is very difficult to process or list records in the order of their keys, while it is simple to do so with an indexed organization. □

A method of searching an index that can be superior to binary search is known as *interpolation,* or *address calculation search.* This method is predicated on our knowing the statistics of the expected distribution of key values, and on that distribution being fairly reliable. For example, if we are asked to look up John Smith in the phone book, we do not open it to the middle, but to about 75% of the way through, "knowing" that this is roughly where we find the S's. If we find ourselves among the T's, we go back perhaps 5% of the way, not halfway to the beginning as we would for the second step of a binary search.

In general, suppose we have an algorithm that given a key value v_1, tells us what fraction of the way between two other key values, v_2 and v_3, we can expect v_1 to lie. Call this fraction $f(v_1, v_2, v_3)$. If an index or part of an index lies on blocks $B_1, \ldots, B_n$, let v_2 be the first key value in b_1 and v_3 the last key value in B_n.† Look at block B_i, where $i=\lceil nf(v_1, v_2, v_3)\rceil$ to see how its first key value compares with v_1. Then, as in binary search, repeat the process on either $B_1, \ldots, B_{i-1}$ or $B_i, \ldots, B_n$, whichever could contain the value that covers v_1, until only one block remains.

It can be shown that if we know the expected distribution of keys, then we can expect to examine about $1+\log_2\log_2 n$ blocks of the index file. When we add to this the two accesses to read and write a block of the main file, we get $3+\log_2\log_2 n$. For example, under the assumptions of Example 2.3, this number is a little over 6, compared with 13 for binary search.

Operating on a Sorted File with Unpinned Records

Let us consider how to do the operations of lookup, insertion, deletion, and modification on a sorted file with records that are not pinned down, by pointers, to a fixed location. These four operations will require insertions, deletions and modifications to the index file, so it is important to bear in mind that the index file itself is sorted and has unpinned records. Thus in describing operations on the main file, we call for the same operations to be done to the index file, assuming that the reader sees how to implement

---

† If $B_1, \ldots, B_n$ is the entire index, then we can estimate v_2 and v_3 without looking at B_1 and B_n, since we assume the distribution of keys is known.

these operations on the index. Note that since the index file has no index, and lookup strategies for the index file have been described already, we are not using circular reasoning.

The original sorted file is kept on a sequence of blocks $B_1, B_2, \ldots, B_k$, with the records of each block in sorted order, and the records of B_i preceding those of B_{i+1} in the ordering, for $i=1, 2, \ldots, k-1$. In the header of each block is information indicating which of the sub-blocks hold records and which are empty, as for the blocks used in the hashed organization. We now describe each of the four operations, assuming no errors such as trying to modify a nonexistent record occur. Such errors are detected in the same manner as for the hashed organization.

Lookup

Suppose we want to find the record in the main file with key value v_1. Examine the index file to find the block whose first record has a key value v_2 that covers v_1. Search this block for a record with the key v_1. The search of the block may as well be linear, since reading the block normally takes more time than searching it, but we can use a binary search if we wish. We must make sure to consult the bits in the header so we don't accidentally find an empty subblock and decide it holds a record with key value v_1.

Modification

To modify a record with key value v_1, use the lookup procedure to find the record. If the modification changes the key, treat the operation as an insertion and deletion. If not, make the modification and rewrite the record.

Insertion

To insert a record with key value v_1, use the lookup procedure to find the block B_i on which a record with key value v_1 would be found. In the special case that v_1 precedes the key value of the first record of B_1 (and hence v_1 precedes every key value in the file) let $i=1$. Place the new record in its correct place in block B_i, keeping the records sorted and moving records with key values greater than v_1 to the right, to make room for the new record. If block B_i had at least one empty subblock, all records will fit. If v_1 precedes the key value v_2 of the first record of B_i (this can only happen if $i=1$) then we must modify the index file entry for B_i, for which we use the modification procedure just described. Note that even though the record in the index file with key value v_2 has its key value changed to v_1, we do not have to delete and insert, since the position of this record in the index file will not change. Finally, we must change the full/empty information in the header of B_i to reflect the additional record. On the assumption that B_i had at least one empty subblock, we are now done.

Now suppose B_i was originally full, so the last record has no place to go. There are a variety of strategies we could follow here. In the next section we shall discuss a strategy in which B_i is split into two half-empty blocks, and this strategy could be used here. An alternative is to examine B_{i+1}. We can find B_{i+1}, if it exists, through the index file, since a pointer to B_{i+1} is in the record of the index file that follows the record just accessed to find B_i. If B_{i+1} has an empty subblock, move the excess record from B_i to the first subblock of B_{i+1}, shifting other records right until the first empty subblock is filled. Change the full/empty information in the header of B_{i+1} appropriately, and modify the index record for B_{i+1} to reflect the new key value in its first record.

If B_{i+1} does not exist, because $i=k$, or B_{i+1} exists but is full, we must get a new block, which will follow B_i in the order. Place the excess record from B_i in the new block, and insert a record for the new block in the index file, using the same strategy as we have described for inserting a record into the main file.

Deletion

As for insertion, a variety of strategies exist, and in the next section we shall discuss one in which blocks are not allowed to get less than half full. Here, let us mention only the simplest strategy, which is appropriate if relatively few deletions are made. To delete the record with key value v_1, use lookup to find it. Move any records to its right one subblock left to close the gap,† and adjust the full/empty bits in the header. If the block is now completely empty, return it to the file system, and delete the record for that block in the index, using the same deletion strategy. If the block is not empty after deleting the record with key value v_1, we are done unless the deleted record was the first in the block. In that case we must modify the index record for that block.

Example 2.4: Suppose we again have our file of dinosaurs, with blocks of 100 bytes. Recall from Example 2.1 that a dinosaur record takes 44 bytes, so we can pack two to a block. An index record consists of the dinosaur name (20 bytes) plus a pointer to a block, which we assume takes 4 bytes. Thus we can pack four to a block. The initial database is shown in Fig. 2.4. The information about the dinosaurs is omitted.

Suppose now that we add Elasmosaurus to the file. Examination of the index file, say by linear search, discloses that "Elasmosaurus" is covered by "Diplodocus." We follow the pointer in the Diplodocus record of the index file to the third block of the dinosaur file. Scanning that

---

† This step is not essential. If we do choose to close up gaps, we can use a count of the full subblocks in the header in place of a full/empty bit for each subblock.

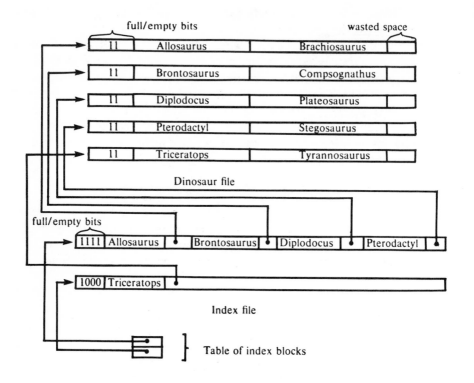

Fig. 2.4. Sorted, indexed dinosaur file.

block, we ascertain that "Elasmosaurus" comes between "Diplodocus" and "Plateosaurus." We therefore move the Elasmosaurus record into the sub-block that held the Plateosaurus record, and the latter record becomes excess. We locate the fourth block of the dinosaur file through the index file and find that the fourth block is also full. We therefore create a new block, placed between the third and fourth blocks in the order, initially holding only the Plateosaurus record.

We then insert a record for this block in the index file. That record replaces the Pterodactyl record in the first block of the index file, and the latter record becomes excess. By consulting the table of index blocks, we find the next index block, discover it has room, and insert the Pterodactyl index record ahead of the Triceratops record. The database at this time is shown in Fig. 2.5.

Now recall that the true name of Brontosaurus is Apatosaurus. We therefore find the Brontosaurus record through the index and delete it from the second dinosaur file block, moving the Compsognathus record left and setting the full/empty bits to 10. We modify the record in the index file for

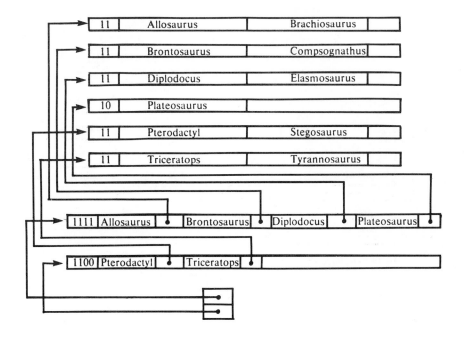

Fig. 2.5. Dinosaur file with added Elasmosaurus record.

block 2 of the dinosaur file by changing its key value from "Brontosaurus" to "Compsognathus." Notice that although the key field is changed, the order of this record is not changed, so we do not have to delete and insert in the index file.

Now we add the Apatosaurus record. We find "Apatosaurus" is covered by "Allosaurus" in the index file, so we are sent to block 1 of the index file. There we insert the Apatosaurus record in the second subblock, and the Brachiosaurus record becomes excess. Fortunately, there is room in the next block, and we insert it ahead of Compsognathus, which is moved back to where it began. We modify the index record for the second dinosaur block, changing its key value to "Brachiosaurus." The final organization is shown in Fig. 2.6. □

Chaining the Files

We should observe that when inserting it is sometimes necessary to find the next block of the main file. Instead of going through the index file we could put a pointer in the header of each block to the next block in the file. Similarly, we could put a pointer to the next block in each index file block. This would obviate the need for a table of index blocks if linear search of the index file were used. We would then need only the address of the first

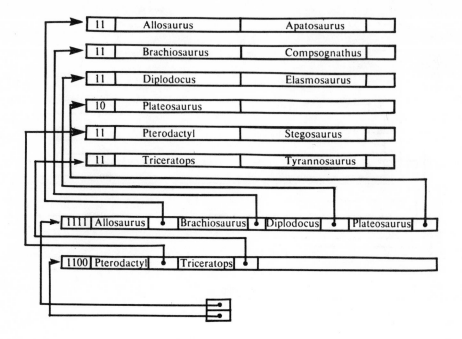

Fig. 2.6. Dinosaur file after changing "Brontosaurus" to "Apatosaurus."
block of the index file.

An Organization for Sorted Files with Pinned Records

If records are pinned down to the place in which they are first stored, we cannot in general keep records sorted within a block. We can even have trouble making sure that the records of each block precede the records of the next block. One solution is to start the file with essentially the same organization as if records were unpinned, as in Fig. 2.4. However, we view each block of the main file as the first block of a bucket. As records are inserted, additional blocks will be added to the bucket, and new blocks are chained by a series of pointers extending from the original block for that bucket. We also create an empty block to begin a bucket that will hold any records that precede the first record of the first block in the initial file. The index never changes in this organization, and the first records of each block of the initial file determine the distribution of records into buckets forever, or at least until the file has gotten so large that it is worthwhile reorganizing it into a larger number of buckets. Let us now describe the way in which operations are performed on a file with this organization.

Initialization

Sort the file and distribute its records among blocks. We might consider filling each block to less than its capacity to make room for expected growth and avoid long chains of blocks in one bucket. Get one additional block to head the bucket for those records inserted later that precede all records of the initial file. Create the index with a record for each block, including the empty block at the front. The index record for the latter block has no key, just a pointer.

Lookup

Find the index record whose key value v_2 covers the desired key value v_1. If v_1 is less than than the first key value of the index file (note that the second index record has the first key value) then the desired index record is the first record. Follow the pointer in the selected index record to the first block of the desired bucket. Scan this block and any blocks of the bucket chained to it to find the record with key v_1.

Modification

The strategy to use here is analogous to that described for the previous organization.

Insertion

Use the lookup procedure to find the desired bucket. Scan the blocks of the bucket to find the first empty place. If no empty subblock exists, get a new block and place a pointer to it in the header of the last block of the bucket. Insert the new record in the new block.

Deletion

Use the lookup procedure to find the desired record. Set the full/empty bit for its subblock to 0. However, as discussed in Section 2.2, if there may exist pointers to the record being deleted, another strategy must be used. The full/empty bit is kept at 1, and to indicate removal of the record, a deletion bit in the record itself is set to 1.

Example 2.5: Suppose we start with a database consisting of the five dinosaurs Brachiosaurus, Diplodocus, Plateosaurus, Stegosaurus and Tyrannosaurus, and we fill blocks as completely as possible in the original database. As in previous examples, blocks are 100 bytes long and so can hold two dinosaur records. The initial database is shown in Fig. 2.7. There are four buckets, which will contain

1.   any name preceding "Brachiosaurus."

2. · any name from "Brachiosaurus" up to but not including "Plateosaurus."

3.   any name from "Plateosaurus" up to but not including "Tyrannosaurus."

4.   "Tyrannosaurus" and any following names.

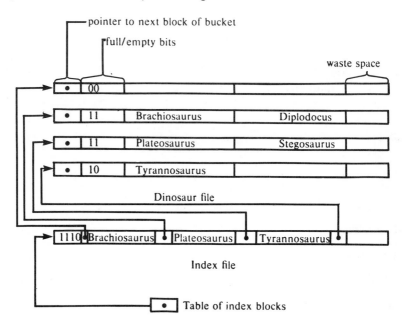

Fig. 2.7. Initial file organization.

Now we add the following dinosaurs. After each name we indicate where the corresponding record goes.

i)   Allosaurus. This record goes in the first subblock of the initially empty block for the first bucket.

ii) Brontosaurus. This record is put into the second bucket. As the only block for that bucket is full, we get a new block and place the Brontosaurus record in the first subblock of that block.

iii) Compsognathus. Another record for bucket 2, it is placed in the second subblock of the second block.

iv)   Elasmosaurus. Again the record is destined for bucket 2. We get a third block for that bucket and place Elasmosaurus in its first sub-block.

v)   Pterodactyl. This record blongs in bucket 3, and goes in a new block.

vi)   Triceratops. Another record for bucket 3, we place it in the second subblock of the second block of that bucket.

Now we discover that the name of Brontosaurus is changed to Apatosaurus. We delete the record for Brontosaurus from bucket 2; no other records for that bucket are moved. The Apatosaurus record is placed in bucket 1 and it occupies the second subblock of the first block for that bucket. The resulting structure is shown in Fig. 2.8. □

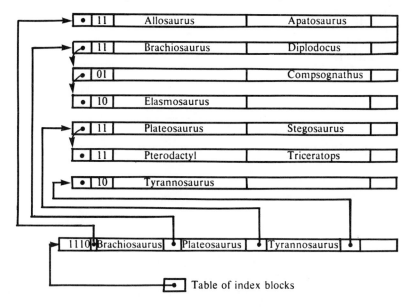

Fig. 2.8. Final file organization.

Additional Links

As for the sorted organization with unpinned links, we may find it useful to link the index blocks in order. We can also link the buckets in order. One way to do so is to leave space for another pointer in each header, and link the first blocks of successive buckets. A way that may save space is to replace the null pointer at the end of the chain for each bucket by a pointer to the first block of the next bucket. A single bit in the header tells whether the pointer is to the next bucket or to the next block of the same bucket.

As records are not placed in a bucket in sorted order after the initialization, we may have difficulty if we wish to examine records in sorted order. To help we can add a pointer in each record to the next record in sorted order. These pointers are somewhat different from the pointers we have been using, since they not only indicate a block, but they indicate an offset within the block; the offset is the number of the byte that begins the stored record, relative to the beginning of the block. The algorithms needed to maintain such pointers should be familiar from an elementary study of list processing.

Example 2.6: The second bucket of Fig. 2.8 with pointers indicating the sorted order is shown in Fig. 2.9. □

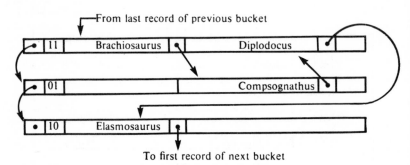

Fig. 2.9. A bucket with pointers to indicate sorted order.

2.4 B-trees

An index being nothing more than a file with unpinned records, there is no reason why we cannot have an index of an index, an index of that, and so on, until an index fits on one block. In fact, such an arrangement can be considerably more efficient than a file with a single level of indexing. A common scheme for extremely large files is to induce a hierarchy of indices that follows the hierarchical nature of the secondary storage devices on which the file resides.

For example, if the file covers several disk units, we could arrange that all records on the first disk unit have key values that precede those on unit 2, which have key values that precede those on unit 3, and so on. The first level index gives the first key value on each unit. Within a unit, the cylinders are ordered, and the second level of index gives the first key value on each cylinder. Then, perhaps, within a cylinder we may order the tracks and use a third level of index to give the first key value of each track. Tracks may be partitioned into blocks and a fourth level of index used. If this organization is used, it is helpful, when the file is initialized, to leave free blocks on each track, free tracks on each cylinder, and so on, to allow the database to exist for a long time without reorganization.

With an adequate file system, we can use a more general scheme in which blocks are treated uniformly, independent of where they are in secondary storage. We can view the hierarchy of indices as a tree, as suggested by Fig. 2.10. We assume in that figure that each block used as an index has space for five records, although, as discussed in Section 2.3, some blocks will hold fewer than the maximum number of records. Since records of an index are not pinned, we shall assume that the full subblocks of any block are to the left of any empty subblocks in that block. In Fig. 2.10 we take key values to be integers, and we have filled in sample key values in the original file, as well as filling in as many key values in the index files as can be determined.

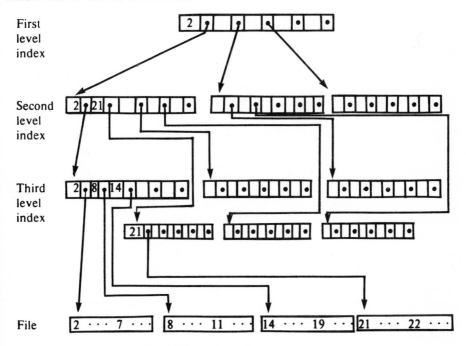

Fig. 2.10. An index hierarchy.

The method for performing lookups, modifications, insertions, and deletions on a multilevel index is a straightforward generalization of the techniques discussed previously. The only problem is what happens when the first level index exceeds the capacity of a block. It should be apparent that the multilevel index idea is not dependent on how may levels of index there are, so we are free to add another level of index, to index what was formerly the first level, should the first level grow beyond the capacity of a block. We are thus led to the idea of a *B-tree* (balanced tree), which is a tree structure similar to that illustrated in Fig. 2.10, but with an unspecified number of levels. We do insist, however, that the tree be *balanced,* that is, every path from the root (the first level index block) to a leaf be of the same length.

We shall assume that the records of the main file are unpinned, although the necessary modification to handle pinned files, where the leaves are the first blocks of buckets, is an easy exercise for the reader to devise. The variant of B-trees that we shall describe shows the blocks of the main file as part of the B-tree. Another approach, which saves space in most situations, is described in Section 2.5. We may keep the main file packed tightly on blocks with records in no particular order. Then the leaves of the B-tree contain not the main file records, but pointers to those records.

For insertion and deletion on a B-tree, we could use the same strategy as was described in the previous section, applying the insertion and deletion operations to the nodes (blocks) of the tree at all levels. This strategy would result in nodes with between one and the maximum possible number of records. Rather, B-trees are usually defined to use a particular insertion/deletion strategy that ensures no node, except possibly the root, is less than half full. For convenience, we assume that the number of index records a block can hold is an odd integer $2d-1 \geqslant 3$, and the number of records of the main file a block can hold is also an odd integer $2e-1 \geqslant 3$.

Before proceeding, let us point out one more difference between B-trees and the index hierarchy depicted in Fig. 2.10. In index blocks of a B-tree the key value in the first record is omitted, to save space. During lookups, all key values less than the value in the second record of a block are deemed to be covered by the first key value.

Lookup

Let us search for a record with key value v. We find a path from the root of the B-tree to some leaf, where the desired record will be found if it exists. We begin our path at the root. Suppose at some time during the search we have reached node (block) B. If B is a leaf (we can tell when we reach a leaf if we keep the current number of levels of the tree available) then simply examine block B for a record with key value v.

If B is not a leaf, it is an index block. Determine which key value in block B covers v. Recall that the first record in B holds no key value, and the missing value is deemed to cover any value less than the key value in the second record. In the record of B that covers v is a pointer to another block. That block follows B in the path being constructed, and we repeat the above steps with the block just found in place of B.

Modification

As with the other organizations discussed, a modification involving a key field is really a deletion and insertion, while a modification that leaves the key value fixed is a lookup followed by the rewriting of the record involved.

Insertion

To insert a record with key value v, apply the lookup procedure to find the block B in which this record belongs. If there are fewer than $2e-1$ records in B, simply insert the new record in sorted order in the block. One can show that the new record can never be the first in block B, unless B is the leftmost leaf. It follows that in no circumstances is it necessary to modify a key value in an ancestor of B, since the first record in each index block omits the key value anyway.

If there are already $2e-1$ records in block B, create a new block B_1 and divide the records from B and the inserted record into two groups of e records each. The first e records go in block B and the remaining e go in block B_1.

Now let P be the parent block of B. Recall that the lookup procedure finds the path from the root to B, so P is already known. Apply the insert procedure recursively, with constant d in place of e, to insert a record for B_1 to the right of the record for B in index block P. Notice that if many ancestors of block B have the maximum $2d-1$ records, the effects of inserting a record into B can ripple up the tree for several levels. However, it is only ancestors of B that are affected. If the effects ripple up to the root, we split the root, and create a new root with two children. This is the only situation in which an index block may have fewer than d records.

Deletion

If we wish to delete the record with key value v, we use the lookup procedure to find the path from the root to a block B containing this record. If after deletion, block B still has e or more records, we are usually done. However, if the deleted record was the first in block B, then we must go to the parent of B to change the key value in the record for B, to agree with the new first key value of B. If B is the first child of its parent, the parent has no key value for B, so we must go to the parent's parent, the parent of that, and so on, until we find an ancestor A_1 of B such that A_1 is not the first child of its parent A_2. Then the new lowest key value of B goes in the record of A_2 that points to A_1. In this manner, every record (v_1, p_1) in every index block has key value v_1 equal to the lowest of all those key values of the original file found among the leaves that are descendants of the block pointed to by p_1. That is, the B-tree, even after deletion, continues to behave as a multilevel index.†

---

† This property is not essential, and we could dispense with the modification of keys in index blocks.

If, after deletion, block B has $e-1$ records, we look at the block B_1 having the same parent as B and residing either immediately to the left or right of B. If B_1 has more than e records, we distribute the records of B and B_1 as evenly as possible, keeping the order sorted, of course. We then modify the key values for B and/or B_1 in the parent of B, and if necessary, ripple the change to as many ancestors of B as have their key values affected. If B_1 has only e records, then combine B with B_1, which will then have exactly $2e-1$ records, and in the parent of B, modify the record for B_1 (which may require modification of some ancestors of B) and delete the record for B. The deletion of this record requires a recursive use of the deletion procedure, with constant d in place of e.

If the deletion ripples all the way up to the children of the root, we may find that we combine the only two children of the root. In this case, the node formed from the combined children becomes the root, and the old root is deleted. This is the one situation in which the number of levels decreases.

Example 2.7: Nontrivial examples of B-trees are hard to show on the page. Let us therefore take the minimum possible values of d and e, namely two. That is, each block, whether interior or a leaf, holds three records. Also to save space, we shall use small integers as key values and shall omit any other fields, including full/empty bits in the header. In Fig. 2.11 we see an initial B-tree.

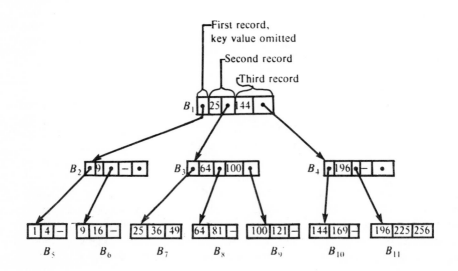

Fig. 2.11. Initial B-tree.

Suppose we wish to insert a record with key value 32. We find a path to the block in which this record belongs by starting at the root, B_1. We find that 32 is covered by 25, the key value in the second record of B_1. We therefore progress to B_3, the block pointed to by the second record of B_1. At B_3 we find that 32 is less than 64, the value in the second record of B_3, so we follow the first pointer in B_3, to arrive at B_7. Clearly 32 belongs between 25 and 36 in B_7, but now B_7 has four records. We therefore get a new block, B_{12}, and place 25 and 32 in B_7, while 36 and 49 go in B_{12}.

We now must insert a record with key value 36 and a pointer to B_{12} into B_3. This causes B_3 to have four records, so we get a new block B_{13}. The records with pointers to B_7 and B_{12} go in B_3, while the records with pointers to B_8 and B_9 go in B_{13}. Next, we insert a record with key value 64 and a pointer to B_{13} into B_1. Now B_1 has four records, so we get a new block B_{14}, and place the records with pointers to B_2 and B_3 in B_1, while the records with pointers to B_{13} and B_4 go in B_{14}. As B_1 was the root, we create a new block B_{15}, which becomes the root and has pointers to B_1 and B_{14}. The resulting B-tree is shown in Fig. 2.12.

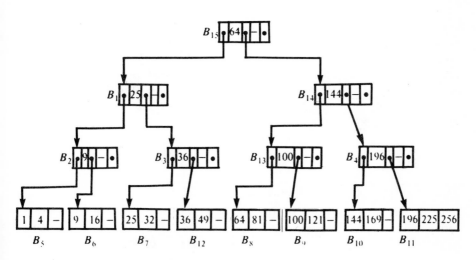

Fig. 2.12. B-tree after insertion of 32.

Next, let us delete the record with key value 64. The lookup procedure tells us the path to the block that holds this record is B_{15}, B_{14}, B_{13}, B_8. We delete the record from B_8 and find that it was the first record of that block. We therefore must propagate upwards the fact that the new lowest key value in B_8 is 81. As B_8 is the leftmost child of B_{13}, we do not change B_{13}, nor do we change B_{14}, since B_{13} is its leftmost child. However, B_{14} is not the leftmost child of B_{15}, so there is a key value in B_{15} that must be changed, and we change 64 to 81 there. Notice that a deletion never causes more than one key value to be changed.

We have another problem when we delete 64. Block B_8 now has only one record. We go to its parent, B_{13}, and find that B_8 has no sibling to its left. We therefore examine B_8's right sibling, B_9. As B_9 has only two records, we can combine B_9 with B_8. Now we discover that B_{13} has only one child, and we must combine B_{13} with a sibling, B_4. Block B_{13} will now have pointers to B_{10} and B_{11}. The key value 196 to go with the pointer to B_{11} is found in B_4, while the key value 144 to go with B_{10} is found in B_{14}. In general, when we merge blocks in a deletion, the necessary key values are found either in the merged blocks or in their common parent.

On combining B_{13} and B_4, we find B_{14} has only one child, and so combine B_{14} with B_1. At this time, B_{15} has only one child, and since it is the root, we delete it, leaving the B-tree of Fig. 2.13. □

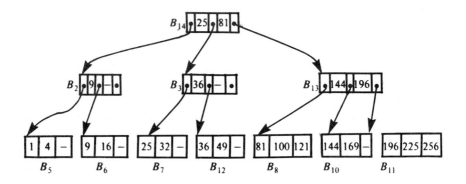

Fig. 2.13. B-tree after deleting 64.

Time Analysis of B-tree Operations

Suppose we have a file with n records organized into a B-tree with parameters d and e. The tree will have no more than n/e leaves, no more than n/de parents of leaves, n/d^2e parents of parents of leaves and so on. If there are i nodes on paths from the root to leaves, then $n \geqslant d^{i-1}e$, or else there would be fewer than one node at the level of the root, which is impossible. It follows that

$$i \leqslant 1 + \frac{\log_2(n/e)}{\log_2 d} = 1 + \log_d(n/e)$$

To perform a lookup, i read operations on blocks suffices. For an insertion, deletion or modification, usually only one block, the leaf holding the record involved, needs to be written, although in pathological cases, about i additional reads and i additional writes may be necessary. Exact analysis of the probability of finding blocks with too many records in an insert or too few records in a delete is very difficult. However, it is not hard to show that even for $d=e=2$, the expected number of extra reads and writes (in excess of the i reads to find the leaf and one write to store the leaf) is a proper fraction. We shall thus neglect this fraction and estimate the number of read/writes at $2+\log_d(n/e)$. Even this figure is conservative, since in the expected case many blocks will have more than the minimum number of records, and therefore the height of the tree may well be less than $1+\log_d(n/e)$.

Example 2.8: If $n=1,000,000$, $e=5$, and $d=50$, the expected number of read/writes of blocks in an operation is $2+\log_{50}(200000) \leqslant 6$. This figure is greater than for hashed access (about 3 read/writes), but is superior to methods using a single level of indexing, except perhaps in those situations where an interpolation search can be performed. The B-tree shares with the methods of Section 2.3 the advantage over hashed access of permitting the file to be listed or searched conveniently in sorted order. $\Box$

2.5 Files with a Dense Index

Suppose we do not wish to keep our file sorted. By allowing records to appear in a random order, we can avoid having many partially filled blocks in the main file. Moreover, insertions are easily made. We have only to keep track of the last block in the file and insert a new record there. When the last block is filled up, we simply get a new block from the file system. If deletions are frequent, "holes" will appear in the file. We could simply ignore the fact that certain subblocks are made empty by deletions, or we could keep a separate file with records consisting of one field, that being a pointer to a block with one or more empty subblocks. We could even make the pointers point to an empty subblock within the block, although doing so will not save block accesses.

The problem with using an unsorted file is that we must have a way of finding a record, given its key value. To do so efficiently, we need another file, called a *dense index*, that consists of records (v, p) for each key value v in the main file, where p is a pointer to the main file record having key value v.

To lookup, modify, or delete a record of the main file we perform a lookup on the dense index file, which tells us the block of the main file we must search for the desired record. We must then read this block of the main file and rewrite it in the case of a modification or deletion; we thus make two more block accesses than are necessary to perform a lookup in the dense index file. (Recall that an "access" is either a read or write of a block.) To perform an insertion, we insert the record at the end of the main file and then insert a pointer to that record in the dense index file. Again this operation takes two more accesses than does the operation on the dense index file.

It would thus seem that a file with a dense index always requires two more accesses than if we used, for the main file, whatever organization (e.g., hashed, indexed, or B-tree) we use on the dense index file. However, there are two factors that work in the opposite direction, to justify the use of dense indices in some situations.

1. The records of the main file may be pinned, but the records of the dense index file are never pinned, so we may use a simpler or more efficient organization on the dense index file than we could on the main file.

2. If records of the main file are large, the total number of blocks used in the dense index may be much less than would be used for a sparse index or B-tree on the main file. By the same token, the number of buckets, or the average number of blocks per bucket, need not be so great if hashed access is used on the dense index as if hashed access were used on the main file.

Example 2.9. Let us consider the same file discussed in Example 2.8, where we used a B-tree with $d=50$ and $e=5$ on a file of a million records. Since dense index records are the same size as the records in the interior nodes of a B-tree, if we use a B-tree organization for the dense index, we may take $d=e=50$. Thus the typical number of accesses to search the dense index is $2+\log_{50}(20000)$, which is less than 5. To this we must add 2 accesses of the main file, so the dense index plus B-tree organization takes slightly less than two more block accesses (the actual figure is $2-\log_{50}(10)$) than the simple B-tree organization.

There are, however, compensating factors for the dense index. We can pack the blocks of the main file fully, if a dense index is used, while in the B-tree organization, the leaf blocks, which contain the main file, are between half full and completely full, so we can save about 25% in storage space for the main file. The space used for the leaves of the B-tree in the dense index is only 10% of the space of the main file, so we still have a net savings of approximately 15% of the space. Moreover, if the main file has pinned records, we could not use the B-tree organization described in Section 2.4 at all, but would have to resort to a B-tree organization where leaves are buckets, perhaps containing several blocks. In this way, the dense index plus B-tree scheme might well prove more efficient than the simple B-tree scheme with buckets. □

Summary

In Fig. 2.14 we list the four types of organizations for files allowing lookup, modification, insertion, and deletion of records given the key value. In the timing analyses, we take n to be the number of records in the main file and, for uniformity with B-trees, we assume the records of the main file can be packed $2e-1$ to a block and records of any index files can be packed

$2d-1$ to a block.

Organization	Time per Operation	Advantages and Disadvantages	Problems with Pinned Records
Hashed	$\geqslant 3$	Fastest of all methods. If file grows, access slows, as buckets get large. Cannot access records easily in order of sorted key values.	Must search buckets for empty space during insertion or allow more blocks per bucket than optimal
sparse index	$\sim 2+\log n$ for binary search $\sim 2+\log\log n$ if address calculation is feasible and is used.	Fast access if address calculation can be used. Records can be accessed in sorted order.	Same as above.
B-tree	$\sim 2+\log_d(n/e)$	Fast access. Records can be accessed in sorted order. Blocks tend not to be solidly packed.	Same as above.
dense index	$\leqslant 2 +$ time for operation on dense index file.	Often slower by one or two block accesses than if same access method used for index file were used for the main file. May save space.	None.

Fig. 2.14. Summary of access methods.

2.6 Files with Variable Length Records

There are many situations in which it is useful to store files whose records have more general structure than those considered in the previous section. In particular, it is convenient to allow fields to be replaced by repeating groups of fields, each field in the group representing the same kind of object. For example, one way to store a many-many mapping from entity set E_1 to entity set E_2 is to create a file with one variable length record for each entity of type E_1. Such records consist of fields representing an entity, say e, of type E_1, and a repeating group of values, each of which is an entity of type E_2 related to e.

Example 2.10: Suppose we have a file of the states and the interstate highways within their boundaries. The states will form entity set E_1 and the highways form set E_2. A variable length record for this file consists of a field whose value is the state name, say a character string of length 15, and a repeating group of values, each of which is a character string of length 3. The file might begin as shown in Fig. 2.15. Notice that the Alaska record has zero elements in its repeating group of highways. □

| Alabama I10 I20 I59 I65 | Alaska | Arizona I8 I10 I17 I19 I40 | · · · |

record for Alabama   record   record for Arizona
                for Alaska

Fig. 2.15. File of states and highways.

We should emphasize that a file such as Fig. 2.15 is a *logical file*, that is, a file at a higher level of abstraction than the files of fixed length records considered in previous sections. Indeed, the principal point of the present section is how one goes about implementing a logical file of variable length records with a file or files of fixed length records.

While in Fig. 2.15 we show actual values for entities, they could just as well be replaced by pointers to records for the states and highways, and attributes of those entities could be kept in another file. In fact, it would be wasteful to keep information about highways in the repeating groups, as this information would have to be repeated once for each state that the highway entered. Moreover, there would be the danger that two copies of the information about a highway could differ. However there is nothing inefficient or dangerous about keeping attributes of the states in their records, as each state appears only once in the file. In fact, if the relationship between entity sets E_1 and E_2 is many-one from E_2 to E_1 (note that the states-highways relationship is not many-one), we could just as well keep the attributes of an entity of type E_2 in the unique record for the entity of type E_1 to which it belongs.

We are thus led to the possibility that elements of repeating groups consist of more than one field. In fact, the fields of a repeating group could themselves be repeating groups, and in this manner we could represent in one file a many-one relationship from entity set E_2 to entity set E_1, another many-one relationship from an entity set E_3 to E_2, and so on. The general definition of a *variable length record format* we shall use is:

1. A variable length record format is a list of "elements."

2. An *element* is either a single field name or a variable length record format, which represents a repeating group of zero or more variable length records with that format.

We can represent variable length record formats in a regular-expression-like notation as follows. An element that is a field name is represented by that name. An element that is a repeating group with format α we represent by $(\alpha)^*$. A variable length record format consisting of elements with representations $\alpha_1, \alpha_2, \ldots, \alpha_k$ is represented by $\alpha_1 \alpha_2 \cdots \alpha_k$. The reader who is familar with regular expressions will notice that the set of possible sequences of field names in a record with the given format is exactly the language denoted by the regular expression constructed in this manner, but it is not essential to one's understanding of variable length record formats that one know about regular expressions. It suffices to remember that * applied to a formula means "repeat zero or more times."

We call a sequence of values that match the fields of a variable length record format an *occurrence* of that record format. Thus the term "occurrence" applies not only to full records, but we may talk about occurrences of a repeating group that is an element of some larger variable length record format. Recall that the possible formats for a repeating group and for a variable length record are one and the same.

Example 2.11:

a) The record format for the file of Example 2.10 is STATE(HIGHWAY)*. That is, the record format consists of two elements. The first is a field, named STATE, and the second is a repeating group of "variable length records." The latter records are not really varying in length and each consists of one field, called HIGHWAY. A typical occurrence of the repeating group HIGHWAY is I95, and an occurrence of the entire record format is:

New Jersey I78 I80 I95

b) If we wished to include the attribute POPULATION in these records we could use the record format

STATE POPULATION (HIGHWAY)*

An example of an occurrence of this format is:

New Jersey 7,168,164 178 180 195

c)   For a more complicated example, we might include with each highway
      in each state the number of miles of roadway and the set of terminal
      or entry points for that highway within the state. The format for
      records with this information is

STATE POPULATION (HIGHWAY LENGTH (TERMINAL)*)*

A typical record with this format is

New Jersey 7,168,164 178 55 Phillipsburg Newark
180 73 Hainesburg Ft. Lee 195 68 W. Trenton Ft. Lee

☐

Storing Variable Length Records

A record with repeating groups cannot be indiscriminately placed in a block
or blocks of storage, because we shall have no way of knowing what type of
field appears where. One possibility is to store each field in sequence, pack-
ing as many to a block as will fit; it is not usual to allow fields to extend
across two blocks, however. A moment's reflection will indicate that if we
simply pack fields into blocks, we shall have great trouble decoding a block
into fields, since to determine where a field begins, we have to know how
long the previous field is. We cannot know how long a field is unless we
know its type. Thus there must be an indication of the field name or data
type along with each field.

This information could be kept in a block header or with the fields
themselves. The former approach requires us to leave space in the header
for the maximum possible number of fields in a block, and most of this
space may be unused in the average block. The latter approach requires
that we examine the entire block from the beginning to isolate any given
field in that block. Some alternative methods for solving this problem
have been implemented in IMS, a database system whose storage structures are discussed in Section 8.4.†

It is often a better approach to represent each variable length record
by one or more fixed length records, and there are three basic strategies for
doing so.

---

† In IMS the objects stored are not fields but "segments," which are records, usually of fixed
length. The analogy between IMS segments and fields as discussed here is a valid one, however.

The Reserved Space Method.

Assume there is a limit c to the number of occurrences of a repeating group. Replace the repeating group by c groups of fields. For example, in Example 2.11(c) we could assume that no highway enters, leaves and then reenters a state. If so, then the repeating group (TERMINAL)* could be replaced by TERMINAL1 TERMINAL2, and the revised record format

>STATE POPULATION (HIGHWAY LENGTH
>TERMINAL1 TERMINAL2)*

would suffice.

If the repeating group occurs no more than c times but could occur fewer than c times, we must have a way of indicating empty fields. One way is by using a "null value," one that could not be a legitimate value in that field. An alternative, which must be used if there is no suitable null value, is to add a field giving the actual number of occurrences of the repeating group; we assume that the empty fields follow the nonempty fields in the group. Thus we might decide that no state has more than ten highways and replace the repeating group for highways by a field COUNT and ten copies of the group. That is, the new record format is:

>STATE POPULATION COUNT
>HIGHWAY1 LENGTH1 TERMINAL1.1 TERMINAL2.1 $\cdots$
>HIGHWAY10 LENGTH10 TERMINAL1.10 TERMINAL2.10

We now have a fixed length record format and can store a file of such records as discussed in Sections 2.2–2.5.

The Pointer Method.

We could replace a repeating group by a pointer to the first block of a chain of blocks used to store the occurrences of the repeating group. For example, we could replace the variable length record format of Example 2.11(c) by the three fixed length record formats

>STATE POPULATION HPTR
>HIGHWAY LENGTH TPTR
>TERMINAL

Figure 2.16 shows how our variable length record might be stored on blocks.

The Combined Method.

There are various combinations of strategies (1) and (2) that can be used. Obviously, we could use pointers for one repeating group and a fixed repetition for another group. In general, we would prefer fixed repetition if there were a reliable maximum number of occurrences, and the average

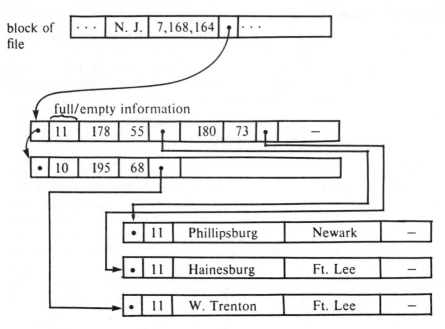

Fig. 2.16. Representing a variable length record with pointers.

number of occurrences was close to this maximum. If the average and maximum number of occurrences differed greatly, we would waste too much
space. Pointer based methods tend to use less space, but they require more
block accesses to find a field than do fixed repetition methods. As an
example, for the record format of Example 2.11(c), we might prefer to use
fixed repetition for the TERMINAL repeating group and pointers for the
HIGHWAY repeating group.

Another mode of combination of strategies (1) and (2) is to replace a
repeating group by room for a small number of occurrences and a pointer
to a chain of blocks where additional occurrences may be found. This strategy is useful if the number of occurrences tends to cluster around the
average number. Then if we choose to make room for slightly more than
the average number of occurrences in the fixed length record, we shall have
few pointers to chase and we shall not waste too much space.

Example 2.12: Let us reconsider Example 2.11(a), where the record format
was STATE(HIGHWAY)*. Suppose we decide to allow room for three
highways in the record for a state. The format of a fixed length record
would then be

STATE COUNT HIGHWAY1 HIGHWAY2 HIGHWAY3 POINTER

Field COUNT indicates how many of the three highway fields are filled.
We assume it is possible to fill these fields from the left, so the count is

sufficient to tell us which fields are full. If values in the three highway fields were pinned, we could, instead of a count, use a bit vector indicating which fields were empty. The field POINTER will indicate the first block of a chain of blocks holding highways in excess of three for a state. The null pointer indicates that there are no extra highways. In Fig. 2.17 we see the records for three states; assuming two state records and four highway records fit in a block. □

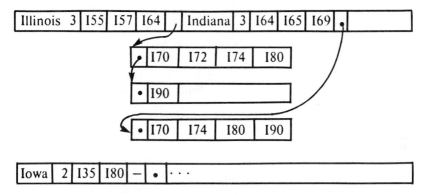

Fig. 2.17. State-highway records using reserved space and pointers.

Operations on Variable Length Records

Suppose we have a logical file of variable length records that we have implemented by a main file with a fixed length record format, perhaps with additional pointers and blocks not part of the main file, as discussed in connection with implementation methods (2) and (3) above. We shall assume that some subset of the fields in the fixed length record format (excluding fields that are pointers to blocks holding occurrences of repeating groups) serves as a key for the variable length records of the logical file. This assumption makes sense if we recall our original motivation for considering variable length records, the representation of a many-many or many-one relationship from an entity set E_2 to another entity set E_1. Then the records will contain the attributes of a unique entity of type E_1, with the repeating group used for the associated entities of type E_2. In this case, the attributes of the key for entity set E_1 serve as a key for both the logical file and the file used in its implementation. Files with variable length records could be used for purposes other than the representation of relationships, and in those cases the main file of the implementation might not possess a key other than the entire set of fields. However, such situations occur rarely.

   Assuming now that some set of fields of the implementing file of fixed length records forms a key, we can organize the implementing file for lookup, insertion, deletion, and modification using any of the organizations of previous sections. The only additional details concern the creation of blocks or chains of blocks for repeating groups during an insertion, if a pointer based implementation is used, and the return of such blocks to the file system if a deletion occurs. The algorithms involved are straightforward and we shall not elaborate on them.

We must also consider a new class of operations on variable length records, operations that have no counterpart for fixed length records. We should consider insertion and deletion of occurrences within a repeating group. These operations correspond to modifications of a relationship, if that is what the logical file represents. Whether the repeating groups are represented by the reserved space method, the pointer method, or a combination, we can view each repeating group as a small file by itself. As for the main file, we assume that there is a key for the repeating group; this key is formed from the fields of the repeating group, but does not include any pointer fields.

We could use any of the methods of previous sections to maintain a small file for a repeating group, but these files are usually sufficiently short that no special organization is used, and given a key value for the repeating group, we simply search linearly through the occurrences of the group. In that case, given a key value, lookup within the group is straightforward; we can delete an occurrence once this occurrence is found, and we can insert, either at the beginning, at the end, or in sorted order, once we have searched the occurrences and determined that no occurrence with the given key value exists.

If occurrences within a repeating group are pinned by pointers to those occurrences, then we must exercise care in how we do insertions and deletions. The ideas are covered in Section 2.2 (hashed files), where we discussed these operations on a bucket of pinned records.

2.7 Data Structures for Lookup on Nonkey Fields

Until now, we have considered only those operations on files where, given a key value, we searched for a record with that key value, and perhaps did something to that record. However, a versatile database system allows queries in which we obtain information from records that are identified by values in a field or fields that do not form a key. For example, referring to our dinosaur file introduced in Example 2.1, the data manipulation language might well allow us to express commands such as:

1.   Find all dinosaurs from the Jurassic period.

2.   Find the habitats with carnivorous dinosaurs.

3.   Find all dinosaurs that lived on land and were at least 50 feet long.

In this section we shall consider how to organize a file so that given values for some particular sets of fields, other than the key, we can obtain efficiently those records with the correct values. The method most generally useful is the creation of "secondary indices," relating values of a field or fields to the records with those values. We consider secondary indices in the present section; the next section considers the more general "partial match retrieval" problem of finding matching records given values for an arbitrary subset of the fields.

Secondary Indices

Let us consider a file whose records have a certain field F whose possible values are taken from the set of values D, the *domain* for F. Field F may be part of a set of fields that form a key, or it may be outside the key. It is possible that the value of field F uniquely determines a record, although we do not assume so. A *secondary index* for field F is a relationship between domain D and the set of records of the file in question.[†] A file with a secondary index on a field F is said to be an *inverted file* (on field F). In terms of Section 2.6, we can represent a secondary index as a logical file with format

VALUE (RECORD)*

An instance of VALUE is a value from D. An instance of RECORD could be either

1. a pointer to a record with the associated value in field F, or
2. a key value for a record with the desired value in field F.

If option (1) is used, the pointer could point to the subblock containing the record, or it could point to the block containing the record, in which case a search of the block would be necessary to find the desired record or records. In either case, the records of the file are consequently pinned, at least to within the block. The pointer could also point to the bucket (for those organizations of fixed length records using buckets) containing the desired record or records. In this case search of a whole bucket for the record is necessary, but records are not pinned (except to within the bucket) unless there are pointers to the file other than those used by the secondary index.

With option (2), records of the main file are not pinned by pointers from the secondary index. However, compared with method (1), method (2) will require several additional block accesses to perform a lookup of a record given its key value, while method (1) goes directly to that record, or at least to its block or bucket.

Example 2.13: In Fig. 2.18 we see a file of dinosaurs again. Presumably there is some sort of primary index on the key field, NAME, but we do not

---

[†] In contrast, the index discussed in Section 2.3, relating key values to records, is called a *primary index*.

show this index, nor do we indicate how the records are distributed among blocks. We do show a secondary index on the field PERIOD, using method (2). This secondary index has only three variable length records, implemented using the pointer method. The secondary index has no index on its own key field VALUE; as there are only three geological periods during which dinosaurs flourished, there is no need for one.

We also show a secondary index on the WEIGHT field. This index uses approach (1) with pointers to the records of the main file. This secondary index has records sorted by their key, the VALUE field, and lookup is by a sparse primary index as discussed in Section 2.3.

Suppose we wish to find the lengths of all dinosaurs from the Jurassic period. We examine the initial block for this index and find a record for "Jurassic." We follow that pointer to a chain of blocks holding the names of these dinosaurs. We then look up in the main file each of the records with these names as key values, using whatever lookup algorithm is appropriate for the unspecified primary index organization of the main file.

Next consider the query: find the names of all dinosaurs with weights between 5 and 10 tons. We begin at the primary index for the secondary index on WEIGHT. The only two records there have WEIGHT values 0 and 15. Since 0 covers both 5 and 10, we need only follow the pointer for 0. In general, if we are looking for the range between m and n we shall have to follow the pointers in the records whose key values cover m and n, and the pointers in any records between those two. In this example, we follow only one pointer, and this leads to a block with WEIGHT values 0, 2, 5, 8, and 10. The last three of these are in the desired range, so we follow their pointers. The pointer for 5 sends us to a block with three pointers to records of the main file, and when we follow these we obtain the names "Allosaurus," "Elasmosaurus," and "Plateosaurus." The pointers for 8 and 10 each lead to a block with one pointer, and following these pointers we obtain the names "Tyrannosaurus" and "Triceratops." □

2.8 Partial Match Retrieval

Many times we are given a query in which the values from two or more fields are specified, yet these fields do not include all of the key fields. Suppose we are told to find the records with value v_1 in field F_1, v_2 in field $F_2, \ldots, v_k$ in field F_k. If S_i is the set of records with value v_i in field F_i, for $i = 1, 2, \ldots, k$, what we want is $S_1 \cap S_2 \cap \cdots \cap S_k$. We shall describe two methods to solve this problem. The first uses multiple secondary indices, and the second involves a specialized form of hashing function. Since the problem involves finding partially specified records, it has become known as the *partial match retrieval* problem.

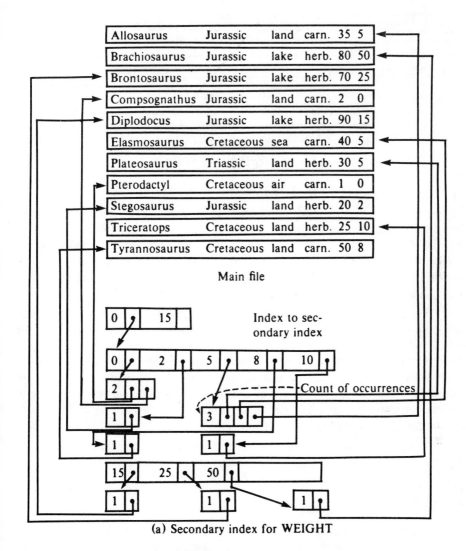

Allosaurus	Jurassic	land	carn.	35	5
Brachiosaurus	Jurassic	lake	herb.	80	50
Brontosaurus	Jurassic	lake	herb.	70	25
Compsognathus	Jurassic	land	carn.	2	0
Diplodocus	Jurassic	lake	herb.	90	15
Elasmosaurus	Cretaceous	sea	carn.	40	5
Plateosaurus	Triassic	land	herb.	30	5
Pterodactyl	Cretaceous	air	carn.	1	0
Stegosaurus	Jurassic	land	herb.	20	2
Triceratops	Cretaceous	land	herb.	25	10
Tyrannosaurus	Cretaceous	land	carn.	50	8

Main file

Index to secondary index

Count of occurrences

(a) Secondary index for WEIGHT

Use of Multiple Secondary Indices

To solve the above problem, we do not actually have to retrieve all the records in S_1, then those in S_2, and so on. Rather, if we have secondary indices for some or all of the fields F_i, we can obtain only the pointers to the records in those sets S_i for which a secondary index for F_i exists. These sets of pointers can, if they are not too large, be intersected in main memory. Then we follow each pointer in the intersection and check that the record pointed to has the desired value in the remaining fields, those for which no secondary index exists. Note that if pointers are to blocks or buckets, rather than to individual records, we have to consider each record

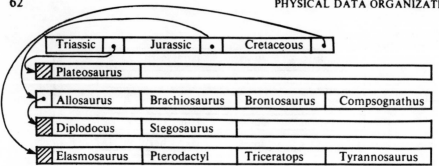

(b) Secondary Index for PERIOD

Fig. 2.18. Secondary indices.

in the block or bucket, and we cannot be sure that even one record there has all the specified values in all the fields with secondary indices. It might be, for example, that a block has one record with value v_1 in field F_1 and a different record with value v_2 in field F_2. In that case a pointer to the block would be in $S_1 \cap S_2$ even though no record of the block had v_1 in F_1 and v_2 in F_2. Such a situation is called a *false drop*.

To minimize the size of the list of pointers with which we must deal, we should first get the set S_i for that field F_i, having a secondary index, for which we expect S_i to be smallest. As a heuristic, we might choose that field F_i with the largest set of different values present in the database, if such statistics are known or can be guessed at. For example, if we are asked for carnivorous dinosaurs of the Jurassic period, we might first look up the secondary index for PERIOD, then DIET, assuming such indices existed, as there are three periods but only two diets.

Extending this principle, the second set S_j in the intersection should be that with the second smallest expected size, and so on. Thus the intersection will shrink as rapidly as possible, on the average.

Partitioned Hash Functions

We shall now mention an interesting method of organization that uses no indices whatsoever, either primary or secondary, yet the organization usually provides significant help in narrowing down the search for records when any set of values for any set of fields is given. Naturally, the more fields there are for which values are specified, the faster the search will be.

The number of blocks to be accessed, when the method to be described is used, is large compared with the number of blocks accessed when the file organization has secondary indices for all fields, so we would not recommend this method of partial match retrieval for extremely large files. However, because no space is used for indices, this method may be a suitable alternative for files requiring a thousand blocks or so. Also, as no secondary indices are present, no time is spent modifying these indices during insertions or deletions to the main file.

The essential idea is that we take all the fields to be the key, even if some subset of the fields could serve as a key, and we hash records using the full set of fields as the key. Now if we used an ordinary hash function, we could obtain the bucket to which a record belongs only if we knew the record exactly. However, if we design the hash function carefully, we can limit the number of buckets in which matching records could be found whenever we know the value of one or more fields. The "trick" is to divide the bits of the bucket number into several pieces and let each field determine one of the pieces. Then, whenever we know one or more fields, we know something about the numbers of the bucket in which the desired record or records could lie.

First, we assume the number of buckets is a power of two, say 2^B, and that a logical bucket address is a sequence of B bits. Translation of logical bucket addresses to physical block addresses can be done by a simple calculation if we can choose the physical addresses ourselves; if the file system assigns block addresses, a table translating logical to physical addresses must be used. Next, we partition the B bits of bucket addresses into groups, one group for each field (a field may be assigned zero bits for its group).

If the fields are F_1, F_2, . . . , F_k, and field F_i is assigned b_i bits, we determine the bucket of a record $(v_1, v_2, . . . , v_k)$, where v_i is the value in field F_i, by computing $h_i(v_i)$ for $i=1, 2, . . . , k$. Here, h_i is a hash function for values in field i, and the value produced by h_i is an integer between 0 and $2^{b_i}-1$. Thus $h_i(v_i)$ is a sequence of b_i bits. We take the logical address of the bucket for record $(v_1, v_2, . . . , v_k)$ to be the sequence of B bits $h_1(v_1)h_2(v_2) \cdots h_k(v_k)$.

Example 2.14: Suppose we have records with three fields

```
EMP_NO   INTEGER(5)
SS_NO    INTEGER(9)   /* Social Security number */
DEPT     CHAR(10)
```

and we wish to store records in $2^9 = 512$ buckets. Suppose also that the nine bits of a bucket address are divided, four for EMP_NO, three for SS_NO, and two for DEPT. The hash function we use for EMP_NO is to divide the employee number by 16 and take the remainder. For SS_NO we divide by 8 and take the remainder. For DEPT we divide the number of nonblank characters in the department name by 4 and take the remainder.†

---

† As with dinosaur names, this hash function is probably inadequate for department names but will make the example easier.

If we are given the record (58651, 130326734, Sales) we divide 58651 by 16 to get the remainder, eleven, or 1011 as a four-bit binary number. The social security number modulo 8 is 6, or 110 in binary, and the length of "Sales" modulo 4 is 1, or 01 as a two-bit binary number. Thus the bucket in which this record will be found is 101111001, the concatenation of hash values 1011, 110, and 01. □

Whenever we are given the value for field F_i, we can compute b_i bits of the bucket address, independently of whether the values in the other fields are known or unknown. Thus, if we know the value in field F_i, we cut down the number of buckets we must search by a factor of 2^{b_i}. For example, if we are looking for the department of the employee with number 58651 in Example 2.14, we must search 32 buckets, corresponding to the 32 possible values of the five bits belonging to fields SS_NO and DEPT. If we know both the EMP_NO and SS_NO of an employee, we need look at only four buckets.

Optimizing the Distribution of Bits Among Fields

Suppose we know the statistics of queries; that is, we know the probability that any given set of fields will have their values specified in a query. Suppose also that when we specify a value for field F_i, any of the possible values for F_i are equally likely. The following theorem provides an important result on bucket addressing in this case.

Theorem 2.1: If all values for a field are equally likely when a value for that field is specified, then the minimum expected number of buckets to be examined to satisfy a query is obtained when, for some $n_1, n_2, \ldots, n_k$ whose product equals the number of buckets, the bucket address for record $(v_1, v_2, \ldots, v_k)$ is expressed as

$$h_k(v_k)+n_k(h_{k-1}(v_{k-1})+n_{k-1}(h_{k-2}(v_{k-2})+ \cdots +n_2h_1(v_1) \cdots))$$

where hash function $h_i(v_i)$ ranges from 0 to n_i. □

The above formula is really a generalization of our approach of using a sequence of bits, calculated separately from the various fields, as a bucket address. That is, in our formulation, $n_i = 2^{b_i}$. Thus our approach is not guaranteed to be optimal, but it is never too far from optimal, and the simplicity of using a sequence of independently derived bits as a bucket address, rather than a formula such as $h_3(v_3) + 3h_2(v_2) + 12h_1(v_1)$, is worthwhile.

The proof of Theorem 2.1 is beyond the scope of this book. It should be intuitively clear that by having each bit of the bucket address only depend on the value of one field, as opposed to the values of two or more fields, we are most likely to know the value of a bit, and therefore are most likely to be able to eliminate a given bucket from the search dictated by a random query. The generalization of this plausibility argument to the bucket address formula of Theorem 2.1, which can be viewed as a variable radix notation for integers† is straightfoward. A proof of Theorem 2.1 is found in Bolour [1979].

While Theorem 2.1 supports our approach of building bucket addresses by concatenating bit strings obtained independently from the several fields, it gives us no hint as to what the values of the n_i's should be, or in our restriction, where $n_i = 2^{b_i}$, what the integer b_i should be. Obviously, the b_i's depend on the frequencies with which various sets of fields have their values specified in a query.

For example, if all queries specified a value for field F_1 and no other field, then we would be best off setting $b_1 = B$ and $b_2 = b_3 = \cdots = b_k = 0$. This situation corresponds to the case where F_1 is a key and in this case, our organization is the same as the hashing scheme of Section 2.2. In this example, each query requires that only one bucket be examined.

As another example, if half the queries only specify F_1 while the other half specify F_2 and F_3, we would expect to be best off if we set $b_1 = B/2$ and $b_2 = b_3 = B/4$, with $b_i = 0$ for $i > 3$. Then we would examine $2^{B/2}$ buckets per query, not only on the average, but in all cases. □

In only a few cases has the formula for the b_i's been obtained in closed form. We mention these cases here.

If a Value is Specified for Only One Field

One such case is when a value is specified for only one field. The following theorem determines the value of b_i that minimizes the expected number of bucket searches in this case.

Theorem 2.2: If all queries specify one field, and p_i is the probability that F_i is the field specified, then assuming no b_i is less than 0 or greater than B, the expected number of buckets to be searched is minimized if we set

$$b_i = \frac{B - \sum_{j=1}^{k} \log_2 p_j}{k} + \log_2 p_i$$

where k is the number of fields and 2^B is the number of buckets. Note that only the last term, $\log_2 p_i$, depends on i.

Proof: If F_i is specified, we look at 2^{B-b_i} buckets. Thus the expected number of buckets searched is $\sum_{i=1}^{k} p_i 2^{B-b_i}$. As $\sum_{i=1}^{k} b^i = B$, using the method

---

† The rightmost digit is the one's place, the next digit the "n_k's place" the third digit the "$n_{k-1} n_k$'s place" and so on.

of Lagrangian multipliers, we know the above expression will be minimized when for all i,

$$\frac{\partial}{\partial b_i} \sum_{i=1}^{k} p_i 2^{B-b_i} + \lambda \left(B - \sum_{j=1}^{k} b_j\right) = 0$$

or equivalently:

$$-(\log_e 2) p_i 2^{B-b_i} - \lambda = 0$$

for all i. Thus there is some constant c such that for all i,

$$p_i 2^{-b_i} = c$$

or

$$\log_2 p_i = b_i + \log_2 c \tag{2.1}$$

Since the b_i's sum to B we see that summing (2.1) gives:

$$\sum_{j=1}^{k} \log_2 p_j = B + k \log_2 c$$

so

$$\log_2 c = \frac{\sum\limits_{j=1}^{k} \log_2 p_j - B}{k}$$

and substituting for $\log_2 c$ in (2.1):

$$b_i = \log_2 p_i - \log_2 c = \frac{B - \sum\limits_{j=1}^{k} \log_2 p_i}{k} + \log_2 p_i$$

as was to be proved. □

There are several problems with the formula of Theorem 2.2. First, what if $b_i < 0$ or $b_i > B$. In the former case, we set b_i to 0, eliminate field F_i from consideration and reapply Theorem 2.2. Note that more than one reapplication of the theorem may be necessary, as some b_j that was positive may become negative on the second application. In the case $b_i > B$, we set $b_i = B$, set all other b_i's to 0, and we are done.

Another problem is that the formula for b_i in Theorem 2.2 may yield a nonintegral number of bits. The rule to be followed to find the optimal apportionment of bits is this. Let $b_i = c_i + d_i$, where c_i is an integer and $0 \leqslant d_i < 1$. Then the d_i's will always sum to an integer if B is an integer. Let $\sum_{i=1}^{k} d_i = D$. Then pick the D b_i's with the largest values of d_i, and raise them to $c_i + 1$. Lower the remaining b_j's to c_j.

Example 2.15: Let us consider the file of Example 2.14. Suppose 75% of the queries specify an employee's EMP_NO, 24% specify the SS_NO, and 1% specify the DEPT. That is, $p_1 = .75$, $p_2 = .24$, and $p_3 = .01$. Suppose $B=9$. As $k=3$, and $\sum_{j=1}^{3} \log_2 p_j = (-0.41) + (-2.05) + (-6.64) = -9.10$, the formula of Theorem 2.2 tells us

$$b_i = \frac{9-(-9.10)}{3} + \log_2 p_i = 6.03 + \log_2 p_i$$

Thus $b_1=5.62$, $b_2=3.98$, and $b_3=-0.61$.

As b_3 is negative, we set b_3, the number of bits allocated to field DEPT, to 0 and resolve the problem as though there were only two fields with probabilities $p_1 = \dfrac{.75}{1-.01} = .758$, and $p_2 = \dfrac{.24}{1-.01} = .242$. Now, $k=2$, so $\sum_{j=1}^{2} \log_2 p_j = (-0.40) + (-2.04) = -2.44$, and

$$b_i = \frac{9-(-2.44)}{2} + \log_2 p_i = 5.72 + \log_2 p_i$$

Whereupon we obtain $b_1=5.32$ and $b_2=3.68$. As the proper fractions in 5.32 and 3.68 total 1, we select the larger fraction, .68, and raise it to 1; the other fraction, .32 is lowered to 0. Thus the optimal apportionment of bits is $b_1=5$, $b_2=4$, and $b_3=0$. that is, five bits from the EMP_NO field, four from the SS_NO field and none from the DEPT field. With this distribution, the expected number of buckets to be searched is

$$.75(2^4) + .24(2^5) + .01(2^9) = 24.8 \text{ buckets}$$

□

If Values for Fields are Specified Independently

The second known case where the values of the b_i's can be found explicitly is if there is a probability p_i that a value will be specified for field i, and this probability is independent of which, if any, of the other fields have values specified. For example, if there are three fields, then the probability that a query specifies values for the first two fields but not the third is $p_1 p_2 (1-p_3)$. Notice that unlike the case of Theorem 2.2, the p_i's need not sum to one.

Theorem 2.3: If the probability is p_i that a value for field F_i is specified, independent of which other fields have values specified, then assuming no b_i is less than zero or greater than B, the expected number of buckets to be searched is minimized when we set

$$b_i = \frac{B - \sum_{j=1}^{k} \log_2(\frac{p_j}{1-p_j})}{k} + \log_2(\frac{p_i}{1-p_i})$$

Notice that the above formula is the formula of Theorem 2.2 with p_m replaced by $\frac{p_m}{1-p_m}$.

Proof: The expected number of buckets searched is

$$\sum_{S \subseteq \{1,2,\ldots,k\}} \prod_{i \text{ in } S} p_i \prod_{i \text{ not in } S} (1-p_i) 2^{b_i}$$

The key observations are first that the above formula is equivalent to

$$2^B \prod_{i=1}^{k} (1-p_i) \sum_{S \subseteq \{1,2,\ldots,k\}} \prod_{i \text{ in } S} (\frac{p_i}{1-p_i}) 2^{-b_i}$$

and then that

$$\sum_{S \subseteq \{1,2,\ldots,k\}} \prod_{i \text{ in } S} a_i = \prod_{i=1}^{k} (1+a_i)$$

Letting $a_i = (\frac{p_i}{1-p_i}) 2^{-B_i}$, we see that the original formula is equivalent to

$$2^B \prod_{i=1}^{k} (1-p_i)(1 + \frac{p_i}{1-p_i} 2^{-B_i}) \tag{2.2}$$

The balance of the proof follows the lines of Theorem 2.2; we use Lagrangian multipliers and take partial derivatives with respect to each b_i. We leave this part as an exercise for the reader. □

We deal with b_i's that are negative or exceed B as in Theorem 2.2. We also adjust fractions in the optimal b_i's as discussed following that theorem.

Example 2.16: Suppose we have a billing file with the following fields

F_1: NAME   CHAR(20)   /* the purchaser */
F_2: ITEM   CHAR(20)   /* the item purchased */
F_3: QUANTITY   INTEGER(9)
F_4: DATE   INTEGER(6)

Let us assume that the probabilities that the various fields are specified in a query are $p_1 = .8$, $p_2 = .5$, $p_3 = .01$, and $p_4 = .2$. and that these probabilities are independent of the other fields specified. For example, the probability of a query like: "find the names and/or quantities of all bills for shirts on July 20, 1978" is $(1-.8)(.5)(1-.01)(.2) = .0198$. That is, about 2% of the queries specify the ITEM and DATE but not the other two fields. Let $B = 9$. Then

$$\sum_{j=1}^{4} \log_2(\frac{p_j}{1-p_j})$$
$$= \log_2(\frac{.8}{1-.8}) + \log_2(\frac{.5}{1-.5}) + \log_2(\frac{.01}{1-.01}) + \log_2(\frac{.2}{1-.2})$$
$$= 2 + 0 + (-6.63) + (-2) = -6.63$$

Thus Theorem 2.3 tells us

$$b_i = \frac{9-(-6.63)}{4} + \log_2(\frac{p_i}{1-p_i}) = 3.91 + \log_2(\frac{p_i}{1-p_i})$$

That is, $b_1 = 5.91$, $b_2 = 3.91$, $b_3 = -2.73$, and $b_4 = 1.91$.

As b_3 is negative, we eliminate the QUANTITY field from consideration and set $b_3 = 0$. Note that unlike Theorem 2.2, no adjustment of probabilities is necessary when we eliminate a field. On reapplying Theorem
2.3 we obtain

$$b_i = 3 + \log_2(\frac{p_i}{1-p_i})$$

for $i=1, \ldots, 4$. Thus $b_1 = 5$, $b_2 = 3$, $b_3 = 0$, and $b_4 = 1$. and no adjustment
of fractions is necessary.

If we apply formula (2.2) to get the average number of buckets, we
obtain

$$2^9 \prod_{i=1}^{4} (1-p_i)(1+\frac{p_i}{1-p_i} 2^{-b_i})$$
$$= 2^9(.2)(1+\frac{4}{2^5})(.5)(1+\frac{1}{2^3})(.99)(1+\frac{.0101}{2^0})(.8)(1+\frac{.25}{2^1})$$
$$= 58.3 \text{ buckets}$$

□

Exercises

2.1: Suppose we have a file of one million records. Each record takes 200
bytes, of which 50 are for the fields of the key. A block has room for
1000 bytes, exclusive of space for the header. A pointer to a block or
subblock takes 5 bytes.

a) If we use a hashed file organization with 1000 buckets, how
many blocks are needed for the bucket directory?

b) How many blocks are needed for the buckets, assuming all
buckets have the average number of records?

c) On the assumption of (b), what is the average number of block
accesses to lookup a record that is actually present in the file?

    d)   If we assume pinned records and use a sparse index that has just been created for the file (all file blocks are full, with no overflow), how many blocks are used for the index?

    e)   If we use binary search of the index, how many block accesses are needed to lookup a record?

    f)   If we use a B-tree, and assume all blocks are as full as possible, how many index blocks are used (among all non-leaf levels)?

2.2:   Suppose keys are integers and our file consists of records with keys $1, 4, 9, \ldots, 15^2 = 225$. Assume that three records will fit in a block.

    a)   If we use the hashed organization of Section 2.2, with the hash function "divide by 7 and take the remainder," what is the distribution of records in buckets?

  **b)   Explain why the perfect squares hash so nonuniformly in part (a).

    c)   Suppose we begin a sparse index organization as in Section 2.3 by packing the odd perfect squares into blocks as tightly as possible. Assuming records are unpinned, show the file organization after inserting the even perfect squares.

    d)   Repeat part (c) assuming pinned records.

    e)   Show a B-tree organization of the file if the fifteen records are inserted in order of their keys. Assume the parameters of the B-tree are $d=e=2$.

    f)   Suppose we use a B-tree with $d=2$ as a dense index on the file. Show the organization if the records are inserted even squares first, in numerical order, then the odd squares in numerical order.

2.3:   Suppose we keep a file of information about states. Each state has a variable length record with a field for the state name and a repeating group for the counties in the state. Each county group has fields for the name and population, a repeating group of township names and a repeating group of city names. Give the record format for variable length state records.

2.4:   Suppose we have variable length records of format $A(B)^*$. An A field takes 20 bytes and a B field 30 bytes. A pointer requires 4 bytes and a count field one byte. Each A has associated with it from 2 to 8 B's, with probabilities .05, .1, .2, .3, .2, .1, .05, respectively. If blocks are 100 bytes long compare the average number of blocks per record used if we adopt

a) the reserved space method,

b) the pointer method, with as many records as possible packed into one block, but with blocks of B fields separated according to their associated A fields, and

c) the mixed method with room for p B fields along with each A field.

What is the optimal value of p?

*2.5: Suppose we have a file with three fields F, G, and H. There are 10 possible values for F, 100 possible values for G, and 20 possible values for H. All 20000 possible (F, G, H) records are equally likely to appear in the file. We assume that all queries specify values for exactly two fields; with probability .8, F and G are specified, with probability .15, F and H are specified, and with probability .05, G and H are specified. Finally, suppose that we are allowed to select two fields on which to create secondary indices. Which two fields should have secondary indices in order that the expected number of retrieved records be minimized? We may assume that in the case where secondary indices for both specified fields exist, we may intersect sets of pointers in memory before we retrieve any records.

2.6: When we create secondary indices, there is a tradeoff between insertion/deletion time and lookup time. Suppose, as an oversimplified example, that if we use s secondary indices, the expected time to find a record is 3^{-s} seconds, while the insertion/deletion is $.1(s+1)$ seconds. If on the average there are 100 lookups for every insertion or deletion, what value of s gives the minimum expected time per operation?

2.7: Complete the proof of Theorem 2.3.

2.8: Suppose we use a partitioned hashing scheme for partial match retrieval as discussed in Section 2.8, and bucket addresses have 12 bits. If there are four fields, and each query specifies exactly one field, with probabilities 1/2, 1/4, 1/8, and 1/8, what is the optimal distribution of bits in the bucket addresses to the fields?

2.9: Suppose all is as in Exercise 2.8, but queries specify any number of fields independently, and the probability that values are specified for the four fields are 8/9, 1/2, 1/9, and 1/17. What is the optimal distribution of bits in the bucket address?

Bibliographic Notes

A variety of books discuss data structures. Among those that emphasize structures for organization of large scale secondary storage are Knuth [1973], Horowitz and Sahni [1976], Martin [1977], and Gotlieb and Gotlieb

[1978]. Hashing techniques are surveyed in Morris [1968], Knuth [1973], and Maurer and Lewis [1975]. The selection of a physical database scheme from among alternatives is discussed by Gotlieb and Tompa [1973].

Fast ordered list searching is discussed by Yao and Yao [1976]. The log log n complexity of interpolation search is shown there; see also Perl, Itai and Avni [1978]. The B-tree is from Bayer and McCreight [1972], where it was presented as a dense index, as described in Section 2.6, rather than in the general form of Section 2.5. The articles by Held and Stonebraker [1978] and Snyder [1978] contain an interesting discussion of the merits of their use in database systems. Yao [1978] analyzes the expected occupancy of 2-3 trees (B-trees with two or three children per node) and shows that on the average, interior nodes have somewhere between 21% and 30% waste space.

The choice of secondary indices is discussed by many people, including Lum and Ling [1970] and Shkolnick [1975]. The point of view generally taken is that the contents of the database can be known before indices are selected. Comer [1978] shows optimal selection NP-complete. (See Aho, Hopcroft, and Ullman [1974] or Garey and Johnson [1979] for a discussion of how NP-completeness implies a problem cannot be solved efficiently.)

The use of partitioned hashing functions for partial match retrieval was considered in its generality by Rivest [1976], and the design of such hashing functions was also investigated by Burkhard [1976]. Theorem 2.1 on the shape of optimal hashing functions is by Bolour [1979]; Theorem 2.2, the case where queries specify one field, is from Rothnie and Lozano [1974], and Theorem 2.3 is from Bolour [1979] and Aho and Ullman [1979]. A related idea, called superimposed codes, also has applications to database systems, as described in Roberts [1978], for example.

3
The Three Great Data Models

In Chapter 1 we mentioned the role of a data model as a basis for data definition and manipulation languages. Now let us consider the three most important such models — the relational, network, and hierarchical. In subsequent chapters we shall explore the relational model predominantly, for reasons we shall discuss at the end of the chapter, after we have had a chance to see the three models in detail. Briefly, the relational model provides the descriptive power of the other models with fewer distinct concepts to learn or special cases to handle. Chapters 4–6 will discuss aspects of the relational model in detail, including a number of high-level data manipulation languages that have been developed for this model.

However, the present state of the art is such that existing commercial systems are almost exclusively based on one of the other two models, a situation that is expected to change slowly. We shall in later chapters consider the hierarchical and network models in some detail too, covering the dominant system designs in these two categories, IBM's hierarchical IMS (Information Management System) and the DBTG (data base task group) network proposal.

3.1 The Relational Data Model

The mathematical concept underlying the relational model is the set-theoretic *relation,* which is a subset of the Cartesian product of a list of domains. A *domain* is simply a set of values. For example, the set of integers is a domain. So are the set of character strings, the set of character strings of length 20, the real numbers, the set $\{0, 1\}$, and so on. The *Cartesian product* of domains $D_1, D_2, \ldots, D_k$, written $D_1 \times D_2 \times \cdots \times D_k$, is the set of all k-tuples $(v_1, v_2, \ldots, v_k)$ such that v_1 is in D_1, v_2 is in D_2, and so on. For example, if $k=2$, $D_1 = \{0, 1\}$, and $D_2 = \{a, b, c\}$, then $D_1 \times D_2$ is $\{(0,a), (0,b), (0,c), (1,a), (1,b), (1,c)\}$.

A *relation* is any subset of the Cartesian product of one or more domains. As far as databases are concerned, it is pointless to discuss infinite relations, so we shall assume that a relation is finite unless we state otherwise. For example, $\{(0,a), (0,c), (1,b)\}$ is a relation, a subset of $D_1 \times D_2$ defined above. The empty set is another example of a relation.

The members of a relation are called *tuples*. Each relation that is a subset of $D_1 \times D_2 \times \cdots \times D_k$ is said to have *arity* k. A tuple $(v_1, v_2, \ldots, v_k)$ has k *components;* the ith component is v_i. Often we use the shorthand $v_1 v_2 \cdots v_k$ to denote the tuple $(v_1, v_2, \ldots, v_k)$.

It helps to view a relation as a table, where each row is a tuple and each column corresponds to one component. The columns are often given names, called *attributes*.

Example 3.1: In Fig. 3.1 we see a relation whose attributes are CITY, STATE, and POP. The arity of the relation is three. For example,

(Miami, Oklahoma, 13880)

is a tuple. □

CITY	STATE	POP
San Diego	Texas	4490
Miami	Oklahoma	13880
Pittsburg	Iowa	509

Fig. 3.1. A relation.

An Alternative Formulation of Relations

If we attach attribute names to columns of a relation, then the order of the columns becomes unimportant. In mathematical terms we view tuples as mappings from attributes' names to values in the domains of the attributes. This change in viewpoint makes certain relations equal that were not equal under the more traditional definition of a relation.

Example 3.2: Figure 3.2 shows two versions of the same relation in the set-of-mappings point of view. For example, as a mapping f, the tuple (Buffalo, W. Va., 831) is defined by $f(\text{CITY}) = \text{Buffalo}$, $f(\text{STATE}) = \text{W. Va.}$, and $f(\text{POP}) = 831$. Note that the order in which the tuples are listed makes no difference in either viewpoint. However, in the traditional view of a tuple as a list of values, the tuples (Buffalo, W. Va., 831) and (W. Va., 831, Buffalo) would not be the same, and the two relations of Fig. 3.2 would not be considered the same. □

As existing relational systems allow the printing of columns of a relation in any order, we shall take the set-of-mappings definition of relations as the standard one. However, there are situations, such as when we discuss relational algebra in Section 4.1, where we shall want to use the set-of-lists definition for relations. Fortunately, there is an obvious method of converting between the two viewpoints. Given a relation in the set-of-lists

CITY	STATE	POP
Buffalo	W. Va.	831
Providence	Utah	1608
Las Vegas	N. M.	13865

STATE	POP	CITY
Utah	1608	Providence
W. Va.	831	Buffalo
N.M.	13865	Las Vegas

Fig. 3.2. Two presentations of the same relations.

sense, we can give arbitrary attribute names to its columns, whereupon it can be viewed as a set of mappings. Conversely, given a relation in the set-of-mappings sense, we can fix an order for the attributes and convert it to a set of lists.

Relation Schemes

The list of attribute names for a relation is called the *relation scheme.* If we name a relation REL, and its relation scheme has attributes $A_1, A_2, \ldots, A_k$, we often write the relation scheme as $REL(A_1, A_2, \ldots, A_k)$. We should observe the analogy between a relation scheme and a record format as well as similar analogies between a relation and a file and between a tuple and a record. The difference in each case is one of the level of abstraction. That is, one possible implementation, among others, for a relation is as a file of records with a record format equal to the list of attributes in the relation scheme, and with one record for each tuple. However, one can conceive of many other implementations for a relation, and some of these will be discussed later in this section.

Representing Data in the Relational Model

The collection of relation schemes used to represent information is called a *(relational) database scheme,* and the current values of the corresponding relations is called the *(relational) database.* We are, of course, free to create relations with any set of attributes for a relation scheme, and we can place any interpretation we wish on tuples. However, we can observe the typical pattern of usage if we recall one discussion of the entity-relationship model from Section 1.4. The data of an entity-relationship diagram is represented by two sorts of relations.

1. An entity set can be represented by a relation whose relation scheme consists of all the attributes of the entity set. If this entity set is one whose entities are identified by a relationship with some other entity set, then the relation scheme also has the attributes in the key for the second entity set, but not its non-key attributes. Each tuple in the relation represents one entity in the entity set.

2.   A relationship among entity sets E_1, E_2, . . . , E_k is represented by a relation whose relation scheme consists of the attributes in the keys for each of E_1, E_2, . . . , E_k. We assume, by renaming attributes if necessary, that no two entity sets have attributes with the same name. A tuple t in this relation denotes a list of entities e_1, e_2, . . . , e_k, where e_i is a member of set E_i, for each i. That is, e_i is the unique entity in E_i whose attribute values for the key attributes of E_i are found in the components of tuple t for these attributes. The presence of tuple t in the relation indicates that the entities e_1, e_2, . . . , e_k are related by the relationship in question.

Example 3.3: Let us explore a database that records baseball players, the teams they played for, their batting averages and positions played. Before showing how data of this nature can be represented as relations, let us consider the entity-relationship diagram that represents the "real world" as it pertains to this example. The entities are

1.   PLAYERS, with attributes

> NAME
> HOME   /* place of birth */
> BDATE   /* date of birth */

attribute NAME is a key.

2.   POSITIONS, with attributes

> POSNAME   /* e.g., pitcher */
> POSNUMBER   /* 1 for pitcher, 2 for catcher · · · */

Either attribute can serve as a key, but we shall take POSNAME as the key.

3.   TEAMS, with attributes

> FRANCHISE /* explained below */
> CITY
> YEAR

The FRANCHISE attribute is a unique identifier we give to a baseball franchise. As a franchise is property, it has existence as an entity even when it moves to another city or changes its name (e.g., the Cincinnati "Reds" have been called the "Redlegs" for two different periods of their history). In all example cases, we use the current name of the franchise as the value of FRANCHISE. A *team* (as opposed to a franchise) is the collection of players, coaches, etc., working for a franchise in a given year. The key for the entity set TEAMS is FRANCHISE and YEAR.

4. BA, the set of batting averages. This entity set has one attribute, PCT, whose values are three digit decimal numbers between 0 and 1. Clearly, PCT is the key.

We shall also discuss the following relationships.

1. The relationship SEASON, between PLAYERS, TEAMS, and BA. Player *p*, team *t* and batting average *b* are related by SEASON if *p* played on team *t*, and his batting average was *b*. Notice that SEASON is a ternary relationship. It is many-one from PLAYERS and TEAMS to BA, in the sense that given a player and a team, that player has a unique batting average. Recall that a "team" exists for one particular year, so the typical player is on many teams and has many batting averages, but just one batting average per year.

2. The relationship PLAYS between PLAYERS and POSITIONS. This is a many-many relationship indicating what positions were played by a player, over the course of his career.

The entity-relationship diagram is shown in Fig. 3.3. We draw an arrow from SEASON to BA to indicate that SEASON is many-one from PLAYERS-TEAMS to BA.

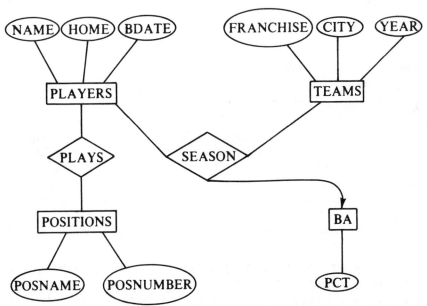

Fig. 3.3. The entity-relationship diagram for the baseball database.

Now let us select relation schemes to represent the entity sets and relationships. First, we have a relation scheme for each entity except BA. While there is no prohibition against a one-component relation (called a *unary* relation), such a relation would tell us nothing. It is merely a set consisting of all the possible batting averages. The three relations for the other entity sets are:

PLAYERS(NAME, HOME, BDATE)
TEAMS(FRANCHISE, CITY, YEAR)
POSITIONS(POSNAME, POSNUMBER)

The relationship PLAYS is represented by a relation whose attributes form the keys for entity sets PLAYERS and POSITIONS. Each of these sets has a one-attribute key, NAME and POSNAME, respectively. Thus we introduce a relation

PLAYS(NAME, POSNAME)

For relationship SEASON we need the keys of PLAYERS, TEAMS and BA. These are NAME, (FRANCHISE, YEAR), and PCT, respectively, so we also have the relation

SEASON(NAME, FRANCHISE, YEAR, PCT)

In Fig. 3.4 we see some sample tuples that would appear in these five relations if they contained all current data.† Notice that tuples need not appear in any particular order, and we certainly do not show all of them. For example, the SEASON relation has tuples for Ruth for all years between 1914 and 1935. □

Implementing a Relational Database

The obvious way to represent a relation is as a file whose record format consists of fields corresponding to the attributes in the relation scheme, in some particular order. Many data definition languages based on the relational model allow the user to specify, from among options, the organization of the file. The options available are usually a subset of those described in Sections 2.2 through 2.5, such as hashed or indexed. Another alternative, which may be the best for relations with few tuples, is the "heap," where the tuples are listed as records in the file in no particular order. A second useful feature found in many relational data manipulation languages is the ability for the user to specify secondary indices on certain attributes or sets of attributes.

As many file organizations are dependent on the existence of a key for records, a relational data definition language should also provide a mechanism for specifying one attribute or set of attributes that forms a key for the relation. The notion of a *key* for a relation is essentially the same as that of "key" in the context of files or entity sets. A relation is

---

† Source: Turkin and Thompson *The Official Encyclopedia of Baseball.* Barnes and Co.

NAME	HOME	BDATE
Ruth, George	Baltimore, Md.	2/6/1895
Cobb, Tyrus	Narrows, Ga.	2/18/1866
Robinson, Jack	Cairo, Ga.	1/31/1919
.	.	.
.	.	.
.	.	.

PLAYERS

FRANCHISE	CITY	YEAR
Red Sox	Boston	1917
Dodgers	Brooklyn	1949
Tigers	Detroit	1911
.	.	.
.	.	.
.	.	.

TEAMS

POSNAME	POSNUMBER
Pitcher	1
Catcher	2
First base	3
.	.
.	.
.	.

POSITIONS

NAME	POSNAME
Musial, Stanley	First base
Cobb, Tyrus	Center field
Cobb, Tyrus	First base
.	.
.	.
.	.

PLAYS

NAME	FRANCHISE	YEAR	PCT
Musial, Stanley	Cardinals	1948	.376
Ruth, George	Red Sox	1917	.325
Ruth, George	Yankees	1923	.393
Cobb, Tyrus	Tigers	1911	.420
Robinson, Jack	Dodgers	1949	.342
.	.	.	.
.	.	.	.
.	.	.	.

SEASON

Fig. 3.4. Part of the five relations for the baseball database.

presumed not to have two tuples that agree on all the attributes of the key. For example, NAME and YEAR form a key for the relation SEASON in Fig. 3.4. We do not expect to find two tuples like

NAME	FRANCHISE	YEAR	PCT
Ruth, George	Red Sox	1917	.325
Ruth, George	Yankees	1917	.302

since we assume each player played for one team only in a given year (or in the case of a trade, we record only the team on which the player finished the season).

Clearly the attributes that form a key for the relation also serve as a key for the file. It is interesting to note that if we design our relation schemes according to the method outlined above, the relations for the entity sets adopt a key from the entity set. Also relations constructed to represent many-one relations from entity set E_1 to set E_2 can adopt the key of E_1. It is only relations for many-many relations that may have no key smaller than the trivial key consisting of all attributes. The general subject of finding and using keys in relations has been well developed, and we shall explore some of the theory in Chapter 5.

Let us emphasize that there is no requirement that each tuple be represented by a record, although this arrangement is by far the preferred implementation in existing systems. For example, a relation with attributes A, B, and C could be represented by a logical file with variable length records of format $A(B(C)^*)^*$, and this logical file could be implemented in one of the ways suggested in Section 2.6. This arrangement saves space if there are relatively few values in the domain of attributes A and/or B. For example, the TEAMS relation of Example 3.3 could be represented conveniently as the logical file FRANCHISE(CITY(YEAR)*)*. FRANCHISE has the smallest domain, there being only two dozen or so franchises. In the logical file each franchise occurs exactly once, while in the relation TEAMS, each franchise occurs in a number of tuples equal to the number of years of its existence. Similarly, in the logical file, each city in which the franchise has resided appears once, while in relation TEAMS, each city appears in one tuple for each year the franchise was located in that city.

Operations on Relational Databases

The basic operations by which a database is modified are the insert, delete, and modify instructions, essentially as introduced in Chapter 2. If the relational data model is used to describe the database, it is natural for these operations to apply to tuples. We shall describe the implementation of these three operations on the assumption that relations are represented by files in which tuples and records are in one-to-one correspondence, and the file is organized by one of the methods of Chapter 2. However, the reader should be able to supply the details of implementation if logical files of variable length records are used. If yet another implementation is used, it is the implementor's responsibility to see that insert, delete and modify can be executed without undue difficulty.

1. *Insert.* For this operation, we are given the tuple to insert and the relation into which it is to be inserted. Select from the tuple the values of those attributes that form a key for the file. With these values, we have only to follow the directions given in Chapter 2 for the appropriate file organization, to insert the record made from the tuple. Conversion of a tuple to a record is not hard. As a tuple is a logical data item it may, for example, have for an attribute value a character string that is too short for the corresponding field of the record, which holds character strings of fixed length. Therefore we must pad the attribute value with blanks to make a field value. Similarly, the value of an attribute could be an integer while the corresponding field takes real values; again a straightforward conversion is necessary.

2. *Delete.* Suppose we are given a relation and values for at least those attributes that form a key for that relation and its underlying file. We may therefore apply the deletion procedure for the appropriate organization directly to the underlying file. Many systems allow deletion of a set of tuples even if the key is not given. In this case we must scan the entire file no matter which of the standard organizations are used.

3. *Modify.* Here we are given a relation, values for the key attributes and new values for those attributes that must change. Again the translation from attribute values to field values is straightforward, and we may apply the appropriate modification procedure to the file as described in Chapter 2. If we are not given values for attributes in the key, we are again forced to scan the entire file.

Interrogation of a Relational Database

The lookup operation on a relation also presents no surprises. However, data manipulation languages using the relational model generally have a rich set of commands, from which we can build a variety of "queries" that obtain data from one or more relations. Some examples of how queries are expressed in existing relational database management systems will be given in the next chapter. However, let us here give some idea of typical queries and the problems they entail.

Example 3.4: Consider the relational database that was described in Fig. 3.4. One type of query asks for the values of certain attributes in those tuples of a relation that satisfy a particular condition. For example, we might ask for the name and franchise of all those players that batted .300 or over for at least one season while playing for that franchise. To implement this query we must scan the tuples of the SEASON relation, or strictly speaking, we scan the records of the file representing the relation. Each time we encounter a tuple for which PCT is at least .300, we collect the NAME and FRANCHISE values from that tuple. To avoid examining the record for every tuple, it would be useful to have a secondary index on attribute PCT for the file. We would also find it convenient if the secondary index, which is a logical file of variable length records of the form PCT(RECORD)*, were sorted on its key, PCT. However, none of these conveniences are essential; they merely speed up processing.

Once we have collected all the desired pairs (NAME, FRANCHISE), we could print them out as is. Strictly speaking, we have produced a relation with relation scheme (NAME, FRANCHISE), and the mathematical notion of a relation does not permit duplicate tuples. Therefore, we should, in principle, remove duplicate tuples, which will occur whenever a player batted .300 or more for two or more seasons for the same franchise. We could, for example, sort the relation by NAME and, within each group of tuples with the same NAME, sort by FRANCHISE. Then duplicate tuples will be adjacent in the order, and can be removed easily. However, many relational DBMS's will not eliminate duplicate tuples unless specifically directed to do so by the user.

As a further example, let us again consider the database of Fig. 3.4, and suppose we ask for the franchise for which Ty Cobb played in 1911. Since NAME and YEAR form a key for the SEASON relation, it is straightforward to execute a lookup on the file representing SEASON, finding the desired record, and determining that the FRANCHISE attribute for the record is "Tigers."

Now suppose that instead of asking for Cobb's franchise in 1911, we asked for the city in which he played that year. This information is not available from the SEASON relation. However, we can obtain the answer by proceeding as above to determine that Cobb played for the Tigers in 1911, then using ("Tigers", 1911) as a key value in the TEAMS relation to discover that the Tigers franchise was in Detroit in 1911. □

The process of following logically connected data from relation to relation in order to obtain desired information is called *navigation*. We saw our first example of navigation in the last part of Example 3.4. In the next chapter we shall consider some of the ways that relational data manipulation languages allow the user to navigate, that is, to connect information from two or more relations. In general, navigation in a broader sense, meaning to follow connections between several parts of that database, is part of any data manipulation language, regardless of the model.

3.2 The Network Data Model

Roughly, the network data model is the entity-relationship model with all relationships restricted to be binary, many-one relationships.† This restriction allows us to use a simple directed graph model for data. It also makes implementation of relationships simpler, as we shall see when we discuss a concrete implementation of the network model in Chapter 7.

There is no consistent terminology for the network model, so we shall adopt our own, trying to be consistent with terms we have used, or shall use, for files and for the other data models. In place of entity sets, we shall talk about *logical record types,* in the network model. A logical record type is essentially a relation, that is, a named set of tuples. However, as in the entity-relationship model, we admit the possibility that two identical records of the same logical record type exist; these records are distinguished only by their relationship to records of another logical type. In the network model, we use the term *logical record* in place of "tuple," and *logical record format* ‡ in place of "relation scheme." We call the component names in a logical record format *fields.*

Let us at the outset justify our decision to change terminology between the relational and the network model by reminding the reader that in the network model, logical record types are used principally to represent what we have called entity sets, while in the relational model, we use relations to represent both entities and relationships. While we cannot rule out bizarre uses of any data model, we feel it would do violence to the intuitive purposes of relations and logical record types if we tried to merge the two concepts.

Instead of "binary many-one relationships" we talk about *links.* We draw a directed graph, called a *network,* which is really a simplified entity-relationship diagram, to represent record types and their links. Nodes correspond to record types. If there is a link between two record types T_1 and T_2, and the link is many-one from T_1 to T_2, then we draw an arc from the node for T_1 to that for T_2,§ and we say the link is from T_1 to T_2. Nodes and arcs are labeled by the names of their record types and links.

---

† Some rather general definitions of the network model allow many-many relationships, requiring only that they be binary.
‡ We drop the word "logical" from "logical record," or "logical record type/format" whenever there is no confusion with the terms for files.
§ Some works on the subject draw the arc in the opposite direction. However, we chose this direction to be consistent with the notion of functional dependency discussed in Chapter 5. Our point of view is that arrows mean "determines uniquely." Thus, as each record of type T_1 is linked to at most one record of type T_2, we draw the arrow into T_2.

Representing Entity-Relationship Diagrams in the Network Model

As we have stated, entity sets are represented directly by logical record types. The attributes of an entity set are fields of the logical record format. In the case that an entity is determined uniquely only through a relationship with another entity, we shall add another field that is a serial number for the entity set, uniquely identifying each entity. This serial number might be a field only on the logical level; in the implementation we could use the location of the record representing the entity as its "serial number."

Among relationships, only those that are binary and many-one (or one-one as a special case) are representable directly by links. However, we can use the following trick to represent arbitrary relationships. Say we have a relationship R among entity sets $E_1, E_2, \ldots, E_k$. We create a new logical record type T representing k-tuples $(e_1, e_2, \ldots, e_k)$ of entities that stand in the relationship R. The format for this record type might consist of a single field that is a serial number identifying logical records of that type, although there are many situations where it is convenient to add other information-carrying fields in the format for the new record type T. We then create links $L_1, L_2, \ldots, L_k$. Link L_i is from record type T to the record type T_i for entity set E_i. The intention is that the record of type T for $(e_1, e_2, \ldots, e_k)$ is linked to the record of type T_i for e_i, so each link is many-one.

Example 3.5: Let us represent in the network model the information about baseball players and teams shown in the entity-relationship diagram of Fig. 3.3. First we shall have logical record types PLAYERS, TEAMS and POSITIONS. The fields of their logical record formats are the same as the attributes of the relations of the same name, from Example 3.3. There is no logical record type for entity set BA, for reasons we shall discuss in connection with the relationship SEASON.

Consider now the many-many relationship PLAYS, between PLAYERS and POSITIONS. To represent PLAYS we need a new record type, which we call PP. The record format for PP consists of a serial number PPID. There are two links, PP_PLAYERS from PP to PLAYERS and PP_POSITIONS, from PP to POSITIONS.

We also need to represent the ternary relationship SEASON among entity sets PLAYERS, TEAMS, and BA. We create a new logical record type PTB with a serial number field named PTBID. We create links PTB_PLAYERS, from PTB to PLAYERS, and PTB_TEAMS, from PTB to TEAMS. We could also create a link from PTB to BA, but we do not need to do so, because the SEASON relationship uniquely determines a batting average, given a player and team. Thus we could include the PCT attribute in the PTB record format, allowing us to avoid the existence of a BA record type and a link from PTB to BA. Notice that we could, in principle, include the attributes of PLAYERS and TEAMS in the PTB format, as well, but to do so would waste a considerable amount of space; the attribute values for each team would be repeated once for each player on the team, and the attributes of a player would be repeated once for each team he was on.

The logical record types we have defined are listed below. As for relation schemes, we use the notation $R(A_1, A_2, \ldots, A_k)$ for record type R with format $A_1, A_2, \ldots, A_k$.

> PLAYERS(NAME, HOME, BDATE)
> TEAMS(FRANCHISE, CITY, YEAR)
> POSITIONS(POSNAME, POSNUMBER)
> PP(PPID)
> PTB(PTBID, PCT)

The links are:

> PP_PLAYERS from PP to PLAYERS
> PP_POSITIONS from PP to POSITIONS
> PTB_PLAYERS from PTB to PLAYERS
> PTB_TEAMS from PTB to TEAMS

The network is shown in Fig. 3.5.

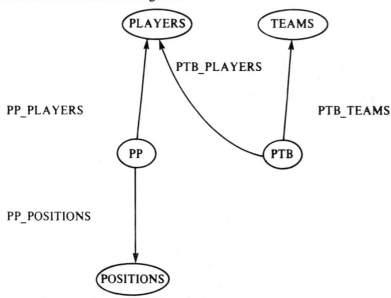

Fig. 3.5 Network for baseball database.

In Fig. 3.6 we show some sample logical records of each type and the occurrences of links among these records. There may, of course, be other link occurrences involving some of the records shown. □

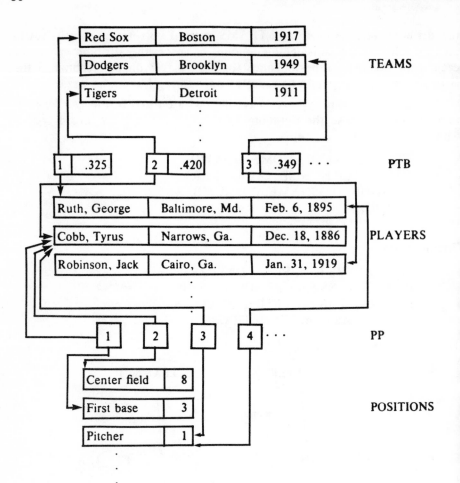

Fig. 3.6. Some logical records in the baseball database.

Implementation of a Network

We can represent the logical records of a given record type by a file in the obvious manner, with one field of each record for each field of the logical record. We may dispense with fields for artificially created serial number attributes as in PP or PTB of Example 3.5, by using the location of the records to identify records uniquely. As we shall see, even if a logical record format consists only of the serial number attribute, its records need not disappear entirely, and the presence of those records surely will influence the organization of the database, no matter what representation we choose for the network.

Suppose we have a link from record type T_1 to record type T_2. Since the link is many-one from T_1 to T_2, we could represent it by variable length records of the format $T_2(T_1)^*$. That is, after each record of type T_2, list all the associated records of type T_1. The variable length records can then be represented in one of the ways discussed in Section 2.6. If there is another link from record type T_3 to T_2, we can list the occurrences of T_3 records with the corresponding T_2 records, using a variable length record format like $T_2(T_1)^*(T_3)^*$. Again, the methodology of Section 2.6 can be used to implement such variable length records.

However, suppose there is another link from T_1 to some record type T_4. We cannot list T_1 records after T_2 records and also list them after T_4 records, or at least, it would hardly be efficient or convenient to do so. We therefore need another way of representing links, one that does not force records of one type to be adjacent to records of another type. In this organization, called a *multilist*, each record has one pointer for each link in which it is involved, although there is the option of eliminating the pointer for one link and representing that link by variable length records as discussed above.

Suppose we have a link L from T_1 to T_2. For each record R of type T_2 we create a circular chain from R, to all the records R_1, R_2, ..., R_k of type T_1 linked to R by L, and then back to R. The pointers for link L in records of types T_1 and T_2 are used for this purpose. We show an example chain in Fig. 3.7. Note how we can follow the chain from R to visit each of R_1, R_2, ..., R_k and, if records of type T_2 are identifiable in some way (e.g., each record begins with a few bits indicating its record type, or the record address determines the type) we can go from any of R_1, R_2, ..., R_k to R.

It is important to remember that in a multilist organization, each record has as many pointers as its record type has links. As the pointers are fields in the records, and therefore appear in fixed positions, we can follow the chain for a particular link without fear of accidentally following some other link. Also remember that since links are many-one, each circular chain has exactly one record of one type and zero or more records of the second type. Notice that if we tried to represent many-many relationships by multilists we would face severe problems, since each record could be on many chains for the same relationship. We would not know in advance how many pointers were needed in a record for each link, and we would have trouble determining which link was for which chain. The problem is not conveniently solved, which explains why the network model emphasizes many-one links.

Example 3.6: Let us take a simple example of a many-many relationship implemented by two many-one links and a dummy record type. The two entity sets involved in the relationship are DEPTS (of a department store) and ITEMS, and the relationship is SELLS. As most departments sell more than one item, and an item could be sold by more than one department,

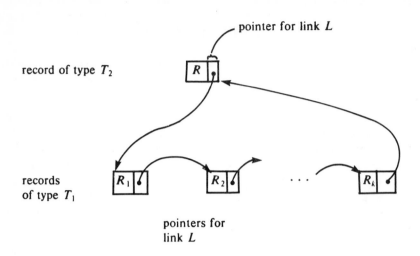

Fig. 3.7. A circular chain.

SELLS is a many-many relationship. To represent SELLS in the network model, we need the intermediate record type DI and two links:

1.   SELLING_DEPT from DI to DEPTS, and

2.   ITEM_SOLD from DI to ITEMS.

In Fig. 3.8 we see a portion of the physical database, where links are represented by multilists. We see two departments, Clothing and Toys, and five items,

1.   Shirts, sold by the Clothing Dept.

2.   Skirts, sold by the Clothing Dept.

3.   "G.I. Jack" dolls, sold by the Toy Dept.

4.   G.I. Jack Flak Jackets, sold by both the Toy and Clothing Depts.

5.   Basilisk collars, sold by no department, due to insufficient demand.

We see in Fig. 3.8 two pointers in each DI record; the first is for link SELLING_DEPT and the second for ITEM_SOLD. The DEPTS records show only the pointer for SELLING_DEPT; there could be other links involving DEPTS. Similarly, we show in ITEMS records only the pointer for the ITEM_SOLD link. SELLING_DEPT pointers are shown with solid lines and ITEM_SOLD pointers are dashed lines. □

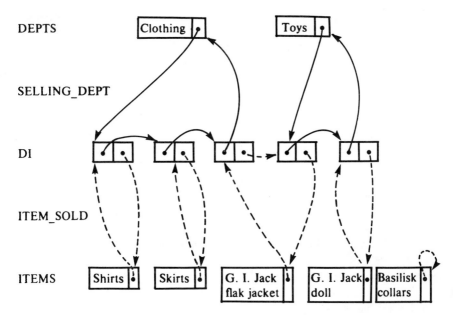

Fig. 3.8 A multilist implementation of a network.

Operations on Networks

As in the relational model, the basic commands to change the database are insertions, deletions and modifications. But while in the relational model we had only to consider these operations on relations, for the network model we must consider the operations on both logical record types and on links. The principles are the same for all three operations, in that each operation is implemented by the corresponding operation on a file, so let us discuss only insertion.

To insert a logical record into a logical record type, we create a physical record from the logical record just as we converted a tuple to a record in the relational model. We then insert the record into the file representing the logical record type, using the appropriate technique from Chapter 2, depending on the file organization.

Suppose now that we have a link L from record type T_1 to record type T_2, and we wish to add to this link the fact that record R_1 of type T_1 is associated with record R_2 of type T_2. First, if necessary, we insert R_1 and R_2 into the files for T_1 and T_2, respectively. If link L is represented by variable length records of the format $T_2(T_1)^*$, we look up the record for R_2 in the file representing the variable length records, and insert R_1 onto the list of associated records of type T_1, using an algorithm from Section 2.6; the exact algorithm depends on how variable length records are represented.

If link L is represented by a multilist organization, we again look up the record for R_2 in the file for T_2. We also look up the record for R_1 in the file for T_1. We then link the latter onto the chain of the former, using elementary list processing operations on the fields of R_1 and R_2 that hold the pointers associated with L.

Note that for both the above representations of links we assume that R_1 was not previously linked to any record of type T_2. If that assumption is false we must first look up R_1 in the file for T_1. If the multilist strategy is used it is a simple matter to remove R_1 from whatever chain for L on which R_1 appears. If the variable length record approach is used to represent L, matters are not so simple. There may be no convenient way to get from R_1 to the record R_3 of type T_2 with which it is currently linked. Fortunately, an easy fixup for each of the representations of variable length records exists to allow us to get from R_1 to R_3. For example, if the records of type T_2 have a pointer to a chain of blocks with associated records of type T_1, we can end the chain with a pointer back to the type T_2 record to which the chain belongs.

Queries on Networks

The simplest queries to answer about a database represented by the network model, involve only attributes of one record type. For example, referring to the database of Example 3.5, we could answer: "What is Ruth's birthday?" by doing a lookup on the file for record type PLAYERS, with value "Ruth, George" for the attribute NAME. Since NAME is the key for PLAYERS, this lookup can be done efficiently. If the query gives us the values of attributes that do not form a key, then we need secondary indices for the file on at least some of the given attributes, or we must search the entire file.

Next, in order of difficulty, come queries that involve following a link. We may be given a key value for a record of type T_2 and be asked to find a record or records of type T_1 to which it is linked by link L from T_1 to T_2. Referring again to Example 3.5, we may be asked "Did Robinson ever bat over .340?" We find the PLAYERS record for Robinson, which gives us access to the list of PTB records for Robinson, by following the PTB_PLAYERS link. We can scan these records for one with a PCT value above .340 and find one with .342.

It is also possible that we are given a key value for a record R of type T_1 and are asked to find the unique record of type T_2 linked to it by link L from T_1 to T_2. If L is represented in multilist fashion, this task is easy; we follow the chain for L on which R appears, until we come to the record of type T_2 on the chain. If L is represented by variable length records, we must have available a pointer that gets us from R to the beginning of the variable length record of which it is part, as discussed in connection with the deletion of links. If the pointer exists, we have no problem; if not we shall have to scan the entire file of records of type T_2 to discover which one has R associated with it.

The hardest kind of query to handle is one that involves following two or more links. For example, suppose we ask: "What center fielders batted over .400?" We begin by finding the POSITIONS record for "Center field," which is easy, since POSNAME is a key for that record type. Next we examine each of the PP records linked to "Center field" by the PP_POSITIONS link. We follow the PP_PLAYERS link to obtain a unique PLAYERS record for each PP record. Lastly, from each PLAYERS record found, we examine the PTB records linked to it by the PTB_PLAYERS link, and if one or more PTB records for that player have a PCT value above .400, we print the name of the player.

3.3 The Hierarchical Data Model

A *hierarchy* is simply a network that is a *forest* (collection of trees) in which all links point in the direction from child to parent. We shall continue to use network terminology "logical record type," and so on, when we speak of hierarchies. One additional concept that is useful when dealing with hierarchies is the *virtual* logical record type, which is a pointer to a record of a given logical type. Virtual record types are needed in situations where intuitively we would like to place a record type in two or more trees of a hierarchy, or even in several places in one tree. We do not wish to place two copies of a record in two positions in the database; to do so wastes space and invites the possibility that we might change one copy without changing the other. Therefore, each logical record type appears in one place in the hierarchy, and other places where we would like that record type are given virtual records instead.

Using virtual types, we can convert any network to a hierarchy. Begin with any logical record type R, which becomes the root of the first tree. If possible, choose R to have no links leaving. The children of record type R are any types that have links entering R. Their children are found by following links backward from them, from head to tail, and so on. However, if we ever encounter a type we have already placed in the hierarchy, we create a virtual record type, put this virtual record type in the hierarchy instead of the logical type encountered, and do not add any children of the virtual type. When we can add no more children to the tree under construction, look for a logical record type not already placed in the hierarchy. If we find none, we are done. Otherwise, repeat the tree construction process with one of the previously unplaced logical record types.

Example 3.7: Let us convert the network of Fig. 3.5 to a hierarchy. We might begin with PLAYERS, which has arcs from PP and PTB entering, but no arcs leaving. The latter two record types have no arcs entering, so we are done with the first tree; it has PLAYERS as root and PP and PTB as children. Our second tree might start with TEAMS. There is one entering arc, from PTB, which we have already placed in the hierarchy. Thus we give TEAMS a virtual record type "pointer to PTB" as child and go on to the third tree, which consists of root POSITIONS with virtual PP as child. The entire hierarchy is shown in Fig. 3.9. Let us observe now that this hierarchy is a poor way to represent the baseball database, because the sorts of queries about this database that are phrased easily in hierarchy-based data manipulation languages do not include some very natural queries. We shall justify this remark about queries and give a better hierarchical representation shortly.

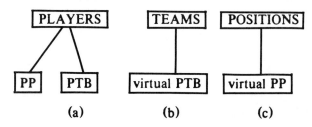

Fig. 3.9. A hierarchical representation of the baseball database.

An instance of the database described by a tree of logical record types may be viewed as a forest. For each logical record type in the hierarchy, the database will have zero or more nodes, each representing a record of that type. It is sometimes useful to draw each tree in the database with a dummy root, whose children are the record occurrences of the root record type. For example, part of the database tree for scheme (a) of Fig. 3.9 is shown in Fig. 3.10. The numbers 1 through 5 are serial numbers, which identity PP and PTB records. The serial numbers disappear in an implementation. □

Direct Representation of Many-Many Relationships in a Hierarchy

Sometimes, hierarchies designed directly from a network can lead to awkwardness when we try to answer queries. Consider the hierarchy of Fig. 3.9, and suppose we wanted to know what positions Cobb played. We would start at the root of Fig. 3.10 and search for the PLAYER record for Cobb. We might be aided in our search by an appropriate organization of the file of PLAYER records, so suppose we find the Cobb record easily. We scan those children of that record that are of PP type. Say we examine the record with serial number 1. We must now go to the database corresponding to tree (c) of Fig. 3.9 and examine each POSITION record. For each such record, we look at its children. which are virtual PP records, that is, pointers to PP records in the database for tree (a). If we find a

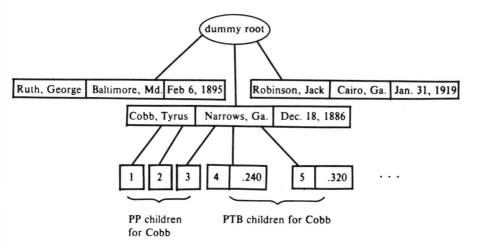

Fig. 3.10. Part of a database in the form of a tree.

virtual PP record for a position that points to the PP record with serial number 1, then we know Cobb played that position.

We might ask why it is much easier to answer this query in the network of Fig. 3.5 than in the hierarchy of Fig. 3.9. The reason is that links in a network are essentially two-way connectors, and in Fig. 3.5 we are able to go directly from a PP record to a POSITIONS record. However, the algorithm above for converting a network to a hierarchy broke the link from PP to POSITIONS, although the link from POSITIONS to PP exists due to the pointers in the virtual PP records. There is an inherent tendency for links to get broken when we go from a network to a hierarchy, although they can be maintained by introducing extra pointer fields into the logical record types of the hierarchy.

Another problem with a poorly designed hierarchy is that while we can navigate wholly within a database built along the lines of the network data model, in a hierarchy we must sometimes jump from tree to tree. This can only be accomplished by reading a value from the database into the workspace of the application program (e.g., the serial number 1 in Example 3.7) and using that value to access information in another tree.

For these reasons, one must often exercise care in designing a hierarchy, so values will be available where needed. One useful idea is the following. Suppose we have entity sets E_1 and E_2 with a many-many relationship R between them. We can represent R in a hierarchy by selecting either E_1 or E_2, say E_1, to be the root of a tree. We give the root a child logical record type T consisting of

1.   a serial number, to identify records, and

2.   attributes forming a key for E_2.

As in networks, the serial number might not appear in the implementation, being replaced, in essence, by the address of the record. We do not wish to place all attributes of E_2 in the format for record type T, because we would then have the task of making sure that several E_2 records representing the same entity had the same information. Instead, we create another logical record type with all the attributes of E_2; this record type will be placed somewhere in the hierarchy — at the root of its own tree if no more convenient place can be found.

In some applications it is only necessary to find E_2 entities associated with a given E_1 entity, and if so, the above arrangement is ideal. However, in other cases it may also be essential that we be able to find the E_1's associated with an E_2 conveniently. If this is the case, we can include, as a child of the E_2 record type, a new record type consisting of the key fields of E_1.

Another possibility is to replace the record types consisting of the keys for E_1 and/or E_2 by pointers to E_1 or E_2 records, respectively. This arrangement pins the records pointed to, but it allows direct access to those records. In comparison, using key values to indicate records requires us to search for the desired record. The reader is referred to Chapter 8 for a detailed example of how a major hierarchical DBMS facilitates the implemation and use of many-many relationships in practice.

Example 3.8: Let us redesign the hierarchy for the baseball database. Remember, the original definition of the database scheme is the entity-relationship diagram of Fig. 3.3. To express the PLAYS relationship we shall have a tree whose root is the logical record type

(NAME, HOME, BDATE)

representing PLAYERS. The root has a child logical record type

(SERIAL1, POSNAME)

representing the names of the positions each player plays. The attribute SERIAL1 is a serial number used to identify records, and it will probably disappear in an implementation, being represented by the location of the record.

To represent the association between position names and numbers there will be a second tree with only a root logical record type:

(POSNAME, POSNUMBER)

We could use the attributes of entity set TEAMS as the root of a third tree, but since we are designing a hierarchy, we may as well take advantage of the fact that there is a hierarchical structure to the set of teams. We choose as root for the third tree a logical record type consisting only of FRANCHISE. A franchise can be viewed as composed of teams, one for each year, so the root of the third tree has one child, which is the logical record type

(SERIAL2, CITY, YEAR)

In the database itself, each record of the above type represents a team, which is determined by the value of YEAR and the value of FRANCHISE in the parent of the record. Again, SERIAL2 is a dummy serial number used to distinguish records of this type, since there may be two franchises in a given city in a given year.

The above logical record type has a child logical record type representing the players on a team and the batting average of that player for that year;, its logical record format is:

(SERIAL3, NAME, PCT)

We expect SERIAL3, like the other serial numbers to disappear in an implementation, and it is present in the conceptual database scheme to prevent us from identifying records with the same NAME and PCT if they represent the batting average of a player for two different seasons. The entire hierarchy is shown in Fig. 3.11.

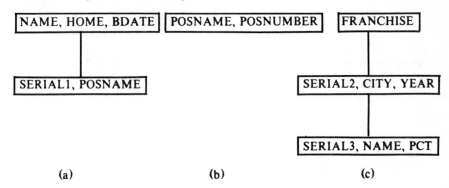

      (a)   (b)   (c)

Fig. 3.11. An improved hierarchy for the baseball database.

In the hierarchy of Fig. 3.11, we can answer a query such as: "What positions did Cobb play?" by finding the Cobb record in the file for the root record type in a tree (a) and examining its children, each of which has the name of a position Cobb played. We could even find the numbers of the positions Cobb played by proceeding as above, then looking in tree (b) for the record for each position, to get the position's number. □

Implementation of Hierarchical Databases

The ideas used in the implementation of a network database carry over to the hierarchical model directly, since hierarchies are special cases of networks. Representation by files of variable length records is especially suitable for hierarchies. To construct a variable length record format for a tree, use the following two rules, working up the tree.

1.   The format for a leaf is (α) *, where α is the list of attributes in the logical record format for this leaf.

2.   If a node has k children with variable length record formats $\alpha_1, \alpha_2, \ldots, \alpha_k$, and the list of attributes in the logical record format for this node is β, then the variable length record format for the node is $(\beta\alpha_1\alpha_2 \cdots \alpha_k)$ *.

In following the above rules, we construct one file of variable length records for each tree in the hierarchy. Of course, each such file must be implemented, as discussed in Section 2.6, such as by one or more files of fixed length records.

Example 3.9: The variable length record format for the tree of Fig. 3.11(c) is

(FRANCHISE(SERIAL2 CITY YEAR (SERIAL3 NAME PCT)*)*)*

and for Fig. 3.9(a) it is:

(NAME HOME BDATE(SERIAL1)* (SERIAL2 PCT)*)*

□

Another possible implementation of a hierarchy is to list the records of each tree in preorder as we suggested in Section 2.6 for fields of a variable length record format. A preorder traversal, or listing, of a tree is defined recursively, as follows.

1.   list the root.

2.   **for** each child c of the root, from the left **do**
      list the subtree with root c, in preorder

Example 3.10: Suppose we have the tree of Fig. 3.12. To list it in preorder, we list A, the root, and then list the tree of B, D, and E, in preorder. To do so, we list B and then the tree consisting of D alone, then the tree of E alone. Thus the first four nodes in preorder are $ABDE$. To complete the preorder listing we list the tree whose root is C, which gives $ABDECF$ as the complete preorder. □

When we list in preorder a tree of records in a database, we must identify each record by some bits at the beginning that indicate its logical record type. This is necessary so we know how to find and interpret the values of fields in the record. It is also convenient to make available in

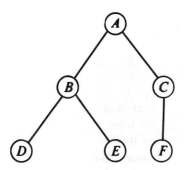

Fig. 3.12. A tree.

each block over which the records are spread, information telling where in the block each begins, since we do not know *a priori* what type each record is or how long it is. As we shall discuss in Section 8.4, it is also useful to thread the list with pointers of various sorts to provide easy access to siblings.

Example 3.11: We may view Fig. 3.12 as a conceptual schema described using the hierarchical model, where $A, B, \cdots$ represent logical record types. In Fig. 3.13 is a possible database represented by the schema of Fig. 3.12. We could list each of the records represented by a node in Fig. 3.13 in preorder, over as many blocks as needed, as follows:

$$a_1b_1d_1d_2d_3e_1b_2d_4c_1f_1f_2c_2f_3a_2b_3d_5e_2c_3f_4f_5f_6c_4f_7$$

Notice that the above string is an instance of the variable length record format $(A(B(D)^*(E)^*)^*(C(F)^*)^*)^*$ constructed from Fig. 3.12. □

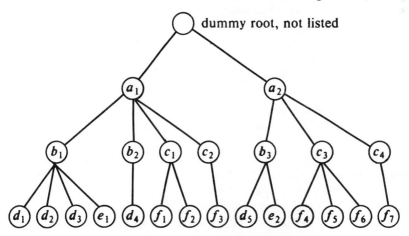

Fig. 3.13. A tree-structured database.

3.4 Comparison of the Models

To evaluate the three models discussed in this chapter we must first state the criteria by which they should be judged. We see two primary concerns.

1. *Ease of use.* Especially in small databases, on the order of thousands or tens of thousands of records, the principal cost may be the time spent by the programmer writing applications programs and by the user posing queries. We want a model that makes accurate programming and the phrasing of queries easy.

2. *Efficiency of implementation.* When databases are large, the cost of storage space and computer time dominate the total cost of implementing a database. We need a data model in which it is easy for the DBMS to translate a specification of the conceptual scheme and the conceptual-to-physical mapping into an implementation that is space efficient and in which queries can be answered efficiently.

By the criterion of easy use, there is no doubt that the relational model is superior. It provides only one construct that the programmer or user must understand. Moreover, as we shall see, there are rich, high-level languages for expressing queries on data represented by the relational model. These languages make systems based on the relational model available to persons whose programming skill is not great.

In comparison, the network model requires our understanding of both record types and links, and their interrelationships. The implementation of many-many relationships and relationships on three or more entity sets is not straightforward, although with practice one gets used to the technique, discussed in Section 3.2, of introducing dummy record types. Similarly, the hierarchical model requires understanding the use of pointers (virtual record types) and has the same problems as the network model regarding the representation of relationships that are more complex than many-one relationships between two entity sets.

When we consider the potential for efficient implementation, the network and hierarchical models score high marks. We saw in Section 3.2 how implementations of variable length records can facilitate the task of following links. We also mentioned that data structures such as the multilist and the pointer-based implementation of variable length records do not generalize readily to many-many mappings. Since relations can, and often do, represent many-many mappings, we see that efficient implementation can be more difficult for relations than for networks or hierarchies. Fortunately, some specialized data structures can be used to implement relations, as well. In Section 4.5 we shall discuss how the multilist and other ideas have been adapted to relations in one existing system.

Efficient utilization of space sometimes can be easier using hierarchies (or networks in the form of a hierarchy) than relations. As a case in point, consider the hierarchy of Fig. 3.14(a) and an example database in Fig. 3.14(b). If we wished to represent the same structure by relations, we would probably choose one relation with attributes A and B, another with attributes A and C, and a third with attributes C and D. The corresponding relations are shown in Fig. 3.15. Observe how a_1, c_1, and c_2 are each repeated several times, resulting in a waste of space, compared with Fig. 3.14(b).

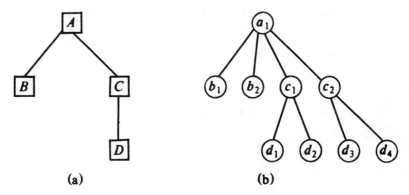

(a) (b)

Fig. 3.14. A hierarchy and database.

A	B
a_1	b_1
a_1	b_2

A	C
a_1	c_1
a_1	c_2

C	D
c_1	d_1
c_1	d_2
c_2	d_3
c_2	d_4

Fig. 3.15. Relations.

The above effect would not be important if it were not that data frequently forms a natural hierarchy. While we are free to implement relations by a hierarchical structure such as Fig. 3.14(b), it is not always clear how to do so. Consider, for example, what the hierarchy corresponding to Fig. 3.15 would look like if C were chosen as the root of the conceptual scheme, rather than A.

Language Level

The level of the data manipulation language can affect profoundly the ease with which a DBMS can be used, just as it is easier to program in FORTRAN than in assembly language, and easier to program in APL than in FORTRAN. It has been the case that relational DBMS's have stressed languages of very high-level, while DBMS's based on the other models have tended to have languages of lower-level. We shall see in Chapter 4 some of the high-level relational languages, while Chapters 7 and 8 exhibit two of the principal low-level languages in which navigation details are expressed in the network and hierarchical models.

One might wonder if there is an inherent reason why these examples are typical. It is hard to argue that there is, although we should point out that the principal general-purpose languages of very high level, such as APL, SNOBOL, LISP, or SETL, are each based on a single data type (the array, string, list structure, and set, respectively), just as the relational model provides but a single data type, the relation. In contrast, lower level languages, like PL/I, have a variety of data types at the programmer's disposal.

Conclusions

In the past, commercial database systems have almost uniformly been based on the network or hierarchical model, because the emphasis of such systems has been on the maintenance of large databases, and these models lend themselves most easily to the necessary efficient implementation. However, it is felt that the relational model will receive the bulk of attention in the future for two reasons. First, it is becoming clearer that the same concepts used to design large databases apply as well to small and medium scale databases, and there are many more small (i.e., thousands of records rather than millions) databases than large ones. With small databases, the ease of use inherent in the relational model assumes increased importance.

Second, many of the apparent inefficiencies of the relational model can be eliminated. Chapter 6 discusses some of the optimization techniques for relational data manipulation languages that allow these languages to use time efficiently. Research aimed at producing good physical implementations of relations is also underway. We shall discuss some of the progress connected with IBM's System R in Section 4.5, and Section 4.7 discusses Query-by-Example, an existing commercial system suitable for medium size databases. Just as general-purpose very high level languages such as APL are winning converts as the rather difficult optimization problems associated with these languages gradually are solved, we suspect that the relational model will become more attractive as the optimization problems associated with this model are likewise solved.

Exercises

3.1: In Fig. 3.16 we see the entity-relationship diagram of an insurance company. The keys for EMPLOYEES and POLICIES are EMP# and P#, respectively; SALESMEN are identified by their isa relationship to EMPLOYEES. Represent this diagram in the (a) relational (b) network (c) hierarchical models.

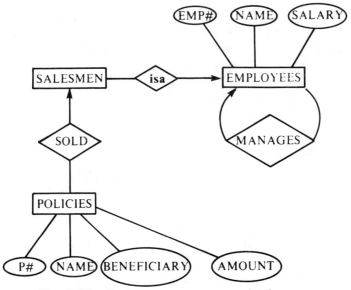

Fig. 3.16. An insurance company database.

3.2: Figure 3.17 shows a genealogy database, with key attributes NAME and LIC#. Represent this diagram in the (a) relational (b) network, and (c) hierarchical models.

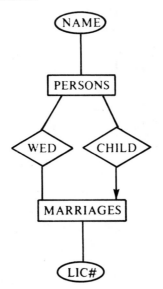

Fig. 3.17. A genealogy database.

3.3: The recipe for *moo shoo roe* includes bamboo shoots, sliced pork, wood ears, golden needles, and assorted vegetables. *Hot and sour soup* is made from wood ears, bean curd, and golden needles, while *family style bean curd* is made from bean curd, sliced pork, and assorted vegetables.

  a) Suppose we wish to store this information in a relation RECIPE(DISH, INGREDIENT). Show the current value of the relation as a table (use suitable abbreviations for the dishes and ingredients).

  b) Suppose we wish to represent the above information as a network with record types DISH, INGREDIENT and DUMMY, where a DUMMY record represents a pair consisting of one ingredient for one dish. Suppose also that there are links USES from DUMMY to DISH and PART_OF from DUMMY to INGREDIENT. Draw the DISH, INGREDIENT, and DUMMY record occurrences and represent the links USES and PART_OF by the multilist structure.

  c) Do the same as in part (b), but represent USES by variable length records with format DISH(DUMMY)*; represent PART_OF by a multilist structure.

  d) Suppose we use the hierarchy of Fig. 3.18 as a conceptual scheme for the above information. Show the actual database, including pointers in the virtual records.

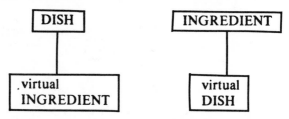

Fig. 3.18. A hierarchy.

*3.4: While database systems generally have their own specialized data manipulation languages, we can get a feel for how our three models facilitate querying the database if we use a conventional language like PL/I† to set up a database and write queries.

  a) Write PL/I record structure declarations for the relations from Exercise 3.3(a).

---

† Any language with record structures, such as PASCAL or C will do as well.

b) Write a PL/I program to print all the dishes using wood ears, using the structure from (a).

c) Write PL/I record structures to represent the record types from Exercise 3.3(b). Include fields for the pointers needed to represent the multilist structure.

d) Write a PL/I program to print all the dishes using wood ears. Start by finding the ingredient record for wood ears, and search its ring for the PART_OF link.

e) Write record structures for the hierarchy of Fig. 3.18. You must find a way of representing the children of DISH and INGREDIENT records, for example, by creating linked lists of virtual INGREDIENT and virtual DISH records.

f) Write a program to print all the dishes using wood ears, using the structure from (e).

*3.5: We mentioned in Section 3.1 that two tables represent the same relation if one can be converted to the other by permuting rows and/or columns, provided the attribute heading a column moves along with the column. If a relation has a scheme with m attributes and the relation has n tuples, how many tables represent this relation?

Bibliographic Notes

The reader should see the bibliographies of Chapters 4, 7, and 8 for references to a variety of systems that use the relational, network, and hierarchical models, respectively. We previously mentioned in Chapter 1 a variety of other models for conceptual schemes; these are generally at a somewhat higher level than the three of this chapter and are intended primarily as database design tools to be translated into one of the three covered here.

Of the three models, only the relational has its origin in theoretical proposals predating any true implementations. The concept is attributed to a series of papers by Codd [1970, 1972a, 1972b] although Codd [1970] acknowledges some earlier work of Childs [1968]. Several works have been devoted to comparisons of the three models, of which we note the compendium Rustin [1974] and the issue of *Computer Surveys*, Sibley [1976].

4
Data Manipulation Languages for the Relational Model

In this chapter we discuss the three principal approaches to the design of languages for expressing queries about relations. The notation for expressing queries is usually the most significant part of a data manipulation language. The nonquery aspects of a relational data manipulation language, or "query language," are often straightforward, being concerned with the insertion, deletion and modification of tuples. On the other hand, queries, which in the most general case are arbitrary functions applied to relations, often use a rich, high-level language for their expression.

Query languages for the relational model break down into two broad classes:

1. Algebraic languages, where queries are expressed by applying specialized operators to relations, and

2. Predicate calculus languages, where queries describe a desired set of tuples by specifying a predicate the tuples must satisfy.

We further divide the calculus-based languages into two classes, depending on whether the primitive objects are tuples or are elements of the domain of some attribute, making a total of three distinct kinds of query languages.

In this chapter we begin by introducing relational algebra and the two forms of relational calculus, called tuple relational calculus and domain relational calculus. These abstract query languages are not implemented exactly as stated in any existing DBMS, but they serve as a benchmark for evaluating existing systems. That is, each of the three abstract query languages is equivalent in expressive power to the others, and they were proposed by Codd [1972b] to represent the minimum capability of any reasonable query language using the relational model. Real query languages usually provide the capabilities of the abstract languages and additional capabilities as well. We shall discuss one typical query language of each of the three types: ISBL, an algebraic language, QUEL, a tuple calculus language, and Query-by-Example, a domain calculus language. We shall also discuss SQUARE and its cousin, SEQUEL, which are languages intermediate between algebra and calculus.

4.1 Relational Algebra

Recall that a relation is a set of k-tuples for some fixed k, the arity of the relation. We sometimes find it convenient to give the components of the tuples names, called attributes, while sometimes it is convenient to let the components be anonymous and to refer to them by number. When defining relational algebra, we assume columns need not be named, and order in tuples is significant. This point of view differs from that of Section 3.1, but is compatible, when we use the obvious conversions. When dealing with relations as a database, it is assumed that all relations are finite, and we shall adopt this assumption without explicit mention in the future. The constraint of finiteness introduces some difficulties into the definition of relational algebra and calculus. For example, we cannot allow the algebraic operation of complementation, since $-R$ generally denotes an infinite relation, the set of all tuples not in R. There is no way to list the relation $-R$, even if the query language permitted such an expression.

The operands of relational algebra are either constant relations or variables denoting relations of a fixed arity. The arity associated with a variable will be mentioned only when it is important. There are five basic operations that serve to define relational algebra. After introducing them we shall mention a few more operations that do not add to the set of functions expressible in the language, but serve as useful shorthand.

1. *Union.* The union of relations R or S, denoted $R \cup S$, is the set of tuples that are in R or S or both. We only apply the union operator to relations of the same arity, so all tuples in the result have the same number of components.

2. *Set difference.* The difference of relations R and S, denoted $R-S$, is the set of tuples in R but not in S. We again require that R and S have the same arity.

3. *Cartesian product.* Let R and S be relations of arity k_1 and k_2, respectively. Then $R \times S$, the Cartesian product of R and S, is the set of (k_1+k_2)-tuples whose first k_1 components form a tuple in R and whose last k_2 components form a tuple in S.

4. *Projection.* The idea behind this operation is that we take a relation R, remove some of the components and/or rearrange some of the remaining components. If R is a relation of arity k, we let $\pi_{i_1, i_2, \ldots, i_m}(R)$, where the i_j's are distinct integers in the range 1 to k, denote the projection of R onto components $i_1, i_2, \ldots, i_m$, that is, the set of m-tuples $a_1 a_2 \cdots a_m$ such that there is some k-tuple

$b_1 b_2 \cdots b_k$ in R for which $a_j = b_{i_j}$ for $j = 1, 2, \ldots, m$. For example, $\pi_{3,1}(R)$ is formed by taking each tuple t in R and forming a 2-tuple from the third and first components of t, in that order. If R has attributes labeling its columns, then we may substitute attribute names for component numbers, and we may use the same attribute names in the projected relation. For example, if relation R is $R(A, B, C, D)$, then $\pi_{C,A}(R)$ is the same as $\pi_{3,1}(R)$, and the resulting relation has attribute C naming its first column and attribute A naming its second column.

5.   *Selection.* Let F be a formula involving

    i)   operands that are constants or component numbers,

    ii)   the arithmetic comparison operators, $<, =, >, \leqslant, \neq,$ and $\geqslant$, and

    iii)   the logical operators $\wedge$ (and), $\vee$ (or), and $\neg$ (not).

Then $\sigma_F(R)$ is the set of tuples t in R such that when for all i, we substitute the ith component of t for any occurrences of the number i in formula F, the formula F becomes true. For example, $\sigma_{2>3}(R)$ denotes the set of tuples in R whose second component exceeds its third component, while $\sigma_{1=\text{'Smith'} \vee 1=\text{'Jones'}}(R)$ is the set of tuples in R whose first component has the value Smith or Jones. As with projection, if a relation has named columns, then the formula in a selection can refer to columns by name instead of number. Notice also that constants must be quoted in formulas to distinguish them from column numbers or names.

Example 4.1: Let R and S be the two relations of Fig. 4.1. In Fig. 4.2(a) and (b), respectively, we see the relations $R \cup S$ and $R - S$. Note that we can take unions and differences even though the columns of the two relations have different names, as long as the relations have the same number of components. However, the resulting relation has no obvious names for its columns. Figure 4.2(c) shows $R \times S$. Since R and S have disjoint sets of attributes, we can carry the column names over to $R \times S$. If R and S had a column name in common, say G, we could distinguish the two columns by calling them $R.G$ and $S.G$. Figure 4.2(d) shows $\pi_{A,C}(R)$, and Fig. 4.2(e) shows $\sigma_{B=b}(R)$ □

Some Additional Algebraic Operations

There are a number of useful operations that can be expressed in terms of the five previously mentioned operations, but which have been given names in the literature and sometimes used as primitive operations.

A	B	C
a	b	c
d	a	f
c	b	d

D	E	F
b	g	a
d	a	f

(a) Relation R (b) Relation S

Fig. 4.1. Two relations.

a	b	c
d	a	f
c	b	d
b	g	a

a	b	c
c	b	d

(a) $R \cup S$ (b) $R - S$

A	B	C	D	E	F
a	b	c	b	g	a
a	b	c	d	a	f
d	a	f	b	g	a
d	a	f	d	a	f
c	b	d	b	g	a
c	b	d	d	a	f

(c) $R \times S$

A	C
a	c
d	f
c	d

A	B	C
a	b	c
c	b	d

(d) $\pi_{A,C}(R)$ (e) $\sigma_{B=b}(R)$

Fig. 4.2. Results of some relational algebra operations.

1. *Intersection.* $R \cap S$ is shorthand for $R - (R - S)$.

2. *Quotient.* Let R and S be relations of arity r and s, respectively, where $r > s$, and $S \neq \varnothing$. Then $R \div S$ is the set of $(r-s)$-tuples t such that for all s-tuples u in S, the tuple tu is in R. To express $R \div S$ using the five basic relational algebra operations, let T stand for $\pi_{1,2,\ldots,r-s}(R)$. Then $(T \times S) - R$ is the set of r-tuples that are not in R, but are formed by taking the first $r-s$ components of a tuple in R and following it by a tuple in S. Then let

$$V = \pi_{1, 2, \ldots, r-s}((T \times S) - R).$$

V is the set of $(r-s)$-tuples t that are the first $r-s$ components of a tuple in R such that for some s-tuple u in S, tu is not in R. Hence $T-V$ is $R \div S$. We can write $R \div S$ as a single expression in relational algebra by replacing T and V by the expressions they stand for. That is,

$$R \div S = \pi_{1, 2, \ldots, r-s}(R) - \pi_{1, 2, \ldots, r-s}((\pi_{1, 2, \ldots, r-s}(R) \times S) - R)$$

Example 4.2: Let R and S be the relations shown in Fig. 4.3(a) and (b). Then $R \div S$ is the relation shown in Fig. 4.3(c). Tuple ab is in $R \div S$ because $abcd$ and $abef$ are in R, and tuple ed is in $R \div S$ for a similar reason. Tuple bc, which is the only other pair appearing in the first two columns of R, is not in $R \div S$ because $bccd$ is not in R. ◻

a	b	c	d
a	b	e	f
b	c	e	f
e	d	c	d
e	d	e	f
a	b	d	e

c	d
e	f

a	b
e	d

(a) relation R (b) relation S (c) $R \div S$

Fig. 4.3. Example of a quotient calculation.

3.   *Join.* The θ-join of R and S on columns i and j written $R \underset{i\theta j}{\bowtie} S$, where θ is an arithmetic comparison operator ($=$, $<$, and so on), is shorthand for $\sigma_{i\theta(r+j)}(R \times S)$, if R is of arity r. That is, the θ-join of R and S is those tuples in the Cartesian product of R and S such that the ith component of R stands in relation θ to the jth component of S. If θ is $=$, the operation is often called an *equijoin*.

Example 4.3: Let R and S be the relations given in Fig. 4.4(a) and (b). Then $R \underset{B<D}{\bowtie} S$ is given in Fig. 4.4(c). As with all algebraic operations, when columns have names we are free to use them. Thus $\underset{B<D}{\bowtie}$ is the same as $\underset{2<1}{\bowtie}$ in this case. ◻

4.   *Natural Join.* The natural join, written $R \bowtie S$, is applicable only when both R and S have columns that are named by attributes. To compute $R \bowtie S$ we

    i)   Compute $R \times S$.

A	B	C
1	2	3
4	5	6
7	8	9

D	E
3	1
6	2

A	B	C	D	E
1	2	3	3	1
1	2	3	6	2
4	5	6	6	2

(a) relation R (b) relation S (c) $R \bowtie_{B<D} S$

Fig. 4.4. Example of a $<$-join.

ii) For each attribute A that names both a column in R and a column in S select from $R \times S$ those tuples whose values agree in the columns for $R.A$ and $S.A$. Recall that $R.A$ is the name of the column of $R \times S$ corresponding to the column A of R, and $S.A$ is defined analogously.

iii) For each attribute A above, project out the column $S.A$.

Formally then, if $A_1, A_2, \ldots, A_k$ are all the attribute names used for both R and S, $R \bowtie S$ is $\pi_{i_1, i_2, \ldots, i_m} \sigma_{R.A_1 = S.A_1 \wedge \cdots \wedge R.A_k = S.A_k}(R \times S)$ where $i_1, i_2, \ldots, i_m$ is the list of all components of $R \times S$, in order, except the components $S.A_1, \ldots, S.A_k$.

Example 4.4: Let R and S be the relations given in Fig. 4.5(a) and (b). Then $R \bowtie S$ stands for $\pi_{A.R.B.R.C.D} \sigma_{R.B = S.B \wedge R.C = S.C}(R \times S)$. To construct $R \bowtie S$, we consider each tuple in R to see which tuples of S agree with it in both columns B and C. For example, *abc* in R agrees with *bcd* and *bce* in S, so we get *abcd* and *abce* in $R \bowtie S$. Similarly, *dbc* gives us *dbcd* and *dbce* for $R \bowtie S$. Tuple *bbf* agrees with no tuple of S in columns B and C, so we obtain no tuple in $R \bowtie S$ that begins with *bbf*. Lastly, *cad* matches *adb*, so we get tuple *cadb*. □

A	B	C
a	b	c
d	b	c
b	b	f
c	a	d

B	C	D
b	c	d
b	c	e
a	d	b

A	B	C	D
a	b	c	d
a	b	c	e
d	b	c	d
d	b	c	e
c	a	d	b

(a) Relation R (b) Relation S (c) $R \bowtie S$

Fig. 4.5. Example of a natural join.

The significance of the natural join will become clear when we discuss the theory of decomposition of relations in the next chapter.

4.2 Relational Calculus.

We shall begin our study of relational calculus by first defining the tuple relational calculus. To make things easy, we shall initially present a calculus that permits infinite relations to be defined. Then we shall discuss the modifications needed to assure that each formula in relational calculus denotes a finite relation. Incidentally, the term "relational calculus" does not imply any connection with the branch of mathematics usually called "calculus," or more precisely, "differential and integral calculus."

Formulas in relational calculus are of the form $\{t \mid \psi(t)\}$, where t is a *tuple variable,* that is, a variable denoting a tuple of some fixed length,† and ψ is a formula built from atoms and a collection of operators to be defined shortly.

The *atoms* of formulas ψ are of three types.

1. $R(s)$, where R is a relation name and s is a tuple variable. This atom stands for the assertion that s is a tuple in relation R.

2. $s[i]\theta u[j]$, where s and u are tuple variables and θ is an arithmetic comparison operator ($<$, $=$, and so on). This atom stands for the assertion that the ith component of s stands in relation θ to the jth component of u. For example, $s[1]<u[2]$ means that the first component of s is less than the second component of u.

3. $s[i]\theta a$ and $a\theta s[i]$, where θ and $s[i]$ are as in (2) above, and a is a constant. The first of these atoms asserts that the ith component of s stands in relation θ to the constant a, and the second has an analogous meaning. For example, $s[1]=3$ means that the value of the first component of s is 3.

When defining the operators of relational calculus, it is useful simultaneously to define the notions of "free" and "bound" tuple variables. These notions are exactly the same as in predicate calculus. (A familiarity with predicate calculus is not a prerequisite for what follows.) Informally, an occurrence of a variable in a formula is "bound" if that variable has been introduced by a "for all" or "there exists" quantifier, and we say the variable is "free" if not.

The notion of a "free variable" is analogous to that of a global variable in a programming language, that is, a variable defined outside the current procedure. A "bound variable" is like a local variable, one that is defined in the procedure at hand. In effect, the quantifiers of relational calculus play the role of declarations in a programming language.

Formulas, and *free* and *bound* occurrences of tuple variables in these formulas, are defined recursively, as follows.

---

† We use $t^{(i)}$ to denote the fact that t is of arity i.

1. Every atom is a formula. All occurrences of tuple variables mentioned in the atom are free in this formula.

2. If ψ_1 and ψ_2 are formulas, then $\psi_1 \wedge \psi_2$, $\psi_1 \vee \psi_2$, and $\neg\psi_1$ are formulas asserting "ψ_1 and ψ_2 are both true," "ψ_1 or ψ_2, or both, are true," and "ψ_1 is not true," respectively. Occurrences of tuple variables are free or bound in $\psi_1 \wedge \psi_2$, $\psi_1 \vee \psi_2$, and $\neg\psi_1$ as they are free or bound in ψ_1 or ψ_2, depending on where they occur. Note that an occurrence of a variable s could be bound in ψ_1, while another occurrence of s is free in ψ_2, for example.

3. If ψ is a formula, then $(\exists s)(\psi)$ is a formula. The symbol $\exists$ is a *quantifier*, read "there exists." The only other quantifier used is $\forall$, "for all," described in (4) below. Occurrences of s that are free in ψ are bound to $(\exists s)$ in $(\exists s)(\psi)$.† Other occurrences of tuple variables in ψ, including possible occurrences of s that were bound in ψ, are free or bound in $(\exists s)(\psi)$ as they were in ψ. The formula $(\exists s)(\psi)$ asserts that there exists a value of s such that when we substitute this value for all free occurrences of s in ψ, the formula ψ becomes true. For example, $(\exists s)(R(s))$ says that relation R is not empty, that is, there exists a tuple s in R.

4. If ψ is a formula, then $(\forall s)(\psi)$ is a formula. Free occurrences of s in ψ are bound to $(\forall s)$ in $(\forall s)(\psi)$, and other occurrences of variables in ψ are treated as in (3) above. The formula $(\forall s)(\psi)$ asserts that whatever value of the appropriate arity we substitute for free occurrences of s in ψ, the formula ψ becomes true.

5. Parentheses may be placed around formulas as needed. We assume the order of precedence is: arithmetic comparison operators highest, then the quantifiers $\exists$ and $\forall$, then $\neg$, $\wedge$, and $\vee$, in that order.

6. Nothing else is a formula.

A *tuple relational calculus expression* is an expression of the form $\{t \mid \psi(t)\}$, where t is the only free tuple variable in ψ.

Example 4.5: The union of R and S is expressed by the calculus expression

$$\{t \mid R(t) \vee S(t)\}$$

In words, the above is "the set of tuples t such that t is in R or t is in S." Note that union only makes sense if R and S have the same arity, and similarly, the formula $R(t) \vee S(t)$ only makes sense if R and S have the same arity, since tuple variable t is assumed to have some fixed length.

---

† If we think of free variable s of ψ as "global" to ψ, then $(\exists s)$ constitutes the "declaration" of s.

The difference $R-S$ is expressed by

$$\{t \mid R(t) \wedge \neg S(t)\}$$

If R and S are relations of arity r and s, respectively, then $R \times S$ can be expressed in calculus by:

$$\{t^{(r+s)} \mid (\exists u^{(r)})(\exists v^{(s)})(R(u) \wedge S(v)$$
$$\wedge\ t[1]=u[1] \wedge \cdots \wedge t[r]=u[r]$$
$$\wedge\ t[r+1]=v[1] \wedge \cdots \wedge t[r+s]=v[s])\}$$

Recall that $t^{(i)}$ indicates that t has arity i. In words, $R \times S$ is the set of tuples t (which we understand to be of length $r+s$) such that there exist u and v, with u in R, v in S; the first r components of t form u, and the next s components of t form v.

The projection $\pi_{i_1, i_2, \ldots, i_k}(R)$ is expressed by

$$\{t^{(k)} \mid (\exists u)(R(u) \wedge t[1]=u[i_1] \wedge \cdots \wedge t[k]=u[i_k])\}$$

The selection $\sigma_F(R)$ is expressed by

$$\{t \mid R(t) \wedge F'\}$$

where F' is the formula F with each operand i, denoting the ith component, replaced by $t[i]$.

As a last example, if R is a relation of arity two, then

$$\{t^{(2)} \mid (\exists u)(R(t) \wedge R(u) \wedge (t[1] \neq u[1] \vee t[2] \neq u[2]))\}$$

is a calculus expression that denotes R if R has two or more members and denotes the empty relation if R is empty or has only one member. $\square$

Restricting Relational Calculus to Yield only Finite Relations

The tuple relational calculus as we have defined it allows us to define some infinite relations such as $\{t \mid \neg R(t)\}$, which denotes all possible tuples that are not in R, but are of the length we associate with t (that length must also be the arity of R for the expression to make sense). As we could not expect to print "all possible tuples" (over what domain?), we must rule out such meaningless expressions. What is usually done is to restrict consideration to those expressions $\{t \mid \psi(t)\}$, called "safe," for which it can be demonstrated that each component of any t that satisfies ψ must be a member of $DOM(\psi)$, which is defined to be the set of symbols that either appear explicitly in ψ or are components of some tuple in some relation R mentioned in ψ. This choice of $\text{DOM}(\psi)$ is not necessarily the smallest set of symbols we could use, but it will suffice.

Notice that $\text{DOM}(\psi)$ is not determined by looking at ψ, but is a function of the actual relations to be substituted for the relation variables in ψ.

However, as all relations are assumed finite, $DOM(\psi)$ is always finite. For example, if $\psi(t)$ is $t[1]=a \lor R(t)$, where R is a binary relation, then $DOM(\psi)$ is the unary relation† given by the relational algebra formula

$$\{a\} \cup \pi_1(R) \cup \pi_2(R)$$

We say a tuple calculus expression $\{t \mid \psi(t)\}$ is *safe* if

1. Whenever t satisfies ψ, each component of t is a member of $DOM(\psi)$.

2. For each subexpression of ψ of the form $(\exists u)(\omega(u))$, if ω is satisfied by u, then each component of u is a member of $DOM(\omega)$.

3. For each subexpression of ψ of the form $(\forall u)(\omega(u))$, if any component of u is not in $DOM(\omega)$, then u satisfies ω.

The purpose of points (2) and (3) is to assure that we can determine the truth of a quantified formula $(\exists u)(\omega(u))$ or $(\forall u)(\omega(u))$ by considering only those u's composed of symbols in $DOM(\omega)$. For example, any formula $(\exists u)(R(u) \land \cdots)$ satisfies (2), and any formula

$$(\forall u)(\neg R(u) \lor \cdots)$$

satisfies (3).

While rule (3) may appear unintuitive, we should observe that the formula $(\forall u)(\omega(u))$ is logically equivalent to $\neg(\exists u)(\neg \omega(u))$. The latter formula is unsafe if and only if there is a u_0 for which $\neg\omega(u_0)$ is true, and u_0 is not in the domain of the formula $\neg\omega$. As the domains of ω and $\neg\omega$ are the same, rule (3) says that formula $(\forall u)(\omega(u))$ is safe exactly when formula $\neg(\exists u)(\neg\omega(u))$ is safe.

We shall see that the safe expressions of tuple relational calculus are equivalent to relational algebra. It is an interesting and nontrivial exercise to determine those tuple calculus expressions that are safe. Fortunately, in showing the equivalence of relational algebra and calculus, we never need to know exactly which calculus expressions are safe. However, we can give some examples of constructions in the tuple calculus that are guaranteed to be safe.

Example 4.6: In what follows, let $\psi(t)$ be a formula such that no subformula of the form $(\exists u)(\omega(u))$ or $(\forall u)(\omega(u))$ violates safety. Then any expression of the form $\{t \mid R(t) \land \psi(t)\}$ is safe, since any tuple t satisfying $R(t) \land \psi(t)$ is in R, whereupon each of its components is in $DOM(R(t) \land \psi(t))$. For example, the formula for set difference,

---

† For all practical purposes, a unary relation is a set of symbols, and we shall so treat it here.

$$\{t \mid R(t) \land \neg S(t)\}$$

is of this form, with $\psi(t) = \neg S(t)$. The formula for selection is also of this form, with $\psi(t) = F$.

As a generalization of the above, we observe that any formula $\{t \mid (R_1(t) \lor R_2(t) \lor \cdots \lor R_k(t)) \land \psi(t)\}$ is also safe; $t[i]$ must be a symbol appearing in the ith component of some tuple of some relation R_j. For example, the formula for union in Example 4.5 is of this form, but ψ is missing, i.e., we may take ψ to be an always true formula like $t[1]=t[1]$.

Another form of safe expression is

$$\{t^{(m)} \mid (\exists u_1)(\exists u_2) \cdots (\exists u_k)(R_1(u_1) \land R_2(u_2) \land \cdots \land R_k(u_k)$$
$$\land\ t[1]=u_{i_1}[j_1] \land t[2]=u_{i_2}[j_2] \land \cdots \land t[m]=u_{i_m}[j_m]$$
$$\land\ \psi(t, u_1, u_2, \ldots, u_k))\}$$

Component $t[l]$ is resricted to be a symbol appearing in the j_l^{th} component of a tuple of R_{i_l}. The formulas for Cartesian product and projection in Example 4.5 are of the above form. □

Reduction of Relational Algebra to Tuple Relational Calculus

We shall prove that the set of functions of relations expressible in relational algebra is exactly the same as the set of functions expressible by safe formulas in the tuple relational calculus. One direction of this equivalence will be proved now, and the other direction will be shown after we introduce the domain relational calculus, which is a third equivalent notation.

Theorem 4.1: If E is a relational algebra expression, then there is a safe expression in tuple relational calculus equivalent to E.

Proof: We proceed by induction on the number of occurrences of operators in E.

Basis: Zero operators. Then E is either a constant relation $\{t_1, t_2, \ldots, t_n\}$ or a relation variable R. In the latter case, E is equivalent to $\{t \mid R(t)\}$, which is a safe expression, as pointed out in Example 4.6. In the former case, E is equivalent to

$$\{t \mid t=t_1 \lor t=t_2 \lor \cdots \lor t=t_n\}$$

where $t=t_i$ is shorthand for $t[1]=t_i[1] \land \cdots \land t[k]=t_i[k]$; k is the assumed arity of t. It is easy to see that $t[i]$ is one of the finite set of symbols appearing explicitly as the ith component of some constant tuple t_j.

Induction: Assume that E has at least one operator, and that the theorem is true for expressions with fewer occurrences of operators than E has.

Case 1: $E = E_1 \cup E_2$. Then E_1 and E_2 each have fewer operator occurrences than E, and by the inductive hypothesis we can find safe relational calculus expressions $\{t \mid \psi_1(t)\}$ and $\{t \mid \psi_2(t)\}$ equivalent to E_1 and

E_2, respectively. Then E is equivalent to $\{t \mid \psi_1(t) \vee \psi_2(t)\}$. If t satisfies $\psi_1(t) \vee \psi_2(t)$, then each component of t is in DOM(ψ_1) or each component is in DOM(ψ_2). As DOM$(\psi_1(t) \vee \psi_2(t))$ = DOM(ψ_1) $\cup$ DOM(ψ_2), E is equivalent to a safe expression. That is, the complete formula $\psi(t) = \psi_1(t) \vee \psi_2(t)$ is true only when t is in DOM(ψ), and any subformula $(\exists u)(\omega(u))$ or $(\forall u)(\omega(u))$ in ψ must be within ψ_1 or ψ_2, so the inductive hypothesis assures that these subformulas do not violate safety.

Case 2: $E = E_1 - E_2$. Then E_1 and E_2 have safe expressions, as in Case 1. Clearly E is equivalent to $\{t \mid \psi_1(t) \wedge \neg\psi_2(t)\}$. As DOM$(\psi_1(t) \wedge \neg\psi_2(t))$ = DOM(ψ_1) $\cup$ DOM(ψ_2), the above expression is safe.

Case 3: $E = E_1 \times E_2$. Let E_1 and E_2 be equivalent to safe expressions as in Case 1, and let E_1 and E_2 denote relations of arity k and m, respectively. Then E is equivalent to

$$\{t^{(k+m)} \mid (\exists u)(\exists v)(\psi_1(u) \wedge \psi_2(v)$$
$$\wedge\ t[1]=u[1] \wedge \cdots \wedge t[k]=u[k]$$
$$\wedge\ t[k+1]=v[1] \wedge \cdots \wedge t[k+m]=v[m])\}$$

It is easy to check that the above expression is safe, since $t[i]$ is restricted to values that $u[i]$ may take, if $i \leqslant k$, and to values that $v[i-k]$ may take if $k < i \leqslant k+m$.

Case 4: $E = \pi_{i_1, i_2, \ldots, i_k}(E_1)$. Let E_1 be equivalent to safe expression $\{t \mid \psi_1(t)\}$. Then E is equivalent to

$$\{t^{(k)} \mid (\exists u)(\psi_1(u) \wedge t[1]=u[i_1] \wedge \cdots \wedge t[k]=u[i_k])\}$$

Safety of the above expression is easy to show, as in Case 3.

Case 5: $E = \sigma_F(R)$. Let E_1 be equivalent to the safe expression $\{t \mid \psi_1(t)\}$. Then E is equivalent to $\{t \mid \psi_1(t) \wedge F'\}$, where F' is F with each operand that denotes component i replaced by $t[i]$. This expression is safe, because each component of t is restricted to those symbols to which $\psi_1(t)$ restricts the component. $\square$

Example 4.7: If R and S are binary relations, their composition in the ordinary set-theoretic sense is expressed by the relational algebra expression $\pi_{1,4}(\sigma_{2=3}(R \times S))$. Using the algorithm of Theorem 4.1, we construct for $R \times S$ the relational calculus expression

$$\{t \mid (\exists u)(\exists v)(R(u) \wedge S(v)$$
$$\wedge\ t[1]=u[1] \wedge t[2]=u[2] \wedge t[3]=v[1] \wedge t[4]=v[2])\}$$

For $\sigma_{2=3}(R \times S)$ we add to the above formula the term $\wedge\ t[2]=t[3]$. Then, for $\pi_{1,4}(\sigma_{2=3}(R \times S))$ we get the expression

$$\{w \mid (\exists t)(\exists u)(\exists v)(R(u) \wedge S(v)$$
$$\wedge\ t[1]=u[1] \wedge t[2]=u[2] \wedge t[3]=v[1] \wedge t[4]=v[2]$$
$$\wedge\ t[2]=t[3] \wedge w[1]=t[1] \wedge w[2]=t[4])\}$$

Note that the above expression is not as succinct as possible; we can eliminate t if we replace each of its components by the appropriate component
of u or v. If we do so, we get

$$\{w \mid (\exists u)(\exists v)(R(u) \wedge S(v) \wedge u[2]=v[1] \wedge w[1]=u[1] \wedge w[2]=v[2])\}$$

The above expression should be recognizable as the usual set-theoretic
definition of composition, translated into the language of tuple relational
calculus. $\square$

Domain Relational Calculus

The domain relational calculus is built from the same operators as the tuple
relational calculus. The essential differences are that

1.   There are no tuple variables in the domain calculus, but there are
      domain variables to represent components of tuples, instead.

2.   An atom is either of the form

      i) $R(x_1 x_2 \cdots x_k)$, where R is a k-ary relation and every x_i is a
              constant or domain variable, or

      ii) $x\theta y$, where x and y are constants or domain variables and θ is an
              arithmetic relational operator.

      $R(x_1 x_2 \cdots x_k)$ asserts that the values of those x_i's that are variables
      must be chosen so that $x_1 x_2 \cdots x_k$ is a tuple in R. The meaning of
      atom $x\theta y$ is that x and y must have values that make $x\theta y$ true.

3.   Formulas in the domain relational calculus use the connectives $\wedge$, $\vee$,
      and $\neg$, as in the tuple calculus. We also use $(\exists x)$ and $(\forall x)$ to form
      expressions of the domain calculus, but x is a domain variable instead
      of a tuple variable.

      The notions of free and bound domain variables and the scope of a
bound variable are defined in the domain calculus exactly as in the tuple
calculus, and we shall not repeat these definitions here. A domain calculus
expression is of the form $\{x_1 x_2 \cdots x_k \mid \psi(x_1, x_2, \ldots, x_k)\}$, where ψ is a
formula whose only free domain variables are the distinct variables
$x_1, x_2, \ldots, x_k$.

      In analogy with tuple calculus, we define a domain calculus expres-
sion $\{x_1 x_2 \cdots x_k \mid \psi(x_1, x_2, \ldots, x_k)\}$ to be *safe* if

1. $\psi(x_1, x_2, \ldots, x_k)$ true implies x_i is in $\text{DOM}(\psi)$,

2.   if $(\exists u)(\omega(u))$ is a subformula of ψ, then $\omega(u)$ true implies that u is in DOM(ω), and

3.   if $(\forall u)(\omega(u))$ is a subformula of ψ, then $\omega(u)$ false implies u is in DOM(ω).

Example 4.8: Let us reconsider the last part of Example 4.5, where we were given a binary relation R and asked to write an expression that was equal to R if R had two or more members and was the empty set otherwise. In domain relational calculus, one such expression is

$$\{wx \mid (\exists y)(\exists z)(R(wx) \wedge R(yz) \wedge (w \neq y \vee x \neq z))\}$$

Let $\psi(w, x, y, z)$ stand for the formula

$$R(wx) \wedge R(yz) \wedge (w \neq y \vee x \neq z)$$

and let R be the relation $\{12, 13\}$. If we let $w=1$ and $x=2$, then the formula

$$(\exists y)(\exists z)(\psi(1, 2, y, z))$$

is true, since we may pick $y=1$ and $z=3$ to make ψ true. Similarly, if we let $w=1$ and $x=3$, this formula is true, as we may pick $y=1$ and $z=2$. Thus tuples 12 and 13 are both in the set denoted by our domain calculus expression. However, if we pick any other values for w and x, then

$$(\exists y)(\exists z)(\psi(w, x, y, z))$$

must be false, since the clause $R(wx)$ of ψ will be false. Thus the domain calculus expression denotes a set equal to R when $R = \{12, 13\}$.

If we let R be a singleton set, like $\{12\}$, then no values of w and x satisfy $(\exists y)(\exists z)(\psi(w, x, y, z))$, since the first clause of ψ, $R(wx)$, is only satisfied if $w=1$ and $x=2$, the second clause $R(yz)$ is only satisfied if $y=1$ and $z=2$, and then the third clause, $(w \neq y \vee x \neq z)$ is not satisfied. □

Reducing Tuple Calculus to Domain Calculus

The construction of a domain calculus expression equivalent to a given tuple calculus expression $\{t \mid \psi(t)\}$ is straightforward. If t has arity k, introduce k new domain variables $t_1, t_2, \ldots, t_k$ and replace the expression by $t_1 t_2 \cdots t_k \mid \psi'(t_1, t_2, \ldots, t_k)$, where ψ' is ψ with any atom $R(t)$ replaced by $R(t_1 t_2 \cdots t_k)$, and each free occurrence of $t[i]$ replaced by t_i. Note that there could be bound occurrences of t within ψ, if there were a quantifier $(\exists t)$ or $(\forall t)$; uses of this t refer to a "different" tuple variable and are not replaced.†

---

† This situation is analogous to a local and global variable having the same identifier, in an ordinary programming language possessing block structure.

Next, for each quantifier $(\exists u)$ or $(\forall u)$, if u has arity m, introduce m new domain variables $u_1, u_2 \cdots u_m$, and, within the scope of this quantification of u, replace $u[i]$ by u_i and $R(u)$ by $R(u_1 u_2 \cdots u_m)$. Replace $(\exists u)$ by $(\exists u_1) \cdots (\exists u_m)$ and replace $(\forall u)$ by $(\forall u_1) \cdots (\forall u_m)$. The result is an expression in the domain calculus that is obviously equivalent to the original tuple calculus expression.

It should also be clear that the values that may be assumed by t_i are exactly those that could be assumed by $t[i]$ in the original expression. Thus if $\{t \mid \psi(t)\}$ is safe, so is the resulting domain calculus expression. We therefore state the following theorem without further proof.

Theorem 4.2: For every safe tuple relational calculus expression there is an equivalent safe domain relational calculus expression. □

Example 4.9: The algorithm described above was used to produce the domain calculus expression of Example 4.8 from the last tuple calculus expression of Example 4.5.

For another example, let us take the simpler expression for composition given in Example 4.7, that is:

$$\{w \mid (\exists u)(\exists v)(R(u) \wedge S(v)$$
$$\wedge \ u[2]=v[1] \wedge w[1]=u[1] \wedge w[2]=v[2])\}$$

We replace w by $w_1 w_2$, u by $u_1 u_2$ and v by $v_1 v_2$ to get

$$\{w_1 w_2 \mid (\exists u_1)(\exists u_2)(\exists v_1)(\exists v_2)(R(u_1 u_2) \wedge S(v_1 v_2)$$
$$\wedge \ u_2=v_1 \wedge w_1=u_1 \wedge w_2=v_2)\}$$

□

Reduction of Domain Calculus to Relational Algebra

Our plan is to take any safe domain calculus formula $\psi(x_1, x_2, \ldots, x_k)$, with free variables $x_1, x_2, \ldots, x_k$, and construct, by induction on the number of operators in ψ, an algebraic expression whose value is

$$\{x_1 x_2 \cdots x_k \mid \psi(x_1, x_2, \ldots, x_k)\}$$

Even though the given expression is safe, some subformulas of its formula may not be safe, so we prove by induction on the size (number of operators) of a subformula ω of ψ with free variables $y_1, y_2, \ldots, y_m$, that there is a relational algebra expression for

$$(DOM(\psi))^m \cap \{y_1 y_2 \cdots y_m \mid \omega(y_1, y_2, \ldots, y_m)\}$$

where D^m denotes $D \times D \times \cdots \times D$, ($m$ times). The following lemmas will be useful in the proof.

Lemma 4.1: If ψ is any formula in domain calculus (or tuple calculus, for that matter) then there is an expression in relational algebra denoting the unary relation (set) DOM(ψ).

Proof: If R is a relation of arity k, let

$$E(R) = \pi_1(R) \cup \pi_2(R) \cup \cdots \cup \pi_k(R)$$

Then the desired expression is the union of $E(R)$, for each relation variable appearing in ψ, and the constant relation $\{a_1, a_2, \ldots, a_n\}$, where the a_i's are all the constant symbols appearing in ψ. □

Lemma 4.2: If ψ is any formula in domain calculus (or tuple calculus, for that matter) then there is a formula ψ' of domain calculus (respectively tuple calculus) with no occurrences of $\wedge$ or $\forall$. If ψ is safe, so is ψ'.

Proof: Replace each subformula $\psi_1 \wedge \psi_2$ of ψ by $\neg(\neg\psi_1 \vee \neg\psi_2)$. This equivalence-preserving transformation is called *DeMorgan's law*, and says that ψ_1 and ψ_2 are both true if and only if it is not true that ψ_1 or ψ_2 is false. Next, replace each subformula $(\forall u)(\psi_1(u))$ by $\neg(\exists u)(\neg\psi_1(u))$. This transformation also preserves equivalence, saying in essence that ψ_1 is true for all u if and only if there does not exist a u for which ψ_1 is false.

Let the resulting formula be ψ'. Surely ψ' is equivalent to ψ. If ψ is safe, then for each subformula $(\forall u)(\psi_1(u))$, we know that $\psi_1(u)$ is true whenever u has a value outside the set DOM(ψ_1). Hence $\neg\psi_1(u)$ is false whenever u is outside DOM(ψ_1), which equals DOM$(\neg\psi_1)$. Thus the introduced formula $(\exists u)(\neg\psi_1(u))$ satisfies the safety condition. □

Theorem 4.3: For every safe expression of the domain relational calculus, there is an equivalent expression in relational algebra.

Proof: Let $\{x_1 \cdots x_k \mid \psi(x_1, \ldots, x_k)\}$ be a safe formula of domain calculus. By Lemma 4.2 we may assume that ψ has only the operators $\vee$, $\neg$, and $\exists$. By Lemma 4.1, we may take E to be a relational algebra expression for the set DOM(ψ), and as usual, we let E^k stand for $E \times E \cdots \times E$ (k times). We prove by induction on the number of operators in a subformula ω of ψ that if ω has free domain variables $y_1, y_2, \ldots, y_m$, then DOM$(\psi)^m \cap \{y_1 \cdots y_m \mid \omega(y_1, \ldots, y_m)\}$ has an equivalent expression in relational algebra. Then, as a special case, when ω is ψ itself, we have an algebraic expression for DOM$(\psi)^k \cap \{x_1 \cdots x_k \mid \psi(x_1, \ldots, x_k)\}$. Since ψ is safe, intersection with DOM$(\psi)^k$ does not change the relation denoted, so we shall have proved the theorem. We therefore turn to the inductive proof.

Basis: Zero operators in ω. Then ω is an atom, which we may take to be in one of the forms $x_1 \theta x_2$, $x_1 \theta x_1$, $x_1 \theta a$, or $R(x_{i_1} x_{i_2} \cdots x_{i_l})$, where θ is an arithmetic comparison operator, and a is a constant. If the atom is $x_1 \theta x_2$, then the desired algebraic expression is $\sigma_{1\theta 2}(E \times E)$. Atoms $x_1 \theta x_1$ and $x_1 \theta a$ are handled similarly.

Finally, if the atom is $R(x_{i_1} x_{i_2} \cdots x_{i_l})$ we construct the expression

$$\pi_{j_1, j_2, \ldots, j_k}(\sigma_F(R))$$

where F is a formula that has term $u=v$ whenever x_{i_u} and x_{i_v} are the same variable, and $u < v$; all terms are connected by the $\wedge$ operator.[†] The list $j_1, j_2, \ldots, j_k$ is any list such that $x_{i_{j_1}} = x_1, \ldots, x_{i_{j_k}} = x_k$. For example, if ψ is $R(x_2 x_1 x_2 x_3)$, then our expression is $\pi_{2,1,4}(\sigma_{1=3}(R))$.

Induction: Assume ω has at least one operator and that the inductive hypothesis is true for all subformulas of ψ having fewer operators than ω.

Case 1: $\omega(y_1, \ldots, y_m) = \omega_1(u_1, \ldots, u_n) \vee \omega_2(v_1, \ldots, v_p)$, where each u_i is a distinct y_j and each v_i is a distinct y_j (although some of the u's and v's may be the same y_j). Let E_1 be an algebraic expression for

$$\text{DOM}(\psi)^n \cap \{u_1 \cdots u_n \mid \omega_1(u_1, \ldots, u_n)\}$$

and E_2 an algebraic expression for

$$\text{DOM}(\psi)^p \cap \{v_1 \cdots v_p \mid \omega_2(v_1, \ldots, v_p)\}$$

Define E_1', by:

$$E_1' = \pi_{i_1, \ldots, i_m}(E_1 \times E^{m-n})$$

where i_l is that q such that $u_q = y_l$ if such a u_q exists, and i_l is a unique integer between $n+1$ and m otherwise. Similarly define

$$E_2' = \pi_{j_1, \ldots, j_m}(E_2 \times E^{m-p})$$

where j_l is that q such that $v_q = y_l$ if such a v_q exists, and j_l is a unique integer beteen $p+1$ and m otherwise. Then the desired expression is $E_1' \cup E_2'$.

For example, if $\omega(y_1, y_2, y_3, y_4)$ is

$$\omega_1(y_1, y_3, y_4) \vee \omega_2(y_2, y_4)$$

then

$$E_1' = \pi_{1,4,2,3}(E_1 \times E)$$

and

$$E_2' = \pi_{3,1,4,2}(E_2 \times E \times E)$$

The correctness of the formula $E_1' \cup E_2'$ follows from the fact that E_1' denotes $\text{DOM}(\psi)^m \cap \{y_1 \cdots y_m \mid \omega_1(u_1, \ldots, u_n)\}$ and E_2' denotes $\text{DOM}(\psi)^m \cap \{y_1 \cdots y_m \mid w_2(v_1, \ldots, v_p)\}$. (Recall that each of the u's and v's is one of the y's.) It follows that $E_1' \cup E_2'$ denotes

---

[†] Note that if there are three or more occurrences of one variable, some of these terms will be redundant and can be eliminated.

$DOM(\psi)^m \cap \{y_1 \cdots y_m \mid \omega(y_1, \ldots, y_m)\}$.

Case 2: $\omega(y_1, \ldots, y_m) = \neg\omega_1(y_1, \ldots, y_m)$. Let E_1 be an algebraic expression for $DOM(\psi)^m \cap \{y_1 \cdots y_m \mid \omega_1(y_1, \ldots, y_m)\}$. Then $E^m - E_1$ is an expression for $DOM(\psi)^m - \{y_1 \cdots y_m \mid \omega_1(y_1, \ldots, y_m)\}$, which is equivalent to $DOM(\psi)^m \cap \{y_1 \cdots y_m \mid \neg\omega_1(y_1, \ldots, y_m)\}$.

Case 3: $\omega(y_1, \ldots, y_m) = (\exists y_{m+1})(\omega_1(y_1, \ldots, y_{m+1}))$. Let E_1 be an algebraic expression for $DOM(\psi)^{m+1} \cap \{y_1 \cdots y_{m+1} \mid \omega_1(y_1, \ldots, y_{m+1})\}$. Since ψ is safe, $\omega_1(y_1, \ldots, y_{m+1})$ is never true unless y_{m+1} is in the set $DOM(\omega_1)$, which is a subset of $DOM(\psi)$. Therefore $\pi_{1,2,\ldots,m}(E_1)$ denotes the relation $DOM(\psi)^m \cap \{y_1 \cdots y_m \mid (\exists y_{m+1})(\omega_1(y_1, \ldots, y_{m+1}))\}$, which completes the induction and proves the theorem. $\square$

Example 4.10: Let R and S be binary relations. The domain calculus expression

$$\{wx \mid R(wx) \wedge (\forall y)(\neg S(wy) \wedge \neg S(xy))\}$$

denotes the set of tuples in R neither of whose components are the first component of any tuple in S. This expression is safe, since

1. The formula is not satisfied for w and x unless wx is a tuple of R, and

2. Whenever y is not a symbol appearing in a tuple of S, $\neg S(wy) \wedge \neg S(xy)$ is surely true.

Let E stand for $\pi_1(R) \cup \pi_2(R) \cup \pi_1(S) \cup \pi_2(S)$. We begin by eliminating $\wedge$ and $\forall$ using the construction of Lemma 4.2. After "cancelling" pairs of $\neg$'s, we obtain the expression:

$$\{wx \mid \neg(\neg R(wx) \vee (\exists y)(S(wy) \vee S(xy)))\}$$

Now we apply the construction of Theorem 4.3, beginning at the atoms and progressing to larger subformulas. The expression R denotes $E^2 \cap \{wx \mid R(wx)\}$, while the expression S denotes $E^2 \cap \{wy \mid S(wy)\}$ as well as $E^2 \cap \{xy \mid S(xy)\}$.[†] Next, let us apply Case 1 of Theorem 4.3 to get an expression for $E^3 \cap \{wxy \mid S(wy) \vee S(xy)\}$. This expression is

$$E_1 = \pi_{1,3,2}(S \times E) \cup \pi_{3,1,2}(S \times E)$$

Then, apply Case 3 to get an expression for

$$E^2 \cap \{wx \mid (\exists y)(S(wy) \vee S(xy))\}.$$

We obtain $\pi_{1,2}(E_1)$. If we compose cascaded projections in the obvious way we obtain

---

† The "formulas" R and S are substantially simpler than the formulas given in the basis of Theorem 4.3. We can use the relations themselves here, because no atom has a domain variable appearing in two components.

$$E_2 = \pi_{1,3}(S \times E) \cup \pi_{3,1}(S \times E)$$

This expression denotes the set of pairs one of whose components is a first component of a tuple of S and whose other component appears in some tuple of R or S.

The expression for $E^2 \cap \{wx \mid \neg R(wx)\}$ is $E^2 - R$ by Case 2. By Case 1, the formula for $\{wx \mid \neg R(wx) \vee (\exists y)(S(wy) \vee S(xy))\}$ is $(E^2 - R) \cup E_2$. Notice that no projection is necessary, since the projections for both $E^2 - R$ and E_2 are $\pi_{1,2}$, which leaves all tuples intact. Finally, the entire domain calculus expression has algebraic expression $E^2 - ((E^2 - R) \cup E_2)$. Since R and E_2 both denote subsets of E^2, this expression is equivalent to $R - E_2$, that is:

$$R - (\pi_{1,3}(S \times E) \cup \pi_{3,1}(S \times E)).$$

□

4.3 General Comments Regarding Query Languages

We have seen three abstract notations that can serve as the part of a data manupulation language that extracts information from relations. These notations are relational algebra, tuple relational calculus, and domain relational calculus. As we saw in Theorems 4.1, 4.2, and 4.3, the three notations are equivalent in their expressive power.

Historically, Codd [1972b] first proposed tuple relational calculus (in a formulation somewhat different from that given in Section 4.2) as a benchmark for evaluating data manipulation languages based on the relational model. That is, a language that does not at least have the expressive power of the safe formulas of relational calculus, or equivalently of relational algebra, was deemed inadequate. It is the case that almost all modern query languages embed within them one of the three notations discussed in the previous section; some are best viewed as embedding a combination of these notations. A language that can (at least) simulate tuple calculus, or equivalently, relational algebra or domain calculus, is said to be *complete*. We shall in the remainder of this chapter consider some example languages and show their completeness.

Additional Features of Data Manipulation Languages

In truth, data manipulation languages generally have capabilities beyond those of relational calculus. Of course, all data manipulation languages include insertion, deletion, and modification commands, which are not part of relational algebra or calculus. Some additional features frequently available are:

1. *Arithmetic capability.* Often, atoms in calculus expressions or selections in algebraic expressions can involve arithmetic computation as well as comparisons, such as $A < B+3$. Note that $+$ and other arithmetic operators appear in neither relational algebra or calculus.

2. *Assignment and Print Commands.* Languages generally allow the printing of the relation constructed by an algebraic or calculus expression or the assignment of a computed relation to be the value of a relation name.

3. *Aggregate Functions.* Operations such as average, sum, min, or max can often be applied to columns of a relation to obtain a single quantity.

For these reasons, the languages we shall discuss are really "more than complete," that is, they can compute functions that have no counterpart in relational algebra or calculus. Many, but not all, become equivalent to relational calculus when we throw away arithmetic and aggregate operators. It is an interesting exercise to prove this by showing how to convert to relational calculus or algebra all expressions in the language that do not involve arithmetic or aggregation. However, the reader should be warned that we do not give the entire set of features of those languages we discuss, so the design document for the language must be consulted before attempting such a proof. Also, some languages, like Query-by-Example (Section 4.7), are more than complete even after eliminating arithmetic and aggregation. In particular, Query-by-Example allows computation of the transitive closure of a relation, although we do not discuss this feature here.

Comparison of Algebraic and Calculus Languages

It is often said that relational calculus-based languages are higher-level than the algebraic languages because the algebra specifies the order of operations while the calculus leaves it to a compiler or interpreter to determine the most efficient order of evaluation. For example, if we have relations $R(A, B)$ and $S(B, C)$, we might write an algebraic expression such as

$$\pi_C \sigma_{A=a_0}(R \bowtie S) \qquad (4.1)$$

where $\bowtie$ stands for the natural join and a_0 is a constant. This query says: "print the C-values associated with A-value a_0 in the joined relation with columns A, B, and C." An equivalent domain calculus expression is

$$\{c \mid (\exists b)(R(a_0 b) \land S(bc))\} \qquad (4.2)$$

If we compare (4.1) and (4.2) we see that the calculus expression does in fact tell only what we want, not how to get it; that is, (4.2) only specifies the properties of the desired value c. In comparison, (4.1) specifies a particular order of operations. It is not immediately obvious that

(4.1) is equivalent to:

$$\pi_C(\pi_B(\sigma_{A=a_0}(R)) \bowtie S) \qquad (4.3)$$

To evaluate (4.3) we need only look up R for the tuples with A-value a_0 and find the associated B-values. This computes $\pi_B(\sigma_{A=a_0}(R))$. Then we look up the tuples of S with those B-values and print the associated C-values.

    In comparison, (4.1) requires that we evaluate the natural join of R and S, which could involve sorting both relations on their B-values and running through the sorted relations. Depending on the file organizations used to represent R and S, the evaluation of (4.1) could take much more time than (4.3), even though the answers are the same.

    In principle, we can always evaluate (4.2) like (4.3) rather than (4.1), which appears to be an advantage of calculus over algebra, especially as (4.1) is more likely to be written in an algebraic language than is (4.3). However, an optimization pass in the query language compiler can convert (4.1) into (4.3) immediately, and relational calculus expressions require optimization as well if we are to receive the full benefit of their nonprocedurality.†

    We shall consider such optimization in Chapter 6. Thus we feel that it is specious to regard calculus as higher-level than algebra, if for no other reason than that the first step in the optimization of an algebraic expression could be to convert it by Theorem 4.1 to an equivalent calculus expression. We must admit, however, that calculus-based languages are today more prevalent than algebraic languages. We prefer to attribute the dominance of calculus languages to the desirability of their nonprocedurality from the programmer's point of view, rather than from the point of view of efficiency or ease of compilation.

Select-Project-Join Expressions

While we expect a query language to be complete, there is a subset of the expressions of relational algebra that appear with great frequency, and it is important to consider how easily a language handles these expressions. The class of expressions we have in mind is formed from the operators select, project, and natural join. Intuitively, many queries can be viewed as taking an entity (described by the selection clause), connecting it to an entity of another type, perhaps through many relationships (the natural join expresses the connection), and then printing some attributes of the latter entity (the projection determines the attributes printed). We call such

---

† A *nonprocedural* language is one that expresses what we want without necessarily saying how to obtain it.

expressions *select-project-join* expressions. The reader is encouraged to look at how the query languages to be described each handle select-project-join queries in a succinct way.

4.4 ISBL: A "Pure" Relational Algebra Language.

ISBL (Information System Base Language) is a query language developed at the IBM United Kingdom Scientific Center in Peterlee, England, for use in the experimental PRTV (Peterlee Relational Test Vehicle) system. It closely approximates the relational algebra given in Section 4.1, so the completeness of ISBL is easy to show. The correspondence of syntax is shown in Fig. 4.6. In both ISBL and relational algebra, R and S can be any relational expressions, and F is a Boolean formula. Components of a relation are given names, and we refer to components by these names in F.

Relational algebra	ISBL
$R \cup S$	$R + S$
$R - S$	$R - S$
$R \cap S$	$R \cdot S$
$\sigma_F(R)$	$R : F$
$\pi_{A_1, \ldots, A_n}(R)$	$R \% A_1, \ldots, A_n$
$R \bowtie S$	$R * S$

Fig. 4.6. Correspondence between ISBL and relational algebra.

To print the value of an expression, preceed it by LIST. To assign the value of an expression E to a relation named R, we write $R = E$. An interesting feature of assignment is that we can delay the binding of relations to names in an expression until the name on the left of the assignment is used. To delay evaluation of a name, preceed it by N!. The N! calls for evaluation "by name."

Example 4.11: Suppose we want to use the composition of binary relations $R(A, B)$ and $S(C, D)$ from time to time. If we write

    RCS = R * S : B=C % A,D

the composition of the current relations R and S would be computed and assigned to relation name RCS. Note that as R and S have attributes with different names, the *, or natural join, operator is here a Cartesian product.

However, suppose we wanted RCS to stand not for the composition of the current values of $R(A, B)$ and $S(C, D)$ but for the formula for composing R and S. Then we could write

    RCS = N!R * N!S : B=C % A,D

The above ISBL statement causes no evaluation of relations. Rather, it defines RCS to stand for the formula R * S : B=C % A,D. If we ever use RCS in a statement that requires its evaluation, such as

    LIST RCS

or

    T = RCS + U

the values of R and S are at that time substituted into the formula for RCS to get a value for RCS. □

    The delayed evaluation operator N! serves two important purposes. First, large relational expressions are hard to write down correctly the first time. Delayed evaluation allows the programmer to construct an expression in easy stages, by giving temporary names to important subexpressions. More importantly, delayed evaluation serves as a rudimentary facility for defining views. By defining relation names by expressions with delayed evaluation, the programmer can use these names as if the defined relations really existed. Thus, a set of defined relations forms a view of the data-base.

Renaming of Attributes

The purely set theoretic operators, union, intersection, and difference, have definitions that are modified from their standard definitions in relational algebra, to take account of the fact that components have attribute names. The union and intersection operators are only applicable when the two relations involved have the same set of attribute names. The difference operator, $R-S$, is the ordinary set-theoretic difference when R and S have the same set of attribute names. However, if some of the attributes of R and S differ, then $R-S$ denotes the set of tuples t in R such that t agrees with no tuple in S on those attributes that R and S have in common. Thus, for example, in ISBL the expression $R-S$, where R is $R(A, B)$ and S is $S(A, C)$, denotes the relational algebra expression

$$R - \pi_A(S) \times \pi_B(R)$$

    To allow these operators to be used at will, a special form of projection permits the renaming of attributes. In a list of attributes following the projection (%) operator, an item $A \rightarrow B$ means that the component for attribute A is included in the projection but is renamed B. For example, to take the union of $R(A, B)$ with $S(C, D)$ we could write

    (R % A, B→C) + S

The resulting relation has attributes A and C.

    We can also use renaming to take the Cartesian product of relations whose sets of attributes are not disjoint. Observe that the natural join

$R(A, B) * S(C, D)$ is really a Cartesian product, but $R(A, B) * S(B, C)$ is a natural join in which the B-components of R and S are equated. If we want to take the Cartesian product of $R(A, B)$ with $S(B, C)$ we can write

(R % A, B→D) * S

As the left operand of the * has attributes A and D, while S has attibutes B and C, the result is a Cartesian product.

With attribute renaming, we have a way to simulate any of the five basic relational algebra operations in ISBL. Thus it is immediately obvious that ISBL is complete.

Some Sample Queries

Example 4.12: Let us now introduce a sample database that we shall use as we discuss various query languages. The Happy Valley Food Coop (HVFC) keeps a database in which its members' balances, their orders, and possible suppliers and prices are recorded. The three relation schemes used are

MEMBERS(NAME, ADDRESS, BALANCE)
ORDERS(NAME, ITEM, QUANTITY)
SUPPLIERS(SNAME, SADDRESS, ITEM, PRICE)

In Fig. 4.7 we see what we shall regard as the "current value" of the corresponding relations for the duration of this chapter. There follow some typical queries and their expression in ISBL.

1. The simplest queries often involve a selection and projection on a single relation. That is, we specify some condition that tuples must have, and we print some or all of the components of these tuples. The specific example query we shall use is

    Print the names of members with negative balances.

    In ISBL we can write

    LIST MEMBERS : BALANCE < 0 % NAME

    The clause BALANCE < 0 selects the third and fourth tuples, because their values in column 3 (BALANCE) is negative. The projection operator leaves only the first column, NAME, so LIST causes the table

    Robin, R.
    Hart, W.

    to be printed.

NAME	ADDRESS	BALANCE
Brooks, B.	7 Apple Rd.	+10.50
Field, W.	43 Cherry La.	0
Robin, R.	12 Heather St.	−123.45
Hart, W.	65 Lark Rd.	−43.00

(a) MEMBERS

NAME	ITEM	QUANTITY
Brooks, B.	Granola	5
Brooks, B.	Unbleached Flour	10
Robin, R.	Granola	3
Hart, W.	Whey	5
Robin, R.	Sunflower Seeds	2
Robin, R.	Lettuce	8

(b) ORDERS

SNAME	SADDRESS	ITEM	PRICE
Sunshine Produce	16 River St.	Granola	1.29
Sunshine Produce	16 River St.	Lettuce	.89
Sunshine Produce	16 River St.	Sunflower Seeds	1.09
Purity Foodstuffs	180 Industrial Rd.	Whey	.70
Purity Foodstuffs	180 Industrial Rd.	Curds	.80
Purity Foodstuffs	180 Industrial Rd.	Granola	1.25
Purity Foodstuffs	180 Industrial Rd.	Unbleached Flour	.65
Tasti Supply Co.	17 River St.	Lettuce	.79
Tasti Supply Co.	17 River St.	Whey	.79
Tasti Supply Co.	17 River St.	Sunflower Seeds	1.19

(c) SUPPLIERS

Fig. 4.7. Current relations in HVFC database.

Notes: All addresses are in the town of Happy Valley. QUANTITY is in pounds.
PRICE is per pound. Lettuce is union-picked only.

2. A more complicated type of query involves taking the natural join, or perhaps a more general join or Cartesian product of several relations, then selecting tuples from this relation and printing some of the components. Our example query is:

    Print the supplier names, items, and prices of all suppliers
    that supply at least one item ordered by Brooks.

We could write the expression for this query directly, but it is conceptually simpler first to define the natural join of ORDERS and SUPPLIERS by

OS = N!ORDERS * N!SUPPLIERS

Note that the evaluation of OS is deferred. Now with the natural join

OS(NAME, ITEM, QUANTITY, SNAME, SADDRESS, PRICE)

available, we select NAME = "Brooks,B." and project onto the desired attributes SNAME, ITEM, and PRICE. The formula is

LIST OS : NAME = "Brooks,B" % SNAME ITEM PRICE

The result of this expression is the table of Fig. 4.8.

SNAME	ITEM	PRICE
Sunshine Produce	Granola	1.29
Purity Foodstuffs	Granola	1.25
Purity Foodstuffs	Unbleached Flour	.65

Fig. 4.8. Result of the second query.

3. A still more complicated sort of query involves what amounts to a "for all" quantifier. The particular query we shall consider is:

    Print the suppliers that supply every item ordered by Brooks.

Such queries are easier in calculus languages than algebraic languages. The reader will note that in the proof of Theorem 4.3 we eliminated ∀ quantifiers before converting to algebra, by converting them to ∃ quantifiers with negations. The same strategy works here. We first construct the set of suppliers that do not supply some item ordered by Brooks. Define

> S = N!SUPPLIERS % SNAME   /* the set of suppliers */
> I = N!SUPPLIERS % ITEM   /* the set of supplied items */
> B = N!ORDERS; NAME="Brooks,B." % ITEM
>   /* the items ordered by Brooks */
> NS = N!S * N!I − (N!SUPPLIERS % SNAME, ITEM)
>   /* the pairs of suppliers and items not supplied
>   by that supplier */
> NSB = N!NS . (N!S * N!B)   /* the set of supplier-
>   item pairs such that the supplier doesn't supply the
>   item, and Brooks ordered the item */

Then the desired expression is S − (NSB % SNAME). It evaluates to the list consisting of one entry: Purity Foodstuffs. □

ISBL Extensions

The ISBL language is fairly limited, when compared with query languages to be discussed in the next sections. For example, it has no aggregate operators (e.g., average, min), and there are no facilities for insertion, deletion, or modification of tuples. However, there exists in the surrounding PRTV system the facility to write arbitrary PL/I programs and integrate them into the processing of relations.

The simplest use of PL/I programs in ISBL is as tuple-at-a-time processors, which serve as generalized selection operators. For example, we could write a PL/I program LOWADDR(S) that examines the character string S and determines whether S, as a street address, has a number lower than 50, returning "true" if so. We can then apply LOWADDR to an attribute in an ISBL expression, with the result that the component for that attribute in each tuple is passed to LOWADDR, and the tuple is "selected" if LOWADDR returns "true." The syntax of ISBL calls for the join operator to be used for these generalized selections. Thus

LIST (MEMBERS * LOWADDR(ADDRESS)) % NAME

prints the names of members whose street number does not exceed 49.

PL/I programs that operate on whole relations, rather than tuples, can also be defined. To facilitate such processing, the PRTV system allows relations to be passed to PL/I programs, either as *relational read files,* or *relational write files.* These are ordinary files in the PL/I sense, opened for reading or writing, respectively. A PL/I program can read or write the next record, which is a tuple of the underlying relation, into or from a PL/I record structure. The reader should be able to envision how to write PL/I programs to compute aggregate operators like sums or averages, to delete or modify tuples in arbitrarily specified ways, or to read tuples from an input file (not necessarily a relational read file; it could be a terminal, e.g.) and append them to a relation.

4.5 SQUARE and SEQUEL: Evolutionary Steps Between Algebraic and Calculus Languages

The language SQUARE is one step in the development of a query language for the System-R DBMS under development at IBM in San Jose. It has evolved into a language called SEQUEL, which is similar in concept to SQUARE, but has a syntax that is reminiscent of tuple relational calculus. We shall discuss the evolution of SQUARE into SEQUEL after presenting the important ideas in SQUARE.

SQUARE itself has a number of features not present in pure relational algebra, such as the ability to name tuples in relations or to compare sets by conditions such as $\subseteq$. In SQUARE, the union and difference operators are expressed as in relational algebra; intersection is treated likewise. The Cartesian product of R and S is expressed by

$$r \in R, \ s \in S$$

Projection of relation R onto attributes $A_1, A_2, \ldots, A_n$ is expressed:

$$_{A_1, A_2, \ldots, A_n} R$$

Selection is not done exactly as in relational algebra. Rather, the style is that of tuple calculus. The expression of $\sigma_F(R)$ in SQUARE is

$$r \in R : F'$$

where F' is F with r_A replacing the attribute A or the component number of that attribute in F.

We can immediately confirm that SQUARE is complete, since in SQUARE there is the capability to assign a computed relation to another relation name, using the assignment operator $\leftarrow$. An assignment

$$R_{A_1, A_2, \ldots, A_n} \leftarrow \ <\text{expression}>$$

where the $<\text{expression}>$ denotes an n-component relation, causes the expression to be evaluated and the result to be assigned to relation name R, whose attributes are then named $A_1, A_2, \ldots, A_n$. Thus, if no more convenient feature is present in the language, we can evaluate any relational expression by applying one operator at a time and assigning the result a temporary name. Note that unlike ISBL, assignment in SQUARE always implies immediate evaluation; deferred evaluation is not possible.

Mappings

One of the central features of SQUARE is the *mapping*, which is a special kind of selection followed by a projection. The general form of a mapping is

$$A_1, A_2, \ldots, A_n R_{B_1, B_2, \ldots, B_m}(\theta_1 b_1, \ \theta_2 b_2, \ \ldots, \theta_m b_m)$$

where R is a relation name, the A's and B's are lists of attributes of R, θ_i is a comparison operator ($=$, $\neq$, $<$, $\leq$, $>$, or $\geq$) and is followed by a constant, b_i. The operator $=$ is understood if θ_i is missing. This mapping stands for

$$\pi_{A_1, A_2, \ldots, A_n}(\sigma_{B_1 \theta_1 b_1 \wedge \cdots \wedge B_m \theta_m b_m}(R))$$

Mappings can be composed using the operator o. Composition will be seen to effect an equijoin of relations, so to a large extent the mapping embodies the select-project-join core of relational algebra.

Example 4.13: The first query of Example 4.12 can be expressed in SQUARE as

$$_{\text{NAME}}\text{MEMBERS}_{\text{BALANCE}}(<0)$$

and the second query can be expressed

$$_{\text{SNAME,ITEM,PRICE}}\text{SUPPLIERS}_{\text{ITEM}} \ o \ _{\text{ITEM}}\text{ORDERS}_{\text{NAME}}(\text{"Brooks,B."})$$

The mapping on the right is applied first, and it produces the set of items ordered by Brooks. Notice that the equality operator before "Brooks,B" is assumed, since no other operator is present. Then the second mapping looks up the tuples in SUPPLIERS with one of those items in the third component and produces the first, third and fourth components of those tuples. □

Free Variables

SQUARE permits tuple variables, called *free variables*, just as the tuple relational calculus does. We have met free variables already, in the formulas for Cartesian product and selection. In SQUARE, free variables may be subscripted by a list of attribute names to indicate which components of the tuple represented by the variable are to be taken. The following expressions in SQUARE can be likened to tuple relational calculus expressions.

$$(t_1)_{\alpha_1} \epsilon R_1, \ \ldots, \ (t_k)_{\alpha_k} \epsilon R_k : \psi \tag{4.4}$$

Here, t_i is a free variable denoting a tuple in R_i; α_i is the list of attributes of R_i that we want printed. If α_i is missing, then the list of all attributes of R_i is understood. Formula ψ takes operands that are constants or variables among the t_i's, perhaps subscripted by arbitrary lists of attributes.

The meaning of (4.4) is

$$\{u \mid (\exists t_1) \cdots (\exists t_k)(R_1(t_1) \wedge \cdots \wedge R_k(t_k) \wedge \omega \wedge \psi)\}$$

where ω asserts that $u[j] = t_i[m]$, if i and m are chosen such that the sum of the lengths of lists $\alpha_1, \alpha_2, \ldots, \alpha_{i-1}$ plus m totals j, and the length of α_i

is no more than m. That is, form the list of components represented by $(t_1)_{\alpha_1}$, then those represented by $(t_2)_{\alpha_2}$, and so on. The jth component of u is equal to the jth component on this list. The form of ω plus the clause $R_i(t_i)$ guarantees safety of the expression, since ψ is not allowed to have quantifiers.

The operators that can appear in ψ include mappings, as defined previously, the algebraic operations $\cup$, $\cap$, and $-$, the Boolean operators, arithmetic operators and comparisons, and set comparisons ($=$, $\neq$, $\subseteq$, and so on).

Example 4.14: The first query of Example 4.12 can be written with free variables as:

$$t_{NAME} \in MEMBERS: t_{BALANCE} < 0$$

The second query is not expressed in a very convenient way using free variables, but the third query, asking for suppliers that supply every item ordered by Brooks can be expressed succinctly as:

$$s_{SNAME} \in SUPPLIERS: (_{ITEM}ORDERS_{NAME}(\text{"Brooks,B."})$$
$$\subseteq {}_{ITEM}SUPPLIERS_{SNAME}(s_{SNAME}))$$

That is, $_{ITEM}ORDERS_{NAME}(\text{"Brooks,B."})$ is a mapping that produces the set of items ordered by Brooks. $_{ITEM}SUPPLIERS_{SNAME}(s_{SNAME})$ gives the set of items supplied by the supplier whose name is in the SNAME component of the tuple s. Therefore, the formula to the right of the colon is true exactly when the supplier mentioned in the tuple s supplies all items ordered by Brooks. As s ranges over all tuples in the SUPPLIERS relation, the expression causes all suppliers that supply all items ordered by Brooks to be printed.

As a last example, note that the expression for $R \times S$ given earlier:

$$r \in R, s \in S$$

is a special case of a free variable expression where the formula ψ is missing, and therefore considered always true. Thus the concatenation of every tuple in R with every tuple in S is printed. $\square$

Insertions, Deletions, and Modifications

The way to insert a tuple into relation R is to write $\downarrow R_{A_1,\ldots,A_n}(a_1,\ldots,a_n)$, where $A_1,\ldots,A_n$ is a list of some or all of the attributes of relation scheme R, and a_i is the value of attribute A_i in the new tuple. If R has attributes not listed among $A_1,\ldots,A_n$, the new tuple has the *null value* in the components for the unlisted attributes.

Example 4.15: The tuple ("Sunshine, L.M.", "29 Blue Sky Dr.", 0) can be added to the MEMBERS relation of Example 4.12 by the SQUARE statement

$$\downarrow MEMBERS_{NAME,ADDRESS,BALANCE}("Sunshine,L.M.", "29 \ Blue \ Sky \ Dr.", 0)$$

□

It is also permitted to write

$$\downarrow R_{A_1, \ldots, A_n}(<expression>)$$

where the $<expression>$'s value is an n-ary relation S. This statement has the same effect as the sequence of statements

$$\downarrow R_{A_1, \ldots, A_n}(a_1, \ldots, a_n)$$

where $(a_1, \ldots, a_n)$ ranges over all tuples in S.

The deletion statement has the same syntax as insertion, but $\uparrow$ is used in place of $\downarrow$.

$$\uparrow R_{A_1, \ldots, A_n}(a_1, \ldots, a_n)$$

deletes from R all tuples whose value in the component for attribute A_i is a_i, for each i between 1 and n. The command

$$\uparrow R_{A_1, \ldots, A_n}(<expression>)$$

where $<expression>$ evaluates to an n-ary relation S, deletes from R all tuples that match some tuple of S in the components for $A_1, \ldots, A_n$.

Example 4.16: If Tasti Supply Co. stops selling lettuce, we could update the database of Example 4.12 by

$$\uparrow SUPPLIERS_{SNAME,ITEM}("Tasti \ Supply \ Co.", "lettuce")$$

This will delete the tuple

("Tasti Supply Co.", "17 River St.", "lettuce", .79)

from SUPPLIERS.

If we wish to cancel the orders of all members with negative balances, we can use the expression $_{NAME}MEMBERS_{BALANCE}(<0)$ to denote the set of all members with negative balances. A set is a unary relation, so we may use it as the argument of a deletion and write

$$\uparrow ORDERS_{NAME}(_{NAME}MEMBERS_{BALANCE}(<0))$$

□

The syntax for a modification is

$$\rightarrow R_{A_1, \ldots, A_n; B_1, \ldots, B_m}(a_1, \ldots, a_n, b_1, \ldots, b_m)$$

The A's and B's are (not necessarily disjoint) lists of attributes of relation

R; the B's, but not the A's, may be preceded by arithmetic operators, $+$, $-$, $\times$, or $/$. The a's and b's are constants. The statement causes R to be searched for tuples whose value in the A_i component is a_i, for all i between 1 and n. For each such tuple, it replaces the value in the component B_i by b_i, for $1 \leqslant i \leqslant m$. However, if B_i is preceded by arithmetic operator α, the old value c in component B_i is replaced by $c \alpha b_i$. For example, $+B_i$ causes c to be replaced by $c + b_i$.

Example 4.17: To set Hart's balance to 0, write

$$\rightarrow \text{MEMBERS}_{\text{NAME:BALANCE}}(\text{"Hart,W."}, 0)$$

If Robin pays 200 dollars, we can increase her balance by that amount if we write

$$\rightarrow \text{MEMBERS}_{\text{NAME:+BALANCE}}(\text{"Robin,R."}, 200)$$

If Purity Foodstuffs cuts the price of whey in half we can write

$$\rightarrow \text{SUPPLIERS}_{\text{SNAME,ITEM:/PRICE}}(\text{"Purity Foodstuffs"}, \text{"Whey"}, 2)$$

□

Aggregate Functions

Functions such as COUNT, AVG, SUM, MIN, or MAX can be applied to the collection of values in a set (unary relation). For example, if we wished to determine the net balance of all members of the HVFC, we could write

$$\text{SUM}(_{\text{BALANCE}}\text{MEMBERS'})$$

As another example, if we wished to find the supplier or suppliers with the lowest price for granola we could write

$$s_{\text{SNAME}} \in \text{SUPPLIERS}: s_{\text{ITEM}}=\text{"Granola"}$$
$$\wedge \; s_{\text{PRICE}}=\text{MIN}(_{\text{PRICE}}\text{SUPPLIERS}_{\text{ITEM}}(\text{"Granola"}))$$

The reader may note the prime on MEMBERS in the first of these formulas. Its presence is to remind SQUARE not to merge two identical elements when it computes a set. That is, if we wrote

$$\text{SUM}(_{\text{BALANCE}}\text{MEMBERS})$$

two members balances that happened to be the same would be counted only once in the sum. The prime indicates that the result of the mapping $_{\text{BALANCE}}\text{MEMBERS}$ is to be a multiset, with repetitions allowed, rather than the usual set, with repetitions combined.

The Query Language SEQUEL

One of the problems with SQUARE is its reliance on subscripts in its syntax. While we can develop a syntax that places everything on a line (and we must do this for use with a computer) such syntax is not appealing. One way in which SEQUEL differs from SQUARE is in the use of keywords to indicate the role of relation and attribute names.

The SQUARE mapping

$$A_1, \ldots, A_n R_{B_1, \ldots, B_m}(\theta_1 b_1, \ldots, \theta_m b_m)$$

is expressed in SEQUEL by

> SELECT $A_1, \ldots, A_n$
> FROM R
> WHERE $B_1\theta_1 b_1 \wedge \cdots \wedge B_m\theta_m b_m$

Recall that if θ_i is missing in the SQUARE mapping, it is assumed to be =. Thus the first query of Example 4.12 can be written

> SELECT NAME
> FROM MEMBERS
> WHERE BALANCE < 0

Once we have adopted this style of representation for mappings, we see that the restrictions on what follows the WHERE can be relaxed somewhat. In SEQUEL the expression following WHERE can be any expression involving the attributes of the relation followng FROM, arithmetic comparisons and operations, Boolean connectives (written AND, OR, NOT), set operations (UNION, INTERSECT, MINUS), set membership (X IN S, where S is a set, or equivalently S CONTAINS X) and the negation of set membership (X NOT IN S or S DOES NOT CONTAIN X). The same operators can serve for set inclusion if X is a set rather than an element or tuple. The expression following WHERE can also contain operands that are relations formed from another SELECT-FROM-WHERE clause.

Example 4.18: To print the names and addresses of suppliers that supply either curds or whey, we write

> SELECT UNIQUE SNAME, SADDRESS
> FROM SUPPLIERS
> WHERE ITEM = 'curds' OR ITEM = 'whey'

The word UNIQUE is needed after SELECT here because unlike SQUARE, when SEQUEL applies a mapping it does not eliminate duplicates unless told to do so by the keyword UNIQUE. Without UNIQUE, this query would print Purity Foodstuffs twice, since it supplies both curds and whey.

The composition of mappings is achieved by nesting SELECT-FROM-WHERE clauses and using the set membership (IN) operator.

Thus the second query of Example 4.12 in SEQUEL is:

    SELECT UNIQUE SNAME, ITEM, PRICE
    FROM SUPPLIERS
    WHERE ITEM IN
        SELECT ITEM
        FROM ORDERS
        WHERE NAME = 'Brooks,B.'

□

There are two features of SEQUEL that are like free variable expressions in SQUARE. First, we can give a name T to a typical tuple of relation R by writing

    SELECT ··· FROM R T WHERE ···

Then, inside the WHERE clause we may refer to the value of component A of tuple T by $T.A$.

Example 4.19: To print the names of all members who have ordered ten or more pounds of food, we could write

    SELECT NAME
    FROM MEMBERS T
    WHERE 10 < =
        SELECT SUM(QUANTITY)
        FROM ORDERS
        WHERE NAME = T.NAME

Here SUM is an aggregate function as in SQUARE. In the clause WHERE NAME = T.NAME, the attribute NAME refers to the NAME component of ORDERS, while T.NAME refers to the NAME component of the tuple T from MEMBERS. The result printed is

    Brooks,B.
    Robin, R.

The third query of Example 4.12 can be written as in Fig. 4.9. □

Another feature of SEQUEL that can be used like free variables in SQUARE is the ability to list more than one relation in the FROM-clause. The values of attributes of any of the relations following FROM can be referred to either in the SELECT- or WHERE-clauses. If there is potential ambiguity, because A is an attribute of more than one relation, we can use $R.A$ to indicate that attribute A from relation R is meant.

If we have clause FROM $R_1, \ldots, R_n$ in a query, we consider all lists $t_1, \ldots, t_n$ of tuples, where t_i is taken from R_i. If the list satisfies the conditions following WHERE, we include in the output, the list of components specified in the SELECT-clause.

```
SELECT SNAME
FROM SUPPLIERS T
WHERE
        (SELECT ITEM
        FROM SUPPLIERS
        WHERE SNAME = T.SNAME)
CONTAINS
        (SELECT ITEM
        FROM ORDERS
        WHERE NAME = 'Brooks,B.')
```

Fig. 4.9. A SEQUEL query.

Example 4.20: We can produce the join of relations by listing them in the FROM-clause and putting the necessary relationships among the attributes in the WHERE-clause. Thus, the second query in Example 4.12 could be written

```
SELECT SNAME, SUPPLIERS.ITEM, PRICE
FROM SUPPLIERS, ORDERS
WHERE NAME = 'Brooks,B.' AND
        SUPPLIERS.ITEM = ORDERS.ITEM
```

Note that as ITEM appears in both relations SUPPLIERS and ORDERS, it must be qualified by the relation from which it comes. Other attributes appear in only one of the two relations and need not be qualified.

As another example, we can take the Cartesian product of relations R and S by

```
SELECT *
FROM R, S
```

The symbol * stands for all components of all the relations folllowing FROM. □

The insertion, deletion and modification operations of SEQUEL are syntactically-sugared versions of the corresponding operations of SQUARE, just as the SELECT-FROM-WHERE construction is a syntactically sugared version of the SQUARE mapping. We shall not go into these operations here.

Completeness of SEQUEL

We saw in Example 4.20 how to compute a Cartesian product. The operations union and set difference are obtained by the UNION and MINUS operations. For example, the union of R and S is

```
(SELECT *
FROM R)
UNION
(SELECT *
FROM S)
```

The SELECT-FROM-WHERE construct obviously includes both the selection and projection operators of relational algebra. In SEQUEL, assignment is indicated by preceding a query by

ASSIGN TO R:

if we wish to assign the result to relation R. Thus we have the means to evaluate any relational algebra expression in SEQUEL by applying one operator at a time and thereby computing each subexpression. hence SEQUEL is complete.

SEQUEL and System R

As we have mentioned, SEQUEL is the principal query language used by the experimental System R DBMS. SEQUEL can be used as a "stand alone" query language, in which the user simply expresses SEQUEL queries and database updates and has these operations executed directly by System R. It is also possible to embed SEQUEL queries in PL/1 programs. The SEQUEL statements are prefixed with a *, and a preprocessor translates them into calls from the surrounding PL/1 program. These calls are to special procedures provided by System R. For example, the procedure named SEQUEL takes a string argument that is the query itself, and a call to this procedure causes the string to be interpreted and executed.

When used with PL/1 as a host language, SEQUEL queries can use variables of the surrounding program. For example, we could write a program to read an item I and then print all suppliers of I, by embedding the SEQUEL query

```
SELECT SNAME
FROM SUPPLIERS
WHERE ITEM = I
```

in the program. It is also possible, using a mechanism we shall not discuss in detail, to retrieve the result of a query, one tuple at a time, into designated variables of the surrounding program.

Implementation of Relations in System R

Let us conclude our discussion of SEQUEL by mentioning how relations are stored in System R. This discussion does not pertain to SEQUEL exclusively, since all data, regardless of the query language involved, is stored the same way, and System R is designed to support a variety of query languages, including languages not based on the relational data model.

System R divides the tuples of a relation among 4096-byte pages, which play the role of blocks as described in Chapter 2. A page can hold tuples from more than one relation, and sometimes it is advantageous to do so. The database administrator has three tools at his disposal to make those queries he expects to occur frequently run efficiently.

1. Tuples from two different relations can be grouped together on pages. The purpose of this arrangement is to make the traversal of implied links between relations (many-one relationships, as in the network model) efficient. The efficiency is gained by limiting the number of pages that have to be brought into main memory in response to a query. For example, there is an implied link between MEMBERS and ORDERS tuples in Example 4.12. That is, each member tuple can be viewed as linked to those ORDERS tuples representing orders by that member. The implied link can be represented by a collection of variable length records of format MEMBERS(ORDERS)*. We can implement this link by, whenever there is room, storing an ORDERS tuple with a given NAME on the same page as the MEMBERS tuple with the same NAME.

2. We can create an *index* to a relation on any collection of attributes of that relation. The index is a dense index as described in Section 2.5, with a B-tree structure. The interior nodes of the B-tree are pages filled with pairs consisting of pointers to other pages and associated values for the attributes on which the index is defined. Leaf nodes of the B-tree consist of values for these attributes and associated lists of *tuple identifiers;* there is one tuple identifier on the list for each tuple having the given values for the attributes of the index. Tuple identifiers are essentially pointers to the tuples, but there is a degree of indirection involved. Actually, tuple identifiers point to a place near the bottom of a page where a pointer to the tuple itself can be found. This arrangement allows for compaction of the tuples on a page as insertions and deletions occur.† Effectively, this degree of indirection allows us to treat tuples as unpinned records, even though they are pointed to by pointers from the B-tree. Figure 4.10 shows an example page.

---

† In System R, tuples can have variable length, so it is not always possible to leave tuples where they are without wasting space.

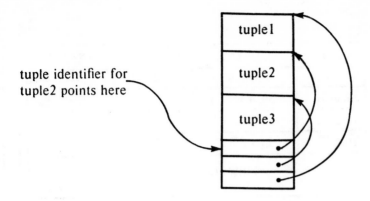

tuple identifier for
tuple2 points here

Fig. 4.10. Use of indirection in pages.

3.   *Links* can be used to connect a tuple *t* in one relation *R* to the tuples
      in relation *S* having the same values, in a designated list of attributes,
      as *t* has in a corresponding list of attributes. A relation can be
      involved in any number of links. This arrangement is very much like
      the multilist structure described in Section 3.2, there being a ring of
      pointers from each tuple *t* in *R*, threading the associated tuples of *S*,
      and returning to *t*. Recall that all pointers are tuple identifiers, and
      point indirectly to the tuples, as in Fig. 4.10.

Example 4.21: Suppose we wish to use a link that associates members with
their orders. Imagine that the MEMBERS and ORDERS relations of Fig.
4.7 each fit on one page. A link from MEMBERS to ORDERS based on
equality of the NAME fields looks schematically like Fig. 4.11. However,
the reader should remember that all pointers are really tuple identifiers, and
point to a place near the bottom of the page where a pointer to the tuple
itself is found. □

4.6 QUEL: A Tuple Relational Calculus Language

QUEL is the query language of INGRES, a relational DBMS developed at
the University of California, Berkeley. It has a powerful statement form
that covers a wide variety of tuple calculus statements. The calculus statement

$$\{u^{(r)} \mid (\exists t_1) \cdots (\exists t_k)(R_1(t_1) \wedge \cdots \wedge R_k(t_k) \tag{4.5}$$
$$\wedge\, u[1]=t_{i_1}[j_1] \wedge \cdots \wedge u[r]=t_{i_r}[j_r]$$
$$\wedge\, \psi\,\}$$

states that t_i is in R_i, that u is composed of r particular components of the
t_i's, and also asserts some additional condition ψ. If ψ is any tuple calculus
formula with no quantifiers, (4.5) can be written in QUEL as:

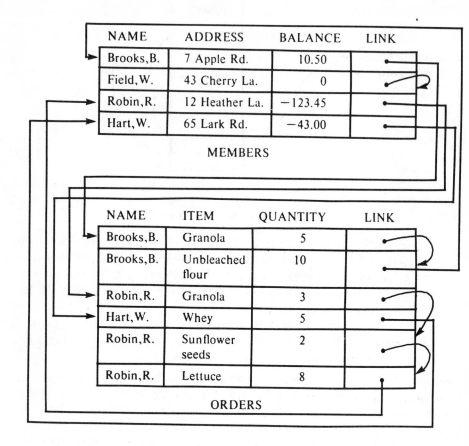

Fig. 4.11. Example of a link.

range of t_1 is R_1

.

.

.

range of t_k is R_k
retrieve $(t_{i_1}.A_1, \ldots, t_{i_r}.A_r)$
    where ψ'

In the above, A_m is the j_mth attribute of relation R_{i_m}, for $m = 1, 2, \ldots, k$, and ψ' is the translation of condition ψ into a QUEL expression. To perform the translation we must:

1. replace ψ's references to a component $u[m]$ by a reference to $t_{i_m}[j_m]$. Note that $u[m]$ and $t_{i_m}[j_m]$ are equated by formula (4.5).

2. replace any reference to $t_m[n]$ by $t_m.B$, where B is the nth attribute of relation R_m, for any n and m.

3. replace $\leqslant$ by $<=$, $\geqslant$ by $>=$, and $\neq$ by $!=$.

4. replace $\wedge$, $\vee$, $\neg$ by and, or, not, respectively.

The intuitive meaning of statement

　　range of t is R

is that any subsequent operations, until t is redeclared by another range statement, are to be carried out once for each tuple in R, with t equal to each of these tuples in turn.

The retrieve statement prints a table whose columns are headed $A_{j_1}, \ldots, A_{j_k}$. If we wish a different name, say TITLE, for column m, use TITLE $= t_{i_m}.A_{j_m}$ in place of $t_{i_m}.A_{j_m}$.

Example 4.22: The first query of Example 4.12 is written

　　range of t is MEMBERS
　　retrieve (t.NAME)
　　　　where t.BALANCE < 0

The second query of that example can be written

　　range of t is ORDERS
　　range of s is SUPPLIERS
　　retrieve (s.SNAME, s.ITEM, s.PRICE)
　　　　where t.NAME = "Brooks,B." and t.ITEM = s.ITEM.

□

The reader should observe that since ψ in (4.5) has no quantifiers, it is easy to show that expression (4.5) is always safe. The form of (4.5) is not quite general enough to be complete; in particular, we cannot express the union or difference of relations. Fortunately, QUEL provides a delete statement to compute set differences among other functions. One can write

　　range of t is R
　　delete t
　　　　where $\psi(t)$

Here, $\psi(t)$ is a QUEL expression like those that can follow "where" in the retrieve statement. The effect of this statement is to delete from R all tuples t that satisfy ψ.

Similarly, QUEL has an append statement to perform unions, among other tasks. We can write range of t_1 is R_1

.

.

.

range of t_k is R_k
append to $S(A_1 = \omega_1, \ldots, A_n = \omega_n)$
  where $\psi(t_1, \ldots, t_k)$

Here ψ is a QUEL expression as above, and the ω_i's are expressions involving components of the t_i's and/or constants, connected by arithmetic operators. For each assignment of values to the t_i's such that $\psi(t_1, \ldots, t_k)$ is true, we add to relation S the tuple whose component for attribute A_p is the value of ω_p, for $p = 1, 2, \ldots, n$. For example, if we wish to add an order for 10 pounds of curds for each member of HVFC with a nonnegative balance we could write

range of t is MEMBERS
append to ORDERS(NAME=t.NAME,
  ITEM="Curds", QUANTITY=10)
  where t.BALANCE $\geqslant$ 0

Note that the where clause is not required in the append statement, and it is possible, indeed usual, for the append statement to be used with no tuple variables, for the purpose of appending a single tuple to a relation.

We are still not ready to simulate any relational algebra expression in QUEL; we need the capability to assign values to new relations. If S is the name of a new relation we can write

range of t_1 is R_1

.

.

.

range of t_k is R_k
retrieve into $S(A_1=\omega_1, \ldots, A_n=\omega_n)$
  where $\psi(t_1, \ldots, t_k)$

this statement will find all lists of tuples $t_1, \ldots, t_k$ such that t_i is in R_i, and $\psi(t_1, \ldots, t_k)$ is true, and create a tuple for new relation S whose i^{th} component is ω_i. Here, ω_i is a formula as in the append statement.

The attribute names $A_1, \ldots, A_n$ become the names of the components of S. We may omit "$A_i=$" if ω_i is of the form t_j.NAME, whereupon NAME becomes the name of the ith attribute of S.

Example 4.23: QUEL, like SEQUEL, does not automatically remove duplicates when it computes a relation. Suppose we wanted to print the names and addresses of all suppliers. We could write

range of t is SUPPLIERS
retrieve (t.SNAME, t.SADDRESS)

but then each supplier would be printed once for each item it supplied. QUEL provides a sort command to eliminate duplicates while it sorts a relation, initially on the first component, then on the second component for tuples with the same first component, and so on. To print each supplier only once, and incidentally print them in alphabetical order, we could write

range of t is SUPPLIERS
retrieve into JUNK(NAME=t.SNAME, ADDR=t.SADDRESS)
sort JUNK
print JUNK

The columns of JUNK would be headed NAME and ADDR. □

Completeness of QUEL

Since we now know how to create temporary relations, all we have to do to evaluate any relational algebra expression is to show how to apply the five basic operators. Suppose in what follows that $R(A_1, \ldots, A_n)$ and $S(B_1, \ldots, B_m)$ are relations, and T is a new relation name. To compute $T = R \cup S$ (assuming $m=n$) we could write

range of r is R
append to $T(C_1=r.A_1, \ldots, C_n=r.A_n)$
range of s is S
append to $T(C_1=s.B_1, \ldots, C_n=s.B_n)$

To compute $T = R-S$, write

range of r is R
append to $T(C_1=r.A_1, \ldots, C_n=r.A_n)$
range of s is S
range of t is T
delete t
    where $s.B_1=t.C_1$ and $\cdots$ and $s.B_n=t.C_n$

For $T = R \times S$ write

range of r is R
range of s is S
append to $T(C_1=r.A_1, \ldots, C_n=r.A_n,$
    $C_{n+1}=s.B_1, \ldots, C_{n+m}=s.B_m)$

To compute the selection $\sigma_F(R)$, write

range of r is R
append to $T(C_1=r.A_1, \ldots, C_n=r.A_n)$
   where F'

Here F' is the formula F translated into QUEL notation (component i of R becomes $r.A_i$, $\wedge$ becomes "and," and so on). Finally, to express the projection $\psi_{i_1, \ldots, i_k}(R)$ we can write

range of r is R
append to $T(C_1=r.A_{i_1}, \ldots, C_k=r.A_{i_k})$

Example 4.24: The third query of Example 4.12 can be evaluated in QUEL by following the relational algebra formula developed in that example. Let us first write a program to compute the set of supplier-item pairs.

range of s is SUPPLIERS
range of i is SUPPLIERS
retrieve into DUMMY(S=s.SNAME, I=i.ITEM)

Now we follow this by statements to delete from DUMMY those supplier-item pairs (S, I) such that S supplies I. The result is those (S, I) pairs such that S does not supply I.

range of s is SUPPLIERS
range of t is DUMMY
delete t
   where t.S=s.SNAME and t.I=s.ITEM

Next create a relation of (S, I) pairs such that S is any supplier and I is not supplied by S but I is ordered by Brooks by writing

range of r is ORDERS
range of t is DUMMY
retrieve into JUNK(S=t.S, I=t.I)
   where r.NAME="Brooks,B." and r.ITEM=t.I

Then, we list only those SUPPLIERS that do not appear as a first component of a tuple in JUNK. To get the set of suppliers, write

range of s is SUPPLIERS
retrieve into SUPS(S=s.SNAME)

Finally, to print the desired set, say

```
range of u is SUPS
range of j is JUNK
delete u
    where u.S=j.S
sort SUPS
print SUPS
```

While the above may look like a lot of code, it can be simplified if we realize that range statements declare a variable to range over a particular relation "forever," or until another range statement for that variable is given. Thus we could condense range statements and write the QUEL program of Fig. 4.12.

```
range of s is SUPPLIERS
range of i is SUPPLIERS
retrieve into DUMMY(S=s.SNAME, I=i.ITEM)
range of t is DUMMY
delete t
    where t.S=s.SNAME and t.I=s.ITEM
range of r is ORDERS
retrieve into JUNK(S=t.S, I=t.I)
    where r.NAME="Brooks,B." and r.ITEM=t.I
retrieve into SUPS(S=s.SNAME)
range of u is SUPS
range of j is JUNK
delete u
    where u.S=j.S
sort SUPS
print SUPS
```

Fig. 4.12. QUEL program for query three.

Aggregate Operators

QUEL uses the aggregate functions sum, avg, count, min, and max, as do SQUARE or SEQUEL. The argument of such a function can be any expression involving components of a single relation, constants and arithmetic operators. The components must all be referred to as $t.A$ for some one tuple variable t and various attributes A. For example, if we want the net balance of all members of HVFC, we could write

```
range of t is MEMBERS
retrieve(sum(t.BALANCE))
```

We can also partition the tuples of a relation according to the value of one or more expressions computed from each tuple and take aggregates separately for each set of tuples having values in common for each of the expressions.† This partitioning is achieved by writing

$$\text{ag\_op}(E \text{ by } F_1, F_2, \ldots, F_k) \tag{4.6}$$

where E and the F's are expressions whose operands are constants and components $t.A$ for one tuple variable t. The operands in an expression may be connected by arithmetic operators. If t ranges over R, the value of (4.6) for a given value of t is computed by finding all those tuples of R that give the same value as t for $F_1, \ldots, F_k$. Then, apply the aggregate operator ag_op to the value of E for each of those tuples.

Example 4.23: To print the items supplied with their average prices, we could write

```
range of s is SUPPLIERS
retrieve into DUMMY(ITEM=s.ITEM,
   AP = avg(s.PRICE by s.ITEM))
sort DUMMY
print DUMMY
```

We sort DUMMY to remove duplicates, as DUMMY will have for each item, as many tuples as the SUPPLIERS relation has for that item. The result of running the above program on relation SUPPLIERS of Fig. 4.7 is shown in Fig. 4.13. □

ITEM	AP
Curds	.80
Granola	1.27
Lettuce	.84
Sunflower Seeds	1.14
Unbleached Flour	.65
Whey	.74

Fig. 4.13. Average prices of items.

Storage Organization in INGRES

In INGRES there is a create command to create a new relation name. The command allows the user to specify the attributes of the relation and the data types of these attributes. Data types are restricted to integers of one, two or four bytes, real numbers of four or eight bytes, and fixed length character strings of up to 255 bytes. Thus, the number of bytes taken by each tuple of the relation is known, and a relation can be stored as a file of

---

† SEQUEL and Query-by-Example (to be discussed in the next section) also have such a feature, although we discuss the concept only in the context of QUEL.

records, one record for each tuple. Records are stored in blocks of 512 bytes, and no record is allowed to overlap two blocks.

If the tuples are in no particular order, the file is called a *heap*. We can arrange for hashed access to the file for relation R, as discussed in Section 2.2, by saying

> modify R to hash on $A_1, \ldots, A_k$

where $A_1, \ldots, A_k$ is the list of attributes of R that serve as a key. The INGRES implementation of the file for R becomes that of Section 2.2; records may be pinned because of secondary indices, which we shall discuss later. As an alternative to a hashed access structure, a primary index can be created for the file R, by writing

> modify R to isam on $A_1, \ldots, A_k$

Again, $A_1, \ldots, A_k$ is the assumed key for R_j. The acronym isam stands for *indexed sequential access method*. The structure created is that of Section 2.3.

We can create a secondary index for R by the statement

> index on R is $S(A_1, \ldots, A_k)$

The relation S becomes a secondary index on attributes $A_1, \ldots, A_k$ for R, using a structure similar to that described in Section 2.7. The relation S has $k+1$ components, the first k being $A_1, \ldots, A_k$, and the last being a pointer to a record of R; the last component has no attribute name, so the user cannot access its values or change them (a good design decision, if you think about it). The file for secondary index S is automatically made isam on $A_1, \ldots, A_k$, although this organization can be changed by a modify command, just as for any other relation, if the user so desires.

4.7 Query-by-Example: A Domain Calculus Language

Query-by-Example *(QBE)* is a language developed at IBM, Yorktown Hts. It contains a number of features not present in relational algebra or calculus, or in any of the implemented query languages we have discussed. Not the least of its special features is that QBE is designed to be used sitting at a terminal, using a special screen editor to compose queries. A button on the terminal allows the user to call for one or more *table skeletons*, as shown in Fig. 4.14, to be displayed on the screen. The user then names the relations and attributes represented by the skeleton, using the screen editor.

Queries are posed by using domain variables and constants, as in domain relational calculus, to form tuples that we assert are in one of the relations whose skeletons appear on the screen. Certain of the variables, indicated by prefixing their name with P., are printed. (All operators in

QBE end in dot, and the dot is not itself an operator.) When a tuple or combination of tuples matching the conditions specified by the query are found, the components for those attributes preceded by P. are printed.

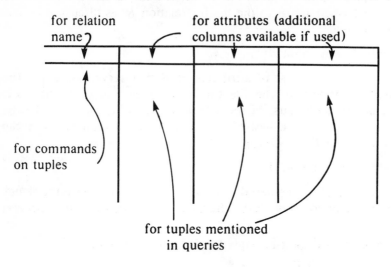

Fig. 4.14. A QBE table skeleton.

Before going into detail regarding the expression and meaning of queries in QBE, let us take an example of what a typical query looks like. Suppose we want to answer the second query of Example 4.12, and we have the ORDERS and SUPPLIERS relations available in the database. We call for two table skeletons to be displayed. In the box reserved for the relation name, in one skeleton, we type ORDERS P. The attributes of ORDERS will appear along the first row of that skeleton, as shown in Fig. 4.15. Similarly, we type SUPPLIERS P. in the upper left corner of the other skeleton to get the attributes of the SUPPLIERS relation.

ORDERS	NAME	ITEM	QUANTITY
	Brooks,B.	_banana	

SUPPLIERS	SNAME	SADDR	ITEM	PRICE
	P.	P.	P._banana	

Fig. 4.15. An example of a query in QBE: for each item ordered by Brooks, print the suppliers, their addresses, and the item.

The essence of query two in Example 4.12 is that we want to find a tuple in the ORDERS relation whose NAME component is "Brooks,B." and whose ITEM component is some item, for example "banana." Then we look for a tuple in the SUPPLIERS relation with the same item in the ITEM component, and we print the SNAME, SADDR, and ITEM components of each such tuple found.

In Fig. 4.15 we see this query expressed in QBE. We write the important features of the tuple we want to find in the ORDERS relation in the second line of the skeleton for that relation. The example item "banana" is preceded by an underscore to indicate that it is only an example. The entry in the NAME component, "Brooks,B.," is written with no quote marks or underscore, to indicate that it is a literal.† In the SUPPLIERS skeleton we see the important feature of the tuple we wish to find in that relation, namely that the item be the same as the item in the tuple found in the ORDERS relation. The fact that the two ITEM components must be the same is expressed by the fact that the domain variable, _banana, is the same in both tuples. We also see, from the tuple written into the SUP-PLIERS skeleton, that components SNAME, SADDR, and ITEM are to be printed. The operator P. in these columns indicates the components printed.

A large family of QBE queries correspond to domain calculus expressions of the form

$$\{a_1 a_2 \cdots a_n | (\exists b_1)(\exists b_2) \cdots (\exists b_m)(R_1(c_{11}, \ldots, c_{1k_1}) \wedge \\ \cdots \wedge R_p(c_{p1}, \ldots, c_{pk_p}))\}$$

where each c_{ij} is an a_l, a b_l, or a constant, and each a_l and b_l appears at least once. To express any such query, we display the table skeletons for all the relations mentioned among $R_1, \ldots, R_p$, and create a variable name for each of the a's and b's. In general, it is a good mnemonic to use variable names that are examples of objects actually found in the appropriate domains, but any character string preceded by an underscore will do. Now, for each term $R_i(c_{i1}, \ldots, c_{ik_i})$ write a tuple in the skeleton for R_i. If c_{ij} is a constant, place that constant in the jth component. If c_{ij} is one of the a's or b's, place the variable corresponding to that symbol there instead. However, if one of the a's or b's appears only once among all the terms, then we can leave the corresponding component blank if we wish.

---

† Note that this convention, preceding names of domain variables by an underscore and leaving literals unadorned, is diametrically opposed to the usual style of query languages and programming languages, where character string literals are adorned with quotes, and variables are unadorned. Also observe that Query-by-Example takes its name from the suggestion that variable names be chosen to be examples of the object desired. However, as with variables of other languages, the name "banana" has no semantic meaning, and it could be replaced in all its occurrences by junk, a, or xyz.

It will often be the case that all the a's appear as components of one term $R_i(c_{i1}, \ldots, c_{ik_i})$. If so, in the tuple for this term we prefix each of the a's by the operator P., and we are done. However, if no such term exists, we can create another table skeleton, whose components we can optionally name, and enter into the table skeleton the tuple

$$P.\_A1 \quad P.\_A2 \quad \cdots \quad P.\_An$$

where $\_Ai$ is the variable name for a_i.

Example 4.25: Suppose we wish to print the name and quantity ordered, for all granola orders. We can express this query in domain calculus as

$$\{a_1 a_2 \mid \text{ORDERS}(a_1 \text{ ``Granola''} a_2)\}$$

and in QBE as

ORDERS	NAME	ITEM	QUANTITY
	P._Oakes	Granola	P.

Here variable _Oakes replaces a_1. We could have omitted _Oakes altogether, since it appears only once. We have taken our option not to create a variable for a_2, since it also appears only once.

Let us consider another problem: print the name, item, quantity and balance of the person named, for each order. In domain calculus this query is:

$$\{a_1 a_2 a_3 a_4 \mid (\exists b_1)(\text{MEMBERS}(a_1 b_1 a_4) \land \text{ORDERS}(a_1 a_2 a_3))\}$$

As no term has all the a's, we call for a new table skeleton, as well as the skeletons of MEMBERS and ORDERS. The query is shown in Fig. 4.16.

MEMBERS	NAME	ADDRESS	BALANCE
	_Oakes		_999

ORDERS	NAME	ITEM	QUANTITY
	_Oakes	_hotdog	_mucho

	P._Oakes	P._hotdog	P._mucho	P._999

Fig. 4.16. Print names, items, quantities ordered, and balances.

It would also have been permissible to write the unnamed relation of Fig. 4.16 as

P.	_Oakes	_hotdog	_mucho	_999

since a command such as P. in the first column (the column corresponding to the relation name) applies to all components of the tuple. □

Implementation of QBE Queries

The general rule for implementing a query in QBE† is that the system creates a tuple variable for each row entered into the table skeletons of existing relations. For the second query of Example 4.25 we would create a tuple variable t for the row (_Oakes, , _999) of MEMBERS and a tuple variable s for the row (_Oakes, _hotdog, _mucho) of ORDERS. Note that no variable is created for the row of the unnamed relation in Fig. 4.16, since that relation does not exist in the database. If there are k such tuple variables we create k nested loops; each loop causes one of the variables to range over all tuples in its relation. For each assignment of values to the tuple variables (each "value" is a tuple in the corresponding relation), we check whether the domain variables of the query can be given consistent values. In the above example, we only have to check that the NAME components of s and t agree, so we can give a consistent value to domain variable _Oakes.

Each time we are successful in obtaining values for the domain variables, we take whatever action the query calls for. For example, if one or more rows of the query has some print commands, we print the values of the domain variables to which P. is prefixed. In Fig. 4.16, only the tuple in the unnamed relation has P. operators, so we obtain the values for the variables mentioned in that tuple and print them. If more than one row has print commands, whether or not the rows are in the same relation, we print the values for those rows in separate tables. Other actions that might be taken when we find a successful match include the insertion or deletion of a tuple into or from a relation; we shall discuss these actions later.

Entries Representing Sets

An entry in a skeleton can be made to match more than one, but less than all, the elements of some domain. A primary example is an entry θc, where θ is an arithmetic comparison and c a constant. For example, $> = 3$ matches any value three or greater. We can also write θv, where v is a

---

† That is not to say that QBE must be implemented this way. Rather, the procedure to be described serves as a definition of queries in QBE.

domain variable. For example, $<$ _amount matches any value less than the value of _amount. Presumably, the value of _amount is determined by some other entry of the query, and that value changes as we allow tuple variables to range over all tuples in the implementation procedure just described.

Example 4.26: To print all orders for at least 5 pounds of granola, we may write the query of Fig. 4.17(a). The query in Fig. 4.17(b) prints all orders for more granola than Robin ordered.

ORDERS	NAME	ITEM	QUANTITY
P.		Granola	$>=5$

(a)

ORDERS	NAME	ITEM	QUANTITY
	Robin,R	Granola	_x
P.		Granola	$>$ _x

(b)

Fig. 4.17. Two queries.

The query of Fig. 4.17(b) is implemented by creating tuple variables *t* and *s* for the rows of the skeleton.† As we allow *t* and *s* to range over the various tuples in ORDERS, we check for matches. Tuple *t* must have NAME component "Robin,R." and ITEM component "Granola." If so, it defines a value for _x. This value happens to be 3 whenever a match occurs (ref. Fig. 4.7). We then look at the tuple *s*. If it has ITEM "Granola," and its QUANTITY exceeds the value of _x, we print *s*. □

Another way to designate a set is to use an entry that is part constant and part variable. Juxtaposition represents concatenation, so if the domain for this entry is character strings, we can try to match any constant character strings in the entry to substrings of the string that forms the corresponding component of some tuple. If we find such a match, we can assign pieces of the remainder of the string to the variables in the entry.

Example 4.27: Suppose we wish to print the names of all suppliers on River St. We could write:

---

† The term *row* is used here to refer to any row except the header, which is the line containing the relation and attribute names.

SUPPLIERS	SNAME	SADDR	ITEM	QUANTITY
	P.	_999 River St.		

Whenever the address ended in "River St.," the variable _999 would take on the street number, and we would have a match. Thus, given the relation of Fig. 4.12(c), we would print

Sunshine Produce
Tasti Supply Co.

Note that QBE, unlike QUEL or SEQUEL, automatically eliminates duplicates. □

Negation of Rows

We may place the symbol ¬ in the first column (the column with the relation name R) of any row. Intuitively, the query then requires that any tuple matching the row not be a tuple of R. We shall try to be more precise later, but first let us consider an example.

Example 4.28: Suppose we wished to print the order or orders with the largest quantity. We could use the aggregate function MAX, to be described later, but we can also do it with a negation. Rephrase the query as: "print an order if there is no order with a larger quantity." This is expressed in QBE in Fig. 4.18. □

ORDERS	NAME	ITEM	QUANTITY
P.			_x
¬			> _x

Fig. 4.18. Print orders such that no order has a larger quantity.

The implementation of queries with a negation requires that we modify the algorithm described earlier. If in Fig. 4.18 we created tuples t and s for the two rows (t for the first row), and we ranged over all possible values of t and s, we would not want to print t just because we found a tuple s whose QUANTITY component was not greater than the QUANTITY of t. This would cause each tuple in ORDERS, whose QUANTITY was not the minimum, to be printed eventually. Rather, we must arrange our loops on the variables so that the variables corresponding to negated rows are the innermost loops. Then for each set of values for the tuples corresponding to unnegated rows, we check that all values of the tuple variables for negated rows fail to produce a consistent assignment of values for the domain variables in the query.

Aggregate Operators

QBE has the usual five aggregate operators, denoted SUM., AVG., MAX., MIN., and CNT. (count). There are two other operators, ALL. and UN. (unique) that often are used in conjunction with aggregate operators. ALL. applied to a domain variable produces the multiset of values that the variable takes on as we run through all the tuples in the relevant relation. Recall that a *multiset* is a set with repetitions allowed, so the ALL. operator effectively leaves duplicates in, while most other QBE operations eliminate duplicates. Thus, to compute the average balance of HVFC members we write

MEMBERS	NAME	ADDRESS	BALANCE
			P.AVG.ALL._999

The operator UN. converts a multiset into a set, by eliminating duplicates. For example, suppose we wanted to know how many suppliers there were in the HVFC database. If we (incorrectly) wrote

SUPPLIERS	SNAME	SADDR	ITEM	PRICE
	P.CNT.ALL._x			

and applied it to the relation of Fig. 4.12(c) we would get the answer 9, since variable _x takes on a multiset of nine values, one for each tuple in the relation. The correct way to pose the query is

SUPPLIERS	SNAME	SADDR	ITEM	PRICE
	P.CNT.UN.ALL._x			

In this way, before counting the set of suppliers produced by the expression ALL._x, the operator UN. removes duplicates.

Insertion and Deletion

If a row in a query has the operator I. or D. in the first column, then when implementing the query we do not create a tuple variable for this row. Rather, when a match for all the tuple variables is found, we insert (I.) or delete (D.) into or from the relation in whose skeleton one of these commands is found. Variables in the row or rows to be inserted, deleted, or updated take their values from the appropriate components of the tuple variables.

Example 4.29: If Sunshine Produce starts selling whey at 59 cents per pound, we write:

SUPPLIERS	SNAME	SADDR	ITEM	PRICE
I.	Sunshine Produce	16 River St.	Whey	.59

Notice that this query is implemented by a special case of the QBE implementation rule. Since there are no tuple variables on which to loop, we simply execute the insert operation once. The row to be inserted has no variables, so the components of the tuple to be inserted are well defined.

If we forget the address of Sunshine Produce, we can obtain it from the database at the same time we perform the insert, as follows.

SUPPLIERS	SNAME	SADDR	ITEM	PRICE
I.	Sunshine Produce	_address	Whey	.59
	Sunshine Produce	_address		

A tuple variable for the second row ranges over all tuples in SUPPLIERS. The value "16 River St." is given to variable _address whenever the tuple variable for the second row takes on a value with "Sunshine Produce" in the first component. □

Updates

The update operation can only be understood if we are aware that the QBE system allows one to define *key* and *nonkey* attributes of relations, by a mechanism to be discussed shortly. The set of key attributes must uniquely determine a tuple; that is, two tuples in a relation cannot agree on all key attributes. If we use the update (U.) operator in the first column of a row, then entries in key fields must match the tuple updated, and any tuple that does match the row in the key attributes will have its nonkey attributes updated to match the values in the row with U.

Example 4.30: In the SUPPLIERS relation, SNAME and ITEM are key attributes and the others are nonkey. If Sunshine Produce changes the price of Granola to \$1.33 per pound, we write

SUPPLIERS	SNAME	SADDR	ITEM	PRICE
U.	Sunshine Produce		Granola	1.33

If all items supplied by Sunshine Produce are increased in price by \$.10 per pound write

SUPPLIERS	SNAME	SADDR	ITEM	PRICE
U.	Sunshine Produce		_hotdog	_x+.10
	Sunshine Produce		_hotdog	_x

Note the use of an arithmetic expression in the row to be updated. The use of arithmetic is permitted where it makes sense, such as in rows to be updated or inserted, and in "condition boxes," a concept to be described next. □

Condition Boxes

There are times when we wish to include a condition on a query, insertion, deletion, or update that is not expressed by terms such as < 3 in the rows of the query. We can then call for a *condition box* to be displayed and enter into the box any relationships we wish satisfied. Entries of a condition box are essentially conditions as in a language like PL/I, but without the use of the "not" operator, $\neg$. Either AND or & can be used for logical "and," while OR or | is used for "or." When the query is implemented, a match is deemed to occur only when the current values of the tuple variables allow a consistent assignment of values to the domain variables in the query, and these values satisfy the conditions.

Example 4.31: Suppose we wish to print all those suppliers of granola that charge more than Tasti Supply Co. charges for sunflower seeds and no more than twice what Purity Foodstuffs charges for curds. The query, expressed with the aid of a condition box, is shown in Fig. 4.19. □

SUPPLIERS	SNAME	SADDR	ITEM	PRICE
	P.		Granola	_p1
	Tasti Supply Co.		Sunflower Seeds	_p2
	Purity Foodstuffs		Curds	_p3

CONDITIONS
_p1 > _p2
_p1 < = _p3 * 2

Fig. 4.19. Example of a condition box.

The Table Directory

The QBE system maintains a list, called the *table directory,* of all the relation names in the database, their attributes and certain information about the attributes. One can query, insert, or delete from this list using the same notation as for general queries. For example, typing P. _relname, or just P., in the upper left hand box of a table skeleton will cause the system to print the current list of relation names. Typing P. _relname P. in that box will print the relation names and their attribute names. The second P. refers to the attribute names. To insert a new relation REL into the table directory, type I.REL I. in the upper left box and then type the attributes of REL along the top of the skeleton. Again, the second I. refers to the attributes, while the first I. refers to the relation name.

　The attributes may be declared to have certain properties. These properties are:

1. KEY, telling whether or not the attribute is part of the key (recall that updates require the system to distinguish between key and nonkey fields). The values of this property are Y (key) and N (nonkey).

2. TYPE, the data type of the attribute, such as CHAR (variable length character string), CHAR(n) (character string of length n), FLOAT (real number), or FIXED (integer).

3. DOMAIN, a name for the domain of values for this attribute. If a domain variable in a query appears in two different columns, those columns must come from the same domain. The system rejects queries that violate this rule, a useful check on the meaningfulness of queries.

4. INVERSION, indicating whether an index on the attribute is (Y) or is not (N) to be created and maintained.

Example 4.32: To create the SUPPLIERS relation we might fill a table skeleton with some of its properties, as shown in Fig. 4.20. The domain AMOUNTS might also be used for the domain of BALANCE in MEMBERS, for example. □

I. SUPPLIERS	I.	SNAME	SADDR	ITEM	PRICE
KEY	I.	Y	N	Y	N
TYPE	I.	CHAR	CHAR	CHAR	FLOAT
DOMAIN	I.	NAMES	ADDRS	ITEMS	AMOUNTS
INVERSION	I.	N	N	N	N

Fig. 4.20. Creation of SUPPLIERS relation.

Completeness of QBE

As with the other languages we have studied, it appears simplest to prove completeness by showing how to apply each of the five relational algebra operations and store the result in a new relation. For instance, to compute $T = R \cup S$ we can execute the QBE command shown in Fig. 4.21, assuming T is initially empty. The operation of set difference is achieved with an insertion command, then a deletion command; Cartesian product and projection are performed with an insertion. We leave these commands as exercises.

The knottiest problem comes when we try to compute the selection $T = \sigma_f(R)$ for an arbitrary condition F.

Conditions in condition boxes do not use the logical "not" operator. However, we can remove ¬'s from the selection condition F as follows. To perform the conversion, the first step is to use DeMorgan's laws:

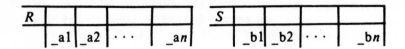

Fig. 4.21. QBE command for taking unions.

$$\neg (F_1 \wedge F_2) = \neg F_1 \vee \neg F_2$$
$$\neg (F_1 \vee F_2) = \neg F_1 \wedge \neg F_2$$

to move all negations inside $\wedge$ and $\vee$ until $\neg$ applies only to atoms. Second, any atom can be negated by changing its comparison. For example $\neg (A \neq B)$ is the same as $A = B$, and $\neg (A < B)$ is the same as $A \geqslant B$. Now we have only $\wedge$ and $\vee$ operators applied to atoms, and the result is a legal QBE formula.

Example 4.33: The formula $\neg (A < B \vee (C = D \wedge E \neq F)$ is first converted by moving $\neg$ inside $\vee$ and $\wedge$, as:

$$\neg (A < B) \wedge \neg (C = D \wedge E \neq F)$$
$$\neg (A < B) \wedge (\neg (C = D) \vee \neg (E \neq F))$$

The negations are applied to the atoms to yield

$$A \geqslant B \wedge (C \neq D \vee E = F)$$

or in the QBE notation

$$A \geqslant B \ \& \ (C \neg = D \ | \ E = F)$$

□

Now, to compute $\sigma_F(R)$ in QBE, we have only to execute the query of Fig. 4.22, where F' is F with "not" operators eliminated as above.

Views

QBE contains a delayed evaluation feature similar to ISBL. When we wish to create a view V, we insert V into the table directly as a relation, prefixing the name V by the keyword VIEW. We then formulate in QBE the method whereby V is to be calculated. V is not actually computed at the time. Rather, it is computed whenever V is used in a subsequent query, and its value is computed then, from the current relations mentioned in the formula for V.

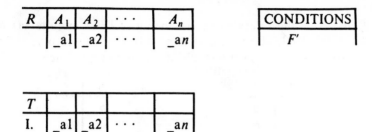

R	A_1	A_2	$\cdots$	A_n
	_a1	_a2	$\cdots$	_an

CONDITIONS
F'

T				
I.	_a1	_a2	$\cdots$	_an

Fig. 4.22. Selection in QBE.

Example 4.34: Suppose we wish to create a view BILLS, that gives the items ordered with the person ordering them, along with a charge for the item. The charge is computed by taking the lowest price for the item among all the suppliers of that item and multiplying the lowest price per pound by the number of pounds ordered. This view can be defined as in Fig. 4.23. We could then use it as a relation in a query such as that of Fig. 4.24. The value of relation BILLS is computed from ORDERS and SUPPLIERS when the query of Fig. 4.24 is executed. □

I. VIEW BILLS	I.	NAME	ITEM	CHARGE
	I.	_Oakes	_hotdog	_q*MIN.ALL._p

ORDERS	NAME	ITEM	QUANTITY
	_Oakes	_hotdog	_q

SUPPLIERS	SNAME	SADDR	ITEM	PRICE
			_hotdog	_p

Fig. 4.23. Definition of View BILLS.

BILLS	NAME	ITEM	CHARGE
P.	Brooks,B.	_hotdog	_999

Fig. 4.24. A query using BILLS: print an itemized bill for Brooks.

Exercises

4.1: Let R and S be the relations shown in Fig. 4.25. Compute (a) $R \cup S$
(b) $R-S$ (c) $R \bowtie S$ (the natural join) (d) $\pi_A(R)$ (e) $\sigma_{A=C}(R \times S)$.
Ignore attribute names in the result of union and diference.

A	B
a	b
c	b
d	e

B	C
b	c
e	a
b	d

Fig. 4.25. Example relations.

4.2: Assuming R and S are of arity 3 and 2, respectively, convert the
expression $\pi_{1,5}(\sigma_{2=4 \vee 3=4}(R \times S))$ to

a)   tuple relational calculus

b)   domain relational calculus.

4.3: Convert the tuple calculus formula

$$\{t^{(2)} \mid R(t) \wedge (\exists u^{(2)})(S(u) \wedge \neg u[1]=t[2])\}$$

to

a)   an English statement

b)   domain relational calculus

c)   relational algebra

4.4: Convert the domain calculus formula

$$\{ab \mid R(ab) \wedge R(ba)\}$$

to

a)   an English statement

b)   tuple relational calculus

c)   relational algebra

4.5: Are the expressions of Exercises 4.3 and 4.4 safe?

4.6: Suppose we have a database consisting of the following three relations

FREQUENTS(DRINKER, BAR)
SERVES(BAR, BEER)
LIKES(DRINKER, BEER)

The first indicates the bars each drinker visits, the second tells what
beers each bar serves, and the last indicates which beers each drinker
likes to drink. Express in (*i*) relational algebra (*ii*) tuple calculus (*iii*)
domain calculus (*iv*) ISBL (*v*) SQUARE (*vi*) SEQUEL (*vii*) QUEL
(*viii*) Query-by-Example the following queries.

a) Print the bars that serve a beer that drinker Charles Chugamug likes.

b) Print the drinkers that frequent at least one bar that serves a beer they like.

*c) Print the drinkers that frequent only bars that serve some beer that they like. (Assume each drinker likes at least one beer and frequents at least one bar.)

*d) Print the drinkers that frequent no bar that serves a beer that they like.

4.7: Using (*i*) SQUARE (*ii*) QUEL (*iii*) Query-by-Example write programs to

a) Delete from SERVES all tuples for Potgold Beer.

b) Insert the fact that drinker Chugamug likes Potgold.

c) Insert the fact that Chugamug likes all beers served at the Bent Elbow Bar and Grill.

4.8: Suppose that the database of Exercise 4.6 has relation SELLS(BAR, BEER, AMOUNT). Write in QUEL, queries to print the (a) sum and (b) average per bar (excluding bars that do not sell the beer) of each beer sold.

4.9: Suppose that in the database of Exercise 4.6 we want a view WHERE(DRINKER, BEER, BAR) containing those tuples (*d, b, r*) such that drinker *d* likes beer *b*, bar *r* serves *b*, and *d* frequents *r*. Write in (a) ISBL and (b) Query-by-Example view definitions for the view WHERE.

*4.10: The *transitive closure* of a binary relation R, denoted R^+, is the set of pairs (*a, b*) such that for some sequence $c_1, c_2, \ldots, c_n$:

i) $c_1 = a$

ii) $c_n = b$

iii) for $i = 1, 2, \ldots, n-1$, we have (c_i, c_{i+1}) in R.

Prove that there is no expression of relational algebra equivalent to the transitive closure operation on finite relations.

*4.11: Show that the five relational algebra operators (union, difference, selection, projection, and Cartesian product) are *independent*, meaning that none can be expressed as a formula involving only the other four operators. *Hint:* For each operator you need to discover a property that is not possessed by any expression in the other four operators. For example, to show independence of union, suppose there were an expression $E(R, S)$ that used only difference, selection, projection, and product, but was equal to $R \cup S$ for any R and S. Let R_0 consist of the single tuple (*a, b*) and S_0 of the single tuple (*c, d*), where

a, b, c, and d do not appear as constants in E. Show by induction on the number of operators used in any subexpression F of E that the relation that is the value of $F(R_0, S_0)$ cannot have a component in which one tuple has a and another tuple has c. Since $R_0 \cup S_0$ has such a component, it follows that $E(R_0, S_0) \neq R_0 \cup S_0$.

Bibliographic Notes

Relational algebra was introduced in Codd [1970], and its equivalence to tuple relational calculus was shown in Codd [1972b]. The latter paper is also the source of the principle that a query language should at least be complete for relational calculus. The notion that predicate calculus could be used for stating queries has been attributed to Kuhns [1967]. Jacobs [1979] generalizes the algebra-calculus correspondence to other data models, such as network and hierarchical. See Gallaire and Minker [1978] for a variety of applications of predicate calculus to relational databases.

ISBL and the PRTV system are discussed in Todd [1976]. The language SQUARE is described in Boyce et al. [1975], while SEQUEL is described in Chamberlin et al. [1976], and an earlier version of the language is covered in Astrahan and Chamberlin [1975]. The System R DBMS is discussed by Astrahan et al. [1976]. For information about QUEL and INGRES see Stonebraker, Wong, Kreps, and Held [1976], Wong and Youssefi [1976], and Zook et al. [1977]. A description of the commercially available Query-by-Example is in IBM [1978a], while the experimental version is described in Zloof [1977].

The survey by Pirotte [1978] mentions a large number of existing relational data manipulation languages and classifies them into algebraic, tuple- and domain-calculus categories, as we have attempted to do here. Greenblatt and Waxman [1978] compare the ease of learning QBE, SEQUEL, and relational algebra; apparently the advantage is with QBE. Additionally of interest is the paper by Aho, Kernighan, and Weinberger [1979], describing a relational database "tool" for use with the UNIX system.

Exercise 4.10, on the transitive closure, is from Aho and Ullman [1979]. That paper and Chandra and Harel [1979] explore the possiblility of relational query languages that perform only manipulation of data (as opposed to arithmetic on data), yet are richer than relational calculus. In contrast, Bancilhon [1978] and Paredaens [1978] attempt to argue that relational calculus can express all operations that do not involve arithmetic. However, they allow functions like R^+ to be computed by a different expression for each R, so there is no contradiction of Exercise 4.10. Zloof [1975] explains how the transitive closure can be computed in QBE (using features of the language that we have not discussed), demonstrating that QBE is more powerful that relational calculus.

A result on operator independence similar to Exercise 4.11 was shown by Beck [1978].

There are a variety of directions that research concerning relational databases has taken. In addition to the design theory discussed in Chapter 5 and query optimization discussed in Chapter 6, we should mention work on natural language as a query language. Typical is the work by Dell'Orco, Spadavecchio, and King [1977] and the Rendezvous system of Codd et al. [1978] and Codd [1978]. While the problem of translating natural languages, such as English, into queries a machine can understand is always difficult, the relational model does provide a useful framework for such translation. In particular, it is possible to identify certain nouns and verbs with relations, attributes, and domain values. The fact that a relation scheme has a fixed set of attributes, known in advance, often provides valuable clues to understanding.

Another important direction is the addition of "semantics" to the relational model. A number of works, such as Schmid and Swenson [1976], Furtado [1978], Codd [1979], and Sciore [1979], have attempted to distinguish the roles played by different attributes. Without going into detail, we noted in Section 3.1 how some attributes in relation schemes might represent entities, while others represent relationships among entities. These distinctions have been further refined in the papers cited. Of additional interest are the concepts called "aggregation and generalization" in Smith and Smith [1977]. Essentially, this paper extends the relational model by allowing the domain of an attribute to be a set of relation names. This extension facilitates generalization (e.g., the entity set "students" generalizes the entity sets "grad students," "female students," and so on) by permitting us to associate with each member of an entity set a relation that gives information germane to that entity (e.g., "advisor" is an attribute appropriate only for grad students).

A third area in which problems remain is the extension of the relational model to handle "null values," that is, entries in tuples that represent unknown, irrelevant, or inconsistent values. Attempts to deal with nulls have been made by Codd [1975], Lacroix and Pirotte [1976], Zaniolo [1977], Lipsky [1978], and Vassilou [1979]. However, problems arise when we try to define algebraic operations. For example, when taking an equijoin, should two nulls be regarded as equal? No answer is wholly satisfactory.

5

Design Theory for Relational Databases

When designing a relational database, we are often faced with a choice among alternative sets of relation schemes.† Some choices are more convenient than others for various reasons. We shall study some of the desirable properties of relation schemes and consider several algorithms for obtaining a database scheme (set of relation schemes) with good properties.

Central to the design of database schemes is the idea of a *data dependency,* that is, a constraint on the possible relations that can be the current value for a relation scheme. For example, if one attribute uniquely determines another, as NAME apparently determines ADDRESS in relation MEMBERS of Example 4.12, we say there is a "functional dependency" of ADDRESS on NAME. We shall consider functional dependencies and a more complex type of dependency called "multivalued," where one or more attributes determine a set of values for one or several other attributes, but that set can have more than one member, unlike the case when the dependency is functional.

After studying dependencies, we shall return to the question of picking a good set of relation schemes to represent given information. The reader should bear in mind that much mathematical preliminaries are needed to deal successfully with the difficult topic of automatic database design, so our digression to study dependencies is a lengthy one.

5.1 What Constitutes a Bad Database Design?
Before telling how to design a good database scheme, let us see why some schemes might prove inadequate. In particular let us focus on the relation scheme

SUPPLIERS(SNAME, SADDRESS, ITEM, PRICE)

of Example 4.12. We can see several problems with this scheme.

---

† Recall a relation scheme is the set of attributes associated with a relation name.

1. *Redundancy.* The address of the supplier is repeated once for each item supplied.

2. *Potential inconsistency (update anomalies).* As a consequence of the redundancy, we could update the address for a supplier in one tuple, while leaving it fixed in another. Thus we would not have a unique address for each supplier as we feel intuitively we should.

3. *Insertion anomalies.* We cannot record an address for a supplier if that supplier does not currently supply at least one item. We might put null values in the ITEM and PRICE components of a tuple for that supplier, but then, should we enter an item for that supplier, will we remember to delete the tuple with the nulls? Worse, ITEM and SNAME form a key for the relation, and it might be awkward or impossible to look up tuples with null values in the key.

4. *Deletion anomalies.* The inverse to problem (3) is that should we delete all the items supplied by one supplier, we unintentionally lose track of his address.

In this example, all the above problems go away if we replace SUP-PLIERS by two relation schemes

    SA(SNAME, SADDRESS)
    SIP(SNAME, ITEM, PRICE)

The first, SA, gives the address for each supplier exactly once; hence there is no redundancy. Moreover, we can enter an address for a supplier even if he currently supplies no items. The second relation scheme, SIP, gives the suppliers, the items they supply, and the price each supplier charges for each item.

Yet some questions remain. For example, there is a disadvantage to the above decomposition; to find the addresses of suppliers of whey, we must now take a join, which is expensive, while with the single relation SUPPLIERS we could simply do a selection and projection. How do we determine that the above replacement is beneficial? Are there other problems of the same four kinds present in the two new relation schemes? How do we find a good replacement for a bad relation scheme? The balance of the chapter is devoted to answering these questions.

5.2 Functional Dependencies

This section and the next represent a digression into the necessary theory of functional dependencies. We shall return to the business at hand, the design of database schemes, in Section 5.4.

In Chapter 3 we asserted that relations could be used to model the "real world" in several ways; for example, each tuple of a relation could represent an entity and its attributes or a relationship between entities. In many cases, the known facts about the real world imply that not every finite set of tuples could be the current value of some relation, even if the tuples were of the right arity and had components chosen from the right domains. We can distinguish two kinds of restrictions on relations.

1. *Restrictions that depend on the semantics of domain elements.* These restrictions depend on understanding what components of tuples mean. For example, no one is 60 feet tall, and no one with an employment history going back 37 years has age 25. It is useful to have a DBMS check for such implausible values, which probably arose due to an error when entering or computing data. Chapter 9 covers the expression and use of this sort of "integrity constraint." Unfortunately, they tell us little or nothing about the design of database schemes.

2. *Restrictions on relations that depend only on the equality or inequality of values.* There are other constraints that do not depend on what value a tuple has in any given component, but only on whether two tuples agree in certain components. We shall discuss the most important of these constraints, called functional dependencies, in this section, but there are other types of value-oblivious constraints that will be touched on in later sections. It is value-oblivious constraints that turn out to have the greatest impact on the design of database schemes.

Let $R(A_1, A_2, \ldots, A_n)$ be a relation scheme, and let X and Y be subsets of $\{A_1, A_2, \ldots, A_n\}$. We say $X \to Y$, read "X functionally determines Y" or "Y functionally depends on X" if whatever relation r is the current value for R, it is not possible that r has two tuples that agree in the components for all attributes in set X yet disagree in one or more components for attributes in set Y.

Functional dependencies arise naturally in many ways. For example, if R represents an entity set, and $A_1, \ldots, A_n$ are the attributes of that entity set, and if X is a set of attributes that forms a key for the entity set, then we may assert $X \to Y$ for any subset Y of the attributes. This follows because the tuples of r represent entities, and entities are identified by the value of attributes in the key. Therefore, two tuples that agreed on the attributes in X would have to represent the same entity and therefore be the same tuple. Similarly, if R represents a many-one mapping from entity set E_1 to entity set E_2, and among the A_i's are attributes that form a key X for E_1 and a key Y for E_2, then $X \to Y$ would hold, and in fact, X functionally determines any set of attributes. However, $Y \to X$ would not hold unless the mapping were one-to-one.

It should be emphasized that functional dependencies are statements about all possible relations that could be the value of relation scheme R. We cannot look at a particular relation r for scheme R and deduce what functional dependencies hold for R. For example, if r is the empty set, then all dependencies appear to hold, but they might not hold in general, as the value of the relation denoted by R changes. We might, however, be able to look at a particular relation for R and discover some dependencies that did not hold.

The only way to determine the functional dependencies that hold for relation scheme R is to consider carefully what the attributes mean. In this sense, dependencies are actually assertions about the real world; they cannot be proved, but we might expect them to be enforced by a DBMS if we told it to do so. Many existing systems will enforce those functional dependencies that follow from the fact that a key determines the other attributes of a relation, and some will even enforce arbitrary functional dependencies.

Let us emphasize that the declaration of a functional dependency in a database is a decision that can be made only by the designer. The advantage of such a declaration is that the database system will then enforce an integrity constraint for the user, and there could even be a more efficient implementation of the relation possible because the functional dependency is asserted to hold. However, there is a price to pay, in that the storage of certain information becomes impossible. For example, if we declare that NAME functionally determines PHONE, then under no circumstances can we store two phone numbers for one person in our database.

Example 5.1: Let us consider the functional dependencies that we expect to hold in the HVFC database of Example 4.12. We might suppose that each member has a unique address and a unique balance, and the co-op will never have two members with the same name. (Perhaps it would use a nickname if the need arose.) If we make these assumptions, then we can assert

NAME → ADDRESS BALANCE

Note that it is customary to use concatenation of attribute names to denote sets of attributes, so $A_1 A_2 \cdots A_n$ is shorthand for $\{A_1, A_2, \ldots, A_n\}$. We also use concatention of sets of attributes in place of union, so XY stands for $X \cup Y$, if X and Y are sets of attributes.

In the relation ORDERS we claim that

NAME ITEM → QUANTITY

This dependency is based on the supposition that it is never valid to have two orders for the same item by the same person. That is, an additional order is implemented by adding to the quantity of the old order, rather than by inserting a new tuple. If one considers the matter, one sees that this restriction is the only reasonable point of view. Otherwise we would be faced with the fact that in Fig. 4.7, Brooks could order another 7 pounds of granola, but could not order another 5 pounds of granola, since a relation, being a set, cannot have two identical tuples. In relation SUPPLIERS, we observe the following dependencies.

SNAME → SADDRESS
SNAME ITEM → PRICE

One might wonder whether a dependency like SADDRESS →
SNAME or ADDRESS → NAME is valid. By looking at Fig. 4.7 we might
suspect they were valid. However, in principle, there is nothing stopping
HVFC from enrolling two members with the same address, or stopping two
suppliers from having the same address. Thus we do not assert these
dependencies. There are other trivial dependencies that do hold, such as

NAME → NAME   or
NAME ITEM → ITEM

and some nontrivial dependencies that follow from those we have already
asserted, such as

SNAME ITEM → SADDRESS PRICE

□

Logical Implications of Dependencies

Suppose R is a relation scheme and A, B, and C are some of its attributes.
Suppose also that the functional dependencies $A \to B$ and $B \to C$ are known
to hold in R. We claim that $A \to C$ must also hold in R. In proof, suppose
r is a relation that satisfies $A \to B$ and $B \to C$, but there are two tuples t and u
in r such that t and u agree in the component for A but disagree in C.
Then we must ask whether t and u agree on attribute B. If not, then r
violates $A \to B$. If they do agree on B, then since they disagree on C, r
violates $B \to C$. Hence r satisfies $A \to C$.

In general, let F be a set of functional dependencies for relation
scheme R, and let $X \to Y$ be a functional dependency. We say F *logically
implies* $X \to Y$ if every relation r for R that satisfies the dependencies in F
also satisfies $X \to Y$. We saw above that if F contains $A \to B$ and $B \to C$, then
$A \to C$ is logically implied by F. Let F^+, the *closure* of F, be the set of functional dependencies that are logically implied by F. If $F = F^+$, we say F is a
full family of dependencies.

Example 5.2: Let $R = ABC$ and $F = \{A \to B,\ B \to C\}$. Then F^+ consists of
all those dependencies $X \to Y$ such that either

1. X contains A, for example $ABC \to AB$, $AB \to BC$, or $A \to C$,

2. X contains B but not A, and Y does not contain A, for example,
     $BC \to B$, $B \to C$, or $B \to \varnothing$, and

3. $X \rightarrow Y$ is one of the two dependencies $C \rightarrow C$ or $C \rightarrow \emptyset$.

We shall discuss how to prove the above contention shortly.   □

Keys

When talking about entity sets we assumed that there was a key, a set of attributes that uniquely determined an entity. There is an analogous concept for relations with functional dependencies. If R is a relation scheme with attributes $A_1 A_2 \cdots A_n$ and functional dependencies F, and X is a subset of $A_1 A_2 \cdots A_n$, we say X is a *key* of R if:

1. $X \rightarrow A_1 A_2 \cdots A_n$ is in F^+, and

2.   for no proper subset $Y \subseteq X$ is $Y \rightarrow A_1 A_2 \cdots A_n$ in F^+.

We should observe that minimality, condition (2) above, was not present when we talked of keys for entity sets in Chapter 1 or keys for files in Chapter 2. The reason is that without a formalism like functional dependencies, we could not verify that a given set of attributes was minimal. The reader should be aware that in this chapter the term "key" does imply minimality. Thus, the given key for an entity set will only be a key for the relation representing that entity set if the given key was minimal. Otherwise, one or more subsets of the entity set key will serve as a key for the relation.

As there may be more than one key for a relation, we sometimes designate one as the primary key. The primary key might serve as the file key when the relation is implemented, for example. However, any key could be the primary key if we desired. The term *candidate key* is sometimes used in the literature to denote any minimal set of attributes that functionally determine all attributes, with the term "key" reserved for one designated candidate key. We also use the term *superkey* for any superset of a key.

Example 5.3. For relation R and set of dependencies F of Example 5.2 there is only one key, A, since $A \rightarrow ABC$ is in F^+, but no X not containing A functionally determines ABC.

A more interesting example is the relation scheme R(CITY, ST, ZIP), where ST stands for street address and ZIP for zip code. We expect tuple (c, s, t) in a relation for R only if city c has a building with street address s, and z is the zip code for that address in that city. It is assumed that the nontrivial functional dependencies are:

$$\text{CITY ST} \rightarrow \text{ZIP}$$
$$\text{ZIP} \rightarrow \text{CITY}$$

That is, the complete address (city and street) determines the zip code, and the zip code determines the city, although not the street address. One can easily check that {CITY, ST} and {ST, ZIP} are both keys.   □

Axioms for Functional Dependencies

To determine keys, and to understand logical implications among functional dependencies in general, we need to compute F^+ from F, or at least, to tell, given F and functional dependency $X \rightarrow Y$, whether $X \rightarrow Y$ is in F^+. To do so requires that we have inference rules telling how one or more dependencies imply other dependencies. In fact, we can do more; we can provide a *complete* set of inference rules, meaning that given set of dependencies F, the rules allow us to deduce all the dependencies in F^+. Moreover, the rules are *sound*, meaning that using them, we cannot deduce from F any dependency that is not in F^+.

The set of rules is often called *Armstrong's axioms*, from Armstrong [1974], although the particular rules we shall present differ from Armstrong's. In what follows we assume we are given a relation scheme with set of attributes U, the *universal set* of attributes, and a set of functional dependencies F involving only attributes in U. The inference rules are:

A1: *(reflexivity).* If $Y \subseteq X \subseteq U$, then $X \rightarrow Y$ is logically implied by F. Note that this rule gives the *trivial dependencies*, those that have a right side contained in the left side. Use of this rule does not depend on F.

A2: *(augmentation).* If $X \rightarrow Y$ holds, and $Z \subseteq U$, then $XZ \rightarrow YZ$. Recall that X, Y, and Z are sets of attributes, and XZ is conventional shorthand for $X \cup Z$. It is also important to remember that the given dependency $X \rightarrow Y$ might be in F, or it might have been derived from dependencies in F using the axioms we are in the process of describing.

A3: *(transitivity)* If $X \rightarrow Y$ and $Y \rightarrow Z$ hold, then $X \rightarrow Z$ holds.

Example 5.4: Let us reconsider the situation of Example 5.3, where we claimed that {ST, ZIP} was a key; that is:

ST ZIP → CITY ST ZIP

In proof we can state the following.

1. ZIP → CITY (given)
2. ST ZIP → CITY ST (augmentation of (1) by ST)
3. CITY ST → ZIP (given)
4. CITY ST → CITY ST ZIP (augmentation of (3) by CITY ST)
5. ST ZIP → CITY ST ZIP (transitivity with (2) and (4)) □

It is relatively easy to prove that Armstrong's axioms are sound; that is, they lead only to true conclusions. It is rather more difficult to prove completeness, that they can be used to make every valid inference about dependencies. We shall tackle the soundness issue first.

Lemma 5.1: Armstrong's axioms are sound. That is, if $X \rightarrow Y$ is deduced from F using the axioms, then $X \rightarrow Y$ is true in any relation in which the dependencies of F are true.

Proof: A1, the reflexivity axiom, is clearly sound. We cannot have a relation r with two tuples that agree on X yet disagree on some subset of X. To prove A2, augmentation, suppose we have a relation r that satisfies $X \rightarrow Y$, yet there are two tuples t and u that agree on the attributes of XZ but disagree on YZ. Since they cannot disagree on any attribute of Z, t and u must disagree on some attribute in Y. But then t and u agree on X but disagree on Y, violating our assumption that $X \rightarrow Y$ holds for r. The soundness of A3, the transitivity axiom, is a simple extension of the argument given previously that $A \rightarrow B$ and $B \rightarrow C$ imply $A \rightarrow C$. We leave this part of the proof as an exercise. $\square$

There are several other inference rules that follow from Armstrong's axioms. We state three of them in the next lemma. Since we have proved the soundness of A1, A2, and A3, we are entitled to use them in the proof that follows.

Lemma 5.2:

a)   *The union rule.* If $X \rightarrow Y$ and $X \rightarrow Z$ hold, then $X \rightarrow YZ$ holds.

b)   *The pseudotransitivity rule.* If $X \rightarrow Y$ and $WY \rightarrow Z$ hold, then $XW \rightarrow Z$ holds.

c)   *The decomposition rule.* If $X \rightarrow Y$ and $Z \subseteq Y$, then $X \rightarrow Z$.

Proof:

a)   We are given $X \rightarrow Y$, so we may augment by X to infer $X \rightarrow XY$. We are also given $X \rightarrow Z$, so we may augment by Y to get $XY \rightarrow YZ$. By transitivity, $X \rightarrow XY$ and $XY \rightarrow YZ$ imply $X \rightarrow YZ$.

b)   Given $X \rightarrow Y$, we may augment by W to get $WX \rightarrow WY$. Since we are given $WY \rightarrow Z$, transitivity tells us $WX \rightarrow Z$.

c)   The decomposition rule follows easily from A1 and A3. $\square$

An important consequence of the union and decomposition rules is that if $A_1, \ldots, A_n$ are attributes, then $X \rightarrow A_1, \ldots, A_n$ holds if and only if $X \rightarrow A_i$ holds for each i.

Before tackling the completeness issue, it is important to define the closure of a set of attributes with respect to a set of functional dependencies. Let F be a set of functional dependencies on set of attributes U, and let X be a subset of U. Then X^+, the *closure* of X (with respect to F) is the set of attributes A such that $X \rightarrow A$ can be deduced from F by Armstrong's axioms. The central fact about the closure of a set of attributes is that it enables us to tell at a glance whether a dependency $X \rightarrow Y$ follows from F by Armstrong's axioms. The next lemma tells how.

Lemma 5.3: $X \rightarrow Y$ follows from Armstrong's axioms if and only if $Y \subseteq X^+$.

Proof: Let $Y = A_1 \cdots A_n$ for attributes $A_1, \ldots, A_n$, and suppose $Y \subseteq X^+$. By definition of X^+, $X \rightarrow A_i$ is implied by Armstrong's axioms for all i. By the union rule, Lemma 5.2(a), $X \rightarrow Y$ follows. Conversely, suppose $X \rightarrow Y$ follows from the axioms. For each i, $X \rightarrow A_i$ holds by the decomposition rule, so $Y \subseteq X^+$. □

We are now ready to prove that Armstrong's axioms are complete. We do so by showing that if F is the given set of dependencies, and $X \rightarrow Y$ cannot be proved by Armstrong's axioms, then there must be a relation in which the dependencies of F all hold but $X \rightarrow Y$ does not; that is, F does not logically imply $X \rightarrow Y$.

Theorem 5.1: Armstrong's axioms are sound and complete.

Proof: Soundness is Lemma 5.1, so we have to prove completeness. Let F be a set of dependencies over attribute set U, and suppose $X \rightarrow Y$ cannot be inferred from the axioms. Consider the relation r with two tuples shown in Fig. 5.1. First we show that all dependencies in F are satisfied by r. Suppose $V \rightarrow W$ is in F but is not satisfied by r. Then $V \subseteq X^+$, or else the two tuples of r disagree on some attribute of V. Also, W cannot be a subset of X^+, or $V \rightarrow W$ is satisfied by the relation r. Let A be an attribute of W not in X^+. Since $V \subseteq X^+$, $X \rightarrow V$ follows from the axioms by Lemma 5.3. Dependency $V \rightarrow W$ is in F, so by transitivity we have $X \rightarrow W$. By reflexivity, $W \rightarrow A$, so by transitivity again, $X \rightarrow A$ follows from the axioms. But then A is in X^+, which we assumed not to be the case. We conclude by contradiction that each $V \rightarrow W$ in F is satisfied by r.

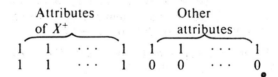

Attributes of X^+			Other attributes		
1	1	$\cdots$ 1	1	1	$\cdots$ 1
1	1	$\cdots$ 1	0	0	$\cdots$ 0

Fig. 5.1. A relation r showing F does not logically imply $X \rightarrow Y$.

Now we must show that $X \rightarrow Y$ is not satisfied by r. Suppose it is satisfied. As $X \subseteq X^+$ is obvious, it follows that $Y \subseteq X^+$, else the two tuples of r agree on X but disagree on Y. But then Lemma 5.3 tells us that $X \rightarrow Y$ can be inferred from the axioms, a contradiction. Therefore, $X \rightarrow Y$ is not satisfied by r, even though each dependency in F is. We conclude that whenever $X \rightarrow Y$ does not follow from F by Armstrong's axioms, F does not logically imply $X \rightarrow Y$. That is, the axioms are complete. □.

Theorem 5.1 has some interesting consequences. We defined X^+ to be the set of attributes A such that $X \rightarrow A$ followed from the given dependencies F using the axioms. We now see that an equivalent definition of X^+ is the set of A such that F logically implies $X \rightarrow A$. Another consequence is that although we defined F^+ to be the set of dependencies that were logically implied by F, we could as well define F^+ to be the set of dependencies that follow from F by Armstrong's axioms.

Computing Closures

It turns out that computing F^+ for a set of dependencies F is a time-consuming task in general, simply because the set of dependencies in F^+ can be large even if F itself is small. Consider the set $F = \{A \to B_1, A \to B_2, \ldots, A \to B_n\}$. Then F^+ includes all the dependencies $A \to Y$, where Y is a subset of $\{B_1, B_2, \ldots, B_n\}$. As there are 2^n such sets Y, we could not expect to list F^+ conveniently, even for reasonably sized n.

At the other extreme, computing X^+, for a set of attributes X, is not hard; it takes time proportional to the length of all the dependencies in F, written out. By Lemma 5.3, telling whether $X \to Y$ is in F^+ is no harder than computing X^+. A simple way to compute X^+ is the following.

Algorithm 5.1: Computation of the closure of a set of attributes with respect to a set of functional dependencies.

Input: A finite set of attributes U, a set of functional dependencies F on U, and a set $X \subseteq U$.

Output: X^+, the closure of X with respect to F.

Method: We compute a sequence of sets of attributes $X^{(0)}$, $X^{(1)}$, . . . , by the rules:

1. $X^{(0)}$ is X.

2. $X^{(i+1)}$ is X plus the set of attributes A such that there is some dependency $Y \to Z$, in F, A is in Z, and $Y \subseteq X^{(i)}$. Since $X = X^{(0)} \subseteq \cdots \subseteq X^{(i)} \subseteq \cdots \subseteq U$, and U is finite, we must eventually reach i such that $X^{(i)} = X^{(i+1)}$. It then follows that $X^{(i)} = X^{(i+1)} = X^{(i+2)} = \cdots$. There is no need to compute beyond $X^{(i)}$ once we discover $X^{(i)} = X^{(i+1)}$. We can (and shall) prove that X^+ is $X^{(i)}$ for this value of i. $\square$

Example 5.5: Let F consist of the following eight dependencies:

$$
\begin{array}{ll}
AB \to C & D \to EG \\
C \to A & BE \to C \\
BC \to D & CG \to BD \\
ACD \to B & CE \to AG
\end{array}
$$

and let $X = BD$. To apply Algorithm 5.1, we let $X^{(0)} = BD$. To compute $X^{(1)}$ we look for dependencies that have a left side B, D, or BD. There is only one, $D \to EG$, so we adjoin E and G to $X^{(0)}$ and make $X^{(1)} = BDEG$. For $X^{(2)}$, we look for left sides contained in $X^{(1)}$ and find $D \to EG$ and $BE \to C$. Thus $X^{(2)} = BCDEG$. Then, for $X^{(3)}$ we look for left sides contained in $BCDEG$ and find, in addition to the two previously found, $C \rightarrow A$, $BC \rightarrow D$, $CG \rightarrow BD$, and $CE \rightarrow AG$. Thus $X^{(3)} = ABCDEG$, the set of all attributes. It therefore comes as no surprise that $X^{(3)} = X^{(4)} = \cdots$. Thus $(BD)^+ = ABCDEG$. $\square$

Algorithm 5.1 can be implemented to run in time proportional to the sum of the lengths of the dependencies if we keep, for each dependency $Y \rightarrow Z$, a count of the number of attributes in Y that are not yet in $X^{(i)}$. We must also create a list, for each attribute A, of the dependencies on whose left side A appears, and when A is adjoined to some $X^{(i)}$, we decrement by one the count for each dependency on A's list. When the count for $Y \rightarrow Z$ becomes 0, we know $Y \subseteq X^{(i)}$. Lastly, we must maintain $X^{(i)}$ as a Boolean array, indexed by attribute numbers, so when we discover $Y \subseteq X^{(i)}$, where $Y \rightarrow Z$ is a dependency, we can tell in time proportional to the size of Z those attributes in Z that need to be adjoined to $X^{(i)}$. When computing $X^{(i+1)}$ from $X^{(i)}$ we have only to set to true the cells of the array corresponding to attributes added to $X^{(i)}$; there is no need to copy $X^{(i)}$. The details of this modification to Algorithm 5.1 are found in Bernstein [1976], although Algorithm 5.1 itself is probably efficient enough for most purposes.

Now we must address ourselves to the problem of proving that Algorithm 5.1 is correct. It is easy to prove that every attribute placed in some $X^{(j)}$ belongs in X^+, but harder to show that every attribute in X^+ is placed in some $X^{(j)}$.

Theorem 5.2: Algorithm 5.1 correctly computes X^+.

Proof: First we show by induction on j that if A is placed in $X^{(j)}$, then A is in X^+.

Basis: $j = 0$. Then A is in X, so surely $X \rightarrow A$.

Induction: Let $j > 0$ and assume that $X^{(j-1)}$ consists only of attributes in X^+. Suppose A is placed in $X^{(j)}$ because A is in Z, $Y \rightarrow Z$ is in F, and $Y \subseteq X^{(j-1)}$. Since $Y \subseteq X^{(j-1)}$, we know $Y \subseteq X^+$ by the inductive hypothesis. Thus $X \rightarrow Y$ by Lemma 5.3. By transitivity, $X \rightarrow Y$ and $Y \rightarrow Z$ imply $X \rightarrow Z$. By reflexivity, $Z \rightarrow A$, so $X \rightarrow A$ by transitivity. Thus A is in X^+.

Now we show the converse, that if A is in X^+, then A is in some $X^{(j)}$. It does not matter whether or not Algorithm 5.1 ends before computing $X^{(j)}$, because if it stops when $X^{(i)} = X^{(i+1)}$, for some $i < j$, we know that $X^{(i)} = X^{(j)}$. Therefore the value returned for X^+, which is $X^{(i)}$, includes A. What we actually show is that if there is a proof by Armstrong's axioms that $X \rightarrow Y$ follows from F, then every attribute of Y is placed in some $X^{(j)}$. The proof is by induction on the number of lines in the proof, where a *line* is a dependency that is either in F, follows from reflexivity or follows from a previous line or lines by augmentation or transitivity; the last line is $X \rightarrow Y$.

Before proceeding to the induction, let us remark on an inference we make repeatedly.

Observation (*) If X_1 and X_2 are two sets of attributes, and $X_1 \subseteq X_2$, then for all j, $X_1^{(j)} \subseteq X_2^{(j)}$.

Informally, when we start Algorithm 5.1 with more attributes, we don't wind up with fewer. A formal proof of (*) by induction on j is easy and left as an exercise. Now we prove by induction on p, the number of lines in a proof of $X \rightarrow A$ from F, that A is in some $X^{(j)}$.

Basis: One line. Then $X \rightarrow Y$ either follows by reflexivity, in which case $Y \subseteq X^{(0)}$, or $X \rightarrow Y$ is in F, in which case each attribute of Y is certainly in $X^{(1)}$.

Induction: Suppose the claim is true for proofs of fewer than p lines, and $X \rightarrow Y$ has a p line proof. If $X \rightarrow Y$ is in F, or follows by reflexivity, then we may argue as in the basis. If $X \rightarrow Y$ follows by transitivity from two previous lines of the proof, say $X \rightarrow Z$ and $Z \rightarrow Y$, then both these dependencies have proofs of fewer than p lines. By the inductive hypothesis there is some $X^{(j)}$ that includes all the attributes of Z, so $Z \subseteq X^{(j)}$. Now consider running Algorithm 5.1 with Z in place of X. By the inductive hypothesis there is some k such that $Z^{(k)}$ contains all the attributes of Y. By observation (*), with $X^{(j)}$ in place of X_2 and Z for X_1, we know that $X^{(j+k)}$ contains all the attributes in Y.

The last case to consider is where $X \rightarrow Y$ follows by augmenting some previous line $V \rightarrow W$ by set of attributes Z. Then $VZ = X$ and $WZ = Y$. We know $V \rightarrow W$ has a proof of fewer than p lines, so by the inductive hypothesis, if we run Algorithm 5.1 starting with V, there is some j such that $W \subseteq V^{(j)}$. By (*), if we run Algorithm 5.1 starting with $X = VZ$, then $W \subseteq X^{(j)}$. Since $Z \subseteq X$, surely $Z \subseteq X^{(j)}$, so WZ, which is Y, is a subset of $X^{(j)}$. This completes the induction.

By Lemma 5.3, if A is in X^+, then $X \rightarrow A$ has a proof from F using the axioms. Therefore, by the above induction, A is in some $X^{(j)}$, and hence A is in the set returned by Algorithm 5.1 as the value of X^+. Hence the algorithm returns neither too much nor too little; it returns exactly X^+. $\square$

Covers of Sets of Dependencies.

Let F and G be sets of dependencies. We say F and G are *equivalent* if $F^+ = G^+$. If F and G are equivalent we sometimes say F *covers* G (and G covers F). It is easy to test whether F and G are equivalent. For each dependency $Y \rightarrow Z$ in F, test whether $Y \rightarrow Z$ is in G^+ using Algorithm 5.1 to compute Y^+ and then checking whether $Z \subseteq Y^+$. If some dependency $Y \rightarrow Z$ in F is not in G^+, then surely $F^+ \neq G^+$. If every dependency in F is in G^+, then every dependency $V \rightarrow W$ in F^+ is in G^+, because a proof that $V \rightarrow W$ is in G^+ can be formed by taking a proof that each $Y \rightarrow Z$ in F is in

G^+, and following it by a proof from F that $V \rightarrow W$ is in F^+. To test whether each dependency in G is also in F^+, we proceed in an analogous manner. Then F and G are equivalent if and only if every dependency in F is in G^+, and every dependency in G is in F^+.

A useful fact about equivalence is stated in the next lemma.

Lemma 5.4: Every set of functional dependencies F is covered by a set of dependencies G in which no right side has more than one attribute.

Proof: Let G be the set of dependencies $X \rightarrow A$ such that for some $X \rightarrow Y$ in F, A is in Y. Then $X \rightarrow A$ follows from $X \rightarrow Y$ by the decomposition rule. Thus $G \subseteq F^+$. But $F \subseteq G^+$, since if $Y = A_1 \cdots A_n$, then $X \rightarrow Y$ follows from $X \rightarrow A_1, \ldots, X \rightarrow A_n$ using the union rule. $\square$

It turns out to be useful, when we develop a design theory for database schemes, to consider a stronger restriction on covers than that the right sides have but one attribute. We say a set of dependencies F is *minimal* if:

1.   Every right side of a dependency in F is a single attribute.

2.   For no $X \rightarrow A$ in F is the set $F - \{X \rightarrow A\}$ equivalent to F.

3.   For no $X \rightarrow A$ in F and proper subset Z of X is $F - \{X \rightarrow A\} \cup \{Z \rightarrow A\}$ equivalent to F.

Intuitively, (2) guarantees that no dependency in F is redundant, and (3) guarantees that no attribute on any left side is redundant. As each right side has only one attribute by (1), surely no attribute on the right is redundant.

Theorem 5.3: Every set of dependencies F is equivalent to a set F' that is minimal.

Proof: By Lemma 5.4, assume no right side in F has more than one attribute. To satisfy condition (2), consider each dependency $X \rightarrow Y$ in F, in some order, and if $F - \{X \rightarrow Y\}$ is equivalent to F, then delete $X \rightarrow Y$ from F. Note that considering dependencies in different orders may result in the elimination of different sets of dependencies. For example, given the set F:

$$\begin{array}{ll} A \rightarrow B & A \rightarrow C \\ B \rightarrow A & C \rightarrow A \\ B \rightarrow C & \end{array}$$

we can eliminate both $B \rightarrow A$ and $A \rightarrow C$, or we can eliminate $B \rightarrow C$, but we cannot eliminate all three.

Having satisfied (2), we proceed to satisfy (3) by considering each dependency remaining in F, and each attribute in its left side, in some order. If we can eliminate an attribute from a left side and still have an equivalent set of attributes, we do so, until no more attributes can be eliminated from any left side. Again, the order in which attributes are eliminated may affect the result. For example, given

$$AB \rightarrow C$$
$$A \rightarrow B$$
$$B \rightarrow A$$

we can eliminate either A or B from $AB \rightarrow C$, but we cannot eliminate them both. □

Example 5.6: Let us consider the dependency set F of Example 5.5. If we use the algorithm of Lemma 5.4 to split right sides we are left with:

AB	$\rightarrow C$	BE	$\rightarrow C$
C	$\rightarrow A$	CG	$\rightarrow B$
BC	$\rightarrow D$	CG	$\rightarrow D$
ACD	$\rightarrow B$	CE	$\rightarrow A$
D	$\rightarrow E$	CE	$\rightarrow G$
D	$\rightarrow G$		

Clearly $CE \rightarrow A$ is redundant, since it is implied by $C \rightarrow A$. $CG \rightarrow B$ is redundant, since $CG \rightarrow D$, $C \rightarrow A$, and $ACD \rightarrow B$ imply $CG \rightarrow B$, as can be checked by computing $(CG)^+$. Then no more dependencies are redundant. However, $ACD \rightarrow B$ can be replaced by $CD \rightarrow B$, since $C \rightarrow A$. Thus one minimal cover for F is shown in Fig. 5.2(a). Another minimal cover, constructed from F by eliminating $CE \rightarrow A$, $CG \rightarrow D$, and $ACD \rightarrow B$, is shown in Fig. 5.2(b). Note that the two minimal covers have different numbers of dependencies. □

AB	$\rightarrow C$	AB	$\rightarrow C$
C	$\rightarrow A$	C	$\rightarrow A$
BC	$\rightarrow D$	BC	$\rightarrow D$
CD	$\rightarrow B$	D	$\rightarrow E$
D	$\rightarrow E$	D	$\rightarrow G$
D	$\rightarrow G$	BE	$\rightarrow C$
BE	$\rightarrow C$	CG	$\rightarrow B$
CG	$\rightarrow D$	CE	$\rightarrow G$
CE	$\rightarrow G$		

(a)	(b)

Fig. 5.2. Two minimal covers.

5.3 Decomposition of Relation Schemes

The *decomposition* of a relation scheme $R = \{A_1, A_2, \ldots, A_n\}$ is it$ replacement by a collection $\rho = \{R_1, R_2, \ldots, R_k\}$ of subsets of R such that $R_1 \cup R_2 \cup \cdots \cup R_k = R$. There is no requirement that the R_i's be disjoint. One of the motivations for performing a decomposition is that i may eliminate some of the problems mentioned in Section 5.1. In general it is the responsibility of the person designing a database (the "database administrator") to decompose an initial set of relation schemes when war ranted.

Example 5.7: Let us reconsider the SUPPLIERS relation scheme introduce in Example 4.12, but as a shorthand, let the attributes be S (SNAME), A (SADDRESS), I (ITEM), and P (PRICE). The functional dependencie$ we shall assume are $S \rightarrow A$ and $SI \rightarrow P$. We mentioned in Section 5.1 tha replacement of the relation scheme $SAIP$ by the two schemes SA and SI makes certain problems go away. For example, in $SAIP$ we cannot store the address of a supplier unless the supplier provides at least one item. I$ SA, there does not have to be an item supplied to record an address for the supplier. $\square$

One might question whether all is as rosey as it looks, when w$ replace $SAIP$ by SA and SIP in Example 5.7. For example, suppose w$ have a relation r as the current value of $SAIP$. If the database uses SA and SIP instead of $SAIP$, we would naturally expect the current relation fo these two relation schemes to be the projection of r onto SA and SIP, tha is $r_{SA} = \pi_{SA}(r)$ and $r_{SIP} = \pi_{SIP}(r)$. How do we know that r_{SA} and r_{SIP} con tain the same information as r? One way is to check that r can be com puted knowing only r_{SA} and r_{SIP}. We claim that the only way to recover r i$ by taking the natural join of r_{SA} and r_{SIP}.[†] The reason is that, as we shal prove in the next lemma, if we let $s = r_{SA} \bowtie r_{SIP}$, then $\pi_{SA}(s) = r_{SA}$, an$ $\pi_{SIP}(s) = r_{SIP}$. If $s \neq r$, then given r_{SA} and r_{SIP} there is no way to tel whether r or s was the original relation for scheme $SAIP$. That is, if the natural join doesn't recover the original relation, then there is no way what soever to recover it uniquely.

Lossless Joins

If R is a relation scheme decomposed into schemes $R_1, R_2, \ldots, R_k$, and L is a set of dependencies, we say the decomposition is a *lossless join decompo sition* (with respect to D) if for every relation r for R satisfying D:

$$r = \pi_{R_1}(r) \bowtie \pi_{R_2}(r) \bowtie \cdots \bowtie \pi_{R_k}(r)$$

that is, r is the natural join of its projections onto the R_i's. From ou

---

† See Section 4.1 for a definition of the natural join.

remarks above, it is apparent that the lossless join property is a desirable condition for a decomposition to satisfy, so we shall study the subject of lossless joins in some detail.

Some basic facts about project-join mappings follow in Lemma 5.5. First we introduce some notation. If $\rho = (R_1, R_2, \ldots, R_k)$, then m_ρ is the mapping defined by $m_\rho(r) = \bowtie_{i=1}^{k} \pi_{R_i}(r)$. That is, $m_\rho(r)$ is the join of the projections of r onto the relation schemes in ρ. Thus the lossless join condition with respect to D can be expressed as: for all r satisfying D, $r = m_\rho(r)$. As another useful notational convention, if t is a tuple, we define $t[X]$, where X is a list of attributes, to be the list of components of t for the attributes of X. For example, we could express $\pi_X(r)$ as $\{t[X] \mid t$ is in $r\}$.

Lemma 5.5: Let R be a relation scheme, $\rho = (R_1, \ldots, R_k)$ a decomposition of R, r a relation for R, and $r_i = \pi_{R_i}(r)$. Then

a) $r \subseteq m_\rho(r)$.

b)   If $s = m_\rho(r)$, then $\pi_{R_i}(s) = r_i$.

c) $m_\rho(m_\rho(r)) = m_\rho(r)$.

Proof:

a)   Let t be in r. Then for each i, $t_i = t[R_i]$ is in r_i. By definition of the natural join, t is in $m_\rho(r)$, since t agrees with t_i on the attributes of R_i for all i.

b)   As $r \subseteq s$ by (a), it follows that $\pi_{R_i}(r) \subseteq \pi_{R_i}(s)$. That is, $r_i \subseteq \pi_{R_i}(s)$. To show $\pi_{R_i}(s) \subseteq r_i$, suppose for some particular i that t_i is in $\pi_{R_i}(s)$. Then there is some tuple t in s such that $t[R_i] = t_i$. As t is in s, there is some u_j in r_j for each j such that $t[R_j] = u_j$. Thus, in particular, $t[R_i]$ is in r_i. But $t[R_i] = t_i$, so t_i is in r_i, and therefore $\pi_{R_i}(s) \subseteq r_i$. We conclude that $r_i = \pi_{R_i}(s)$.

c)   If $s = m_\rho(r)$, then by (b), $\pi_{R_i}(s) = r_i$. Thus $m_\rho(s) = \bowtie_{i=1}^{k} r_i = m_\rho(r)$.

□

Let us observe that if for each i, r_i is some relation for R_i, and $s = \bowtie_{i=1}^{k} r_i$, then $\pi_{R_i}(s)$ is not necessarily equal to r_i. The reason is that r_i may contain "dangling" tuples. For example, if $R_1 = AB$, $R_2 = BC$, $r_1 = \{a_1b_1\}$, and $r_2 = \{b_1c_1, b_2c_2\}$, then $s = \{a_1b_1c_1\}$ (assuming the ordering ABC for the three attributes) and $\pi_{BC}(s) = \{b_1c_1\} \neq r_2$. However, in general, $\pi_{R_i}(s) \subseteq r_i$, and if the r_i's are each the projection of some one relation r, then $\pi_{R_i}(s) = r_i$.

The ability to store "dangling" tuples is an advantage of decomposition. As we mentioned previously, this advantage must be balanced against the need to compute more joins when we answer queries, if relation schemes are decomposed, than if they are not. When all things are considered, it is generally believed that decomposition is desirable when necessary to cure the problems, such as redundancy, described in Section 5.1, but not otherwise.

Testing Lossless Joins

It turns out to be fairly easy to tell whether a decomposition has a lossless join with respect to a set of functional dependencies.

Algorithm 5.2: Testing for a lossless join.

Input: A relation scheme $R = A_1 \cdots A_n$, a set of functional dependencies F, and a decomposition $\rho = (R_1, \ldots, R_k)$.

Output: A decision whether ρ is a decomposition with a lossless join.

Method: We construct a table with n columns and k rows; column j corresponds to attribute A_j, and row i corresponds to relation scheme R_i. In row i and column j put the symbol a_j if A_j is in R_i. If not, put the symbol b_{ij} there.

Repeatedly "consider" each of the dependencies $X \to Y$ in F, until no more changes can be made to the table. Each time we "consider" $X \to Y$, we look for rows that agree in all the columns for the attributes of X. If we find two such rows, equate the symbols of those rows for the attributes of Y. When we equate two symbols, if one of them is a_j, make the other be a_j. If they are b_{ij} and b_{lj}, make them both b_{ij} or b_{lj}, arbitrarily.

If after modifying the rows of the table as above, we discover that some row has become $a_1 \cdots a_k$, then the join is lossless. If not, the join is lossy (not lossless). □

Example 5.8: Let us consider the decomposition of $SAIP$ into SA and SIP as in Example 5.7. The dependencies are $S \to A$ and $SI \to P$, and the initial table is

S	A	I	P
a_1	a_2	b_{13}	b_{14}
a_1	b_{22}	a_3	a_4

Since $S \to A$, and the two rows agree on S, we may equate their symbols for A, making b_{22} become a_2. The resulting table is

S	A	I	P
a_1	a_2	b_{13}	b_{14}
a_1	a_2	a_3	a_4

Since one row has all a's, the join is lossless.

For a more complicated example, let $R = ABCDE$, $R_1 = AD$, $R_2 = AB$, $R_3 = BE$, $R_4 = CDE$, and $R_5 = AE$. Let the functional dependencies be:

$$A \rightarrow C \qquad DE \rightarrow C$$
$$B \rightarrow C \qquad CE \rightarrow A$$
$$C \rightarrow D$$

The initial table is shown in Fig. 5.3(a). We can apply $A \rightarrow C$ to equate b_{13}, b_{23}, and b_{53}. Then we use $B \rightarrow C$ to equate these symbols with b_{33}; the result is shown in Fig. 5.3(b), where b_{13} has been chosen as the representative symbol. Now use $C \rightarrow D$ to equate a_4, b_{24}, b_{34}, and b_{54}; the resulting symbol is a_4. Then $DE \rightarrow C$ enables us to equate b_{13} with a_3, and $CE \rightarrow A$ lets us equate b_{31}, b_{41}, and a_1. The result is shown in Fig. 5.3(c). Since the middle row is all a's, the decomposition has a lossless join. $\square$

It is interesting to note that one might assume Algorithm 5.2 could be simplified by only equating symbols if one was an a_i. The above example shows this is not the case; if we do not begin by equating b_{13}, b_{23}, b_{33}, and b_{53}, we can never get a row of all a's.

Theorem 5.4: Algorithm 5.2 correctly determines if a decomposition has a lossless join.

Proof: Suppose the final table produced by Algorithm 5.2 does not have a row of all a's. We may view this table as a relation r for scheme R; the rows are tuples, and the a_j's and b_{ij}'s are distinct symbols chosen from the domain of A_j. Relation r satisfies the dependencies F, since Algorithm 5.2 modifies the table whenever a violation of the dependencies is found. We claim that $r \neq m_\rho(r)$. Clearly r does not contain the tuple $a_1 a_2 \cdots a_n$. But for each R_i, there is a tuple t_i in r, namely the tuple that is row i, such that $t_i[R_i]$ consists of all a's. Thus the join of the $\pi_{R_i}(r)$'s contains the tuple with all a's, since that tuple agrees with t_i for all i. We conclude that if the final table from Algorithm 5.2 does not have a row with all a's, then the decomposition ρ does not have a lossless join; we have found a relation r for R such that $m_\rho(r) \neq r$.

Conversely, suppose the final table has a row with all a's. We can in general view the table as shorthand for the domain relational calculus expression

$$\{a_1 a_2 \cdots a_n \mid (\exists b_{11}) \cdots (\exists b_{kn})(R(w_1) \wedge \cdots \wedge R(w_k))\} \qquad (5.1)$$

where w_i is the ith row of the initial table. Formula (5.1) defines the function m_ρ, since $m_\rho(r)$ contains an arbitrary tuple $a_1 \cdots a_n$ if and only if for each i, r contains a tuple with a's in the attributes of R_i and arbitrary values in the other attributes.

Since we assume that any relation r for scheme R, to which (5.1)

A	B	C	D	E
a_1	b_{12}	b_{13}	a_4	b_{15}
a_1	a_2	b_{23}	b_{24}	b_{25}
b_{31}	a_2	b_{33}	b_{34}	a_5
b_{41}	b_{42}	a_3	a_4	a_5
a_1	b_{52}	b_{53}	b_{54}	a_5

(a)

A	B	C	D	E
a_1	b_{12}	b_{13}	a_4	b_{15}
a_1	a_2	b_{13}	b_{24}	b_{25}
b_{31}	a_2	b_{13}	b_{34}	a_5
b_{41}	b_{42}	a_3	a_4	a_5
a_1	b_{52}	b_{13}	b_{54}	a_5

(b)

A	B	C	D	E
a_1	b_{12}	a_3	a_4	b_{15}
a_1	a_2	a_3	a_4	b_{25}
a_1	a_2	a_3	a_4	a_5
a_1	b_{42}	a_3	a_4	a_5
a_1	b_{52}	a_3	a_4	a_5

(c)

Fig. 5.3. Applying Algorithm 5.2.

could be applied, satisfies the dependencies F, we can infer that (5.1) is equivalent to a set of similar formulas with some of the a's and/or b's identified. The modifications made to the table by Algorithm 5.2 are such that the table is always shorthand for some formula whose value on relation r is $m_\rho(r)$ whenever r satisfies F, as can be proved by an easy induction on the number of symbols identified. Since the final table contains a row with all a's, the domain calculus expression for the final table is of the form.

$$\{a_1 \cdots a_n \mid R(a_1 \cdots a_n) \wedge \cdots \} \tag{5.2}$$

Clearly the value of (5.2) applied to relation r for R, is a subset of r. However, if r satisfies F, then the value of (5.2) is $m_\rho(r)$, and by Lemma 5.5(a), $r \subseteq m_\rho(r)$. Thus whenever r satisfies F, (5.2) computes r, so $r = m_\rho(r)$. That is to say, the decomposition ρ has a lossless join with respect to F. □

Algorithm 5.2 works for decompositions into any number of relation schemes. However, for decompositions into two schemes we can give a simpler test, the subject of the next theorem.

Theorem 5.5: If $\rho = (R_1, R_2)$ is a decomposition of R, and F is a set of functional dependencies, then ρ has a lossless join with respect to F if and only if $R_1 \cap R_2 \to R_1 - R_2$ or $R_1 \cap R_2 \to R_2 - R_1$. Note that these dependencies need not be in the given set F; it is sufficient that they be in F^+.

	$R_1 \cap R_2$	$R_1 - R_2$	$R_2 - R_1$
row for R_1	$a\,a\,\cdots\,a$	$a\,a\,\cdots\,a$	$b\,b\,\cdots\,b$
row for R_2	$a\,a\,\cdots\,a$	$b\,b\,\cdots\,b$	$a\,a\,\cdots\,a$

Fig. 5.4. A general two row table.

Proof: The initial table used in an application of Algorithm 5.2 is shown in Fig. 5.4, although we have omitted the subscripts on a and b, which are easily determined and immaterial anyway. It is easy to show by induction on the number of symbols identified by Algorithm 5.2 that if the b in the column for attribute A is changed to an a, then A is in $(R_1 \cap R_2)^+$. It is also easy to show by induction on the number of steps needed to prove $R_1 \cap R_2 \to Y$ by Armstrong's axioms, that any b's in the columns for attributes in Y are changed to a's. Thus the row for R_1 becomes all a's if and only if $R_2 - R_1 \subseteq (R_1 \cap R_2)^+$, that is $R_1 \cap R_2 \to R_2 - R_1$, and similarly, the row for R_2 becomes all a's if and only if $R_1 \cap R_2 \to R_1 - R_2$. □

Example 5.9: Suppose $R = ABC$ and $F = \{A \to B\}$. Then the decomposition of R into AB and AC has a lossless join, since $AB \cap AC = A$, $AB - AC = B$,† and $A \to B$ holds. However if we decompose R into $R_1 = AB$ and $R_2 = BC$, we discover that $R_1 \cap R_2 = B$, and B functionally determines neither $R_1 - R_2 = A$ nor $R_2 - R_1 = C$. Thus the decomposition AB and BC does not have a lossless join with respect to $F = \{A \to B\}$, as can be seen by considering the relation $r = \{a_1 b_1 c_1, a_2 b_1 c_2\}$ for R. Then $\pi_{AB}(r) = \{a_1 b_1, a_2 b_1\}$, $\pi_{BC}(r) = \{b_1 c_1, b_1 c_2\}$, and

$$\pi_{AB}(r) \bowtie \pi_{BC}(r) = \{a_1 b_1 c_1, a_1 b_1 c_2, a_2 b_1 c_1, a_2 b_1 c_2\}.$$

□

Decompositions that Preserve Dependencies

We have seen that it is desirable for a decomposition to have the lossless join property, because it guarantees that any relation can be recovered from its projections. Another important property of a decomposition of relation scheme R into $\rho = (R_1, \ldots, R_k)$ is that the set of dependencies F for R be

---

† To make sense of equations like these do not forget that $A_1 A_2 \cdots A_n$ stands for $\{A_1, A_2, \ldots, A_n\}$.

implied by the projection of F onto the R_i's. Formally, the *projection* of F onto a set of attributes Z, denoted $\pi_Z(F)$, is the set of dependencies $X \to Y$ in F^+ such that $XY \subseteq Z$. (Note that $X \to Y$ need not be in F; it need only be in F^+.) We say decomposition ρ *preserves* a set of dependencies F if the union of all the dependencies in $\pi_{R_i}(F)$, for $i = 1, 2, \ldots, k$ logically implies all the dependencies in F.

The reason it is desirable that ρ preserve F is that the dependencies in F can be viewed as integrity constraints for the relation R. If the projected dependencies do not imply F, then should we represent R by $\rho = (R_1, \ldots, R_k)$, we could find that the current value of the R_i's represented a relation R that did not satisfy F, even if ρ had the lossless join property with respect to F. Alternatively, every update to one of the R_i's would require a join to check that the constraints were not violated.

Example 5.10: Let us reconsider the problem of Example 5.3, where we had attributes CITY, ST, and ZIP, which we here abbreviate C, S, and Z. We observed the dependencies $CS \to Z$ and $Z \to C$. The decomposition of the relation scheme CSZ into SZ and CZ has a lossless join, since $(SZ \cap CZ) \to (CZ - SZ)$. However, the projection of $F = \{CS \to Z, Z \to C\}$ onto SZ gives only the trivial dependencies that follow from reflexivity, while the projection onto CZ gives $Z \to C$ and the trivial dependencies. It can be checked that $Z \to C$ and trivial dependencies do not imply $CS \to Z$, so the decomposition does not preserve dependencies.

For example, the join of the two relations in Fig. 5.5(a) and (b) is the relation of Fig. 5.5(c). Figure 5.5(a) satisfies the trivial dependencies, as any relation must. Figure 5.5(b) satisfies the trivial dependencies and the dependency $Z \to C$. However, their join in Fig. 5.5(c) violates $CS \to Z$. □

S	Z
545 Tech Sq.	02138
545 Tech Sq.	02139

(a)

C	Z
Cambridge, Mass.	02138
Cambridge, Mass.	02139

(b)

C	S	Z
Cambridge, Mass.	545 Tech Sq.	02138
Cambridge, Mass.	545 Tech Sq.	02139

(c)

Fig. 5.5. A join violating a functional dependency.

We should note that a decomposition may have a lossless join with respect to set of dependencies F, yet not preserve F. Example 5.10 gave one such instance. Also, the decomposition could preserve F yet not have a lossless join. For example, let $F = \{A \rightarrow B, C \rightarrow D\}$, $R = ABCD$, and $\rho = (AB, CD)$.

5.4 Normal Forms for Relation Schemes

A number of different properties, or "normal forms" for relation schemes with dependencies have been defined. The most significant of these are called "third normal form"† and "Boyce-Codd normal form." These normal forms guarantee that most of the problems of redundancy and anomalies discussed in Section 5.1 do not occur.

To define these terms, we should first agree to call an attribute A in relation scheme R a *prime* attribute if A is a member of any key for R (recall there may be many keys). If A is not a member of any key, then A is *nonprime*.

Example 5.11: In the relation scheme CSZ of Example 5.10, all attributes are prime, since given the dependencies $CS \rightarrow Z$ and $Z \rightarrow C$ we can check that both CS and SZ are keys.

In the relation scheme $ABCD$ with dependencies $AB \rightarrow C$, $B \rightarrow D$, and $BC \rightarrow A$ we see that AB and BC are the only keys, so A, B, and C are prime; D is nonprime. □

Third Normal Form

A relation scheme R is in *third normal form* if there does not exist a key X for R, a set of attributes $Y \subseteq R$, and a nonprime attribute A of R not in X or Y, such that

1. $X \rightarrow Y$ holds in R,
2. $Y \rightarrow A$ holds in R, but
3. $Y \rightarrow X$ does not hold in R.

If Y is a subset of X, and therefore by (3), Y is a proper subset of X, then we say R has a *partial* dependency. If Y is not a subset of X, then R has a *transitive* dependency. If R satisfies the above condition whenever $Y \subseteq X$, but not necessarily otherwise, then R is said to be in *second normal form*.‡

Example 5.12: The relation scheme $SAIP$ from Example 4.12, with dependencies $SI \rightarrow P$ and $S \rightarrow A$ violates third normal form, and in fact violates

---

† Yes Virginia, there is a first normal form and a second normal form. There's even a fourth normal form. All in good time · · ·

‡ O.K., we might as well mention "first normal form." That form simply requires that the domain of each attribute consists of indivisible values, not sets or tuples of values from a more elementary domain or domains. We have not considered set valued domains and so feel free to ignore first normal form. In effect, relation is for us synonymous with "first normal form relation" in some works appearing in the literature.

second normal form. Let $X = SI$ and $Y = S$. A is a nonprime attribute, since the only key is SI. Then $X \rightarrow Y$ and $Y \rightarrow A$ hold, but $Y \rightarrow X$, which is $S \rightarrow SI$, does not hold. Note that in this case, $X \rightarrow Y$ and $Y \rightarrow A$ not only hold in R; they are given dependencies. In general, however, it is sufficient that $X \rightarrow Y$ and $Y \rightarrow A$ follow from the given set of dependencies, even if they are not themselves given.

As another example, the relation scheme CSZ from Example 5.11 is in third normal form. Since all of its attributes are prime, the conditions for third normal form hold vacuously.

For an example of a relation scheme in second normal form but not third, consider the attributes S (Store) I (Item) D (Department number), and M (Manager). The functional dependencies we assume are $SI \rightarrow D$ (each item in each store is sold by at most one department) and $SD \rightarrow M$ (each department in each store has one manager). The only key is SI. If we let $X = SI$, $Y = SD$, and $A = M$, then we violate third normal form. However, there are no partial dependencies, since no proper subset of the key SI functionally determines D or M. $\square$

Motivation Behind Third Normal Form

We may suppose that the functional dependencies $X \rightarrow Y$ not only represent an integrity constraint on relations, but also represent a relationship that the database is intended to store. That is, we regard it important to know, given an assignment of values to the attributes in X, what value for each of the Y attributes is associated with this assignment of values. If we have a partial dependency $Y \rightarrow A$, where X is a key and Y a proper subset of X, then in every tuple used to associate an X-value with values for other attributes besides A and those in X, the same association between Y and A must appear. This situation is best seen in the running example of the $SAIP$ scheme, where $S \rightarrow A$ is a partial dependency, and the supplier's address must be repeated once for each item supplied by the supplier. The third normal form condition eliminates this possibility and the resultant redundancy and update anomalies.

If we have a transitive dependency $X \rightarrow Y \rightarrow A$, then we cannot associate a Y-value with an X-value unless there is an A-value associated with the Y value. This situation leads to insertion and deletion anomalies, where we cannot insert an X-to-Y association without a Y-to-A association, and if we delete the A-value associated with a given Y-value, we lose track of an X-to-Y association. For example, in the relation scheme $SIDM$ with dependencies $SI \rightarrow D$ and $SD \rightarrow M$, mentioned in Example 5.12, we cannot record the department selling hats in Bloomingdales if that department has no manager.

Boyce-Codd Normal Form

A relation scheme R with dependencies F is said to be in *Boyce-Codd normal form* if whenever $X \to A$ holds in R, and A is not in X, then X includes a key for R. Put another way, the only nontrivial dependencies are those in which a key functionally determines one or more other attributes.

Example 5.13: The relation scheme CSZ of Example 5.11, with dependencies $CS \to Z$ and $Z \to C$ is not in Boyce-Codd normal form, although it is in third normal form. The reason is that $Z \to C$ holds (in fact it is a given dependency), but Z is not a key of CSZ. $\square$

As we saw from the above example, a relation scheme can be in third normal form but not Boyce-Codd normal form. However, every Boyce-Codd normal form relation scheme is in third normal form. The benefits of Boyce-Codd normal form are the same as for third normal form — freedom from insertion and deletion anomalies and redundancies. Note from Example 5.13 how Boyce-Codd normal form eliminates some anomalies not prevented by third normal form. For instance, in Example 5.13, we cannot record the city to which a zip code belongs unless we know a street address with that zip code.

It is worth noting that relations intended to represent an entity set or a many-one mapping between entity sets will be in Boyce-Codd normal form unless there are unexpected relationships among attributes.

Theorem 5.6: If a relation scheme R with functional dependencies F is in Boyce-Codd normal form, then it is in third normal form.

Proof: Imagine that R is in Boyce-Codd normal form, but not in third normal form. Then there is a partial or transitive dependency $X \to Y \to A$, where X is a key for R, A is not in X or Y, and $Y \to X$ is not in F^+. Then Y does not include a key for R, or surely $Y \to X$ would hold. But A is not in Y, so $Y \to A$ violates the Boyce-Codd normal form condition. $\square$

Lossless Join Decomposition into Boyce-Codd Normal Form

It turns out that any relation scheme has a lossless join decomposition into Boyce-Codd Normal Form, and it has a decomposition into third normal form that has a lossless join and is also dependency preserving. However, there may be no decomposition of a relation scheme into Boyce-Codd normal form that is dependency preserving. The CSZ relation scheme of Example 5.13 is the canonical example. It is not in Boyce-Codd normal form because the dependency $Z \to C$ holds, yet if we decompose CSZ in any way such that CSZ is not one of the schemes in the decomposition, then the dependency $CS \to Z$ is not implied by the projected dependencies. Before giving the decomposition algorithms, we shall state some properties of natural joins that we shall need.

Lemma 5.6:

a)   Suppose R is a relation scheme with functional dependencies F. Let $\rho = (R_1, \ldots, R_k)$ be a decomposition of R with a lossless join with respect to F. For a particular i, let F_i be the projection of F onto R_i, that is, the set of $X \to Y$ in F^+ such that X and Y are subsets of R_i, and let $\sigma = (S_1, \ldots, S_m)$ be a decomposition of R_i whose join is lossless with respect to F_i. Then the decomposition of R into $(R_1, \ldots, R_{i-1}, S_1, \ldots, S_m, R_{i+1}, \ldots, R_k)$ has a lossless join with respect to F.

b)   Suppose R, F and ρ are as in (a), and let $\tau = (R_1, \ldots, R_k, R_{k+1}, \ldots, R_n)$ be a decomposition of R into a set of relation schemes that includes those of ρ. Then τ also has a lossless join with respect to F.

Proof: Each of these statements follows by algebraic manipulation from the definition of a lossless join decomposition. We shall leave formal proofs as exercises and only give the intuition here. The reason (a) holds is that if we take relation r for R and project it to relation r_i for each R_i, and then project r_i to relation s_p for S_p, the lossless join property tells us we can join the s_p's to recover r_i. Then we can join the r_i's to recover r. Since the natural join is an associative operation (another exercise for the reader) the order in which we perform the join doesn't matter, so we recover r no matter in what order we take the join of the r_i's and the s_p's.

For part (b), we again appeal to the associativity of the natural join. Observe that if we project relation r for R onto the R_i's, $i = 1, 2, \ldots, n$, then when we take the join of the projections onto $R_1, \ldots, R_k$ we recover r. Since $R_1, \ldots, R_k$ include all the attributes of R, further joins can only produce a subset of what we already have, which is r. But by Lemma 5.5(a), $r \subseteq m_\tau(r)$, so we cannot wind up with less than r. That is, $m_\tau(r) = r$, and τ is a lossless join decomposition. $\square$

Algorithm 5.3: Lossless Join Decomposition into Boyce-Codd Normal Form.

Input: Relation scheme R and functional dependencies F.

Output: A decomposition of R with a lossless join, such that every relation scheme in the decomposition is in Boyce-Codd normal form with respect to the projection of F onto that scheme.

Method: We iteratively construct a decomposition ρ for R. At all times, ρ will have a lossless join with respect to F. Initially, ρ consists of R alone. If S is a relation scheme in ρ, and S is not in Boyce-Codd normal form, let $X \to A$ be a dependency that holds in S, where X does not include a key for S, and A is not in X. Then there must be some attribute of S that is not A and is not in X, or else X would include a key for S. Replace S in ρ by S_1 and S_2, where S_1 consists of A and the attributes of X, and S_2 consists of all the attributes of S except for A.

By Theorem 5.5, the decomposition of S into S_1 and S_2 has a lossless join with respect to the set of dependencies projected onto S, since $S_1 \cap S_2 = X$, and $X \to S_1 - S_2 = A$. By Lemma 5.6(a), ρ with S replaced by S_1 and S_2 has a lossless join, if ρ does. As S_1 and S_2 each have fewer attributes then S, we eventually reach a point where each relation scheme in ρ is in Boyce-Codd normal form. At that time, ρ still has a lossless join, since the initial ρ consisting of R alone does, and each modification of ρ preserves the lossless join property. □

Example 5.14: Let us consider the relation scheme CTHRSG, where $C =$ course, $T =$ teacher, $H =$ hour, $R =$ room, $S =$ student, and $G =$ grade. The functional dependencies F we assume are

$$C \to T \qquad \text{each course has one teacher}$$
$$HR \to C \qquad \text{only one course can meet in a room at one time}$$
$$HT \to R \qquad \text{a teacher can be in only one room at one time}$$
$$CS \to G \qquad \text{each student has one grade in each course}$$
$$HS \to R \qquad \text{a student can be in only one room at one time}$$

The only key for CTHRSG is HS.

To decompose this relation scheme into Boyce-Codd normal form, we might first consider the dependency $CS \to G$, which violates the condition, since CS does not contain a key. Thus, by Algorithm 5.3, we first decompose CTHRSG into CSG and CTHRS. For further decompositions we must compute F^+ and project it onto CSG and CTHRS.

Note that this process is in general time consuming, as the size of F^+ can be exponential in the size of F. Even in this relatively simple example, F^+, naturally, has all the trivial dependencies that follow by reflexivity and, in addition to those in F, some other nontrivial dependencies like $CH \to R$, $HS \to C$, and $HR \to T$. Once we have F^+, we select those involving only C, S, and G. This is the set of dependencies F projected onto CSG. This set has a minimal cover consisting of $CS \to G$ alone; all other dependencies in the set follow from this dependency by Armstrong's axioms. We also project F^+ onto CTHRS. The projected set has a minimal cover

$$C \to T \qquad TH \to R$$
$$HR \to C \qquad HS \to R$$

and the only key for CTHRS is HS.

It is easy to check that CSG is in Boyce-Codd normal form with respect to its projected dependencies. CTHRS must be decomposed further, and we might choose the dependency $C \to T$ to break it into CT and CHRS. Minimal covers for the projected dependencies are $C \to T$ for CT and $CH \to R$, $HS \to R$, and $HR \to C$ for CHRS; HS is the only key of the latter scheme. Observe that $CH \to R$ is needed in a cover of CHRS, although in CTHRS it followed from $C \to T$ and $TH \to R$.

   CT is in Boyce-Codd normal form, and one more decomposition of
CHRS, say using *CH→R*, puts the entire database scheme into the desired
form. In Fig. 5.6 we see the tree of decompositions, with the keys and
minimal covers for the sets of projected dependencies also shown.

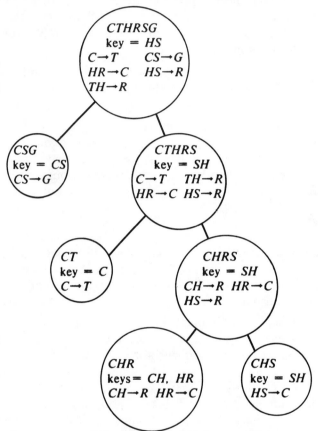

Fig. 5.6. Tree of decomposition.

   The final decomposition of *CTHRSG* is *CSG, CT, CHR,* and *CHS*.
This is not a bad database design, since its four relation schemes tabulate,
respectively,

1.   grades for students in courses,

2.   the teacher of each course,

3.   the hours at which each course meets and the room for each hour,
     and

4.   the schedule of courses and hours for each student.

In fairness it should be noted that not every decomposition produces a database scheme that matches so well our intuition about what information should be tabulated in the database. For example, if at the last decomposition step we had used dependency $HR \rightarrow C$ instead of $CH \rightarrow R$, we would have scheme HRS instead of CHS, and HRS represents the room in which a student can be found at a given hour, rather than the class he is attending. Surely the latter is more fundamental information than the former.

Another problem with the decomposition of Fig. 5.6 is that the dependency $TH \rightarrow R$ is not preserved by the decomposition. That is, the projection of F onto CSG, CT, CHR, and CHS, which can be represented by the cover

$$
\begin{array}{ll}
CS \rightarrow G & HR \rightarrow C \\
C \rightarrow T & HS \rightarrow C \\
CH \rightarrow R &
\end{array}
$$

found by taking the minimal covers in each of the leaves of Fig. 5.6, does not imply $TH \rightarrow R$. For example, the relation for $CTHRSG$ shown below

C	T	H	R	S	G
c_1	t	h	r_1	s_1	g_1
c_2	t	h	r_2	s_2	g_2

does not satisfy $TH \rightarrow R$, yet its projections onto CSG, CT, CHR, and CHS satisfy all the projected dependencies. □

We mentioned that the process of projecting dependencies, where we construct F^+ from F and then select out those with a particular set of attributes, can be exponential in the number of dependencies in F. One might wonder whether Algorithm 5.3 can be made to run in less than exponential time by using another approach to decomposition. Unfortunately, Beeri and Bernstein [1979] proved that it is NP-complete† just to determine whether a relation scheme is in Boyce-Codd normal form. Thus it is extremely unlikely that one will find a substantially better algorithm.

Dependency Preserving Decompositions into Third Normal Form

We saw from Examples 5.10 and 5.13 that it is not always possible to decompose a relation scheme into Boyce-Codd normal form and still preserve the dependencies. However, we can always find a dependency-preserving decomposition into third normal form, as the next algorithm and

---

† NP-completeness of a problem almost certainly implies that it is inherently exponential. See Aho, Hopcroft, and Ullman [1974] or Garey and Johnson [1979] for a description of the theory.

theorem show.

Algorithm 5.4: Dependency-Preserving Decomposition into Third Normal Form.

Input: Relation scheme R and set of functional dependencies F, which we assume without loss of generality to be a minimal cover.

Output: A dependency-preserving decomposition of R such that each relation scheme is in third normal form with respect to the projection of F onto that scheme.

Method: If there are any attributes of R not involved in any dependency of F, either on the left or right, then that attribute can, in principle, form a relation scheme by itself, and we shall eliminate it from R.† If one of the dependencies in F involves all the attributes of R, then output R itself. Otherwise, the decomposition ρ to be output consists of scheme XA for each dependency $X \rightarrow A$ in F. However, if $X \rightarrow A_1$, $X \rightarrow A_2$, ..., $X \rightarrow A_n$ are in F, we may use scheme $XA_1 \cdots A_n$ instead of XA_i for $1 \leqslant i \leqslant n$, and in fact, this substitution is usually preferable. $\square$

Example 5.15: Reconsider the relation scheme $CTHRSG$ of Example 5.14, whose dependencies have minimal cover

$$C \rightarrow T \qquad CS \rightarrow G$$
$$HR \rightarrow C \qquad HS \rightarrow R$$
$$HT \rightarrow R$$

Algorithm 5.4 yields the set of relation schemes CT, CHR, HRT, CGS, and HRS. $\square$

Theorem 5.7: Algorithm 5.4 yields a dependency-preserving decomposition into third normal form.

Proof: Since the projected dependencies include a cover for F, the decomposition clearly preserves dependencies. Suppose there is a dependency $X \rightarrow A$ in F that includes all the attributes of R, after removing any that are not involved in any dependency. In this case, we claim R is in third normal form. First observe that since F is a minimal cover, X must be a key of R. Surely $X \rightarrow R$ holds. If some proper subset $Y \subseteq X$ is a key, then $X \rightarrow A$ may be replaced by $Y \rightarrow A$ in F without changing the closure, which contradicts our assumption that F is a minimal cover. We now show that R is already in third normal form.

---

† Sometimes it is desirable to have two or more attributes, say A and B, appear together in a relation scheme, even though there is no functional dependency involving them. There may simply be a many-many relationship between A and B. An idea of Bernstein [1976] is to introduce a dummy attribute θ and functional dependency $AB \rightarrow \theta$, to force this association. After completing the design, attribute θ is eliminated.

Case 1: Suppose there is a transitive dependency $V \rightarrow W \rightarrow B$ in R. If A is not in V, then let Z be V and the attributes of X excluding B and excluding those in W. Since $V \rightarrow W \rightarrow B$ is transitive, either B or some attribute of $W - V$ is not A, so Z is a proper subset of X. As $Z = V \cup (X - W - B)$, and $V \rightarrow W \rightarrow B$ is given, it follows that $Z \rightarrow X$. Thus, X is not a key for R, a contradiction. If A is in V, let Z be as above. Since $Z \rightarrow R$ holds, there is some subset $U \subseteq Z$ that is a key for R. If A is in U, then R has only prime attributes, since $X = R - A$ is a key also. Thus R is in third normal form vacuously. If A is not in U, then U is a proper subset of X that functionally determines X, contradicting the fact that X is a key.

Case 2: There is a partial dependency $X \rightarrow Y \rightarrow B$. If $B \neq A$, then as $Y \subseteq X$ in a partial dependency, $X - B$ is a proper subset of X that determines X, contradicting the assumption that X is a key. If $B = A$, then $Y \rightarrow A$, and Y is a proper subset of X, contradicting the fact that F is a minimal cover. This concludes the proof that if a dependency in F includes all attributes of R, then R is in third normal form.

Now let $X \rightarrow A$ be a dependency in F that does not include all attributes. We claim that XA is in third normal form with respect to the projection of F onto XA. We have only to observe that X must be a key of XA, else F is not a minimal cover. Then the argument proceeds as above, where XA replaces R. $\square$

Decompositions into Third Normal Form with a Lossless Join and Preservation of Dependencies

We have seen that we can decompose any relation scheme R into a set of schemes $\rho = (R_1, \ldots, R_k)$ such that ρ has a lossless join and each R_i is in Boyce-Codd normal form (and therefore in third normal form). We can also decompose R into $\sigma = (S_1, \ldots, S_m)$ such that σ preserves the set of dependencies F, and each S_j is in third normal form. Can we find a decomposition that has both properties? We can if we simply adjoin to σ a relation scheme X that is a key for R, as the next theorem shows.

Theorem 5.8: Let σ be the third normal form decomposition of R constructed by Algorithm 5.4, and let X be a key for R. Then $\tau = \sigma \cup \{X\}$ is a decomposition of R with all relation schemes in third normal form; the decomposition preserves dependencies and has the lossless join property.

Proof: It is easy to show that any transitive or partial dependency in X implies that a proper subset of X functionally determines X, and therefore R, so X would not be a key in that case. Thus X, as well as the members of σ, are in third normal form. Clearly τ preserves dependencies, since σ does.

To show that τ has a lossless join, apply the tabular test of Algorithm 5.2. We can show that the row for X becomes all a's, as follows. Consider the order $A_1, A_2, \ldots, A_k$ in which the attributes of $R-X$ are added to X^+ in Algorithm 5.1. Surely all attributes are added eventually, since X is a key. We show by induction on i that the column corresponding to A_i in the row for X is set to a_i in the test of Algorithm 5.2.

The basis, $i=0$, is trivial. Assume the result for $i-1$. Then A_i is added to X^+ because of some given functional dependency $Y \rightarrow A_i$, where $Y \subseteq X \cup \{A_1, \ldots, A_{i-1}\}$. Then YA_i is in σ, and the rows for YA_i and X agree on Y (they are all a's) after the columns of the X-row for $A_1, \ldots, A_{i-1}$ are made a's. Thus these rows are made to agree on A_i during the execution of Algorithm 5.2. Since the YA_i-row has a_i there, so must the X-row. □

Obviously, in some cases τ is not the smallest set of relation schemes with the properties of Theorem 5.8. We can throw out relation schemes in τ one at a time as long as the desired properties are preserved. Many different database schemes may result, depending on the order in which we throw out schemes, since eliminating one may preclude the elimination of others.

Example 5.16: We could take the union of the database scheme produced for *CTHRSG* in Example 5.15 with the key *SH*, to get a decomposition that has a lossless join and preserves dependencies. It happens that *SH* is a subset of *HRS*, which is one of the relation schemes already selected. Thus, *SH* may be eliminated, and the database scheme of Example 5.15, that is *CT*, *CHR*, *HRT*, *CGS*, and *HRS*, suffices. Although some proper subsets of this set of five relation schemes are lossless join decompositions, we can check that the projected dependencies for any four of them do not imply the complete set of dependencies F, last mentioned in Example 5.15. □

5.5 Multivalued Dependencies

In previous sections we have assumed that the only possible kind of data dependency is functional. In fact there are many plausible kinds of dependencies, and at least one, the multivalued dependency, merits serious study. Suppose we are given a relation scheme R, and X and Y are subsets of R. Intuitively, we say that $X \twoheadrightarrow Y$, read "X *multidetermines* Y," or "there is a *multivalued dependency* of Y on X," if given values for the attributes of X there is a set of zero or more associated values for the attributes of Y, and this set of Y-values is not connected in any way to values of the attributes in $R-X-Y$.

Formally, we say $X \twoheadrightarrow Y$ holds in R if whenever r is a relation for R, and t and s are two tuples in r, with $t[X]=s[X]$ (that is, t and s agree on the attributes of X), then r also contains tuples u and v, where

1. $u[X] = v[X] = t[X] = s[X]$,
2. $u[Y] = t[Y]$ and $u[R-X-Y] = s[R-X-Y]$, and
3. $v[Y] = s[Y]$ and $v[R-X-Y] = t[R-X-Y]$.†

That is, we can exchange the Y values of t and s to obtain two new tuples that must also be in r. Note that we did not assume X and Y are disjoint in the above definition.

Example 5.17: Let us reconsider the relation scheme *CTHRSG* of the previous section. In Fig. 5.7 we see a possible relation for this relation scheme. In this simple case there is only one course with two students, but we see several salient facts that we would expect to hold in any relation for this relation scheme. A course can meet for several hours, in different rooms each time. Each student has a tuple for each class taken and each session of that class. His grade for the class is repeated for each tuple.

C	T	H	R	S	G
CS101	Deadwood, J.	M9	222	Klunk, A.	B+
CS101	Deadwood, J.	W9	333	Klunk, A.	B+
CS101	Deadwood, J.	F9	222	Klunk, A.	B+
CS101	Deadwood, J.	M9	222	Zonker, B.	C
CS101	Deadwood, J.	W9	333	Zonker, B.	C
CS101	Deadwood, J.	F9	222	Zonker, B.	C

Fig. 5.7. A sample relation for scheme *CTHRSG*.

Thus we expect that in general the multivalued dependency $C \twoheadrightarrow HR$ holds, that is, there is a set of hour-room pairs associated with each course and disassociated from the other attributes. For example, if in the formal definition of a multivalued dependency we let

t = CS101   Deadwood, J.   M9 222 Klunk, A.   B+
s = CS101   Deadwood, J.   W9 333 Zonker, B.   C

then we would expect to be able to exchange (M9, 222) from t with (W9, 333) in s to get the two new tuples

u = CS101   Deadwood, J.   M9 222 Zonker, B.   C
v = CS101   Deadwood, J.   W9 333 Klunk, A.   B+

A glance at Fig. 5.7 affirms that u and v are indeed in r.

It should be emphasized that $C \twoheadrightarrow HR$ holds not because it held in the one relation of Fig. 5.7. It holds because for any course c, if it meets at hour h_1 in room r_1, with teacher t_1 and student s_1 with grade g_1, and it also

---

† Note we could have eliminated clause (3); it follows from (1) and (2) when we interchange t and s.

meets at hour h_2 in room r_2 with teacher t_2 and student s_2 with grade g_2, then we expect from our understanding of the attributes' meanings that the course c also meets at hour h_1 in room r_1 with teacher t_2 and student s_2 with grade g_2.

Note also that $C \longrightarrow\!\!\!\!\!\rightarrow H$ does not hold, nor does $C \longrightarrow\!\!\!\!\!\rightarrow R$. In proof, consider r of Fig. 5.7 with tuples t and s as above. If $C \longrightarrow\!\!\!\!\!\rightarrow H$ held, we would expect to find tuple

      CS101   Deadwood, J.   M9 333 Zonker, B. C

in r, which we do not. There are a number of other multivalued dependencies that hold, however, such as $C \longrightarrow\!\!\!\!\!\rightarrow SG$ and $HR \longrightarrow\!\!\!\!\!\rightarrow SG$. There are also trivial multivalued dependencies like $HR \longrightarrow\!\!\!\!\!\rightarrow R$. We shall also prove that every functional dependency $X \rightarrow Y$ that holds implies that the multivalued dependency $X \longrightarrow\!\!\!\!\!\rightarrow Y$ holds as well. □

Axioms for Functional and Multivalued Dependencies

We shall now present a sound and complete set of axioms for making inferences about a set of functional and multivalued dependencies over a set of attributes U. The first three are Armstrong's axioms for functional dependencies only; we repeat them here.

A1:   *(reflexivity for functional dependencies)* If $Y \subseteq X \subseteq U$, then $X \rightarrow Y$.

A2:   *(augmentation for functional dependencies)* If $X \rightarrow Y$ holds, and $Z \subseteq U$, then $XZ \rightarrow YZ$.

A3:   *(transitivity for functional dependencies)* If $X \rightarrow Y$ and $Y \rightarrow Z$ hold, then $X \rightarrow Z$.

The next three axioms apply to multivalued dependencies.

A4:   *(complementation for multivalued dependencies)* If $X \longrightarrow\!\!\!\!\!\rightarrow Y$, then $X \longrightarrow\!\!\!\!\!\rightarrow U - X - Y$.

A5:   *(augmentation for multivalued dependencies)* If $X \longrightarrow\!\!\!\!\!\rightarrow Y$, and $V \subseteq W$, then $WX \longrightarrow\!\!\!\!\!\rightarrow VY$.

A6:   *(transitivity for multivalued dependencies)* If $X \longrightarrow\!\!\!\!\!\rightarrow Y$ and $Y \longrightarrow\!\!\!\!\!\rightarrow Z$, then $X \longrightarrow\!\!\!\!\!\rightarrow Z - Y$.

It is worthwhile comparing A4-A6 with A1-A3. Axiom A4, the complementation rule, has no counterpart for functional dependencies. Axiom A1, reflexivity, appears to have no counterpart for multivalued dependencies, but the fact that $X \longrightarrow\!\!\!\!\!\rightarrow Y$ whenever $Y \subseteq X$ follows from A1 and the rule (Axiom A7, to be given) that if $X \rightarrow Y$ then $X \longrightarrow\!\!\!\!\!\rightarrow Y$. A6 is more restrictive than its counterpart transitivity axiom, A3. The more general statement, that $X \longrightarrow\!\!\!\!\!\rightarrow Y$ and $Y \longrightarrow\!\!\!\!\!\rightarrow Z$ imply $X \longrightarrow\!\!\!\!\!\rightarrow Z$ is false. For instance, we saw in Example 5.17 that $C \longrightarrow\!\!\!\!\!\rightarrow HR$, and surely $HR \longrightarrow\!\!\!\!\!\rightarrow H$ is true, yet $C \longrightarrow\!\!\!\!\!\rightarrow H$ is false. To compensate partially for the fact that A6 is weaker than A3, we use a stronger version of A5 than the analogous augmentation axiom for functional dependencies, A2. We could have replaced A2 by: $X \rightarrow Y$ and $V \subseteq W$ imply $WX \rightarrow VY$, but for functional dependencies, this rule is easily proved from A1, A2, and A3.

Our last two axioms relate functional and multivalued dependencies.

A7: If $X \rightarrow Y$ then $X \twoheadrightarrow Y$.

A8: If $X \twoheadrightarrow Y$, $Z \subseteq Y$, and for some W disjoint from Y, we have $W \rightarrow Z$, then $X \rightarrow Z$ also holds.

We shall not give a proof that axioms A1-A8 are sound and complete. Rather, we shall prove that some of the axioms are sound, that is, they follow from the definitions of functional and multivalued dependencies, leaving the soundness of the rest of the axioms, as well as a proof that any valid inference can be made using the axioms (completeness of the axioms), for an exercise.

Let us begin by proving A6, the transitivity axiom for multivalued dependencies. Suppose in some relation r over set of attributes U, $X \twoheadrightarrow Y$ and $Y \twoheadrightarrow Z$ hold, but $X \twoheadrightarrow Z - Y$ does not hold. Then there are tuples t and s in r, where $t[X] = s[X]$, but the tuple u, where $u[X] = t[X]$, $u[Z-Y] = t[Z-Y]$, and $u[U-X-(Z-Y)] = s[U-X-(Z-Y)]$, is not in r. Since $X \twoheadrightarrow Y$ holds, it follows that the tuple v, where $v[X] = t[X]$, $v[Y] = s[Y]$, and $v[U-X-Y] = t[U-X-Y]$, is in r. Now v and s agree on Y, so since $Y \twoheadrightarrow Z$, it follows that r has a tuple w, where $w[Y] = s[Y]$, $w[Z] = v[Z]$, and $w[U-Y-Z] = s[U-Y-Z]$.

We claim that $w[X] = t[X]$, since on attributes in $Z \cap X$, w agrees with v, which agrees with t. On attributes of $X-Z$, w agrees with s, and s agrees with t on X. We also claim that $w[Z-Y] = t[Z-Y]$, since w agrees with v on $Z-Y$, and v agrees with t on $Z-Y$. Finally, we claim that $w[V] = s[V]$, where $V = U-X-(Z-Y)$. In proof, surely w agrees with s on $V-Z$, and by manipulating sets we can show $V \cap Z = (Y \cap Z) - X$. But w agrees with v on Z, and v agrees with s on Y, so w agrees with s on $V \cap Z$ as well as on $V-Z$. Therefore w agrees with s on V. If we look at the definition of u, we now see that $w = u$. But we claimed that w is in r, so u is in r, contrary to our assumption. Thus $X \twoheadrightarrow Z - Y$ holds after all, and we have proved A6.

Now let us prove A8. Suppose we have a relation r in which $X \twoheadrightarrow Y$ and $W \rightarrow Z$ hold, where $Z \subseteq Y$, and $W \cap Y$ is empty, but $X \rightarrow Z$ does not hold. Then there are tuples s and t in r such that $s[X] = t[X]$, but $s[Z] \neq t[Z]$. By $X \twoheadrightarrow Y$ applied to s and t, there is a tuple u in r, such that $u[X] = t[X] = s[X]$, $u[Y] = t[Y]$, and $u[U-X-Y] = s[U-X-Y]$. Since $W \cap Y$ is empty, u and s agree on W. As $Z \subseteq Y$, u and t agree on Z. Since s and t disagree on Z, it follows that u and s disagree on Z. But this contradicts $W \rightarrow Z$; since u and s agree on W but disagree on Z. We conclude that $X \rightarrow Z$ did not fail to hold, and we have verified rule A8.

The remainder of the proof of the following theorem is left as an exercise.

Theorem 5.9: (Beeri, Fagin, and Howard [1977]). Axioms A1-A8 are sound and complete for functional and multivalued dependencies. That is, if D is a set of functional and multivalued dependencies over a set of attributes U, and D^+ is the set of functional and multivalued dependencies that follow logically from D, in the sense that every relation over U that satisfies D also satisfies the dependencies in D^+, then D^+ is exactly the set of dependencies that follow from D by A1-A8. □

Additional Inference Rules for Multivalued Dependencies

There are a number of other rules that are useful for making inferences about functional and multivalued dependencies. Of course, the union, pseudotransitivity, and decomposition rules for functional dependencies mentioned in Lemma 5.1 still apply. Some other rules are:

1. *(union rule for multivalued dependencies)* If $X \rightarrow\!\!\!\rightarrow Y$ and $X \rightarrow\!\!\!\rightarrow Z$, then $X \rightarrow\!\!\!\rightarrow YZ$.

2. *(pseudotransitivity rule for multivalued dependencies)* If $X \rightarrow\!\!\!\rightarrow Y$ and $WY \rightarrow\!\!\!\rightarrow Z$, then $WX \rightarrow\!\!\!\rightarrow Z - WY$.

3. *(mixed pseudotransitivity rule)* If $X \rightarrow\!\!\!\rightarrow Y$ and $XY \rightarrow Z$, then $X \rightarrow Z - Y$.

4. *(decomposition rule for multivalued dependencies)* If $X \rightarrow\!\!\!\rightarrow Y$ and $X \rightarrow\!\!\!\rightarrow Z$ hold, then $X \rightarrow\!\!\!\rightarrow Y \cap Z$, $X \rightarrow\!\!\!\rightarrow Y - Z$, and $X \rightarrow\!\!\!\rightarrow Z - Y$ hold.

We leave the proof that these rules are valid as an exercise; the techniques are similar to those used for A6 and A8 above.

We should note that the decomposition rule for multivalued dependencies is weaker than the corresponding rule for functional dependencies. The latter rule allows us to deduce immediately from $X \rightarrow Y$ that $X \rightarrow A$ for each attribute A in Y. The rule for multivalued dependencies only allows us to conclude $X \rightarrow\!\!\!\rightarrow A$ from $X \rightarrow\!\!\!\rightarrow Y$ if we can find some Z such that $X \rightarrow\!\!\!\rightarrow Z$, and either $Z \cap Y = A$ or $Y - Z = A$.

However, the decomposition rule for multivalued dependencies, along with the union rule, allows us to make the following statement about the sets Y such that $X \rightarrow\!\!\!\rightarrow Y$ for a given X.

Theorem 5.10: If U is the set of all attributes, then we can partition $U - X$ into sets of attributes $Y_1, Y_2, \ldots, Y_k$, such that if $Z \subseteq U - X$, then $X \rightarrow\!\!\!\rightarrow Z$ if and only if Z is the union of some of the Y_i's.

Proof: Start the partition of $U - X$ with all of $U - X$ in one block. Suppose at some point we have partition $W_1, \ldots, W_n$, and $X \rightarrow\!\!\!\rightarrow W_i$ for

r $i = 1, 2, \ldots, n$. If $X \longrightarrow\!\!\!\!\!\rightarrow Z$, and Z is not the union of some W_i's, replace each W_i such that $W_i \cap Z$ and $W_i - Z$ are both nonempty by $W_i \cap Z$ ad $W_i - Z$. By the decomposition rule, $X \longrightarrow\!\!\!\!\!\rightarrow W_i \cap Z$ and $X \longrightarrow\!\!\!\!\!\rightarrow W_i - Z$. As e cannot partition a finite set of attributes indefinitely, we shall eventually nd that every Z such that $X \longrightarrow\!\!\!\!\!\rightarrow Z$ is the union of some blocks of the partion. By the union rule, X multidetermines the union of any set of blocks.

We call the above sets $Y_1, \ldots, Y_k$ constructed for X from a set of inctional and multivalued dependencies D the *dependency basis* for X (with espect to D) Note that if $X \to Y_i$, then Y_i must consist of only one attribute y the decomposition rule for functional dependencies and axiom A7 every functional dependency is a multivalued dependency).

xample 5.18: In Example 5.17 we observed that $C \longrightarrow\!\!\!\!\!\rightarrow HR$. Thus, by the omplementation rule, $C \longrightarrow\!\!\!\!\!\rightarrow TSG$. We also know that $C \to T$. Thus, by xiom A7, $C \longrightarrow\!\!\!\!\!\rightarrow T$. By the decomposition rule, $C \longrightarrow\!\!\!\!\!\rightarrow SG$. One can check aat no single attribute except T or C itself is multidetermined by C. Thus ae dependency basis for C is T, HR, SG. □

:losures of Functional and Multivalued Dependencies

given a set of functional and multivalued dependencies D, we would like to nd the set D^+ of all functional and multivalued dependencies logically nplied by D. We can compute D^+ by starting with D and applying axioms A1-A8 until no more new dependencies can be derived. However, this rocess can take time that is exponential in the size of D. Often we only vant to know whether a particular dependency $X \to Y$ or $X \longrightarrow\!\!\!\!\!\rightarrow Y$ follows rom D, if for example, we should wish to eliminate redundant dependenies.

To test whether a multivalued dependency $X \longrightarrow\!\!\!\!\!\rightarrow Y$ holds, it suffices to letermine the dependency basis of X and see whether $Y - X$ is the union of ome sets thereof. Referring to Example 5.18, we know that $C \longrightarrow\!\!\!\!\!\rightarrow CTSG$, ince TSG is the union of T and SG. Also, $C \longrightarrow\!\!\!\!\!\rightarrow HRSG$, but $C \longrightarrow\!\!\!\!\!\rightarrow TH$ is alse, since TH intersects block HR of the dependency basis, yet TH does aot include all of HR. In computing the dependency basis of X with espect to D, a theorem of Beeri [1977] tells us it suffices to compute the pasis with respect to the set of multivalued dependencies M, where M conists of

L.   all multivalued dependencies in D, and

2.   for each functional dependency $X \to Y$ in D, the set of multivalued dependencies $X \longrightarrow\!\!\!\!\!\rightarrow A_1, \ldots, X \longrightarrow\!\!\!\!\!\rightarrow A_n$, where $Y = A_1 \cdots A_n$ for attributes $A_1, \ldots, A_n$.

Another theorem of Beeri [1977] gives us a way to extract the nonrivial functional dependencies from the dependency basis computed according to the set of multivalued dependencies M. It can be shown tha if X does not include A, then $X \to A$ holds if and only if

1. A is a singleton set of the dependency basis for X according to the se of dependencies M, and

2. there is some set of attributes Y, excluding A, such that $Y \to Z$ is in D and A is in Z.

Furthermore, Beeri [1977] gives a polynomial time algorithm for computing the dependency basis of X with respect to M.

Algorithm 5.5: Computing the Dependency Basis.

Input: A set of multivalued dependencies M over set of attributes U, and a set $X \subseteq U$.

Output: The dependency basis for X with respect to M.

Method:

1. Let T be the set of sets $Z \subseteq U$ such that for some $W \twoheadrightarrow Y$ in M, we have $W \subseteq X$, and Z is either $Y - X$ or $U - X - Y$.

2. Until T consists of a disjoint collection of sets, find a pair of sets Z_1 and Z_2 in T that are not disjoint and replace them by $Z_1 - Z_2$, $Z_2 - Z_1$ and $Z_1 \cap Z_2$, throwing away the empty set, in case one of Z_1 and Z_2 is contained in the other. Let S be the final collection of sets.

3. Until no more changes can be made to S, look for dependencies $V \twoheadrightarrow W$ in M and a set Y in S such that Y intersects W but not V. Replace Y by $Y \cap W$ and $Y - W$ in S.

4. The final collection of sets S is the dependency basis for X. □

Since steps (2) and (3) only cause sets to be split, and they terminate when no more splitting can be done, it is straightforward that Algorithm 5.5 takes time that is polynomial in the size of M and U. In fact, careful implementation allows the algorithm to run in time proportional to the number of dependencies in M times the cube of the number of attributes in U. A proof of this fact and a proof of correctness for Algorithm 5.5 can be found in Beeri [1977].

Lossless Joins

Algorithm 5.2 helps us determine when a decomposition of a relation scheme R into $(R_1, \ldots, R_k)$ has a lossless join, on the assumption that the only dependencies to be satisfied by the relations for R are functional. The algorithm can be generalized when there are multivalued dependencies as follows.

1.   Construct the table of a's and b's as in Algorithm 5.2.

2.   Construct a collection of tables by taking some table T already constructed and either (a) identifying two symbols because of a functional dependency, as in Algorithm 5.2, or (b) taking a multivalued dependency $X \longrightarrow\!\!\!\!\!\rightarrow Y$ and two rows t_1 and t_2 of some table such that $t_1[X]=t_2[X]$, and adding the row u, where $u[X]=t_1[X]$, $u[Y]=t_1[Y]$, and $u[R-X-Y]=t_2[R-X-Y]$, if u is not already in T.

3.   As there are no new a's or b's created, there can be only a finite number of such tables. If any of them has a row of all a's then the join is lossless, otherwise not.

However, in the case of a decomposition of R into two schemes, there is a far simpler test for a lossless join.

Theorem 5.11: Let R be a relation scheme and $\rho=(R_1, R_2)$ a decomposition of R. Let D be a set of functional and multivalued dependencies on the attributes of R. Then ρ has a lossless join if and only if $R_1 \cap R_2 \longrightarrow\!\!\!\!\!\rightarrow R_1-R_2$ (or equivalently, by the complementation rule, $R_1 \cap R_2 \longrightarrow\!\!\!\!\!\rightarrow R_2-R_1$).

Proof: ρ has a lossless join if and only if for any relation r satisfying D, and any two tuples t and s in r, the tuple u such that $u[R_1]=t[R_1]$ and $u[R_2]=s[R_2]$ is in r if it exists. But u exists if and only if $t[R_1 \cap R_2] = s[R_1 \cap R_2]$. Thus, the condition that u is always in r is exactly the condition that $R_1 \cap R_2 \longrightarrow\!\!\!\!\!\rightarrow R_1-R_2$, or equivalently, $R_1 \cap R_2 \longrightarrow\!\!\!\!\!\rightarrow R_2-R_1$. ⧠

Note that by axiom A7 Theorem 5.5 implies Theorem 5.11 when the only dependencies are functional, but Theorem 5.5 says nothing at all if there are multivalued dependencies that must be satisfied.

5.6 Fourth Normal Form

There is a generalization of Boyce-Codd normal form, called fourth normal form, that applies to relation schemes with multivalued dependencies. Let R be a relation scheme and D the set of dependencies applicable to R. We say R is in *fourth normal form* if whenever there is a multivalued dependency $X \longrightarrow\!\!\!\!\!\rightarrow Y$, where Y is not empty or a subset of X, and XY does not include all the attributes of R, then X includes a key for R. The definition of "key" has not changed because multivalued dependencies are present; it still means a set of attributes that functionally determines R.

Note that if D includes only functional dependencies, then whenever R is in fourth normal form it is in Boyce-Codd normal form. For then $X \longrightarrow\!\!\!\!\!\rightarrow Y$ must mean that $X \rightarrow Y$. Suppose R is not in Boyce-Codd normal form, because there is some functional dependency $X \rightarrow A$, where X does not include a key. If $XA=R$, then surely X includes a key. Therefore XA does not include all attributes, and a violation of fourth normal form, with $X \rightarrow A$ as a special case of $X \longrightarrow\!\!\!\!\!\rightarrow Y$, is immediate.

We can find a decomposition of R into $\rho = (R_1, \ldots, R_k)$, such that ρ has a lossless join with respect to D, and each R_i is in fourth normal form, as follows. We start with ρ consisting only of R, as in Algorithm 5. (decomposition into Boyce-Codd normal form). If there is a relation scheme in ρ not in fourth normal form with respect to D projected onto S, then there must be in S a dependency $X \twoheadrightarrow Y$, where X does not include key for S, Y is not empty or a subset of X, and $XY \neq S$. We may assume X and Y are disjoint, since $X \twoheadrightarrow Y - X$ follows from $X \twoheadrightarrow Y$ using A1, A1 and the decomposition rule. Then replace S by $S_1 = XY$ and $S_2 = S - Y$ which must be two relation schemes with fewer attributes than S. By Theorem 5.7, since $S_1 \cap S_2 \twoheadrightarrow S_1 - S_2$, the join of S_1 and S_2 is lossless with respect to D projected onto S.

We leave it as an exercise that the repeated decomposition as above produces a set of relation schemes that has a lossless join with respect to D.† The only important detail remaining is to determine how one computes given R, D, and $S \subseteq R$, the set of dependencies that hold in S, that is, the projection of D onto S. It is a theorem of Aho, Beeri, and Ullman [1979] that this set of dependencies can be computed as follows.

1.   Compute D^+.

2.   For each $X \to Y$ in D^+, if $X \subseteq S$, then $X \to Y \cap S$ holds in S.‡

3.   For each $X \twoheadrightarrow Y$ in D^+, if $X \subseteq S$, then $X \twoheadrightarrow Y \cap S$ holds in S.

4.   No other dependencies for S may be deduced from the fact that holds for R.

Example 5.19: Let us reinvestigate the *CTHRSG* relation scheme first introduced in Example 5.14. We have several times noted the minimal cover

$$C \to T \qquad CS \to G$$
$$HR \to C \qquad HS \to R$$
$$HT \to R$$

for the pertinent functional dependencies. It turns out that one multivalued dependency

$$C \twoheadrightarrow HR$$

together with the above functional dependencies, allows us to derive all the multivalued dependencies that we would intuitively feel are valid. We saw for example, that $C \twoheadrightarrow HR$ and $C \to T$ imply $C \twoheadrightarrow SG$. We also know that $HR \to CT$, so $HR \twoheadrightarrow CT$. By the complementation rule, $HR \twoheadrightarrow SG$. That is

---

† We shall discuss later how to find the projection of a set of functional and multivalued dependencies.

‡ Note that since $X \to Y \cap S$ is also in D^+, this rule is equivalent to the rule for projecting functional dependencies given earlier.

o say, given an hour and room, there is an associated set of student-grade pairs, namely the students enrolled in the course meeting in that room and that hour, paired with the grades they got in that course. The reader is invited to explore further the set of multivalued dependencies following from the given five functional dependencies and one multivalued dependency.

To place relation scheme $CTHRSG$ in fourth normal form, we might start with $C \twoheadrightarrow HR$, which violates the fourth normal form conditions since C does not include a key. Recall that SH is the only key for $CTHRSG$. We decompose $CTHRSG$ into CHR and $CTSG$. The relation scheme CHR has key HR. The multivalued dependency $C \twoheadrightarrow HR$ does not violate fourth normal form for CHR, since the left and right sides together include all the attributes of CHR. No other functional or multivalued dependency projected onto CHR violates fourth normal form, so we need not decompose CHR any further.

Such is not the case for $CTSG$. The only key is CS, yet we see the multivalued dependency $C \twoheadrightarrow T$, which follows from $C \rightarrow T$. We therefore split $CTSG$ into CT and CSG. These are both in fourth normal form with respect to their projected dependencies, so we have obtained the decomposition CHR, CT, and CSG, which has a lossless join and all relation schemes in fourth normal form.

It is interesting to note that when in Example 5.14 we decomposed $CTHRSG$ into Boyce-Codd normal form using only functional dependencies, we obtained these three relation schemes and the scheme CHS as well. When we ignore the multivalued dependency $C \twoheadrightarrow HR$, the decomposition into three schemes $\rho = (CHR, CT, CSG)$ does not necessarily have a lossless join, but if we are allowed to use $C \twoheadrightarrow HR$, it is easy to prove by Theorem 5.11 that their join is lossless. As an exercise, the reader should find a relation r for $CTHRSG$ such that $m_\rho(r) \neq r$, yet r satisfies all the given functional dependencies (but not $C \twoheadrightarrow HR$, of course). $\square$

Embedded Multivalued Dependencies

One further complication that enters when we try to decompose a relation scheme R into fourth normal form is that there may be certain multivalued dependencies that we expect to hold when we project any plausible relation r for R onto a subset $X \subseteq R$, yet we do not expect these dependencies to hold in r itself. Such a dependency is said to be *embedded* in R, and we must be alert, when writing down all the constraints that we believe hold in relations r for R, not to ignore an embedded multivalued dependency. Incidentally, embedded functional dependencies never occur; it is easy to show that if $Y \rightarrow Z$ holds when any plausible relation r for R is projected onto X, then $Y \rightarrow Z$ also holds in R. The same is not true for multivalued dependencies, as the following example shows.

Example 5.20: Suppose we have the attributes C (course), S (student), P (prerequisite), and Y (year in which the student took the prerequisite). The only nontrivial functional or multivalued dependency is $SP \rightarrow Y$, so we may decompose $CSPY$ into CSP and SPY; the resulting schemes are apparently in fourth normal form.

The multivalued dependency $C \rightarrow\!\!\!\rightarrow S$ does not hold. For example, we might have in relation r for $CSPY$ the tuples

$$
\begin{array}{llll}
CS402 & \text{Jones} & CS311 & 1978 \\
CS402 & \text{Smith} & CS401 & 1979
\end{array}
$$

yet not find the tuple

$$
\begin{array}{llll}
CS402 & \text{Jones} & CS401 & 1979
\end{array}
$$

Presumably Jones took CS401, since it is a prerequisite, but perhaps he did not take it in 1979. Similarly, $C \rightarrow\!\!\!\rightarrow P$ does not hold in $CSPY$.

However, if we project any legal r for $CSPY$ onto CSP, we would expect $C \rightarrow\!\!\!\rightarrow S$ and, by the complement rule, $C \rightarrow\!\!\!\rightarrow P$ to hold, provided every student enrolled in a course is required to have taken each prerequisite for the course at some time. Thus $C \rightarrow\!\!\!\rightarrow S$ and $C \rightarrow\!\!\!\rightarrow P$ are embedded multivalued dependencies for R. As a consequence, CSP is really not in fourth normal form, and it should be decomposed into CS and CP. This replacement avoids repeating the student name once for each prerequisite of a course in which he is enrolled.

It is interesting to observe that the decomposition $\rho = (CS, CP, SPY)$ has a lossless join if we acknowledge that $C \rightarrow\!\!\!\rightarrow S$ is an embedded dependency for CSP. For then, given any relation r for $CSPY$ that satisfies $SP \rightarrow Y$ and the dependency $C \rightarrow\!\!\!\rightarrow S$ in CSP, we can prove that $m_\rho(r) = r$. Yet we could not prove this assuming only the functional dependency $SP \rightarrow Y$; the reader can as an exercise find a relation r satisfying $SP \rightarrow Y$ (but not the embedded dependency) such that $m_\rho(r) \neq r$. □

Exercises

5.1: Suppose we have a database for an investment firm, consisting of the following attributes: B (broker), O (office of a broker), I (investor), S (stock), Q (quantity of stock owned by an investor), and D (dividend paid by a stock), with the following functional dependencies: $S \rightarrow D$, $I \rightarrow B$, $IS \rightarrow Q$, and $B \rightarrow O$.

a)   Find a key for the relation scheme $R = BOSQID$.

b)   How many keys does relation scheme R have? Prove your answer.

    c)   Find a lossless join decomposition of R into Boyce-Codd normal form.

    d)   Find a decomposition of R into third normal form, having a lossless join and preserving dependencies.

5.2: Suppose we choose to represent the relation scheme R of Exercise 5.1 by the two schemes $ISQD$ and IBO. What redundancies and anomalies do you forsee?

5.3: Suppose we instead represent R by SD, IB, ISQ, and BO. Does this decomposition have a lossless join?

5.4: Suppose we represent R of Exercise 5.1 by ISQ, IB, SD, and ISO. Find minimal covers for the dependencies (from Exercise 5.1) projected onto each of these relation schemes. Find a minimal cover for the union of the projected dependencies. Does this decomposition preserve dependencies?

5.5: In the database of Exercise 5.1, replace the functional dependency $S \rightarrow D$ by the multivalued dependency $S \twoheadrightarrow D$. That is, D now represents the dividend "history" of the stock.

    a)   Find the dependency basis of I.

    b)   Find the dependency basis of BS

    c)   Find a fourth normal form decomposition of R.

5.6: Complete the proof of Theorem 5.5 by providing a formal proof that in the row for R_1, an a is entered if and only if $R_1 \cap R_2 \rightarrow A$.

5.7: Complete the proof of Lemma 5.5 by showing that if $r \subseteq s$ then $\pi_{R_i}(r) \subseteq \pi_{R_i}(s)$.

5.8: In Example 5.10 we contended that $Z \rightarrow C$ does not imply $CS \rightarrow Z$. Prove this contention.

5.9: At the end of Section 5.3 it was claimed that $\rho = (AB, CD)$ was a dependency-preserving, but not lossless join decomposition of $ABCD$, given the dependencies $A \rightarrow B$ and $C \rightarrow D$. Verify this claim.

5.10: Complete the proof of Theorem 5.9 by showing that axioms $A1-A8$ are sound and complete.

5.11: Verify the union, pseudotransitivity, and decomposition rules for multivalued dependencies.

5.12: Give a formal proof of Lemma 5.6(a), that the iteration of lossless join decompositions itself has a lossless join. Also prove Lemma 5.6(b), that the addition of schemes (with no new attributes) to a lossless join decomposition preserves the lossless join property.

*5.13: Verify the contention in Example 5.20, that there is a relation r satis fying $SP \rightarrow Y$, such that $\pi_{CS}(r) \bowtie \pi_{CP}(r) \bowtie \pi_{SP}(r) \neq r$. Check tha your relation does not satisfy $C \rightarrow\!\!\!\rightarrow S$ in CSP.

*5.14: An interesting prospect is that after decomposing a relation R into th set of schemes $(R_1, \ldots, R_k)$, we may pose queries as if R existed i the database, taking a join of R_i's, when necessary to implement th query. Suppose a query involves the set of attributes $S \subseteq R$. Develo as efficient an algorithm as you can to find a smallest subset o $\{R_1, \ldots, R_k\}$ whose union includes S, and such that the join of thi subset is lossless.

*5.15: Another approach to the problem posed in the previous exercise is t retain the decomposition tree constructed by Algorithm 5.3, when A is decomposed into Boyce-Codd normal form. If a query involves th set of attributes S, find a node in the tree with a minimal number o descendant leaves, such that the relation schemes at these leave include all attributes in S. (Note that the join of the descendants o any node in the tree must be lossless.) Give an efficient algorithm fo finding such a node.

*5.16: Give the relative advantages and disadvantages of the approaches out lined in Exercises 5.14 and 5.15.

**5.17: Show that it is NP-complete to determine

    a)   Whether a relation scheme has a key of size k or less.

    b)   If a relation scheme is in Boyce-Codd normal form.

Bibliographic Notes

Functional dependencies were first studied by Codd [1970]. Axioms fo functional dependencies were first given by Armstrong [1974]; the axiom used here are from Beeri, Fagin, and Howard [1977]. Algorithm 5.1, th computation of the closure of a set of attributes, is from Bernstein [1977] Algorithm 5.2, the lossless join test, is from Aho, Beeri, and Ullma [1978]. The special case of the join of two relations, Theorem 5.5, wa shown in the "if" direction by Delobel and Casey [1972] and in the oppo site direction by Rissanen [1977].

Third normal form is defined in Codd [1970] and Boyce-Codd norma form in Codd [1972a]. The dependency-preserving decomposition int third normal form, Algorithm 5.4, is from Bernstein [1976], although h there uses a "synthetic" approach, designing a scheme without startin with a universal relation. Theorem 5.8, giving a third normal form decom position with lossless join and dependency preservation is from Biskup Dayal, and Bernstein [1979]. A related result appears in Osborn [1977] The equivalence problem for decompositions of a given relation was solve by Beeri, Mendelzon, Sagiv, and Ullman [1979]. Ling and Tompa [1978 eneralize the notion of third normal form to account for redundancies cross several different relation schemes.

Multivalued dependencies were invented independently by Fagin 1977], Delobel [1978], and Zaniolo [1976], although the earliest manifes-ation of the concept is in Delobel's thesis in 1973. The axioms for mul-valued dependencies are from Beeri, Fagin, and Howard [1977]. The dependence of subsets of these axioms was considered by Mendelzon 1977], while Biskup [1978] shows that if one does not assume a universal lation, then without the complementation axiom, they form a sound and mplete set. The dependency basis and Algorithm 5.5 are from Beeri 1977]. Hagihara et al. [1979] gives a more efficient test whether a given ultivalued dependency is implied by others. Embedded multivalued ependencies were considered by Fagin [1977], Delobel [1978] and Tanaka, ambayashi, and Yajima [1978].

Multivalued dependencies are a special case of the *join dependency,* here a join of *n* relations, for some $n \geq 2$, is required to be lossless (Ris-nen [1978]). The multivalued dependency is the case $n=2$. Fagin 1979a] provides a "fifth" normal form, based on the absence of nontrivial in dependencies within a relation scheme, and Fagin [1979b] goes beyond is, showing that it is possible to decompose relation schemes so that the nly dependencies remaining are functional dependencies of a nonkey attri-ute on a key and constraints that reflect the limited sizes of domains for ttributes.

Lossless join testing, given multivalued and functional dependencies as considered in Aho, Beeri, and Ullman [1978], while Maier, Mendel-on, and Sagiv [1979] handle the case where join dependencies are cluded. Liu and Demers [1978] provide a more efficient lossless join test.

The problem of adequacy of a decomposition has been considered rom several points of view. Arora and Carlson [1978] regard the lossless in and dependency-preservation conditions as a notion of adequacy, while issanen [1977] defines a decomposition to have *independent components* if here is a one-to-one correspondence between relations for the universal cheme that satisfy the dependencies, and projections of relations that atisfy the projected dependencies. Maier, Mendelzon, Sadri, and Ullman 1979] show that these notions are equivalent for functional dependencies, ut not for multivalued dependencies.

The condition on relations corresponding to a join dependency on heir relation schemes has been studied by Nicolas [1978] and Mendelzon nd Maier [1979].

The problem discussed in Exercises 5.14 and 5.15, finding lossless oins to cover the attributes of a query, has been handled in Schenk and inkert [1977] and Kambayashi [1978].

A number of problems concerning the subject matter of this chapter have been shown NP-complete. For example, testing whether a relation scheme is in Boyce-Codd normal form is NP-complete (Beeri and Bernstein [1979]), and finding a minimal sized key for a relation scheme is also (Lucchesi and Osborn [1978]). A useful survey of relational database design, with additional references, is Beeri, Bernstein, and Goodman [1978].

6
Query Optimization

High level query languages such as those discussed in Chapter 4 allow us to write queries that take a great deal of time to execute, and whose execution time can be reduced greatly if the query language processor rephrases the query before executing it. Such improvements are commonly called "optimizations," although the rephrased query need not be optimal over all possible ways of implementing the query, and the terms "amelioration" or "improvement" would be more appropriate. In this chapter we shall explore methods of optimizing relational algebra expressions and relational calculus expressions. Especially important is the handling of expressions that involve a join or Cartesian product, followed by a selection operator and perhaps a projection, since these are among the most common types of queries and most susceptible to optimization. We saw in Section 4.3 how one such query could be significantly simplified.

6.1 General Remarks About Optimization

One might first ask why certain queries take a long time to execute. The greatest offender, at least in query languages based on the relational model, is the query that involves a join or Cartesian product, or an equivalent construct in relational calculus. For example, consider the expression $AB \times CD$.† If we are to produce the value of this product, we have no choice but to run through one file, say the file for relation AB, and for each record r (representing a tuple) run through the entire file for CD and concatenate r with each record of the latter file.

If we are clever, we shall load main memory with as many blocks of the AB file as we can, while still leaving room for one block of the CD file. Then we can concatenate each AB record in main memory with the records on a block of the CD file, as it is brought into memory. This strategy reduces the number of times we must load each CD block, by a factor equal

---

†In this chapter, we shall frequently use a list of attributes as the name of a relation with those attributes.

to the number of AB records that can fit in main memory. If

1.   relations AB and CD have n_{AB} and n_{CD} records, respectively,

2. b_{AB} and b_{CD} records of AB and CD, respectively, fit on a block, and

3.   main memory can hold m blocks,

then the total number of block accesses is n_{AB}/b_{AB} to read file AB, an $(n_{CD}/b_{CD})(n_{AB}/(m-1)b_{AB})$ to read file CD the necessary $n_{AB}/(m-1)b$ times, a total of

$$\frac{n_{AB}}{b_{AB}}(1+\frac{n_{CD}}{(m-1)b_{CD}})$$

accesses. If $n_{AB}=n_{CD}=10,000$, $b_{AB}=b_{CD}=5$, and $m=100$, the number accesses is 42,400. At 20 block accesses per second, the evaluation of th Cartesian product takes 35 minutes.

If the query asks that the Cartesian product be printed, there is litt better that we can do. However, often the entire query will be somethi like the QUEL program:

> range of x is AB
> range of y is CD
> retrieve $(x.A)$
> > where $x.B=y.C$ and $y.D=99$

In algebraic terms, this query is asking for the value of

$$\pi_A(\sigma_{B=C \wedge D=99}(AB \times CD))$$

If we migrate the selection $D=99$ inside the Cartesian product to get

$$\pi_A(\sigma_{B=C}(AB \times \sigma_{D=99}(CD)))$$

we save considerably, as the following analysis shows. We can also tak advantage of the fact that $\sigma_{B=C}$ converts the Cartesian product into a equijoin; we can write the above formula as

$$\pi_A(AB \underset{B=C}{\bowtie} \sigma_{D=99}(CD))$$

Let us now consider how to evaluate the above formula. Should th file for CD be indexed on D, a few block accesses suffice to find thos records with $D=99$. Even if there is no index, we need only scan the C file once to find all records with $D=99$, which takes n_{CD}/b_{CD} bloc accesses, or 2000 accesses using the above numbers for n_{CD} and b_{CD}. the resulting set of records fits in main memory, we can scan the AB fil once, taking another 2000 accesses to compute the produc $AB \times \sigma_{D=99}(CD)$, and at the same time perform the selection $\sigma_{B=C}$ and th projection onto A. However, if the AB file has an index on B, we can tak into account the selection $\sigma_{B=C}$ when we perform the Cartesian produc and for each *CD* record $(c, 99)$, obtain those *AB* records with $B=c$, in a few block accesses.

We see that the reorganized query takes no more than one tenth the block accesses of the original, given our sample file sizes; if certain indices are present, and there are not too many records with $D=99$, the time to execute the restated query could be many orders of magnitude less than the original.

Implementation of Joins

The implementation of a join, especially a non-equijoin like $AB \underset{B<C}{\bowtie} CD$, can present pitfalls similar to that encountered with the Cartesian product. Even an equijoin, such as $AB \underset{B=C}{\bowtie} CD$ requires careful thought in its implementation. If we run through *AB* and *CD* records looking for $B=C$ we take as much time as the Cartesian product $AB \times CD$. However, we can use indices on *B* and/or *C*, created on the spot if necessary, to make the process take time that is linear in the size of the two relations. As another approach, we could sort *AB* on *B* and sort *CD* on *C* and then scan each file once looking for equality on the *B* and *C* fields. Depending on the data type of *B* and *C*, the sort could be linear in the relation sizes or take on the order of $n \log n$ time to sort a file of *n* records.† If there are comparatively few different values for attributes *B* and *C*, index creation can be done primarily in main memory and therefore takes time proportional to the relation sizes. We would probably prefer index creation to sorting in this situation.

General Strategies for Optimization

The above informal example suggests some general strategies for optimization, and there are others that we might consider as well.

1. *Perform selections as early as possible.* This transformation on queries, more than any other, is responsible for saving orders of magnitude in execution time, since it tends to make intermediate results of the evaluation small.

2. *Preprocess files appropriately* before performing a join (or equivalently, a Cartesian product followed by a selection). We mentioned two important preprocessing ideas: sorting the files and creating indices. Each allows common values in the two files to be associated efficiently.

---

† The reader should refer to Knuth [1973], e.g., for a description of efficient methods for sorting files in secondary storage.

3. *Look for common subexpressions in an expression.* If the result of the common subexpression is not a large relation, and it can be read from secondary memory in much less time than it takes to compute it, it is advantageous to precompute the common subexpression once. Subexpressions involving a join that cannot be modified by moving a selection inside it generally fall into this category. It is interesting to observe that common subexpressions will appear frequently when the query is expressed in terms of views, since to execute the query we must substitute an expression for the view.

4. *Cascade selections and projections.* A sequence of these operations, each taking only one operand, can be performed all at once while we scan through the file for the operand.

5. *Combine projections with a binary operation that precedes or follows it.* There is no need to run through a file just to eliminate certain fields, if we can eliminate those fields either as we create the file, or at the first time we use the file.

6. *Combine certain selections with a prior Cartesian product to make a join.* As we have seen, a join, especially an equijoin, can be considerably cheaper than a Cartesian product of the same relations. When the result of a Cartesian product $R \times S$ is the argument of a selection, and that selection involves the logical "and" of comparisons between attributes of R and S, the product and selection are really a join. Note that a comparison involving no attribute of R or no attribute of S can be moved ahead of the product, which is even better than converting the product to a join.

6.2 Algebraic Manipulation

Most of the above strategies involve transforming algebraic expressions. A good place to begin a study of optimization is therefore by cataloging some of the algebraic laws that apply to the relational algebra operators. We envision a query processor that begins by building a parse tree for an algebraic expression. The query language itself might be a pure relational algebra language, like ISBL, or it might be a language like SQUARE or SEQUEL, with certain algebraic features, in which case the parse of a query might yield a tree in which some of the operators are relational algebra operators, and others are operators special to the language. Yet again, the query language might be a relational calculus language whose calculus-like expressions are translated into algebraic expressions. For example, the QUEL optimizer, to be discussed in the next section, begins by assuming a Cartesian product of relations $R_1 \times R_2 \times \cdots \times R_k$ if the applicable range statements are of the form range of t_i is R_i

for $i = 1, 2, \ldots, k$. Then the where-clause of the QUEL query is replaced by a selection, and the components mentioned in the retrieve-clause are obtained by a projection.

Equivalence of Expressions

Before we can "optimize" expressions we must understand clearly when two expressions are equivalent. First, let us recall that there are two definitions of relations in use (see Section 4.1), and they have somewhat different mathematical properties. The first viewpoint is that a relation is a set of k-tuples for a fixed k, and two relations are equal if and only if they are the same sets of tuples. The second viewpoint is that a relation is a set of mappings from a set of attribute names to values. Two relations are deemed equal if they are the same set of mappings. A relation in the first sense can be converted to a relation in the second sense by providing attribute names for the columns. We can convert from the second definition of relation to the first by picking a fixed order for the attributes.

We shall here use only the second definition, that a relation is a set of mappings from attributes to values. The justification is that existing query languages all allow, or even require, names for columns in a relation. More importantly, in any application of which we are aware, the order in which the columns of a table are printed is not significant, as long as each column is labeled by the proper attribute name. Where possible, we adopt names for attributes of a relation that is the result of an algebraic expression, from the names of attributes for the expression's arguments. We also require that names be provided for the result of a union or set difference.

An expression in relational algebra whose operands are relation variables $R_1, R_2, \ldots, R_k$, plus possible constant relations, defines a mapping from k-tuples of relations $(r_1, r_2, \ldots, r_k)$, where r_i is a relation of the arity appropriate to R_i, to a single relation, the relation that results when we substitute each r_i for R_i and evaluate the expression. Two expressions E_1 and E_2 are *equivalent,* written $E_1 \equiv E_2$ if they represent the same mappings, that is, when we substitute the same relations for identical names in the two expressions, we get the same result. With this definition of equivalence, we can list some useful algebraic transformations.

Laws Involving Joins and Cartesian Products

1. *Commutative laws for joins and products.* If E_1 and E_2 are relational expressions, and F is a condition on attributes of E_1 and E_2,† then

---

† We refer to an attribute by its name. If two or more attributes of the same name A exist, we denote them $R.A$, $S.A$, and so on, to distinguish one from another in a condition such as F.

$$E_1 \underset{F}{\bowtie} E_2 \equiv E_2 \underset{F}{\bowtie} E_1$$

$$E_1 \bowtie E_2 \equiv E_2 \bowtie E_1$$

$$E_1 \times E_2 \equiv E_2 \times E_1$$

Let us prove the first of these, the commutative law for joins. Let E_1 have attributes $A_1, \ldots, A_n$ and E_2 have attributes $B_1, \ldots, B_m$; we do not assume the A's and B's are distinct. Let r_1 and r_2 be arbitrary relations for E_1 and E_2 respectively. Then the value of $E_1 \underset{F}{\bowtie} E_2$ is the set of mappings ν from $A_1, \ldots, A_n, B_1, \ldots, B_m$ to values, such that there are mappings μ_1 and μ_2 in r_1 and r_2, respectively, for which

a) $\nu[A_i] = \mu_1[A_i]$, for $i = 1, 2, \ldots, n$,

b) $\nu[B_i] = \mu_2[B_i]$, for $i = 1, 2, \ldots, m$, and

c)   the condition F becomes true when we substitute $\nu[C]$ for each attribute name C in F.

If we express the value of $E_2 \underset{F}{\bowtie} E_1$ in this style, we see it is exactly the same set, proving the equivalence. Note that if we viewed relations as tuples rather than mappings, the join, natural join, and Cartesian product operations would not be commutative, since the order of components in the resulting relations would be of significance.

2.   *Associative laws for joins and products.* If E_1, E_2, and E_3 are relational expressions, and F_1 and F_2 are conditions, then

$$(E_1 \underset{F_1}{\bowtie} E_2) \underset{F_2}{\bowtie} E_3 \equiv E_1 \underset{F_1}{\bowtie} (E_2 \underset{F_2}{\bowtie} E_3)$$

$$(E_1 \bowtie E_2) \bowtie E_3 \equiv E_1 \bowtie (E_2 \bowtie E_3)$$

$$(E_1 \times E_2) \times E_3 \equiv E_1 \times (E_2 \times E_3)$$

We leave the verification of these laws as easy exercises.

Laws Involving Selections and Projections

The cascade of several projections can be combined into one. We express this fact by:

3.   *Cascade of projections.*

$$\pi_{A_1, \ldots, A_n}(\pi_{B_1, \ldots, B_m}(E)) \equiv \pi_{A_1, \ldots, A_n}(E)$$

Note that the attribute names $A_1, \ldots, A_n$ must be among the B_i's for the cascade to be legal.

Similarly, the cascade of selections can be combined into one selection that checks for all conditions at once, as expressed by:

4.   *Cascade of selections.*

$$\sigma_{F_1}(\sigma_{F_2}(E)) \equiv \sigma_{F_1 \wedge F_2}(E)$$

5.   *Commuting selections and projections.*

$$\sigma_F(\pi_{A_1, \ldots, A_n}(E)) \equiv \pi_{A_1, \ldots, A_n}(\sigma_F(E))$$

More generally, if condition F also involves attributes $B_1, \ldots, B_m$ that are not among $A_1, \ldots, A_n$, then

$$\pi_{A_1, \ldots, A_n}(\sigma_F(E)) \equiv$$
$$\pi_{A_1, \ldots, A_n}(\sigma_F(\pi_{A_1, \ldots, A_n, B_1, \ldots, B_m}(E)))$$

6.   *Commuting selection with Cartesian product.* If all the attributes mentioned in F are attributes of E_1, then

$$\sigma_F(E_1 \times E_2) \equiv \sigma_F(E_1) \times E_2$$

As a useful corollary, if F is of the form $F_1 \wedge F_2$, where F_1 involves only attributes of E_1, and F_2 involves only attributes of E_2, we can use rules (1), (4) and (6) to obtain

$$\sigma_F(E_1 \times E_2) \equiv \sigma_{F_1}(E_1) \times \sigma_{F_2}(E_2)$$

Moreover, if F_1 involves only attributes of E_1, but F_2 involves attributes of both E_1 and E_2, we can still assert

$$\sigma_F(E_1 \times E_2) \equiv \sigma_{F_2}(\sigma_{F_1}(E_1) \times E_2)$$

thereby pushing part of the selection ahead of the product.

7.   *Commuting selection with a union.* If we have an expression $E = E_1 \cup E_2$, we may assume the attributes of E_1 and E_2 have the same names as those of E, or at least, that there is a given correspondence that associates each attribute of E with a unique attribute of E_1 and a unique attribute of E_2. Thus we may write

$$\sigma_F(E_1 \cup E_2) \equiv \sigma_F(E_1) \cup \sigma_F(E_2)$$

If the attribute names for E_1 and/or E_2 actually differ from those of E, then the formulas F on the right must be modified to use the appropriate names.

8.   *Commuting selection with a set difference.*

$$\sigma_F(E_1 - E_2) \equiv \sigma_F(E_1) - \sigma_F(E_2)$$

As in (7), if the attribute names of E_1 and E_2 differ, we must replace the attributes in F on the right by the corresponding names for E_1. Note also that the selection $\sigma_F(E_2)$ is not necessary; we could replace it by E_2 if we wished. However, it is usually at least as efficient to perform the selection, and in many cases, $\sigma_F(E_2)$ is much easier to compute than E_2, because the former is a much smaller set than the latter.

We shall not state the laws for pushing a selection ahead of a join, since a join can always be expressed as a Cartesian product followed by a selection, and, in the case of the natural join, a projection. The rules for passing a selection ahead of a join thus follow from rules (4), (5), and (6).

The rules for moving a projection ahead of a Cartesian product or union are similar to rules (6) and (7). However, note that there is no general way to move a projection ahead of a set difference.

9.   *Commuting a projection with a Cartesian product.* Let E_1 and E_2 be two relational expressions. Let $A_1, \ldots, A_n$ be a list of attributes, of which $B_1, \ldots, B_m$ are attributes of E_1, and the remaining attributes, $C_1, \ldots, C_k$, are from E_2. Then

$$\pi_{A_1, \ldots, A_n}(E_1 \times E_2) \equiv \pi_{B_1, \ldots, B_m}(E_1) \times \pi_{C_1, \ldots, C_k}(E_2)$$

10.   *Commuting a projection with a union.*

$$\pi_{A_1, \ldots, A_n}(E_1 \cup E_2) \equiv \pi_{A_1, \ldots, A_n}(E_1) \cup \pi_{A_1, \ldots, A_n}(E_2)$$

As in rule (7), if the names of attributes for E_1 and/or E_2 differ from those in $E_1 \cup E_2$, we must replace $A_1, \ldots, A_n$ on the right by the appropriate names.

An Algorithm for Optimizing Relational Expressions

We can apply the above laws to "optimize" relational expressions. The resulting "optimized" expressions obey the principles set down in Section 6.1, although they are in no sense guaranteed to be optimal over all equivalent expressions. We shall attempt to move selections and projections as far down the parse tree of the expression as we can, although we want a cascade of these operations to be organized into one selection followed by one projection. We also group selections and projections with the preceding binary operation, such as union, Cartesian product, or set difference, where possible.

Some special cases occur when a binary operation has operands that are selections and/or projections applied to leaves of the tree. We must consider carefully how the binary operation is to be done, and in some cases we wish to incorporate the selection or projection with the binary operation. For example, if the binary operation is union, we can incorporate selections and projections below it in the tree with no loss of efficiency, as we must copy the operands anyway to form the union. However, if the binary operation is Cartesian product, with no following selection to make it an equijoin, we would prefer to do selection and projection first, leaving the result in a temporary file, as the size of the operand files greatly influences the time it takes to execute a full Cartesian product.

The output of our algorithm is a *program,* consisting of the following kinds of steps.

1. the application of a single selection or projection,

2. the application of a selection and projection, or

3. the application of a Cartesian product, union, or set difference to two operands, perhaps preceded by selections and/or projections applied to one or both operands, and possibly followed by these operations.

We assume steps (1) and (2) are implemented by a pass through the operand relation, creating a temporary relation. Steps of type (3) are implemented by applying selection and/or projection to each tuple of operand relations, if appropriate, each time the operand tuple is accessed, and applying the following selection and/or projection, if appropriate, to each tuple generated as part of the resulting relation. The result goes into a temporary relation.

Algorithm 6.1: Optimization of Relational Expressions.

Input: A tree representing an expression of relational algebra.

Output: A program for evaluating that expression.

Method:

1. Use rule (4) to separate each selection $\sigma_{I_1 \wedge \cdots \wedge I_n}(E)$ into the cascade $\sigma_{I_1}(...(\sigma_{I_n}(E))...)$.

2. For each selection, use rules (4)-(8) to move the selection as far down the tree as possible.

3. For each projection, use rules (3), (9), (10), and the generalized rule (5) to move the projection as far down the tree as possible. Note that rule (3) causes some projections to disappear, while the generalized rule (5) splits a projection into two projections, one of which can be migrated down the tree if possible. Also, eliminate a projection if it projects an expression onto all its attributes.

4. Use rules (3)-(5) to combine cascades of selections and projections into a single selection, a single projection, or a selection followed by a projection. Note that this alteration may violate the heuristic "do projection as early as possible," but a moment's reflection will serve to convince one that it is more efficient to do all selections, then all

projections, in one pass over a relation than it is to alternate selections and projections in several passes.

5. Partition the interior nodes of the resulting tree into *groups,* as follows. Every interior node representing a binary operator ($\times$, $\cup$, or $-$) is in a group along with any of its immediate ancestors that are labeled by a unary operator (σ or π). Also include in the group any chain of descendants labeled by unary operators and terminating at a leaf, except in the case that the binary operator is a Cartesian product and not followed by a selection that combines with the product to form an equijoin.

6. Produce a program consisting of a step to evaluate each group in any order such that no group is evaluated prior to its descendant groups. □

Example 6.1: Let us consider a library database consisting of the following relations.

> BOOKS(TITLE, AUTHOR, PNAME, LC_NO)
> PUBLISHERS(PNAME, PADDR, PCITY)
> BORROWERS(NAME, ADDR, CITY, CARD_NO)
> LOANS(CARD_NO, LC_NO, DATE)

The attributes used above that are not self explanatory are:

> PNAME   = publisher's name
> LC_NO   = Library of Congress number
> PADDR   = the street address of a publisher
> PCITY   = the city in which a publisher is located
> CARD_NO = library card number
> DATE   = the date on which a book was borrowed.

To keep track of books, we might suppose that there is a view XLOANS that contains additional information about books borrowed. XLOANS is the natural join of BOOKS, BORROWERS, and LOANS, which might, for example, be defined as

$$\pi_S(\sigma_F(\text{LOANS, BORROWERS, BOOKS}))$$

where

> F = BORROWERS.CARD_NO=LOANS.CARD_NO
> $\wedge$ BOOKS.LC_NO=LOANS.LC_NO

while

> S = TITLE, AUTHOR, PNAME, LC_NO, NAME,
> ADDR, CITY, CARD_NO, DATE

We might wish to list the books that been borrowed before some date in the distant past, say 1/1/78 by:

$$\pi_{TITLE}(\sigma_{DATE \leqslant 1/1/78}(XLOANS))$$

After substituting for XLOANS, the expression above has the parse tree, shown in Fig. 6.1.

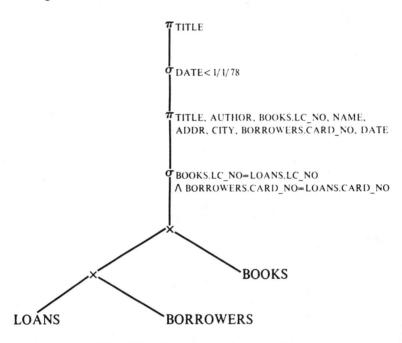

Fig. 6.1. Parse tree of expression.

The first step of the optimization is to split the selection F into two, with conditions BOOKS.LC_NO = LOANS.LC_NO and BORROWERS.CARD_NO = LOANS.CARD_NO, respectively. Then we move each of the three selections as far down the tree as possible. The selection $\sigma_{DATE < 1/1/78}$ moves below the projection and the two selections by rules (4) and (5). This selection then applies to the product (LOANS × BORROWERS) × BOOKS. Since DATE is the only attribute mentioned by the selection, and DATE is an attribute only of LOANS, we can replace

$$\sigma_{DATE < 1/1/78}((LOANS \times BORROWERS) \times BOOKS)$$

by

$$(\sigma_{DATE < 1/1/78}(LOANS \times BORROWERS)) \times BOOKS$$

then by

$$((\sigma_{\text{DATE}<1/1/78}(\text{LOANS})) \times \text{BORROWERS}) \times \text{BOOKS}$$

We have now moved this selection as far down as possible. The selection with condition BOOKS.LC_NO = LOANS.LC_NO cannot be moved below either Cartesian product, since it involves an attribute of BOOKS and an attribute not belonging to BOOKS.† However, the selection on BORROWERS.CARD_NO = LOANS.CARD_NO can be moved down to apply to the product of $\sigma_{\text{DATE}<1/1/78}(\text{LOANS}) \times \text{BORROWERS}$. Note that LOANS.CARD_NO is the name of an attribute of $\sigma_{\text{DATE}<1/1/78}(\text{LOANS})$ since it is an attribute of LOANS.

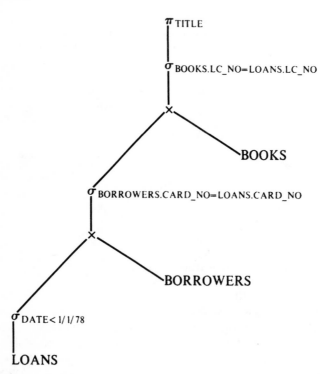

Fig. 6.2 Tree with selections lowered and projections combined.

Next, we can combine the two projections into one, π_{TITLE}, by rule (3). The resulting tree is shown in Fig. 6.2. Then by the extended rule (5) we can replace π_{TITLE} and $\sigma_{\text{BOOKS.LC\_NO=LOANS.LC\_NO}}$ by the cascade

---

† We could use the commutative and associative laws of products and then move this selection down one level, but then we could not move the selection on BORROWERS.CARD NO = LOANS.CARD_NO down.

π TITLE
σ BOOKS.LC_NO=LOANS.LC_NO
π TITLE, BOOKS.LC_NO, LOANS.LC_NO

We apply rule (9) to replace the last of these projections by π TITLE,BOOKS.LC_NO applied to BOOKS and π LOANS.LC_NO applied to the left operand of the higher Cartesian product in Fig. 6.2.

The latter projection interacts with the selection below it by the extended rule (5) to produce the cascade

π LOANS.LC_NO
σ BORROWERS.CARD_NO=LOANS.CARD_NO
π LOANS.LC_NO, BORROWERS.CARD_NO, LOANS.CARD_NO

The last of these projections passes through the Cartesian product by rule (9) and passes partially through the selection $\sigma_{DATE < 1/1/78}$ by the extended rule (5). We then discover that in the expression

π LOANS.LC_NO, LOANS.CARD_NO, DATE (LOANS)

the projection is superfluous, since all attributes of LOANS are mentioned. We therefore eliminate this projection. The final tree is shown in Fig. 6.3. In that figure we have indicated groups of operators by dashed lines. Each of the Cartesian products is effectively an equijoin, when combined with the selection above it. In particular, the selection on LOANS and the projection of BORROWERS below the first product can be successfully combined with that product. Obviously a program executing Fig. 6.3 will perform the lower group of operations before the upper. □

6.3 The QUEL Decomposition Algorithm

We shall now consider in some detail the optimization algorithm used in the QUEL processor. This algorithm, while it is tailored to a calculus based language, has application to algebraic languages as well. In addition to using the idea of the previous section, that selections should be performed as early as possible, the QUEL algorithm has at least one important idea not encountered so far, the judicious decomposition of Cartesian products and joins.

Consider the QUEL query

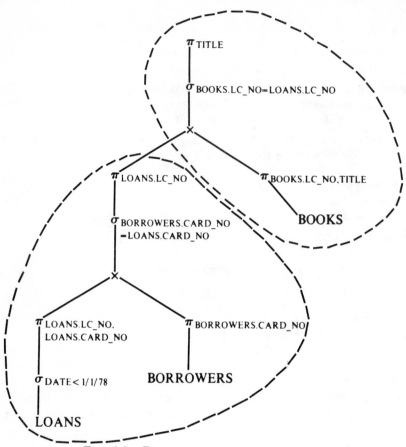

Fig. 6.3. Final tree with grouping of operators.

range of t_1 is R_1

.

.

.

range of t_k is R_k
retrieve (α)
where F

where α is a list of attributes belonging to the relations $R_1, \ldots, R_k$, and F is a condition on attributes of the R_i's. The formal meaning of this query is given by the expression

$$\pi_\alpha(\sigma_F(R_1 \times R_2 \times \cdots \times R_k)) \qquad (6.1)$$

Note that some of the R_i's may be the same relation. Since the attributes in α and F are associated with t_i's, we can determine which copy of a relation is referred to by terms in α and F, should two or more of the R_i's be the same.

If we use the algebraic manipulation techniques of the previous section, we can move the selection and projection as far inside the Cartesian products as possible. However, we can also take advantage of the associativity and commutativity of the product to pick a good ordering for these products. There is a nonobvious technique used in the QUEL optimizer that helps select a good order for the products. To motivate this method, suppose we wish to take the natural join of relations AB, BC, and CD, where A, B, C, and D are attribute names. By the commutative and associative laws, we can join in any order we wish. The worst thing we could do is to start by taking $AB \bowtie CD$, since this join is really a Cartesian product. Better is to take the join $AB \bowtie BC$, and then join the result with CD. Starting with $BC \bowtie CD$ is an equally good way because of the symmetry of the situation.

To analyze the relative merits of approaches to this problem, let us assume for simplicity that each of the three relations has n tuples, and that when we take a natural join of relations with one common attribute, the resulting relation has $p \geqslant 1$ times the maximum of the number of tuples in either operand. We also assume that the domain of each attribute is sufficiently small that we can create conveniently an index on any attribute, and the time to create the index is a constant c times the number of tuples in the relation. We also assume that the time to compute a join, once the necessary indices have been created, is d times the size of the result.

Then the time to compute $AB \bowtie BC$ is cn to create an index for one of the two relations on attribute B, and dpn to compute the join. Then to compute $(AB \bowtie BC) \bowtie CD$ takes cn to compute an index on C for CD, the smaller relation, then dp^2n to compute the join. The total time is thus

$$2cn + d(p^2 + p)n \qquad (6.2)$$

There is another way we might compute the join. First create an index for AB on B and for CD on C. This step takes time $2cn$. Then run through the tuples (b_1, c_1) of BC. Use the indices to find all the tuples in AB with B-value b_1 and all the tuples in CD with C-value c_1. Add the Cartesian product of these sets to produce the value of the join $AB \bowtie BC \bowtie CD$. This step takes time proportional to the number of tuples produced, which is $0(p^2n)$, so the entire join is computed in time

$$2cn + ep^2n \qquad (6.3)$$

for some constant e.

If we consider the details of this process and the details of computing a join like $AB \bowtie BC$, we realize that d and e are about the same. As long as $d=e$, the value of (6.2) exceeds that of (6.3). Furthermore, our second approach uses no extra space, except for indices, while taking two joins requires space for a temporary relation.

Thus we see the desirability of implementing a natural join of three relations, two of which have sets of attributes that do not overlap, by *decomposing* the relation that overlaps the other two, that is, by running through the tuples of the latter relation. If we now reconsider the basic QUEL query, formula (6.1) at the beginning of the section, we see that we have a Cartesian product, not a join. However, suppose condition F is the logical "and" of one or more terms, and each term involves the equality of two attributes. Then the Cartesian product can be viewed as a collection of equijoins. We can apply the decomposition approach to equijoins just as we did to natural joins, simply by taking account of the fact that the attributes providing the link between two relations have different names in the two relations. Of course the selection condition F need not be the logical "and" of terms; it could involve "or" and "not." Moreover, F might involve comparisons other than = among attributes. These situations complicate the decomposition algorithm to be described, but the method works very well on a large fraction of the queries, those for which selection conditions are the logical "and" of equalities among attributes and constant values.

The Connection Graph

Suppose we have the Cartesian product of relations $R_1, \ldots, R_k$, to which a selection $\sigma_{F_1 \wedge \cdots \wedge F_n}$ is to be applied. Each F_i may be an arbitrarily complex condition, but we assume it is not the logical "and" of two or more conditions. We construct a graph $G\dagger$ with a node for each R_i, $i = 1, 2, \ldots, k$, and a node for each occurrence of a constant in any of the F_j's. Two occurrences of the same relation name or the same constant are given two distinct nodes. For each F_j, find the set of relations R_i such that F_j involves one or more attributes of R_i, and find the set of constants appearing in F_j. These sets of relations and constants determine a set of nodes of G. Create an "edge," which in general is a hyperedge, connecting this set of nodes, and label the hyperedge F_j. In the common case where F_j is of the form $R_1.A = a$ or $R_i.A = R_m.B$, the "edge" will be a true edge connecting two nodes, although in more complex cases the "edge" will connect many nodes. A useful observation is that since each occurrence of a constant has a unique node in G, the nodes for constants have only one edge incident upon them.

Example 6.2: Let us reconsider the relations of Example 6.1 and suppose we have the QUEL program of Fig. 6.4. That is, print all persons who have

---

† Technically, G is a *hypergraph* since its "edges" are in general *hyperedges*, that is, sets of one, two, or more nodes, rather than being pairs of nodes as in an ordinary graph. In the most important and frequent case, the edges will turn out to be pairs of nodes.

range of *t* is BOOKS
range of *s* is PUBLISHERS
range of *u* is BORROWERS
range of *v* is LOANS
retrieve (*u*.NAME)
    where *t*.LC_NO = *v*.LC_NO
    and *u*.CARD_NO = *v*.CARD_NO
    and *t*.PNAME = *s*.PNAME
    and *u*.CITY = *s*.PCITY

Fig. 6.4. A QUEL program.

borrowed a book published in the same city that they live in. In algebra, this query is expressed by the Cartesian product

BOOKS×PUBLISHERS×BORROWERS×LOANS

to which we apply the selection indicated in the where-clause and then project onto BORROWERS.NAME. The connection graph for this query is shown in Fig. 6.5. Note that all edges in Fig. 6.5 are hyperedges that happen to be ordinary edges, that is, sets of two nodes. □

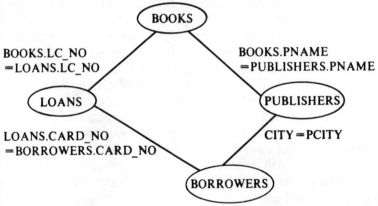

Fig. 6.5. The Connection graph for the program of Fig. 6.4.

Decomposing the Connection Graph

The execution of a query can be viewed as a series of operations on the connection graph, where each operation has the effect of constructing a new relation, used as an intermediate step in the evaluation of the query, as well as changing the graph itself. At the end of this process, the graph disappears, and the relation denoted by the query has been constructed. During the construction, some nodes will symbolize new relations, and others will symbolize new "constants," which may be single tuples or sets of tuples (relations) that we assume are small sets and which we treat as if they were single tuples.

In what follows, we use doubly circled nodes to symbolize constants in this generalized sense. Constant nodes will always have only one incident edge. If an edge runs between two nodes and has a label of the form $A = B$, we call it a *simple edge*. The constructions we use to decompose the connection graph are the following.

1. *Instantiation.* A simple edge connecting a relation to a constant is in effect a selection. We execute the selection as follows. Suppose we have a simple edge between nodes n and m, where n represents a relation r and m represents a constant that is a single value v. We eliminate node m in such a way that the relation denoted by the entire graph does not change. If the constant is a single value v, the label of a simple edge will be $A = v$, for some A that is an attribute for relation r. We eliminate the edge (n, m), eliminate the node m, and make node n represent the relation $\sigma_{A=v}(r)$. This relation is deemed to be "small," so node n now represents a constant that is a small relation.

2. *Dissection.* Suppose we have a node n representing a relation r, and let there be k edges incident upon n. To evaluate the relation denoted by the entire graph, we may run through the tuples t in r and for each t create a graph that denotes the relation of the original graph, with r replaced by $\{t\}$. To do so, let e be an "edge" (which may be incident upon more than two nodes) incident upon n, and let F be the formula associated with e. Replace each occurrence in F of an attribute A of r, by the constant $t[A]$, and for each component of t mentioned in F, create a node representing the constant value of that component. Let e be incident upon all nodes created, but let e no longer be incident upon node n. Do the same for each edge incident upon n and then eliminate node n. After evaluating the resulting graph to yield a relation s, take the Cartesian product $s \times \{t\}$. Take the union of these Cartesian products over all tuples t in r. The result is the relation denoted by the original graph.

We can now give the complete decomposition algorithm for a connection graph. The algorithm is recursive, calling itself on modified graphs and returning a relation that is the value denoted by the graph on which it is called. To get the value of a given query, we construct its connection graph, call the decomposition algorithm on the graph, and then project the resulting relation, which is a selection applied to a product, onto the components mentioned in the retrieve clause. As an exercise, the reader can modify the algorithm to perform projections as soon as possible.

Algorithm 6.2: Query Evaluation by Decomposition.

Input: A connection graph G.

Output: The relation $\text{REL}(G)$ denoted by G.

Method: We choose to apply either instantiation or dissection according to the following preferences.

1. While an instantiation is possible, do it.

2. If no instantiation is possible, select a node n for dissection. In selecting n consider only nodes with an incident edge. Give first priority to nodes all of whose incident edges are simple. If there are one or more such nodes, select one representing a "small" constant relation (these are created during instantiations); if there are none, select a node whose elimination will disconnect the graph,† and if there are none of these, select any node with only simple incident edges. If there are no nodes with only simple incident edges, select any node, giving priority to nodes representing "small" relations and then to nodes whose deletion breaks the graph into two or more connected components.

3. Having selected a node n for dissection, for each tuple t in the relation denoted by n, proceed to replace that node by nodes denoting constant values, as described in the definition of dissection, to obtain a graph G_t. Apply Algorithm 6.2 recursively to G_t, to produce a relation $\text{REL}(G_t)$. Return $\cup (\text{REL}(G_t) \times \{t\})$. Note that the method provided by Algorithm 6.2 to evaluate G_t works for arbitrary t, so the algorithm must be run on only one "generic" G_t. Also, usually t will range over a small set, so the union may not be very large.

4. We reach here only if after using instantiation wherever possible, there are no edges remaining. In this case return the Cartesian product of the relation represented by each of the remaining nodes. □

Example 6.3: Let us apply Algorithm 6.2 to the connection graph of Fig. 6.5. No instantiation is possible, so we turn to a dissection. All edges are simple, but there are no "small" relations, and no node disconnects the graph. Therefore we are free to dissect at any node, and let us choose BOOKS. Letting t be an arbitrary tuple in BOOKS we replace Fig. 6.5 by the graph of Fig. 6.6; there is, in principle, one such graph for each t, although their decompositions are essentially the same, and we need only work on one to discover how to evaluate the relation denoted by any one of them.

---

† It is not trivial to find such nodes, but algorithms exist for finding them; see Aho et al. [1974]. Note that the preference for disconnecting a graph corresponds to our preference to run through the tuples of BC in the join $AB \bowtie BC \bowtie CD$, as discussed in the beginning of the section.

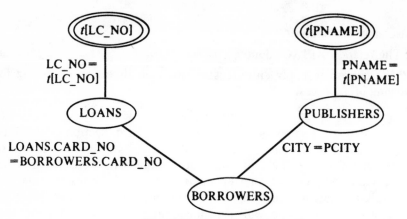

Fig. 6.6. A typical graph G_t.

We now apply Algorithm 6.2 to the graph G_t represented in Fig. 6.6. There are two applications of instantiation to be made, to the constant nodes $t[$LC_NO$]$ and $t[$PNAME$]$. As a result of these operations, the nodes of Fig. 6.6 representing LOANS and PUBLISHERS now represent the "small" relations

$$L_1 = \sigma_{\text{LC\_NO}=t[\text{LC\_NO}]}(\text{LOANS}).$$
$$P_1 = \sigma_{\text{PNAME}=t[\text{PNAME}]}(\text{PUBLISHERS})$$

The resulting graph is shown in Fig. 6.7.

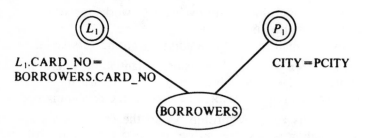

Fig. 6.7. A typical graph G_t after instantiation.

We now prefer to pick either of the "small" relations L_1 or P_1 on which to do dissection; say we pick L_1. Let u be a typical tuple of L_1. We create for each u the graph G_{tu} as shown in Fig. 6.8(a). Instantiation then enables us to replace BORROWERS by the relation

$$B_1 = \sigma_{\text{CARD\_NO}=u[\text{CARD\_NO}]}(\text{BORROWERS})$$

as shown in Fig. 6.8(b). A last dissection, say on B_1, produces a graph G_{tuv}, as in Fig. 6.8(c), for each v in B_1. Then an application of instantiation leaves us with the graph of Fig. 6.8(d), where

$$P_2 = \sigma_{\text{PCITY}=v[\text{CITY}]}(P_1)$$

By step (4) of Algorithm 6.2, $\text{REL}(G_{tuv}) = P_2$. To obtain $\text{REL}(G_{tu})$ we take $\underset{v \text{ in } B_1}{\cup} (\text{REL}(G_{tuv}) \times \{v\})$. Note that B_1 is a "small" relation, and also that the actual value of B_1 depends on t and u. Then we obtain

$$\text{REL}(G_t) = \underset{u \text{ in } L_1}{\cup} (\text{REL}(G_{tu}) \times \{u\})$$

where L_1 is the relation from Fig. 6.7. Note that L_1 depends on t, and $\text{REL}(G) = \underset{t \text{ in } \text{BOOKS}}{\cup} (\text{REL}(G_t) \times \{t\})$. □

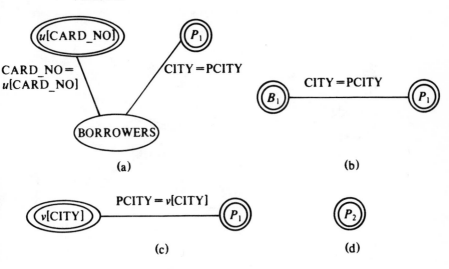

(a) (b) (c) (d)

Fig. 6.8. Further steps in the decomposition process.

Example 6.4: Suppose we have the QUEL program

    range of t is BOOKS
    range of u is LOANS
    range of v is BORROWERS
    retrieve (v.NAME, t.TITLE)
        where v.CARD_NO = u.CARD_NO
        and u.LC_NO = t.LC_NO

That is, print the persons borrowing books and the titles of the books they borrowed. The connection graph G is shown in Fig. 6.9. The first step must be a dissection, and we prefer LOANS, since it alone disconnects the graph, and there are no "small" relations. For each u in LOANS we obtain the graph G_u shown in Fig. 6.10(a). Two instantiations yield the graph of Fig. 6.10(b), where

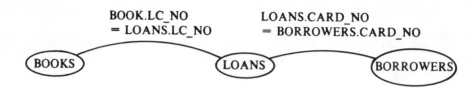

Fig. 6.9 A connection graph G.

$B_1 = \sigma_{LC\_NO=u[LC\_NO]}(\text{BOOKS})$
$B_2 = \sigma_{CARD\_NO = u[CARD\_NO]} (\text{BORROWERS})$

Now we obtain $\text{REL}(G_u) = B_1 \times B_2$, and

$$\text{REL}(G) = \bigcup_{u \text{ in LOANS}} (\text{REL}(G_u) \times \{u\})$$

answering the query. □

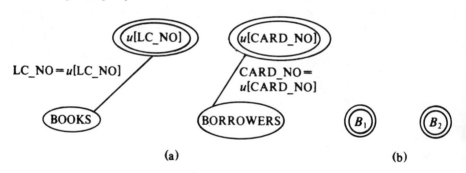

(a)   (b)

Fig. 6.10. Decomposition steps.

6.4 Exact Optimization for a Subset of Relational Queries.

We have seen some sensible ways of transforming queries into equivalent queries that can be evaluated more efficiently than the originals. However, can we be sure that the transformed queries are "optimal"? That is, are they the most efficiently evaluatable of all equivalent queries? In general, we cannot be sure. For one thing, we have not been completely specific regarding the cost measure we use to determine the efficiency with which a given query can be evaluated. We did sketch in Section 6.1 what we believe to be the best algorithms for evaluating relations represented simply as files; but there are other representation techniques, for example, those we mentioned in Sections 4.6 and 4.7 in connection with System R and INGRES.

Even if we have a specific cost measure in mind, it is likely that the problem of finding the query of least cost equivalent to a given query is

ndecidable for most reasonable cost measures. While there is good reason
o believe that the methods of Sections 6.2 and 6.3 perform well in practice,
: is interesting to consider under what circumstances we can achieve exact
ptimization. There is, it turns out, an extensive class of queries, called
"conjunctive queries," for which the equivalence problem is decidable
although it is NP-complete). It is also possible, for these queries, to
ninimize the number of joins and/or Cartesian products needed for their
valuation. On the reasonable assumption that under any possible cost
neasure an optimal query will have a minimum number of joins/products,
it becomes possible to find the optimal query equivalent to a given "con-
unctive query," even if we have to search among all those with a
ninimum number of joins/products. If we can assume that a plausible cost
neasure favors doing selections and projections as early as possible, our
search is further simplified; we have only to worry about the order in which
oins and products are to be done.

　　We are thus led to consider the equivalence problem for "conjunctive
queries." We shall give an algorithm to decide equivalence and then show
now it implies a way to minimize joins and/or products. We shall also
observe that any relational algebra expression involving Cartesian product,
equijoin, intersection, projection, and certain selections can be expressed as
conjunctive queries, so the considered class contains many of the most frequently encountered types of queries. In particular, it contains the select-
project-join core of relational algebra.

Conjunctive Queries

A *conjunctive query* is one that can be expressed in domain relational calculus as

$$\{a_1 \cdots a_n \mid (\exists b_1) \cdots (\exists b_m)(\psi(a_1, \ldots, a_n, b_1, \ldots, b_m, c_1, \ldots, c_r))\}$$

where the a's are domain variables or constants, the b's are domain variables, and the c's are constants, and ψ is of the form
$R_1(w_1) \wedge \cdots \wedge R_k(w_k)$. The R's are (not necessarily distinct) relation
names, and the w's are tuples composed of the a's, b's, and c's. The fact
that ψ must be a conjunction of terms gives the class of queries its name.

　　Conjunctive queries are a natural class to consider. For example,
compositions of SQUARE mappings are conjunctive queries. So are the
simple forms of QBE queries with which we introduced Section 4.7. The
retrieve-statement in QUEL and the SELECT-FROM-WHERE statement in
SEQUEL yield conjunctive queries whenever the where-clauses are the conjunction (logical and) of terms that equate two components of tuples or
equate a component to a constant.

Example 6.5: The query of Fig. 6.4, finding people who have borrowed a
book published in the city where they live, is a conjunctive query

expressable as

$$\{a_1 \mid (\exists b_1) \cdots (\exists b_9)(\text{BOOKS}(b_1 b_2 b_3 b_4) \wedge \text{PUBLISHERS}(b_3 b_5 b_6)$$
$$\wedge \text{LOANS}(b_7 b_4 b_8) \wedge \text{BORROWERS}(a_1 b_9 b_6 b_7))\}$$

See Example 6.1 for an indication of the names and order of the attributes for the four relations involved in the above query.

The query "print the title and date of all books borrowed on card number 12345" is expressed

$$\{a_1 a_2 \mid (\exists b_1)(\exists b_2)(\exists b_3)(\text{BOOKS}(a_1 b_1 b_2 b_3) \wedge \text{LOANS}('12345' b_3 a_2))\}$$

□

The Containment Relationship Between Queries

Recall from Section 6.2 that we defined queries $Q_1(R_1, \ldots, R_k)$ and $Q_2(R_1, \ldots, R_k)$ to be *equivalent*, written $Q_1 \equiv Q_2$, if whatever relations $r_1, \ldots, r_k$ we substitute for arguments $R_1, \ldots, R_k$, the resulting relations $Q_1(r_1, \ldots, r_k)$ and $Q_2(r_1, \ldots, r_k)$ are equal. We could also define Q_1 to be *contained in* Q_2, written $Q_1 \subseteq Q_2$, if for every $r_1, \ldots, r_k$ we have $Q_1(r_1, \ldots, r_k) \subseteq Q_2(r_1, \ldots, r_k)$. It happens that it is easier to test for equivalence of conjunctive queries by testing for containment twice, using the principle that

$$Q_1 \equiv Q_2 \text{ if and only if } Q_1 \subseteq Q_2 \text{ and } Q_2 \subseteq Q_1$$

Example 6.6: To get a feel for query containment, note that if $Q_1 = R_1 \cap R_2$ and $Q_2 = R_1 \cup R_2$, then $Q_1 \subseteq Q_2$, although $Q_1 \equiv Q_2$ and $Q_2 \subseteq Q_1$ are false. That is, the intersection of any two relations r_1 and r_2 is a subset of their union, although it is not generally true that $r_1 \cap r_2 = r_1 \cup r_2$ or $r_1 \cup r_2 \subseteq r_1 \cap r_2$, although these relationships happen to hold in the special case that r_1 and r_2 are the same relation.

Some other interesting containments that are not equivalences are:

$$\pi_S(R_1 \cap R_2) \subseteq \pi_S(R_1) \cap \pi_S(R_2)$$
$$\pi_S(R_1) - \pi_S(R_2) \subseteq \pi_S(R_1 - R_2)$$

□

Foldings

The test for containment of one conjunctive query Q_1 in another, Q_2, is based on the existence of a certain kind of mapping from the symbols used in Q_2 to those used in Q_1. Since the containment $Q_1 \subseteq Q_2$ is possible only if the relations defined by Q_1 and Q_2 are of the same arity, we may assume that

$$Q_1 = \{a_1 \cdots a_n \mid$$
$$(\exists b_1) \cdots (\exists b_m)(\psi_1(a_1, \ldots, a_n, b_1, \ldots, b_m, c_1, \ldots, c_k))\}$$

$$Q_2 = \{a'_1 \cdots a'_n \mid$$
$$(\exists b'_1) \cdots (\exists b'_r)(\psi_2(a'_1, \ldots, a'_n, b'_1, \ldots, b'_m, c'_1, \ldots, c'_s))\}$$

A *folding* from Q_2 to Q_1 is a mapping f from the symbols of Q_2 to the symbols of Q_1 such that:

1. $f(a'_i) = a_i$,

2. $f(c'_i) = c'_i$, and therefore, c'_i must be c_j for some j, †

3. $f(b'_i)$ is any of the a_j's, b_j's, or c_j's,

4. If $R(w)$ is any term of ψ_2, then $R(f(w))$ is a term of ψ_1, where f applied to tuple $w = d_1 \cdots d_j$ is defined by $f(d_1 d_2 \cdots d_j) = f(d_1)f(d_2) \cdots f(d_j)$.

Example 6.7: Let

$$Q_1 = \{a_1 a_2 \mid (\exists b_1)(\exists b_2)(R(a_1 b_1) \wedge S(b_2 a_2) \wedge R(b_2 c))\}$$

$$Q_2 = \{a_3 a_4 \mid (\exists b_3)(\exists b_4)(\exists b_5)(\exists b_6)$$
$$(R(b_3 b_5) \wedge R(a_3 b_6) \wedge R(b_4 c) \wedge S(b_4 a_4))\}$$

Then there is a folding f from Q_2 to Q_1 defined by:

i) $f(a_3) = a_1$ and $f(a_4) = a_2$, as required by rule (1).

ii) $f(c) = c$, as required by rule (2),

iii) $f(b_3) = a_1$, $f(b_4) = b_2$, $f(b_5) = b_1$, and $f(b_6) = b_1$. We can check that each term of Q_2 becomes a term of Q_1 when we replace each symbol d by $f(d)$. For example, $R(b_3 b_5)$ is a term of Q_2, $f(b_3 b_5) = a_1 b_1$, and $R(a_1 b_1)$ is a term of Q_1. It follows that $Q_1 \subseteq Q_2$. That is, whatever relations we substitute for R and S, the result of formula Q_1 will be a subset of the result of Q_2.

It is also true that $Q_2 \subseteq Q_1$, as we can demonstrate with the folding g defined by:

i) $g(a_1) = a_3$ and $g(a_2) = a_4$,

ii) $g(c) = c$,

iii) $g(b_1) = b_6$, and $g(b_2) = b_4$.

Since $Q_1 \supseteq Q_2$ and $Q_2 \supseteq Q_1$, it follows that $Q_1 \equiv Q_2$. □

We must now prove our claim about foldings, that one exists from Q_2 to Q_1 if and only if $Q_1 \subseteq Q_2$. We do so in the next two lemmas.

---

† In the case a'_i is a constant, rules (1) and (2) imply that a_i must be the same constant.

Lemma 6.1: If there is a folding from Q_2 to Q_1, then $Q_1 \subseteq Q_2$.

Proof: Let

$$Q_1 = \{a_1 \cdots a_n \mid$$
$$(\exists b_1) \cdots (\exists b_m)(\psi_1(a_1, \ldots, a_n, b_1, \ldots, b_m, c_1, \ldots, c_k))\}$$

$$Q_2 = \{a'_1 \cdots a'_n \mid$$
$$(\exists b'_1) \cdots (\exists b'_r)(\psi_2(a'_1, \ldots, a'_n, b'_1, \ldots, b'_r, c'_1, \ldots, c'_s))\}$$

and let f be a folding from Q_2 to Q_1. Suppose ψ_1 and ψ_2 involve relations $R_1, \ldots, R_j$, and when relations $r_1, \ldots, r_j$ are substituted for these, the tuple t is in the relation Q_1. We must show t is also in Q_2 when the same substitution for the R_i's is made. For t to be in Q_1, there must be some *valuation* v, that is, an assignment of value $v(d)$ to each symbol d of ψ such that

1. $v(a_1 \cdots a_n) = t$, and

2. if $R_i(w)$ is a term of ψ_1, then $v(w)$ is in r_i, where $v(d_1 \cdots d_l) = v(d_1) \cdots v(d_l)$. But then, if we use valuation $v'(d) = v(f(d))$ for each symbol d of ψ_2, we discover that t is in Q_2 also. That is, $v'(a'_1 \cdots a'_n) = v(f(a'_1 \cdots a'_n)) = v(a_1 \cdots a_n) = t$. Moreover, for each term $R_i(w)$ in ψ_2, $v'(w) = v(f(w))$. We know $R_i(f(w))$ is a term of ψ_1, since f is a folding. But $v(f(w))$ is in r_i, so $v'(w)$ is in r_i, proving that t is in Q_2. □

Lemma 6.2: If $Q_1 \subseteq Q_2$, then there is a folding from Q_2 to Q_1.

Proof: Let Q_1 and Q_2 be as defined in Lemma 6.1. Consider the a's, b's, and c's as distinct values, and let r_i be the relation $\{w \mid R_i(w)$ is a term of $\psi_1\}$. For example, if Q_1 is as in Example 6.7, with $R = R_1$ and $S = R_2$, then $r_1 = \{a_1b_1, b_2c\}$ and $r_2 = \{b_2a_2\}$. Note that a_1, a_2, b_1, b_2, and c are each regarded as constant values here.

When these r_i's are substituted for the R_i's in Q_1, it follows that the particular tuple $a_1 \cdots a_n$ is in Q_1. Since $Q_1 \subseteq Q_2$, this tuple must also be in the relation Q_2 when we substitute r_i for R_i in Q_2. Then there must be a valuation v of the symbols of Q_2 such that

i) $v(a'_1 \cdots a'_n) = a_1 \cdots a_n$, and

ii) for each term $R_i(w)$ in Q_2, $v(w)$ is a member of r_i. We claim that v must be a folding from Q_2 to Q_1, since (i) implies condition (1) of the folding definition, and (ii), together with the fact that the a's, b's, and c's are distinct "constants" implies conditions (2–4). □

Theorem 6.1: a) $Q_1 \subseteq Q_2$ if and only if there is a folding from Q_2 to Q_1.
b) $Q_1 \equiv Q_2$ if and only if there are foldings from Q_1 to Q_2 and from Q_2 to Q_1.

Proof: Immediate from Lemmas 6.1 and 6.2. □

Minimization of Conjunctive Queries

We can use Theorem 6.1 to help us determine, given a conjunctive query Q, the minimum-term conjunctive query equivalent to Q. By minimizing terms, we minimize the number of joins and/or products that must be taken to evaluate the query in the obvious way. As these are the most expensive operations in relational algebra, we see that minimizing terms of a conjunctive query is a good first step, although this step must be followed by other optimizations, such as doing selections and projections early, as discussed in the previous two sections.

It may come as a surprise that for each conjunctive query Q, there is a unique (up to renaming of symbols) conjunctive query Q_0 equivalent to Q and having the fewest possible terms. That is, any minimum-term query equivalent to Q must be Q_0, perhaps with some symbols replaced by other symbols. The proof of this fact involves viewing foldings not as mappings among symbols but among terms. If there is a folding f from Q_1 to Q_2, then each term $R(s)$ of Q_1 is mapped by f to a unique term $R(f(w))$ of Q_2.

Example 6.8: In Fig. 6.11 we see the two foldings f and g of Example 6.7, in their role as mappings from terms to terms. □

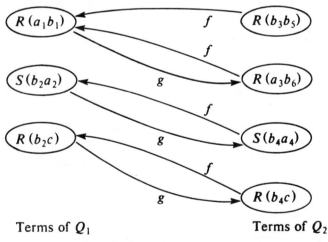

Terms of Q_1 Terms of Q_2

Fig. 6.11. Foldings as mappings on terms.

Another important observation is that the composition of two foldings is itself a folding. The reader should verify this assertion as an exercise. Thus, a folding such as f from Q_2 to Q_1, composed with folding g from Q_1 to Q_2 is a folding from Q_2 to itself. The folding gf from Q_2 to Q_2 shows that Q_2 with term $R(b_3b_5)$ deleted, which we may call Q_3, is equivalent to

Q_2, since the identity mapping is clearly a folding from Q_3 to Q_2. Note, incidentally, that Q_3 and Q_1 are one-to-one symbol renamings of one another. For example, a_1 in Q_1 corresponds to a_3 in Q_3, and b_1 in Q_1 corresponds to b_6 in Q_3. As b_3 and b_5 of Q_2 do not appear in Q_3, they do not need corresponding symbols in Q_1, which is significant, since otherwise we could not choose a unique corresponding symbol for a_1 and b_1. We are now prepared to prove the central theorem about conjunctive queries.

Theorem 6.2: For each conjunctive query Q there is a conjunctive query Q_0 equivalent to Q, such that Q_0 has as few terms as possible, and any other query Q'_0 equivalent to Q, having a minimal number of terms, and with no useless quantified variables, is a one-to-one symbol renaming of Q_0.

Proof: Suppose Q has two minimal-term equivalents Q_0 and Q'_0, each having no useless quantified variables. Then by Theorem 6.1 there are foldings f and g from Q_0 to Q'_0 and from Q'_0 to Q_0, respectively. Suppose f maps two terms of Q_0 to the same term of Q'_0. Then gf is a folding from Q_0 to itself that maps the terms of Q_0 to a proper subset of these terms. Since in the other direction, the identity mapping is a folding from this subset of terms to Q_0, we have shown that Q_0 is not minimum-term, there being a proper subset of Q_0 that is equivalent to Q_0.

Thus f induces a one-to-one correspondence between the terms of Q_0 and the terms of Q'_0. Hence, f is also a one-to-one correspndence of symbols, since if two symbols of Q_0 mapped to one of Q'_0, f would have to map two rows of Q_0 to one of Q'_0, as we assume each quantified symbol of Q_0 appears in a term. It follows that Q_0 and Q'_0 are really one-to-one symbol renamings of each other. □

Corollary: Given any conjunctive query Q we can find a minimum-term equivalent by removing zero or more terms of Q and any quantifiers $(\exists b)$ such that b no longer appears in a term.

Proof: Let Q_0 be a minimum-term equivalent for Q. Then a folding from Q to Q_0 composed with a folding from Q_0 to Q yields a folding from Q to a subset of itself. This subset can consist of no more terms than Q_0 and must be equivalent to Q. □

Example 6.9: If we start with Q_2 of Example 6.7 and 6.8, we find that Q_2 with $R(b_3 b_5)$ removed, that is

$$\{a_3 a_4 \mid (\exists b_4)(\exists b_6)(R(a_3 b_6) \wedge R(b_4 c) \wedge S(b_4 a_4))\}$$

is a minimal equivalent for Q. We had previously called this query Q_3. Checking that a given query is minimal is a hard (NP-complete) problem; essentially we must consider every possible symbol-to-symbol mapping on the symbols of Q_3 and show that none is a folding of Q_3 into a subset of its terms. However, the reader may verify our contention in this small example. □

Exercises

6.1: Verify each of the identities in Section 6.2.

6.2: Show that the equation

$$\pi_S(E_1 - E_2) \equiv \pi_S(E_1) - \pi_S(E_2)$$

is not valid in general.

6.3: Let us recall the beer drinkers' database of Exercise 4.6, with relations

> FREQUENTS(DRINKER,BAR)
> SERVES(BAR,BEER)
> LIKES(DRINKER,BEER)

Write relational algebra expressions for the following queries and optimize them according to Algorithm 6.1.

   a) Find the drinkers that frequent a bar that serves a beer that they like.

   b) Find the drinkers that drink at the same bar with a drinker that likes "Potgold" beer.

   c) Find the drinkers that drink at the same bar with a drinker that likes a brand of beer that the bar serves and Charles Chugamug likes.

6.4: Use Algorithm 6.2 to optimize the queries of Exercise 6.3.

6.5: Which of the queries of Exercise 6.3 are conjunctive queries?

*6.6: Show that every SQUARE mapping defines a conjunctive query.

*6.7: Show that any QUEL retrieve statement, in which a list of attributes is retrieved (no aggregate operators), and the where-clause is the logical "and" of terms equating components of tuples to one another or to constants, is a conjunctive query.

*6.8: Show that QBE queries in which all entries are variables or constants and no condition boxes are used is a conjunctive query.

*6.9: Show that every relational algebra expression using the operators selection (where the conditions are equalities among components and constants), projections, Cartesian products, equijoin, and intersection is a conjunctive query.

6.10: In Example 6.6 we asserted that the containments

$$\pi_S(R_1 \cap R_2) \subseteq \pi_S(R_1) \cap \pi_S(R_2)$$
$$\pi_S(R_1) - \pi_S(R_2) \subseteq \pi_S(R_1 - R_2)$$

held. Prove that this is the case.

6.11: Consider the following four conjunctive queries.

I $\{a_1 a_2 \mid (\exists b_1)(\exists b_2)(R(a_1 b_1) \land R(b_1 b_2) \land R(b_2 a_2))\}$

II $\{a_1 a_2 \mid (\exists b_1)(\exists b_2)(\exists b_3)(R(a_1 b_1) \land R(b_1 b_2) \land R(b_2 b_3)$
$\land R(b_3 a_2))\}$

III $\{a_1 a_2 \mid (\exists b_1)(\exists b_2)(\exists b_3)(\exists b_4)(R(a_1 b_2) \land R(b_3 b_4) \land R(b_1 a_2)$
$\land R(a_1 b_3) \land R(b_2 b_4) \land R(b_4 b_1))\}$

IV $\{a_1 a_2 \mid (\exists b_1)(\exists b_2)(R(a_1 b_1) \land R(b_1 c) \land R(c b_2) \land R(b_2 a_2))\}$

where c is a constant. Find all the equalities and containments among these expressions.

**6.12: Suppose $Q = Q_1 \cup Q_2 \cup \cdots \cup Q_k$, and $P = P_1 \cup P_2 \cup \cdots \cup P_r$, where the Q_i's and P_i's are sets defined by conjunctive queries. Prove that $Q \subseteq P$ if and only if for each Q_i there exists a P_j such that $Q_i \subseteq P_j$.

*6.13: Prove that the composition of foldings is a folding.

**6.14: Show that it is NP-complete to determine the minimum-term equivalent conjunctive query.

Biblographic Notes

A variety of algorithms for optimization of an expression in relational algebra have been proposed in Hall [1976], Minker [1975], Pecherer [1975], and Smith and Chang [1975], for example. The heart of these algorithms is the moving of selections as far down the tree as possible, although a variety of other useful manipulations are suggested. The strategy of optimization by doing selections first is attributed to Palermo [1974]. Gotlieb [1975] discusses alternative ways to compute joins, and S. B. Yao [1979] analyses alternatives for select-project-join queries.

The QUEL decomposition algorithm is from Wong and Youssefi [1976]. ISBL optimization is described in Hall [1976], and SEQUEL optimization in Astrahan et al. [1976] and Griffiths et al. [1979].

The optimization of conjunctive queries is based on Chandra and Merlin [1977], and the solution to Exercise 6.14, the NP-completeness of minimization, is from there. Aho, Sagiv, and Ullman [1979] extended these results to optimizations that take advantage of functional or multivalued dependencies. Sagiv and Yannakakis [1978] extended the equivalence test to unions of conjunctive queries (Exercise 6.12) and to some even more general classes of queries.

7
The DBTG Proposal

The dominant influence in the development of the network data model and database systems using that model has been a series of proposals put forth by the Data Base Task Group (DBTG) of the Conference on Data Systems Languages (CODASYL), the group responsible for the standardization of the programming language COBOL. In addition to proposing a formal notation for the network model the *(Data Definition Language* or *DDL)* and several key concepts for manipulating databases based on this model, the DBTG has proposed a *Subschema Data Definition Language (subschema DDL)* for defining views of a conceptual scheme that was itself defined using the data definition language. Also proposed is a *Data Manipulation Language (DML)* suitable for writing applications programs that manipulate the conceptual scheme or a view.

We shall begin the chapter by defining the DBTG's data model and introducing a number of the key ideas connected with it. Then we introduce the data manipulation language. As the DML proposed by the DBTG is heavily influenced by COBOL and its rather unusual syntax, we shall not write programs in the language formally proposed, but rather in a "pidgin" version designed to approximate the syntax of modern programming languages, as well as to provide the reader with some mnemonic aids in the form of redundant keywords. Our approach is consistent with the spirit of the DBTG proposal, since host languages other than COBOL are envisioned for the data manipulation language, and existing systems based on the DBTG concepts often adopt their own syntax. Finally, after discussing the data manipulation language, we shall return to a more detailed study of the data definition language.

7.1 Basic DBTG Concepts

The underlying model of data is the network model, as discussed in Section 3.2. What we have called logical record types are referred to as *record types* in the DBTG proposal. The fields in a logical record format are called *data items,* and what we called logical records are known simply as *records.* We shall use the terms "record" and "record type," since we are inclined to drop the term "logical" anyway, when no confusion results. However, let us continue to use "field," rather than "data item." The database can, naturally, contain many occurrences of records of the same type. There is no requirement that occurrences of the same type be distinct, and indeed, record types with no fields are possible; they would be used to connect records of other types, and in the implementation, the seemingly empty record occurrences would have one or more pointers.

DBTG Sets

By an unfortunate turn of fate, the concept of a link, that is, a many-one mapping from one record type to another, is known in the DBTG world as a *set*. To avoid the obvious confusions that would occur should the term "set" be allowed this meaning, many substitute names have been proposed; the term *DBTG set* is a common choice, and we shall adopt it here.

When we have a many-one mapping m from records of type R_2 to records of type R_1, we can associate with each record r of type R_1 the set S_r of records s of type R_2, such that $m(s)=r$. Since m is many-one, the sets S_{r_1} and S_{r_2} are disjoint if $r_1 \neq r_2$. If SET is the name of the DBTG set representing the link m, then each set S_r, together with r itself, is said to be a *set occurrence* of SET. Record r is the *owner* of the set occurrence, and each s such that $m(s)=r$ is a *member* of the set occurrence. Record type R_1 is called the *owner type* of SET, and R_2 is the *member type* of SET. We shall observe the DBTG restriction that the owner and member types of a DBTG set are distinct.

The requirement that owner and member types be distinct produces some awkwardness, but it is considered necessary because many DBTG operations assume that we can distinguish the owner from members in a set occurrence. We can get around the requirement by introducing dummy record types. For example, we might have a record type PEOPLE, which we would like to be both the owner and member types of DBTG set MOTHER_OF, where the owner record in a set occurrence is intended to be the mother of all its member records. The solution is to create a record type DUMMY, with the following DBTG sets.

1.   IS, with owner DUMMY and member PEOPLE. The intention is that each DUMMY record owns an IS set occurrence with exactly one PEOPLE record. Thus, each DUMMY record is effectively identified with the person represented by the PEOPLE record owned by that DUMMY record.

2.   MOTHER_OF, with owner PEOPLE and member DUMMY. The intention is that a PEOPLE record *r* owns the DUMMY records that own (in the IS set occurrence) the PEOPLE records of which *r* is the mother.

We now consider an extended example of how a network database can be defined using the data definition language.

Example 7.1: Let us return to Happy Valley (see Example 4.12) and see how the HVFC is getting along since they replaced their relational database system by a system based on the DBTG model. In Fig. 7.1 we see the declaration of the record types and DBTG sets needed to implement the database described in Example 4.12. These declarations are in a "Pidgin" language based on the DBTG proposal. The actual DBTG data manipulation language requires that certain other items of information, the nature of which we have not yet touched upon, be included in the declaration of DBTG sets and record types. We shall summarize the complete data manipulation language in Section 7.5.

The fields for each record type, with the data type of each field, are listed in the declaration of the record type. The integer 1 preceding each field name is a level number, as in the declaration of PL/I record structures. Level numbers up to 99 are permitted, allowing fields to have structure. The typical use of such structure is to declare, within a field such as ADDRESS, subfields like STREET, CITY, and ZIP at level 2.

Fields are represented by their name when no ambiguity arises. If two record types *A* and *B* have fields named *F*, we can use *A.F* and *B.F* to distinguish them. Incidentally, the DBTG proposal uses *F* IN *A* for the more common notation *A.F*.

Figure 7.2 shows the network diagram for the HVFC database. In principle, the HVFC database is two many-many relationships, one between the items and the members (whom we call "persons" here, to avoid confusion with "member of a DBTG set") ordering the items; the other relationship is between suppliers and items supplied. As discussed in Section 3.2, we must represent these two many-many mappings by introducing two new record types, which we call PRICES and ORDERS. A record of type ORDERS represents a pair, one person and one item ordered by the person. The only information from the original HVFC database associated with an ORDERS record is QUANTITY. However, we choose to make ORDERS records be unique, so we have introduced a serial number, ORDER_NO, to serve as an identifier for ORDERS. The introduction of ORDER_NO is not the only way to achieve uniqueness, as the reader will see when we discuss PRICES records. In fact, there is no requirement that records of a type be unique at all.

```
RECORD SUPPLIERS
    1  SNAME    CHAR(20),
    1  SADDR    CHAR(30);

RECORD ITEMS
    1  INAME    CHAR(15);

RECORD PRICES
    1  PRICE    REAL,
    1  INAME    VIRTUAL
             SOURCE IS ITEMS.INAME OF OWNER OF ITEMPR
    1  SNAME    VIRTUAL
             SOURCE IS SUPPLIERS.SNAME OF OWNER OF SUPPR;

RECORD PERSONS
    1  NAME     CHAR(20),
    1  ADDR     CHAR(30),
    1  BALANCE REAL;

RECORD ORDERS
    1  ORDER_NO  INTEGER,
    1  QUANTITY  REAL;

DBTG SET SUPPR
    OWNER IS SUPPLIERS
    MEMBER IS PRICES;

DBTG SET ITEMPR
    OWNER IS ITEMS
    MEMBER IS PRICES;

DBTG SET ITEMORD
    OWNER IS ITEMS
    MEMBER IS ORDERS;

DBTG SET PERSORD
    OWNER IS PERSONS
    MEMBER IS ORDERS;
```

Fig. 7.1. A DDL description of records and DBTG sets.

An ORDERS record r serves not only to represent the quantity ordered, but also to associate a person, the owner of the ORDERS record in the PERSORD set occurrence to which r belongs, with an item that person has ordered. That item is found in the owner record of r in the ITEMORD set occurrence to which r belongs.

Similarly, a PRICES record associates one item with one supplier for that item. We have chosen to make each PRICES record unique by including fields INAME and SNAME. These fields are declared VIRTUAL, meaning that although they are not actually present in PRICES records even as pointers, we may write programs as if they were. The clause

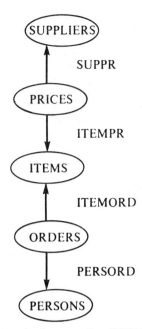

Fig. 7.2 Network diagram for HVFC database.

SOURCE IS ITEMS.INAME OF OWNER OF ITEMPR

n the INAME declaration of PRICES says that to find the value of INAME or a PRICES record, we first find the owner of that record's set occurrence or the ITEMPR DBTG set. This owner must be an ITEMS record (see he declaration of the ITEMPR set), and we can extract its INAME field, which becomes the value of the virtual INAME field in the PRICES record. The virtual field SNAME is evaluated analogously, by going to the owner of he PRICES record in the SUPPR DBTG set occurrence to which it belongs.

Figure 7.1 also contains the declaration of four DBTG sets, corresponding to the four links in Fig. 7.2. Each link is many-one from the member type for the DBTG set to the owner of that DBTG set. For example, one set occurrence of the ITEMORD set consists of an owner, which is n ITEMS record, and zero or more members, which are ORDERS records representing all the orders for that item.

Let us consider how the database of Fig. 4.7 would be represented by records and set occurrences. For example, the PERSORD DBTG set would have four occurrences, each owned by a PERSONS record; the owners are Brooks, Field, Robin, and Hart. Each of these records has a name, address, and balance, as:

Brooks, B   7 Apple Rd.   +10.50

These four set occurrences have ORDERS records as members. If we assume the six orders in Fig. 4.7(b) are given order numbers 1 through 6, then the member records for the set occurrence owned by Brooks has member records (1,5) and (2,10). The first of these records means order number 1, with quantity 5 pounds, and other ORDERS records are interpreted similarly. The set occurrence owned by Robin has member records (3,3), (5,2), and (6,8); the set occurrence owned by Hart has one member record: (4,5), while the set occurrence for Field has no member records.

The ITEMORD DBTG set has six set occurrences, each owned by an ITEMS record. For example, the granola record owns a set occurrence with ORDERS member records (1,5) and (3,3). The other set occurrences are owned by unbleached flour, whey, sunflower seeds, lettuce, and curds. The last of these owns no member records, because no one has ordered curds.

To determine the items ordered by Brooks, we must navigate through PERSORD and ITEMORD set occurrences, taking advantage of the fact that each ORDERS record is owned by both a PERSONS and an ITEMS record. Starting at the record for Brooks, we find its set occurrence in the PERSORD DBTG set. This set occurrence has member records (1,5) and (2,10) of type ORDERS. To find the items these orders represent, we find the owners of their set occurrences in the ITEMORD DBTG set. ORDERS record (1,5) is owned by the granola ITEMS record and (2,10) by the unbleached flour ITEMS record, so these are the items ordered by Brooks.

The SUPPR DBTG set has three occurrences, owned by the three SUPPLIERS records for the three suppliers, Sunshine Produce, Purity Foodstuffs, and Tasti Supply Co. For example, the SUPPR set occurrence for Sunshine Produce owns three member records of PRICES type:

1.29	Granola	Sunshine Produce
.89	Lettuce	Sunshine Produce
1.09	Sunflower seeds	Sunshine Produce

Recall that only the prices actually appear in the records, item and supplier names being virtual fields.

Lastly, the DBTG set ITEMPR has six occurrences, each owned by one of the six items. For example, the ITEMPR set occurrence for lettuce owns the member records of PRICES type:

.89	Lettuce	Sunshine Produce
.79	Lettuce	Tasti Supply Co.

☐

We now consider a variety of additional concepts found in the DBTG proposal.

Database Keys

To distinguish records, each record, of whatever type, is given a unique *database key* when it is created. The database key is, in essence, the location in which the record is stored. It is possible to refer to a record by its database key as well as by the values of its fields.

Location Modes

We may imagine that for each record type there is a file consisting of all of the records of that type. This file is organized in one of several ways, called *location modes,* and we shall cover the options in Section 7.5. The most important location mode is called *CALC,* and is indicated by the clause

LOCATION MODE IS CALC <procedure> USING <field list>

in the declaration of the record type. For example, in Fig. 7.1 we could include with the declaration for SUPPLIERS the information

LOCATION MODE IS CALC PROC1 USING SNAME, SADDR

Presumably, PROC1 is the name of a procedure that takes values for the SNAME and SADDR fields, producing a "hash value." We can imagine that SUPPLIER records are stored in buckets, one bucket for each value that could be returned by PROC1, as discussed in Section 2.2. However, PROC1 could actually be a lookup algorithm for any of the file organizations discussed in Sections 2.2–2.5, and perhaps others; the decision as to how to store a file with location mode CALC is pretty much up to the DBMS implementer, as long as one can "easily" find the record, given the value of the <procedure> applied to the <field list>. For example, the true file organization could have records sorted by the value returned by the <procedure>, with a sparse index on that value, along the lines discussed in Section 2.3.

Despite this freedom, the CALC location mode is usually mentally identified with hashing, and one will not go wrong by doing so. In the next sections we shall assume that all record types have location mode CALC.

Set Selection

There are a number of situations where we need to select a particular occurrence of a given DBTG set. The most common situation is where we create and store a new record r of some type T. The DBTG proposal allows r automatically to be made a member of some set occurrence for each DBTG set S of which T is the member record type, merely by executing a "STORE r" instruction. But which set occurrence of DBTG set S should receive r? By a SET SELECTION clause, we can associate with S an algorithm for selecting this set occurrence. Certain common set selection strategies can be declared in a SET SELECTION clause when the DBTG set itself is declared. We shall consider set selection in Section 7.4.

View Definition

The DBTG proposal calls for a subschema data definition language, in which one can define views. Unlike the view facilities described for ISBL and Query-by-Example in Chapter 4, views in the DBTG proposal are tangible, in the sense that deletions or modifications to the views change the underlying conceptual scheme.

In a view one is permitted to use a different name for any record type, field, or DBTG set. We can omit from the view fields that are present in a record type, we can eliminate record types altogether, and we can eliminate DBTG sets from the view.

As the view facility of the DBTG proposal contains no concepts not present in the data definition language for the conceptual scheme, we shall in the following sections write programs that act on the conceptual scheme directly, as if it were a complete view of itself. Thus, views play no role in what follows.

7.2 The Program Environment

Programs are written in a host language (COBOL in the DBTG proposal) augmented by the commands of the data manipulation language, such as FIND (locate a described record), GET (read a record from the database), and STORE (a record into the database). The environment in which a program operates is depicted in Fig. 7.3. There is a workspace, called the *user working area,* in which is found space for three kinds of data:

1.   Variables defined by the program.

2.   *Currency pointers,* which are the database keys of certain records in the database; we shall describe currency pointers in more detail next.

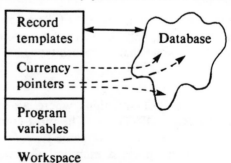

Workspace

Fig. 7.3. The program environment.

3. Templates for the various record types. The template for a record type T consists of space for each field F of the record type, and that space is referred to as $T.F$ (or just F if the field name is unique) in programs. A record is stored into the database only after assembling the record in the template for its type, and the STORE command copies the contents of the template into the database. Similarly, the GET command reads a record from the database into the appropriate template. We also use the template as a way of "passing parameters" to certain commands that at first glance do not appear to have parameters, especially to the FIND command.

Currency Pointers

As a program runs, it is necessary for it to locate various records by a FIND command, and to operate upon them by other commands. To keep track of recently accessed records, a collection of currency pointers is maintained automatically by the database system, and the values of these pointers, which are actually the database keys of the records, are made available to the program. The currency pointers with which we deal are:

1. The *current of run-unit*. The term "run-unit" means "program" in the DBTG proposal. The most recently accessed record, of any type whatsoever, has its database key in a currency pointer called the "current of run-unit."

2. The *current of record type*. For each record type T, the most recently accessed record of this type is pointed to by the "current of T."

3. The *current of set type*. For each DBTG set S, consisting of owner record type T_1 and member record type T_2, the most recently accessed record of type T_1 or T_2 is called the "current of S." Note that sometimes the current of S will be an owner, and sometimes it will be a member. Also understand that the current of S is a record, rather than a set occurrence. Sometimes it is convenient to talk of the set occurrence containing the record "current of S" as if this set occurrence itself were the "current S occurrence," but there is no such thing as a pointer to a set occurrence.

Example 7.2: Let us return to the database of Example 7.1. Suppose we wish to find the items ordered by Brooks. In Example 7.1 we showed how we might use the PERSORD and ITEMORD DBTG sets to navigate from Brooks to the items, granola and unbleached flour, that he ordered. It is convenient to view a set occurrence as a ring of records consisting of the owner and any members, as described in Section 3.2 when we discussed the multilist data structure. Thus the set occurrence of the PERSORD DBTG set for Brooks might consist of an owner record for Brooks and two member records (1,5) and (2,10), in that order around a ring. While we have not yet discussed how the FIND statement works, suffice it to say that one thing we can do, starting at an owner record, is to find each member record around the ring in turn. Another thing we can do is find the owner of a set occurrence if we are given a member of that set occurrence. In Fig. 7.4 we see a sequence of steps that a program might execute, and we indicate the current of the PERSONS, ORDERS, and ITEMS record types, the current of the PERSORD and ITEMORD DBTG sets, and the current of run-unit after each step. □

| | | | Current of | | | |
Step	PERSONS	ORDERS	ITEMS	PERSORD	ITEMORD	run-unit
1. find Brooks record	Brooks	–	–	Brooks	–	Brooks
2. find (1,5) ORDERS record	Brooks	(1,5)	–	(1,5)	(1,5)	(1,5)
3. find owner of (1,5) in ITEMORD	Brooks	(1,5)	Granola	(1,5)	Granola	Granola
4. find (2,10) ORDERS record	Brooks	(2,10)	Granola	(2,10)	(2,10)	(2,10)
5. find owner of (2,10) in ITEMORD	Brooks	(2,10)	Unbleached flour	(2,10)	Unbleached flour	Unbleached flour

Fig. 7.4. A program and its effect on currency pointers.

7.3 Navigation Within the Database

Reading a record from the database to the workspace is a two stage process. First, using a sequence of FIND statements, we locate the desired record; that is, the desired record becomes the current of run-unit. At this point, nothing has been copied into the template for the record type. To copy the record into the template in the workspace, we simply execute the command GET. This command always copies the current of run-unit into the template for whatever record type is the current of run-unit. If we wish to copy only a subset of the fields of the current of run-unit, we can list the desired fields after GET, as in

GET < record type>; < list of fields>

Example 7.3 If the current of run-unit is a PRICES record (we are continuing with the HVFC example), we can read the INAME and PRICE fields by saying

GET PRICES; INAME, PRICE

The SNAME field in the template for PRICES is not affected. Notice that even though INAME is a virtual field of PRICES, we can program as though it actually existed, relying on the system to get the correct value from the ITEMS.INAME field of the owner of the PRICES record in its ITEMPR set occurrence. □

For debugging purposes, we can append the record type to the command GET, even if we want all fields of the record. For example

GET PRICES

will copy the current of run-unit into the PRICES template, if the current of run-unit is a PRICES record. Otherwise, the system will warn the user of an error when the GET PRICES statement is executed. Let us emphasize that one cannot use GET to read a record other than the current of run-unit, even if we follow GET by the type of that record.

The FIND Statement

The FIND command in the DBTG proposal is really a collection of different commands, distinguished by the keywords following FIND, with the common purpose of locating a particular record by some designated strategy. The variety of FIND statements is extensive, and we shall here consider only a useful subset of the possibilities. In brief, the FIND statement can be used in the following ways.†

1. Find a record given its database key.

2. Find a record given values for its CALC-key. Recall that record types are given a location mode, and frequently that location mode is CALC, where there is a "hash function" applied to the values in certain fields (the CALC-key) of any record of that type. Given values for these fields, we can find some record (it need not be unique) with those values in the designated fields.

3. We can scan the file of records of a given type, and in turn find all the records with a given value in the CALC-key field or fields.

4. We can scan all the members of a set occurrence in turn.

5. We can scan a set occurrence for those member records having specified values in certain of the fields.

6. We can find the owner of a given record in a given DBTG set.

7. We can find the current of any record or DBTG set. At first, this statement seems paradoxical, since if a record is "current of something" it is, in principle, "found." However, we observed that GET operates only on the current of run-unit, not on a current of set or

---

† These seven types of FIND statement are not the "seven formats" spoken of in the literature. Rather, we have grouped the formats mentioned in the DBTG proposal into what we regard as logical units.

record. Most of the other commands, which we have not yet introduced, also require the current of run-unit as the sole possible operand. Thus the purpose of this FIND statement is to make a "current of something" record be the current of run-unit, for further processing.

Finding a Record Directly

The first two sorts of FIND access records by a "key," either the database key or the CALC-key. To access by database key in our "Pidgin" language† we write:

FIND < record type> RECORD BY DATABASE KEY < variable>

where the < variable> is a variable in the workspace that has previously been given a database key as value. For example, to read the current of ITEMS into its template in the workspace, we could write:

XYZ := CURRENT OF ITEMS
FIND ITEMS RECORD BY DATABASE KEY XYZ
GET ITEMS

Here XYZ is the name of a variable in the workspace.

To find a record given values for its CALC-key fields, we "pass" those values to FIND by placing the values in the corresponding fields of the template, then issue the command

FIND < record type> RECORD BY CALC-KEY

For example, suppose PERSONS records are given location mode CALC with a CALC-key consisting only of the field NAME. Then we could find the balance for Brooks by:

PERSONS.NAME := "Brooks, B."
FIND PERSONS RECORD BY CALC-KEY
GET PERSONS; BALANCE

Note that PERSONS.NAME and PERSONS.BALANCE could have been written NAME and BALANCE, as no ambiguity would arise. We should also observe that although NAME is a CALC-key, there is no guarantee that two persons with the same name do not exist, and the above sequence of steps will only find one record with NAME = "Brooks, B.,"

---

†There are several differences between the notation used here and that used in the DBTG proposal. First, the proposal calls for many optional "noise words" in its syntax. We have arbitrarily chosen to include or exclude them, with an eye toward maximizing clarity. Second, we have inserted the words RECORD, SET, and other explanatory words, in certain places where they help to remind the reader of what the variables represent.

not all of them.

Scanning a Record Type

To find all the records of a given type with a given value for the CALC-key, we can find the first such record as above, and then find additional records with the same CALC-key by executing, in a loop,

FIND DUPLICATE < record type> RECORD BY CALC-KEY

Assuming the current of run-unit is of the type < record type>, and its values in the CALC-key fields equal the corresponding values in the template for < record type>, then the next < record type> record with those values is found.

When performing any sort of scan, we must be prepared to find no record matching the specifications. In the DBTG proposal, there is a global *error-status* word, that indicates when a FIND operation fails to find a record, among other abnormal conditions. We shall here assume for convenience that a variable FAIL becomes true if and only if a FIND fails to find a record.

Example 7.4: Suppose we wish to print all the suppliers of granola and the prices they charge. Suppose for convenience that the CALC-key for PRICES is INAME. Then the desired table could be printed by the routine shown in Fig. 7.5.

```
print "SUPPLIER", "PRICE" /* print header */
PRICES.INAME := "Granola"
FIND PRICES RECORD BY CALC-KEY
while ¬FAIL do
        GET PRICES; SNAME, PRICE
        print PRICES.SNAME, PRICE
        FIND DUPLICATE PRICES RECORD BY CALC-KEY
end
```

Fig. 7.5. Print suppliers and prices for granola.

Scanning a Set Occurrence

To begin, suppose we have a current set occurrence for some DBTG set *S*. Recall that the set occurrence can be viewed as a ring consisting of the owner and each of the members. If we get to the owner, we can scan around the ring and come back to the owner, causing FAIL to become true when we do. The FIND statement

FIND OWNER OF CURRENT < set name> SET

finds the owner of the current of < set name>, making it the current of run-unit and, most importantly, the current of <set name>.

The statement

    FIND NEXT <record type> RECORD IN
    CURRENT <set name> SET

goes one position around the ring from the current of <set name>, setting
FAIL to true† if the next record is not of the <record type>. Normally,
the <record type> is the member type of the <set name>, so we fail
when we get back to the owner.

An alternative way to scan around the ring is to issue the command

    FIND FIRST <record type> RECORD IN
    CURRENT <set name> SET

to get the first member record of the current <set name> DBTG set. If
there are no members of this set, FAIL becomes true. Otherwise, we can
continue around the ring with a loop containing a FIND NEXT · · · command, as above.

Example 7.5: Let us print the items ordered by Brooks. The program of
Fig. 7.6 does the job. We begin by finding the PERSONS record for
Brooks. This record owns the PERSORD set occurrence we wish to scan.
We find the first member record of this set occurrence, and in the loop, we
check whether we have gone around the ring already. If not, we use FIND
OWNER to get the ITEMS record owning the order and read it, to get the
name of the item. We print the item, find the next member of the PER-
SORD set occurrence owned by Brooks, and go around the loop once more.
□

```
NAME := "Brooks, B."
FIND PERSONS RECORD BY CALC-KEY
/* CALC-key for PERSONS is NAME */
FIND FIRST ORDERS RECORD IN CURRENT PERSORD SET
while ¬FAIL do
        FIND OWNER OF CURRENT ITEMORD SET
        GET ITEMS /* read item that owns current order record */
        PRINT ITEMS.INAME
        FIND NEXT ORDERS RECORD IN CURRENT PERSORD SET
end
```

Fig. 7.6. Print the items ordered by Brooks.

---

† Technically, the error-status word treats reaching the last member of a set occurrence as a
different "abnormality" from failing to find a record, but we trust no confusion will occur if
we use FAIL to indicate all abnormalities.

Singular Sets

There are times when we would like to scan all the records of a certain type, for example, to find all PERSONS with negative balances. We cannot directly access all the PERSONS records by CALC-key or database key, unless we know the name of every person belonging to the HVFC, or if we know all the database keys for these records, which are two unlikely situations. Scanning set occurrences for PERSONS records won't work either, unless we have some way of locating every set occurrence of some DBTG set.

We may define, for a given record type, what is known as a *singular* DBTG set. A singular set has two special properties.

1. The owner type is a special record type called SYSTEM. Having SYSTEM as the owner distinguishes singular DBTG sets.

2. There is exactly one set occurrence, whose members are all the records of the member type. The records are made members automatically, with no specific direction required from the user.

Example 7.6: If we wish the capability of searching all the PERSONS records conveniently, we could add to the DBTG set declarations in Fig. 7.1 the definition of the following singular set.

        DBTG SET ALLPERS
          OWNER IS SYSTEM
          MEMBER IS PERSONS;

To print all the persons with negative balances we could execute the program of Fig. 7.7. □

```
    print "PERSON", "BALANCE"
    FIND FIRST PERSONS RECORD IN CURRENT ALLPERS SET
    /* the lone set occurrence of ALLPERS is always current */
    while ¬FAIL do
        GET PERSONS
        if BALANCE < 0 then
        print NAME, BALANCE
        FIND NEXT PERSONS RECORD IN CURRENT ALLPERS SET
    end
```

Fig. 7.7. Print HVFC members with negative balances.

Scanning a Set Occurrence for Fields of Specified Value

The next type of FIND statement also scans the members of a set occurrence, but it allows us to look at only those records with specified values in certain fields. The values for these fields are stored in the template for the member record type before using the FIND. To get the first member record having the desired values, in the current set occurrence of the <set name> DBTG set, we can write

FIND <record type> RECORD IN CURRENT
<set name> SET USING <field list>

Here, <record type> is the member type for the DBTG set whose name is <set name>, and the <field list> is a list of fields of the <record type> whose values, stored in the template for <record type>, must match the values of these fields in the record found. To get subsequent records in the same set occurrence with the same values we say

FIND DUPLICATE <record type> RECORD IN CURRENT
<set name> SET USING <field list>

Example 7.7: To find the price charged by Tasti Supply Co. for whey, we could use the program of Fig. 7.8. As an example of a situation where we might wish to scan for several matching records, consider Fig. 7.9, where we scan the singular set ALLPERS, introduced in Example 7.6, for all persons with zero balance. □

```
SUPPLIERS.SNAME := "Tasti Supply Co."
FIND SUPPLIERS RECORD USING CALC-KEY
  /* establishes a current SUPPR occurrence */
PRICES.INAME := "Whey"
FIND PRICES RECORD IN CURRENT SUPPR SET USING INAME
GET PRICES; PRICE
print PRICE
```

Fig. 7.8. Find the price charged by Tasti for whey.

```
BALANCE := 0
FIND PERSONS RECORD IN CURRENT ALLPERS
  SET USING BALANCE
while ¬FAIL do
    GET PERSONS; NAME
    print NAME
    FIND DUPLICATE PERSONS RECORD IN
      CURRENT ALLPERS SET USING BALANCE
end
```

Fig. 7.9. Find persons with zero balance.

Establishing a Current of Run-Unit

The last sort of FIND we shall cover is a FIND statement whose purpose is to make a current of record or set become the current of run-unit. The syntax is:

FIND CURRENT OF < set name> SET

or

FIND CURRENT OF < record type> RECORD

Example 7.8: Suppose we wish to find if Brooks ordered granola, and if so, how much. We scan the PERSORD set occurrence owned by Brooks. For each order, we consult its owner in the ITEMORD DBTG set to see if the item is granola. We could read the ORDERS record before consulting its owners, but then we would waste time reading orders for items other than granola. One solution is to reestablish an ORDERS record as the current of run-unit when we discover it is an order for granola.† Remember that having made an ITEMS record be the current of run-unit, we cannot immediately apply GET to any other record. The program is given in Fig. 7.10. □

```
NAME := "Brooks, B."
FIND PERSONS RECORD USING CALC-KEY
LOOP: repeat forever
        FIND NEXT ORDERS RECORD IN CURRENT PERSORD SET
        if FAIL then break LOOP
        FIND OWNER OF CURRENT ITEMORD SET
        GET ITEMS; INAME
        if ITEMS.INAME = "Granola" then do
             FIND CURRENT OF ORDERS RECORD
             GET ORDERS; QUANTITY
             print QUANTITY
             break LOOP
        end
    end LOOP
```

Fig. 7.10. Find how much granola Brooks ordered.

---

† While we do not discuss the matter here, it is possible to suppress the updating of the currency pointers, which provides another solution to this problem.

7.4 Other Database Commands

In addition to FIND and GET, the DBTG proposal includes commands to insert or delete the current of run unit from set occurrences and from the list of records of a type, and a command to modify the current of run unit.

The STORE Command

To store a new record of type *T* into the database, we create the record *r* in the template for record type *T* and then issue the command

> STORE *T*

This command adds *r* to the collection of records of type *T* and makes *r* be the current of run-unit, the current of *T*, and the current of any DBTG set of which *T* is the owner or member type.

There is an interesting side effect the STORE command can have. If *T* is a member type of DBTG set *S*, we can arrange for *r* to become a member of some particular set occurrence of *S* automatically, when *r* is stored into the file for *T*. To do so, we must, when DBTG set *S* is declared, add a clause

> INSERTION IS AUTOMATIC

The opposite of AUTOMATIC is MANUAL, meaning that member records are not inserted into any set occurrence of *S* when the records are stored, and we must "manually" insert records into set occurrences of *S* by an INSERT command, to be discussed later in this chapter.

Set Selection

Granted that we have declared insertion of records of type *T* into set occurrences of *S* to be AUTOMATIC, we need a mechanism for deciding which set occurrence of *S* gets the new record. The STORE command itself cannot specify the correct set occurrence. Rather, when we declare DBTG set *S*, we include a SET SELECTION clause that tells how to select the set occurrence of *S* into which a newly stored member record is to be placed. There are many different ways in which the set occurrence could be chosen. We shall describe two common ways first and a more complex way later. Remember that each of the following statements belongs in the declaration for a set *S*; it is not part of the executable portion of a program. Also note that we use a "Pidgin" syntax to make the meaning of the clauses more apparent.

1. SET SELECTION IS THRU CURRENT OF <set name> SET. Here, before storing a record, the program itself establishes a current set occurrence for the <set name> set (presumably *S* is the set name). When the record is stored, it becomes a member of the current *S* occurrence.

2. SET SELECTION IS THRU OWNER USING <field list>. The <field list> is the CALC-key for the owner type of *S*, which must therefore have location mode CALC, if this particular type of set selection is to be used. The current values of these fields in the template for the owner type must determine a unique record of the owner type for *S*, and the stored record goes into the set occurrence of *S* owned by that record.

Example 7.9: Suppose we wish to store ORDERS records and insert them automatically into PERSORD and ITEMORD set occurrences when we do. If NAME is the CALC-key for PERSONS, we can use a person's name to select the set occurrence for PERSORD, by including in the declaration for PERSORD the clause

SET SELECTION IS THRU OWNER USING NAME

We might choose to select the ITEMORD occurrence through the owner identifier INAME, but for variety, let us select the ITEMORD occurrence by placing

SET SELECTION IS THRU CURRENT OF ITEMORD SET

in the declaration of ITEMORD. The clause

INSERTION IS AUTOMATIC

must be placed in the declarations of both PERSORD and ITEMORD. The program in Fig. 7.11 reads an order, stores it in the ORDERS file, and inserts it into the desired set occurrences of PERSORD and ITEMORD, automatically. □

```
read N, I, Q /* the name, item, and quantity */
NEXTORD := NEXTORD + 1 /* get a new order number */
PERSONS.NAME := N /* prepare PERSORD set selection */
ITEMS.INAME := I
FIND ITEMS RECORD USING CALC-KEY
     /* prepare ITEMORD set selection */
ORDERS.ORDER_NO := NEXTORD
ORDERS.QUANTITY := Q
     /* create new ORDERS record in template */
STORE ORDERS /* automatically places the record in the
     PERSORD set occurrence owned by N and in the current ITEMORD
     set, which is that owned by I */
```

Fig. 7.11. Read and store new order.

There is one other important kind of set selection, in which we chain through a sequence of DBTG sets to find the proper set occurrence of the last DBTG set in the chain. This sort of set selection is used when we have a natural hierarchy of record types, such as STATES, COUNTIES, and TOWNS. Each state consists of many counties, and each county has many towns. Obviously, town names are not unique, although no county has two towns of the same name. Neither are county names unique, although no state has two counties of the same name. For example, there is a Washington County in Alabama, Arkansas, Colorado, Florida, Georgia, and 23 other states.

Suppose we make the declarations of record types and DBTG sets shown in Fig. 7.12. When we store a new TOWN record, we want it to go in the proper set occurrence of T_IN_C, which means we must know its county. But the county name alone does not determine the set occurrence of a county; we must also know the state in which the county (and hence the town) is located. Thus to select the correct occurrence of T_IN_C, we use the state name as a CALC-key to find the correct set occurrence of C_IN_S, then use the county name to find the correct COUNTIES record within that C_IN_S set occurrence. This COUNTIES record is the owner of the correct set occurrence of T_IN_C for the new TOWNS record. The above algorithm can be expressed in a set selection clause for T_IN_C as

SET SELECTION IS THRU C_IN_S OWNER USING SNAME
THEN THRU T_IN_C OWNER USING CNAME

Having made the above set selection declaration for T_IN_C, we could insert a record for Midvale, Washington County, Idaho by the program shown in Fig. 7.13. The record automatically becomes a member of the set occurrence for Washington County, Idaho.

Manual Insertion and Deletion

If we do not wish to use set selection to place records in set occurrences, we can do so by an explicit command. A record type can be declared an AUTOMATIC member of some DBTG sets, in which case set selection is used, and the same record type can be declared

INSERTION IS MANUAL

for some other DBTG set of which it is a member, in which case a record, when stored, is not made a member of any set occurrence for this DBTG set.

To insert a record r (which already exists in the database) of the member type T for DBTG set S, into a designated set occurrence of S, we first make this set occurrence be the current of S, by whatever means we find suitable. Then we make r be the current of run-unit and issue the command

> INSERT *T* INTO *S*

Note that *r* must be the current of run-unit, not just the current of *T*. It is permissible to follow INTO by a list of DBTG sets, and if so, insertion of *r* into the current of each set will occur.

```
RECORD   STATES
    1  SNAME;

RECORD   COUNTIES
    1  CNAME;

RECORD   TOWNS
    1  TNAME;

DBTG SET   C_IN_S
    OWNER IS STATES
    MEMBER IS COUNTIES;

DBTG SET   T_IN_C
    OWNER IS COUNTIES
    MEMBER IS TOWNS;
```

Fig. 7.12.   Declaration of states, counties, and towns.

```
TNAME := "Midvale"
CNAME := "Washington"
SNAME := "Idaho"
STORE TOWNS
```

Fig. 7.13. Storing the TOWNS record for Midvale, Idaho.

Example 7.10: In Example 7.9 we read an ORDERS record and inserted it automatically into PERSONS and ITEMS set occurrences. If we instead declare ORDERS to be a MANUAL member of the PERSORD and ITEMORD DBTG sets, we can do the insertion manually by the procedure of Fig. 7.14. □

To remove the current of run-unit, which is a record of type *T*, from its set occurrence for DBTG set *S*, we issue the command

> REMOVE *T* FROM *S*

As with insertion, *S* could be replaced by a list of DBTG sets. Remember, the record removed must be the current of run-unit, not just the current of *T*. This arrangement, as in other statements, serves as a redundancy check to catch program bugs. The reader should also be warned that a retention declaration for DBTG set *S*, to be discussed in the next section, can make it impossible to remove a record from an *S* occurrence.

```
read N, I, Q
NEXTORD := NEXTORD + 1
PERSONS.NAME := N
FIND PERSONS RECORD USING CALC-KEY
  /* establish the correct current of PERSORD */
ITEMS.INAME := I
FIND ITEMS RECORD USING CALC-KEY
  /* establish the correct current of ITEMORD */
ORDERS.ORDER_NO := NEXTORD
ORDERS.QUANTITY := Q
STORE ORDERS /* new order is now the current of run unit,
  but not a member of any set occurrences */
INSERT ORDERS INTO PERSORD, ITEMORD
```

Fig. 7.14   Manual instertion of a new ORDERS record.

Record Modification

The command

MODIFY < record type>

has the effect of copying the template for < record type> into the current of run-unit. If the current of run-unit is not of the designated record type, it is an error. We can also modify a selected subset of the fields in the current of run-unit by writing

MODIFY < record type>; < field list>

If *T* is the record type for the current of run-unit, the values of the fields in the list are copied from the template for *T* into the fields of the current of run-unit. Other fields in the current of run-unit are unchanged. Thus to change the price charged by Sunshine Produce for lettuce to .75 we could execute the program of Fig. 7.15.

```
PRICES.INAME := "Lettuce"
PRICES.SNAME := "Sunshine Produce"
FIND PRICES RECORD USING CALC-KEY
PRICES.PRICE := .75
MODIFY PRICES; PRICE
```

Fig. 7.15.   Set price of lettuce sold by Sunshine Produce to .75.

Deletion of Records from the Database

The command

> DELETE < record type>

deletes the current of run-unit, which must be of the specified <record type>, from the file of records of that type. Naturally, if the current of run-unit is a member of any set occurrences, it is removed from those occurrences. If the current of run-unit is the owner of any set occurrences, those occurrences must presently have no members, or it is an error, and the deletion cannot take place.

Another form of DELETE statement is

> DELETE < record type> ALL

This instruction is applicable even if the current of run-unit is the owner of some nonempty set occurrences. The DELETE ALL statement not only erases the current of run-unit, as the simple DELETE does, but recursively, DELETE ALL is applied to any members of set occurrences owned by the deleted record. Thus it is conceivable that DELETE ALL could destroy the entire database.

Example 7.11: To cancel an order given its order number we could write

> **read** ORDERS.ORDER_NO
> FIND ORDERS RECORD USING CALC-KEY
> DELETE ORDERS

Since ORDERS records are not owners in any DBTG set, the given order is simply deleted from the file of ORDERS records and from whatever PERSORD and ITEMORD records it belongs to.

As another example, if Robin quits the HVFC, we can execute

> NAME := "Robin, R."
> FIND PERSONS RECORD USING CALC-KEY
> DELETE PERSONS ALL

This erasure has the effect of deleting the record for Robin from the PERSONS file and deleting the entire PERSORD set occurrence of which Robin is the owner. Recursively, each order in the deleted set occurrence is itself deleted from the ORDERS file and from the ITEMORD set occurrence of which it is a member. Since ORDERS records do not own any set occurrences, the recursion stops here, and no further alterations to the database are made. □

7.5 Some Other Features of the DBTG Proposal

In this section we briefly survey some of the salient aspects of the proposa that we have left untouched. These include location and set modes, reten tion declarations, areas, and the ordering of members within se occurrences.

Location Modes

A *location mode* for a record type is a description of the storage structure fo the records of that type. We mentioned previously what is probably th most important location mode:

LOCATION MODE IS CALC <procedure> USING <field list>

The <field list> is the set of fields we have called the CALC-key. Thi location mode suggests, but does not require, that the file for a record typ declared this way be stored in buckets, one for each value produced by th "hashing" <procedure> applied to the values of the fields in the <fiel list>. As a perfectly reasonable alternative, the <procedure> coul examine a sparse index to find the bucket in which a record belongs, a described in Section 2.3, or it could examine a B-tree as described in Sec tion 2.4. There are no fundamental limits on what the <procedure> ca do, but the user is entitled to rely on the assumption that, given values fo the <field list>, locating some record (there may be several) with thos values in the <field list> can be done efficiently; it is the responsibility o the system to provide built-in procedures that make this search efficient.

Let us not forget that if we are to be able to search the file of record of a given type using

FIND (DUPLICATE) <record type> RECORD BY CALC-KEY

then the <record type> must be declared with a CALC location mode.

A second location mode is DIRECT, declared by

LOCATION MODE IS DIRECT

In this case, the database key, rather than a CALC-key, determines th place in which the record is kept. In principle, the file of records of thi type can be kept in any order; a record will be accessed by providing a data base key, which is in essence the location of the record.

The location mode VIA for a record type T_1 is declared by

LOCATION MODE IS VIA <set name> SET

This declaration implies that type T_1 is the member type of the designatec <set name> S, and each record of type T_1 will be grouped with the owne of the S occurrence of which it is a member. That is, if the owner type fo S is T_2, the file of T_2 records can be viewed as a file of variable lengtf ecords, with format $T_2(T_1)$*. This file can be implemented by fixed length ecords as suggested in Section 2.6, or it could be implemented in a reorder sequence as suggested for hierarchies in Section 3.3. Another kely alternative is to place the T_1 records in any order and use the multist structure mentioned in Section 3.2 to link T_2 records to their owner in a ing.

The VIA SET location mode leads to some very complex structures. For example, it is possible that record type T_2 is given declaration

LOCATION MODE IS VIA R SET

where T_2 is the member type for DBTG set R, whose owner type is T_3. Then records of types T_1, T_2, and T_3 are organized as if in variable length ecords with format $T_3(T_2(T_1)*)$*. Observe that if the VIA SET location node is used for a record type T, then its insertion in the DBTG set deter-nining its location must be AUTOMATIC, or else there is no place to put new record.

Set Modes

Like record types, DBTG sets can be declared to have a particular data tructure. The proposal is less specific about the structure of sets than ecord types, allowing the implementor the freedom to design and name his own structures. However, the following two options are called for in any mplementation.

. The *chain* set mode. This is the familiar multilist structure of Section 3.2. An option is to have pointers around the ring in both direc-tions.†

. The *pointer array* set mode. Here each member record points to its owner. Associated with the owner is an array of pointers, one to each member of the set occurrence.

Retention Classes

To provide a check against certain types of program bugs, we can, if we wish, and the intended use warrants it, declare that retention of a member ecord in a DBTG set occurrence is MANDATORY. If we so declare, then every record of type T, once it becomes a member of an S occurrence, ither automatically upon storage, or manually by an INSERT command, must always be a member of some S occurrence. The opposite of MAN-DATORY retention is OPTIONAL.

---

* While we have not mentioned the possibility, FIND can scan DBTG sets in the backward, s well as forward direction.

MANDATORY retention puts some constraints on the way we can deal with T records. We can never remove a T record from an occurrence, although we can copy the T record into the working area, delete it from the database, and then store the copy into another occurrence.

Areas

An area is an abstract representation of a region of secondary storage. While the exact nature of an area is determined by the system, we can think of an area as the name for a cylinder of a disk, and we shall not go far wrong. Each record type must be declared to have its records stored among one or more areas, and several record types can be placed in the same area. For each area used, a "current of area" pointer is maintained in the workspace, just as the currency pointers for records, sets and run-units are maintained. While most areas are part of the permanent database we can declare an area to be TEMPORARY, in which case it is created when an application program, in which it is declared, begins execution, and the temporary area is destroyed upon termination of that program. Such areas can be used for temporary data created by the program.

The area concept is useful for two reasons; it can enhance efficiency and it can provide a measure of security. Efficiency can be improved if, for example, records of a certain type are all placed in one area, and this area is implemented by a cylinder. As searching for records is noticeably faster if the disk heads do not have to switch cylinders, a scan of records of this type is relatively fast.

To facilitate security, a view can declare only a subset of the areas used by the conceptual schema. Then, records used by programs based on one view can be made inaccessible to records used by programs for another view, even if the records have the same record type.

Ordered Set Occurrences

When we insert a member into a set occurrence, it must be placed somewhere in the "ring" consisting of the owner and members of the occurrence. An ORDER clause in the declaration of the DBTG set specifies where in the ring the new member is to appear. The options are the following.

1.   ORDER IS FIRST. The new occurrence is placed immediately after the owner of the occurrence. If the multilist structure is not really used to implement DBTG sets, then the new member is placed first on the list of members, however that list is actually represented.

. ORDER IS LAST. The new member is placed immediately before the owner, that is, last on the list of members.

. ORDER IS PRIOR. The new record is placed just before the current of the DBTG set, which must be a member of this set occurrence.

. ORDER IS NEXT. This option is similar to PRIOR, but the new record immediately follows the current of the set around the ring.

. ORDER IS SORTED. We can specify that the ORDER IS SORTED BY DATABASE KEY, which means that the database keys for the member records are treated as integers, and records with lower database keys precede higher. More commonly, we define one or more fields to serve as a key on which to sort. The sort may be ascending or descending on each of the fields in the sort key. For example, if F_1 and F_2 are two fields of member records for some DBTG set, we could declare

ASCENDING KEY IS F_1, F_2

Then we sort records in a set occurrence first on the value of field F_1 in ascending order (i.e., lexicographic order if F_1 values are strings, or numerical order if F_1 values are numbers). Among records of a given set occurrence with the same F_1 value we sort these by the value in field F_2, in ascending order. Actually, the sort key need not be a key in the usual sense. We can permit records with the same sort key value if we declare

DUPLICATES ARE ALLOWED

The alternative is DUPLICATES ARE NOT ALLOWED, with the obvious effect.

Summary

Let us review the items required or optional in the declarations of records and DBTG sets. Some of these items have not been mentioned previously and will be described briefly here. For a record declaration, the following items are required (or optional if so indicated), and must appear in the order given.

1. RECORD < record type>, the declaration of the name for the record type.

2. LOCATION MODE IS <location mode option>. See this section and Section 7.1 for a description of the options: CALC, DIRECT, and VIA SET. A location mode clause is optional.

3.   WITHIN <area list>, giving a list of areas in which records of th type can appear. See this section for a description of areas.

4.   ON conditions. These are optional procedures that are intended to b invoked by the system before or after the use of the various con mands like STORE. We shall not discuss this aspect of the propos here, but see Section 9.1 for remarks regarding their use as integri checks.

5.   PRIVACY information, giving a password or similar protection info mation for the various data manipulation commands on records of th type being declared. This information is optional and will not be di cussed further.

6.   Information on the fields of the record type, their levels, and dat types. See Section 7.1.

The principal kinds of information in a DBTG set declaration are th following:

1.   DBTG SET <set name>, the declaration of the DBTG set.

2.   MODE IS <set mode>. See this section for the modes of DBT(sets.

3.   ORDER IS <order option>. See this section for a description c how members of a set occurrence may be ordered.

4.   ON conditions. As for the declaration of record types, we ma declare that certain procedures are to be invoked when a comman like INSERT is applied to a DBTG set. This information is optional.

5.   PRIVACY information, protecting set occurrences as for record type Privacy declarations are optional.

6.   OWNER IS <record type>, specifying the owner type of the DBT(set.

7.   MEMBER IS <record type>, giving the member type for the DBT(set, its insertion class (AUTOMATIC/MANUAL), and its retentio class (MANDATORY/OPTIONAL). Insertion classes are discusse in Section 7.4 and retention classes in this section.

8.   KEY information, describing the sort key, if in item (3) above ORDER IS SORTED is declared. See this section.

9.   SEARCH KEY information. The term "search key" means secon dary index, and zero or more search keys for the member record typ can be declared to help find the set occurrence of member record efficiently.

0. SET SELECTION information, as described in Section 7.4.

xercises

.1: Define, using the DBTG data manipulation language, the networks of

    a) Example 3.6

    b) Figure 3.5

.2: Suppose we have the following record types:

       COMPANY(CNAME, CADDR)
       STOCK(SH_NO, QUANTITY)
       PERSON(PNAME, PADDR)

Let there also be the following DBTG sets.

1. EMP, with member PERSON and owner COMPANY, indicating the employees of a company.

2. OWNS, with member STOCK and owner PERSON, indicating which person owns which stock certificates.

3. ST_CO, with member STOCK and owner COMPANY, indicating the company to which a stock certificate pertains.

You may assume the location mode for each record is CALC, with keys CNAME, SH_NO, and PNAME, respectively. Write programs in the "Pidgin" data manipulation language of this chapter, to do the following.

    a) Read a share number and print the name and address of the person owning the share.

    b) List all persons owning stock in IBM. You may list a person owning two certificates twice.

    c) List all persons owning stock in the company they work for. (Assume a singular set of persons exists.)

    d) Determine the total quantity of stock in IBM owned by its employees.

.3: Suppose we wish to enter new shares into the database of exercise 7.2, and we want a new share to be entered into the correct OWNS and ST_CO set occurrences when the stock record is stored.

    a) Suggest set selection clauses that will enable the automatic insertion to be performed.

    b) Write a program to read the necessary data and store the new stock record correctly.

c)   Suppose we wish to use manual insertion instead of automatic
     Write a program to store STOCK records and insert them in th
     proper OWNS and ST_CO occurrences manually.

*7.4:   Discuss the advantages and disadvantages of the various locatio
        modes and set modes defined in the DBTG proposal. What sorts o
        queries make one data structure preferable to another?

*7.5:   A relation can be represented by a record type in the DBTG sense; i
        is convenient if a singular set for this record type is assumed to exist.

   a)   Show how to do each of the relational algebra operations usin
        the DBTG data manipulation language.

   b)   Show how the existence of a dummy record type and DBTG set
        linking it to record types *R* and *S* can be used to facilitate on
        particular join between *R* and *S*.

Bibliographic Notes

The DBTG proposal is contained in the document CODASYL [1971]
Periodic updates are available in the *COBOL Journal of Developmer*
(CODASYL [1978]). Olle [1978] is a tutorial on the network model.

   TOTAL (see Cincom [1978]) is a major commercial system based o
the network model. IDMS (Cullinane [1978]) and ADABAS (Software A(
[1978]) are other important realizations of some of these ideas. Each o
these systems is described in Tsichritzis and Lochovsky [1977], an
TOTAL is also described in Cardenas [1979]. Weiderhold [1977
enumerates many commercial systems based on DBTG ideas.

8
IMS: A Hierarchical System

BM's Information Management System (IMS) is one of the most heavily
ised of commercially available systems and is at least partially responsible
or the importance of the hierarchical data model, on which it is based. For
hese reasons it is incumbent upon us to take a look at the most important
eatures of this system. This examination will also serve to illustrate the
iierarchical approach in general, although IMS's "record at a time" data
nanipulation is not representative of all hierarchical systems any more than
he "record at a time" DBTG proposal, discussed in the previous chapter,
s mandatory for network systems.

8.1 An Overview of IMS

Figure 8.1 shows the way in which the database is made available to an
pplication program and in which the program can use or influence the data.
\t the bottom, data is structured by *physical database descriptions* (DBD's).
\ physical database scheme is a single tree of logical record types, called
egments in IMS terminology. The physical database description includes
he segment names, their fields, the hierarchy into which the segments are
irranged, and a specification of the physical organization of the database.
There are four physical organizations that may be chosen; we shall discuss
hese in Section 8.4.

A "physical database" in IMS terminology is not quite what we meant
by a physical database scheme in Chapter 1, although the concepts are simi-
ar. For one thing, the entire database may be stored in many IMS physical
iatabases. For another, the IMS physical database embodies a conceptual
nodel, the hierarchy, while in Chapter 1, we viewed the physical scheme as
in organization of files, independent of their conceptual meaning at higher
evels of abstraction.

Logical Databases, like physical databases, are hierarchies of segments.
Each logical database is built from one or more physical databases using a
iatabase description quite similar in form to that used to define physical
iatabases. The segments of a logical database do not really exist; they

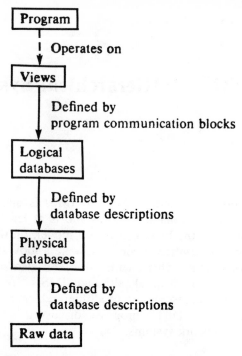

Fig. 8.1. Communication between program and data.

stand for one, or in some cases, more than one, segment of a physical data base. The logical database can utilize pointers, placed in physical database segments intentionally for this purpose, to create a hierarchy quite different from that of the underlying physical database or databases. For example we shall see in Section 8.3 how logical databases can serve to simulate networks or many-many mappings. The collection of logical databases built upon a collection of physical databases forms a good approximation to what we called a conceptual scheme in Chapter 1.

Database Description

The "data definition language" used to write database descriptions for physical or logical databases is actually a collection of assembly language macros.

1. DBD. This macro is the first statement and takes parameters NAME = <database name> and ACCESS = <method>, among others. The NAME gives the name of the database, and the ACCESS parameter gives the access method. The <method> can be HSAM, HISAM, HDAM, or HIDAM, indicating one of the four storage organizations alluded to above and discussed in Section 8.4, or the word LOGICAL, indicating that a logical database is being defined.

. DATASET and its parameters gives additional information about the storage organization and the storage device used. We shall not go into the details of this statement.

. SEGM. This statement introduces a segment definition. Its parameters include NAME, giving the name of the segment, and PARENT, indicating the parent of the segment in the hierarchy being defined. Other parameters give the number of bytes used by a segment, an estimate of the number of occurrences of this segment type as children of each occurrence of its parent segment type in the database, and an indication of the presence of certain pointer fields (to be discussed later) in the segment.

. FIELD. This statement represents a field of the segment. Its parameter NAME gives the name of the field. Other parameters tell the number of bytes used by the field, the offset of the field (number of bytes used by preceding fields of the segment), and the data type for the field. One, and only one, field in a segment can be declared to be a *sequence field.* Occurrences of a segment type that are children of one occurrence of the parent segment type appear in the database in the order of their sequence field values (e.g., lexicographic order if the sequence field has character string data type). Occurrences of the root segment type are likewise normally ordered by their sequence fields. For example, the parameter NAME = (ZAP, SEQ, U) defines field ZAP to be the sequence field for its segment type. The letter U (unique) means that no parent segment occurrence can have two children with the same value for the sequence field. An M in place of U means that there can be multiple segments with the same sequence field value as children of one parent segment occurrence. The sequence field is often referred to as a "key," although even when the U option is specified, there can be two occurrences of the segment with the same sequence field value, as long as they are children of different parent segment occurrences in the database.

. DBDGEN, FINISH, and END, in that order, close the database definition.

In our discussion to follow we shall omit all but the DBD, SEGM, nd FIELD macros and shall omit parameters other than NAME and ARENT.

xample 8.1: The HVFC database does not provide an interesting hierarchy, o we shall introduce the database of a national real estate agency, the cheme for which is shown in Fig. 8.2. The reader should review Section .3 and remember that an actual database represented by this scheme consists of a sequence of trees, called *database records* in the IMS argot, one or each occurrence of the root segment type. The root segment of each ree is a REGIONS segment, and its children are OFFICES segments, one for each office in the region. The children of an OFFICES segment are AGENTS, EMPS, and LISTINGS segments, in that order, and AGENTS segments have children that are CLIENTS segments. No other segments have children. Fig. 8.3 shows the beginning of a possible database with the scheme of Fig. 8.2. Segments $r_1, r_2, \cdots$ are REGIONS segments $o_1, o_2, \cdots$ are OFFICES segments, and so on.

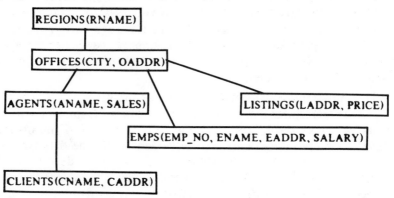

Fig. 8.2. Scheme for the real estate database.

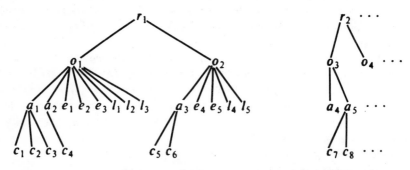

Fig. 8.3. Beginning of a database satisfying the scheme of Fig. 8.2.

In Fig. 8.4 we see the sketch of a database definition for the scheme of Fig. 8.2. It is presumably a physical database implemented by one of the four IMS storage organizations, although with some modifications in the SEGM and FIELD statements it could be a logical database, as described in Section 8.3. □

Application Programs and Views

Each program defines its own views of the various physical and logical databases on which it operates. The view of a single database scheme (tree of segment types) is defined by a sequence of macros called a *program communication block* (PCB), and the collection of communication blocks for a

```
DBD     NAME=RLESTATE
SEGM    NAME=REGIONS
FIELD   NAME=(RNAME, SEQ, U)

SEGM    NAME=OFFICES, PARENT=REGIONS
FIELD   NAME=(CITY, SEQ, U)
FIELD   NAME=OADDR

SEGM    NAME=AGENTS, PARENT=OFFICES
FIELD   NAME=(ANAME, SEQ, U)
FIELD   NAME=SALES

SEGM    NAME=EMPS, PARENT=OFFICES
FIELD   NAME=(EMP_NO, SEQ, U)
FIELD   NAME=ENAME
FIELD   NAME=EADDR
FIELD   NAME=SALARY

SEGM    NAME=LISTINGS, PARENT=OFFICES
FIELD   NAME=(LADDR, SEQ, U)
FIELD   NAME=PRICE

SEGM    NAME=CLIENTS, PARENT=AGENTS
FIELD   NAME=(CNAME, SEQ, U)
FIELD   NAME=CADDR
```

Fig. 8.4. Database definition sketch for the real estate database.

program, one for each database it accesses, is called a *program specification block* (PSB). A view of a physical or logical database consists of a subset of the segments of that database with the property that if a segment is included in the view so is its parent.† Therefore the root of the database is always included in any view.

The following macros are used to form program specification blocks.

PCB. This macro begins a program communication block. Its parameter DBDNAME gives the name of the underlying database definition of which this communication block is a view. Other parameters exist but will not be discussed.

SENSEG. This macro indicates a *sensitive segment,* that is, a segment to be included in the view. The parameter NAME indicates the name of the segment in the underlying physical or logical database, and parameter PARENT tells the parent of this segment. The parameter PROCOPT = < list of letters > gives the *processing options,* that is, operations permitted on the segment. The important options are G

---

† Technically, we can avoid including the parent by specifying "key sensitivity" for the parent; we shall discuss this concept shortly.

(get, meaning read), I (insert), D (delete), and R (replace, meaning modify). The processing option K (key) means that the segment is *key sensitive;* the segment is not really part of the view but had to be mentioned because some of its children are present, and a segment in a view requires that its parent be in the view.

3. PSBGEN and END terminate the program specification block, that is the list of communication blocks, for a program. We shall omit these macros in examples.

Example 8.2: Suppose the payroll department of the real estate agency had program that generated paychecks and mailed them to the appropriate offices. This program needs to see only the OFFICES and EMPS segments of Fig. 8.2, but since it needs OFFICES, its program communication block must include the parent, REGIONS. Figure 8.5 is a sketch of the program specification block for this program. While in this case there is only one communication block, recall that in general there could be many in one specification block, if the program needed access to several physical or logical databases.

```
PCB        DBDNAME=RLESTATE
SENSEG     NAME=REGIONS, PROCOPT=K
SENSEG     NAME=OFFICES, PARENT=REGIONS, PROCOPT=G
SENSEG     NAME=EMPS, PARENT=OFFICES, PROCOPT=G
```

Fig. 8.5. A program specification block.

The PROCOPT for segment REGIONS is K, meaning that it is key sensitive, that is, present on a pro forma basis only, and not accessible The other two segments, OFFICES and EMPS, are given PROCOPT=G meaning that the program can only read them. In general, the PROCOPT could be a sequence of several letters (not including K), for example PROCOPT=GI, allowing reading and insertion only. Observe that, options like I, D, and R are allowed for a program, then changes to the view are reflected in the underlying physical database, just as in the DBTG proposal discussed in the previous chapter, and unlike the view facilities for ISBL and Query-by-Example discussed in Chapter 4.

Figure 8.6 shows the subscheme defined by the program specification block of Fig. 8.5. Observe that the segment REGIONS is not part of the subscheme, because it was defined to be key sensitive only. Also remember that, in general, a subscheme may be a complicated tree, not just one path. □

The program communication block, when assembled, bears little resemblance to Fig. 8.5. It becomes a block of data accessible both to the program and the IMS system. The program, written in a host language

Fig. 8.6. A subscheme

1akes calls to a particular procedure, supplied by IMS, to manipulate the
atabase. After each call, a variety of information is left by this procedure.
'he most important pieces are:

. The *fully concatenated key* of the segment accessed by the call. The
fully concatenated key is the concatenation of the sequence field
values along the path from the root to the target segment, including
any key sensitive segments along the path. Suppose a call by the program using the subscheme of Fig. 8.6 accesses the employee record
for the employee with EMP_NO 12345, and this employee works in
the Princeton office of the Northeast region. Then the fully concaten-
tated key consists of

> Northeast, Princeton, 12345

with each of the three key values occupying as many bytes as were
declared for their fields in the underlying database definition.

. Status information, indicating the success or failure of the call to find
a specified segment. This information is analogous to the variable
FAIL we introduced in our description of the DBTG proposal.

The program communication block also contains information for the
MS procedure called. The important pieces of information are:

) the name of the logical or physical database to be accessed by the call
(taken from the PCB macro), and

·) the PROCOPT information, assembled from SENSEG statements, telling IMS what operations are permitted on the various segments.

.2 The IMS Data Manipulation Language

'he IMS system is prepared to deal with application programs written in
ne of three host languages: COBOL, PL/I, and assembly language. Data
nanipulation commands are effected by calls to a single procedure for each
anguage, for example, the procedure PLITDLI (PL/I to DL/I) is called if
he host language is PL/I, while CBLTDLI is used with COBOL and
\SMTDLI with assembly language. The arguments of the call are, in
ssence, literal strings forming a command in the IMS data manipulation
anguage, DL/I (data language one). We shall first introduce a "Pidgin"
·ersion of DL/I, then indicate how commands actually look as arguments
·f a call.

Currency Pointers

For each view manipulated by the program there is what amounts to "current of view," the most recently accessed segment occurrence. This segment occurrence is represented by the fully concatenated key left in the program communication block for that view. Certain commands also involve a "current parent," most often the parent of the "current of view." In fact, using special "command codes," which are modifiers of the basic commands, we can have a "current of segment" for any segment type. It should be emphasized that the DBTG "current-of" concept is not explicitly part of DL/I; it just helps to think of DL/I marking positions in the database this way.

The GET Command

The basic retrieval command of DL/I, called GET UNIQUE, specifies path from a root segment occurrence to a *(target)* segment of a particular type, not necessarily a leaf segment type. Despite the word UNIQUE, the target segment need not be uniquely determined; IMS will retrieve the left most segment in the sequence of database trees (as in Fig. 8.3) such that it and its ancestors satisfy whatever conditions are placed on them in the GET UNIQUE command. The retrieved segment is put in an *input/output area* which is a data structure, belonging to the application program, whose address is passed to DL/I as a parameter of the call.

The syntax we shall use in our "Pidgin DL/I" for GET UNIQUE is

GET UNIQUE < segment name> WHERE < segment search list>

The < segment search list> consists of a sequence of conditions of the form

. < field name> θ < constant>

possibly connected by "and" and "or." The < field name> is a field of the < segment name>, and θ is one of the arithmetic comparison operators =, <, and so on. We can omit the < segment name> if it is uniquely determined by the field name.

Example 8.3: Let us suppose that the hierarchy of Fig. 8.2 is the view used by our program. Note that since the data model used in views, physical databases and logical databases is the same, the fact that Fig. 8.2 was initially called a physical database should not concern us. The DL/I command

GET UNIQUE AGENTS
WHERE SALES> 1000000

finds the first (leftmost in the list of trees) agent whose sales total exceeds one million dollars.† It is implemented by scanning the database in

---

† Technically, the GET UNIQUE command, but not the other commands, must specify the entire sequence of segment types from the root to the desired type, even if some of them

preorder,‡ effectively examining each AGENTS segment from the left, until finding one whose sales total exceeds one million dollars. When found, this segment is returned to the application program in an input/output area that both the DL/I interpreter and the application program can access.

Suppose now we wished to find an agent in the Princeton office with over a million in sales. We could write.

```
GET UNIQUE AGENTS
    WHERE
        CITY = "Princeton",
        SALES> 1000000
```

If the agency had offices in both Princeton, N.J. and Princeton, Tex., we could specify

```
GET UNIQUE AGENTS
    WHERE
        RNAME = "Northeast",
        CITY  = "Princeton",
        SALES> 1000000
```

assuming that New Jersey is in the Northeast region and Texas is not.

It is also possible to use variables in segment search arguments, even though technically the value appearing to the right of the = sign must be a constant. We shall see how when we give the details of calls to DL/I later. As a consequence, it is perfectly legal to write a program that behaves as the "Pidgin" program, in Fig. 8.7, which reads a region and city, and finds an agent with over a million in sales in that city's office. □

```
read REG, OFF
GET UNIQUE AGENTS
    WHERE
        RNAME=REG,
        CITY =OFF,
        SALES> 1000000
```

Fig. 8.7. Use of variables in segment search arguments.

---

have no associated conditions. In this example, the path is REGIONS, OFFICES, AGENTS. In our "Pidgin" language, we shall omit this redundant information.
‡ It is convenient to assume all REGIONS segments are children of a dummy root. See Section 3.3.

Another version of the GET command allows us to scan the entire database for segments satisfying some conditions. We use the word NEXT in place of UNIQUE to cause a scan rightward from the last segment accessed (i.e., from the "current of view") until we next meet a segment of the same type satisfying the conditions in the GET NEXT statement. These conditions could differ from the conditions that established the "current of view," but in practice they are usually the same.

Example 8.4: Suppose we wish to find all agents with sales over a million. We could write the program of Fig. 8.8 to accomplish this task. Note that from Fig. 8.8 it would appear that the DL/I language is embedded in a host language the way the data manipulation language is embedded in COBOL in the DBTG proposal. The reader should remember that we are using "Pidgin DL/I," and in practice, the DL/I statements would be transmitted as a series of arguments in a call to a special procedure, say PLITDLI if the host language were PL/I.

It should also be understood that in Fig. 8.8 we are using the variable FAIL to denote that portion of the program communication block used to indicate the success or failure of a call to DL/I. The value of FAIL becomes true whenever no segment satisfying the desired conditions can be found. In our example, if no agents have sales over a million, GET UNIQUE will cause FAIL to become true. Otherwise, FAIL becomes true on the execution of GET NEXT immediately after the rightmost agent with sales over a million was found. □

```
GET UNIQUE AGENTS
    WHERE SALES> 1000000
while ¬ FAIL do
    print AGENTS.ANAME /* actually, we print
    a portion of the I/O area where the retrieved
    AGENTS segment is found */
    GET NEXT AGENTS
        WHERE SALES> 1000000
end
```

Fig. 8.8. Print all agents with sales over a million.

A third form of GET, written GET NEXT WITHIN PARENT, permits us to visit all the children of a particular segment occurrence in the actual database. It utilizes the informal concept of "current parent," which is the segment occurrence most recently accessed by any variety of GET other than GET NEXT WITHIN PARENT. The segment type accessed by a GET NEXT WITHIN PARENT command need not be a child segment type for the type of the current parent; it could be any descendant segment type. The important difference between GET NEXT and GET NEXT WITHIN PARENT is that the latter fails when it has scanned all the descendants of the current parent; the former searches rightward for any segment occurrence such that it and its ancestors satisfy the associated conditions.

Example 8.5: In Fig. 8.9 we show a program that prints all the clients of agent Sam Slick, who works in the Princeton office (we assume this information uniquely identifies the agent). If instead, we wanted to print all the clients in the Princeton office (assuming there is only one office with CITY = "Princeton") we could simply change the GET UNIQUE statement in Fig. 8.9 to

> GET UNIQUE OFFICES
>   WHERE CITY = "Princeton"

Note that in this case, "within parent" effectively means "within grandparent," and all clients of all agents in the Princeton office would be printed. □

```
GET UNIQUE AGENTS
    WHERE ANAME = "Slick,Sam"
    /* establishes the current parent */
GET NEXT WITHIN PARENT CLIENTS
    /* get Slick's first client */
while ¬ FAIL do
    print CLIENTS.CNAME /*from the I/O area */
    GET NEXT WITHIN PARENT CLIENTS
end
```

Fig. 8.9. Print all the clients of Slick.

Insertions

An INSERT command, for which we use the same "Pidgin" syntax as for the varieties of GET, allows us to insert a segment of type S, first created in an I/O area, as a child of a designated segment occurrence of the parent type for S. There is also a feature, similar to DBTG's automatic insertion using set selection available with the INSERT command of IMS. If the "current of view" is either of the parent type for S, or any descendant of the parent type, simply writing

> INSERT S

will make the segment of type S sitting in the I/O area a child of that occurrence of the parent type that is the current of view or an ancestor of the current of view. In any case, the segment inserted takes its proper place among the children of its parent, as determined by its sequence field. Recall all children of a segment occurrence are sorted on that field.

Example 8.6: Suppose Joe Nebbish agrees to become Sam Slick's client. We could enter a segment for Nebbish as a child of the segment for Slick, by executing the program of Fig. 8.10. If Slick's segment was already the current of view, or even if some client of Slick were the current of view, we could insert the Nebbish segment by putting the correct field values for the segment in the I/O area, as in Fig. 8.10, and then issuing the command

INSERT CLIENTS

□

CLIENTS.CNAME := "Nebbish, Joe"
CLIENTS.ADDR := "74 Family Way"
/* we assume the I/O area for this command is a structure named
CLIENTS with fields corresponding to the fields of the CLIENTS seg-
ment. The location of the I/O area is passed with the call to DL/I */
INSERT CLIENTS
    WHERE
        CITY="Princeton",
        ANAME="Slick,Sam"

Fig. 8.10. Nebbish becomes a client of Slick.

Deletion and Modification

In order to delete or modify a segment we must first "hold" it by issuing some variety of GET command that will make the desired segment the current of view, but adding the word HOLD after GET in the command. The requirement for holding a segment before deleting or modifying it is motivated by the possibility that there is concurrent processing of the database by two or more application programs. Upon executing GET HOLD, any other program is prevented from accessing the segment. See Chapter 10 for a description of the need for "holding" a segment before modifying it. "Hold" here corresponds to "lock" or "write-lock" in Chapter 10.

To delete a segment after finding and holding it, simply issue the DL/I command

DELETE

The effect of this statement is to delete the segment that is the current of view and also to delete any of its children in the underlying database.† Note that some of the segments deleted may not be sensitive, that is, they are

† In the case the view is built on a logical rather than physical database, the effect of the deletion on the physical databases underlying the logical one must be specified along with the logical database. Normally, though, the children of the deleted segment in the logical database are deleted from the logical database.

not part of the view. Thus the delete command may have effects on segments the programmer did not know existed.

To modify a segment after finding and holding it, we first change the copy of the record found in the I/O area. It is not permissible to change the sequence field, since segments are not moved when they are modified, and children must be sorted on their sequence fields. When we issue the DL/I command

REPLACE

the version of the current segment in the I/O area replaces the corresponding segment in the database. Note that the I/O area is mentioned in the call to DL/I that is represented by our "Pidgin" statement REPLACE.

Example 8.7: Suppose agent Slick sells a lonely tropical island for one hundred thousand dollars. We can add this amount to his sales total with the program shown in Fig. 8.11.

Unfortunately, shortly thereafter, the tropical island swims away. It is therefore decided that Slick must be fired, which is done with the commands

GET HOLD UNIQUE AGENTS
    WHERE
        CITY = "Princeton",
        ANAME = "Slick,Sam"
DELETE

Note that the DELETE command deletes not only Slick's segment but also the segments of all clients of Slick. Perhaps we should have transferred them to another agent first. □

GET HOLD UNIQUE AGENTS
    WHERE
        CITY = "Princeton",
        ANAME = "Slick,Sam"
AGENTS.SALES := AGENTS.SALES + 100000
    /* the above takes place in the I/O area, assumed to be
    a record structure named AGENTS */
REPLACE

Fig. 8.11. Add 100,000 to the sales of Slick.

Details of the Call to DL/I

Remember that we have been using a "Pidgin" DL/I to describe the commands of DL/I, and commands are not really embedded in the program, but rather are effected by calls to a particular procedure, whose name depends on the host language used. We shall assume the host language is

PL/I, so this procedure is PLITDLI. The parameters of this procedure are, in order:

1. The number of parameters in the call, not counting this parameter.

2. The command itself. This parameter is a character string of length four, and the codes for the commands are (filled out with blanks when necessary): GU (get unique), GN (get next), GNP (get next within parent), GHU, GHN, GHNP (the same, with "hold" included), ISRT (insert), DLET (delete), and REPL (replace).

3. The name of the program communication block for the view accessed by the command. Actually the communication block is not part of the data of the application program. Rather, it is outside the program, and the IMS system, when it first gives control to the application program, passes to the program a pointer to the program communication block. The program declares a name for the data pointed to, so the program can refer to this data, e.g., to determine whether a GET command has failed to find any segment.

4. The name of the I/O area, a character string long enough to hold a segment of the type involved in the command.

5. The list of segment search arguments. The GET UNIQUE command requires a segment search argument for each segment type along the path from the root to the target segment type, but in other commands they are optional.

A segment search argument is effectively a string of characters of the form

<command code> (<field name> = <value>)

The <command code> is optional and if present is represented by a * followed by a letter. We shall not discuss command codes here. Suffice it to say that they modify the action of the command. For example, they help us obtain segments that are children of the current parent but not of the segment type of the current of view, they can change the segment type of the current parent, and they allow us to get, insert, or replace an entire path from a root segment to a segment of some descendant type. The parenthesized <field name> = <value> is also optional; recall that for GET UNIQUE the path of segment types to the target segment type must appear in segment search arguments.

As the PL/I compiler cannot know the data types of the parameters of PLITDLI when an application program is compiled (e.g., the argument count is FIXED BINARY(31); the command itself is CHAR(4)), it is necessary to declare variables of the correct type, initialize them to the correct values, and pass the variable names, rather than the values themselves, to PLITDLI. This arrangement has an unexpected benefit. If we use a variable, say SSA, for a particular segment search argument of a particular call, then before the call, we can modify the portion of the value of the SSA to the right of the = sign to become anything we choose.

Example 8.8: If we recall Fig. 8.7, where we read variables REG and OFF and then used them as part of a segment search argument, we now see how the application program actually uses these variables. If we have two variables, SSA1, and SSA2, used as segment search arguments, with initial values

$$SSA1 = \text{'REGIONS(RNAME=XXXXXXXXXX)'}$$
$$SSA2 = \text{'OFFICES(CITY=YYYYYYYYYY)'}$$

we can replace the positions with X's by the value of REG and the positions with Y's by the value of OFF before using these as the first two segment search arguments in a call such as

CALL PLITDLI(#6, GU, AGENCYPCB, IOAREA,
   SSA1, SSA2, SSA3)

Here #6 is a variable declared FIXED BINARY(31) and initialized to 6; GU is declared CHAR(4) and initialized to 'GU ', AGENCYPCB is the name used by the application program for the program communication block, IOAREA, is a variable whose length in characters equals the length of an AGENTS segment, and SSA3 is a variable initialized to the segment search argument for the AGENTS segment in this command, that is,

AGENTS(SALES>1000000)

□

8.3 Logical Databases

Let us reconsider the HVFC database from Example 4.12, but for simplicity, focus on the relationship between members, items and orders, forgetting about suppliers and their relationship to items. One conceivable way to implement this part of the HVFC database in IMS is shown in Fig. 8.12. Each ITEMS segment occurrence has, as children, the orders for that item, including the name, address, and balance of each member ordering the item. While in principle this scheme has all the information of the relations MEMBERS and ORDERS of Example 4.12, it suffers from many of the problems of relations that are not in third normal form. That is, the address and balance of each member is repeated once for each order, and if at some time a member has nothing on order, we would lose track of his address and balance.

   One solution is to create two physical databases, as shown in Fig. 8.13. One physical database has only a root segment type; each occurrence represents a member. The other database has root segment ITEMS, as in

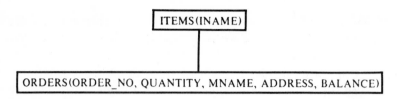

Fig. 8.12. Part of (a bad implementation of) the HVFC database.

Fig. 8.12, and a child segment ORDERS, with a field QUANTITY, as before. Instead of the full information about the member doing the ordering, we substitute a pointer to the appropriate MEMBERS occurrence. This arrangement avoids the problems mentioned above. The address and balance of each member are recorded exactly once, independently of how many orders he has placed.

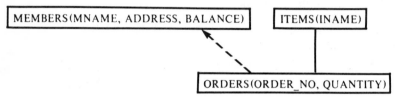

Fig. 8.13. Two physical databases.

Logical Parents and Children

In effect, the ORDERS segment above represents a many-many relationship between the MEMBERS and ITEMS segments. It is possible to link these segments by declaring both MEMBERS and ITEMS to be, in a sense, parents of ORDERS. We can, when we define the two physical databases of Fig. 8.13, declare the existence of a pointer field in ORDERS segments, the target of that pointer being a MEMBERS occurrence. While it might appear that, in effect, we have made MEMBERS a child of ORDERS, in IMS terminology just the opposite is the case. MEMBERS is called a *logical parent* of ORDERS, and ORDERS is a *logical child* of MEMBERS. In general, introduced pointers run from a logical child to a logical parent, and they are called *logical parent pointers*.† When we declare these two databases, we include in the definition of the MEMBERS segment the fact that it has a logical child ORDERS, by using a macro LCHILD. Then, when we declare the ORDERS segment, the PARENT parameter indicates two parents. The syntax for this parameter is

PARENT = ((<actual parent>),(<logical parent>, <database>))

---

† The best way to remember this is to note that, as we shall see when we construct logical databases, a logical child can "inherit" fields of data from its logical parent.

The pair (<logical parent>, <database>)‡ indicates the segment name of the logical parent and the physical database to which it belongs.

Example 8.9: A sketch (recall we omit certain macros and parameters) of the physical database descriptions of the two databases of Fig. 8.13 is shown in Fig. 8.14. Note the difference in the way logical parents and pointers are declared. The macro LCHILD in the MEMBERS segment says that ORDERS is the logical child of MEMBERS. In the ORDERS segment declaration, we see that the existence of a pointer to the logical parent is declared with the POINTER parameter, while the fact that MEMBERS is a logical parent is declared with the PARENT parameter. □

```
DBD       NAME = MEM_DB
SEGM      NAME = MEMBERS
LCHILD    NAME = (ORDERS, ITEM_DB)
FIELD     NAME = (MNAME, SEQ, U)
FIELD     NAME = ADDRESS
FIELD     NAME = BALANCE

DBD       NAME = ITEM_DB
SEGM      NAME = ITEMS
FIELD     NAME = (INAME, SEQ, U)
SEGM      NAME = ORDERS, POINTER = LPARENT,
          PARENT = ((ITEMS), (MEMBERS, MEM_DB))
FIELD     NAME = (ORDER_NO, SEQ, U)
FIELD     NAME = QUANTITY
```

Fig. 8.14. Declaration of databases of Fig. 8.13.

Defining Logical Databases

The reader may have observed that our description of DL/I did not include any way of following pointers such as the logical parent pointer from ORDERS to MEMBERS. One may therefore wonder how such pointers are used. The answer is that they help in the construction of logical databases, where we may combine a logical or physical parent and child into one segment, thus cementing the relationship between the two parents that is implied by the child segment. We may then write application programs on the logical database (actually on a view of that database, which may be the same) as though the pointer did not exist, relying on the implementation to follow the pointer whenever data that actually existed in a MEMBERS segment was required from the combined segment in the logical database.

---

‡ Technically, these pairs are triples, but we shall omit the middle component and not discuss its role.

In the declaration of a logical database, we do not declare the fields of a segment; they are determined from the underlying physical database. We do declare, for each segment in the logical database, a *source* (or sources) using the parameter

$$SOURCE = (<segmentname>,<database>) \qquad (8.1)$$

to declare that the segment in the logical database is really in the database <database>.† In case a logical segment is the combination of a physical segment and its logical or physical parent, then the source is a pair consisting of both segments.

When we create a logical segment consisting of a physical segment S and its logical parent P, the logical segment appears to contain the fields not only of S and P, but the fields in the fully concatenated key of P. Thus, the sequence field of P actually appears twice, since it is part of P and also of its fully concatenated key. Some of this information may be omitted from a logical segment, although we shall not discuss this mechanism. The term *intersection data* is often used for the copy of S in the logical segment, since the information usually tells something about the relationship between the entities represented by the logical parent P and the physical parent of S. Thus, in Fig. 8.13, if S is ORDERS and P is MEMBERS, the intersection data is (ORDER_NO, QUANTITY), which tells about a particular MEMBERS-ITEMS pair.

Similarly, in a logical database we can create a segment consisting of a child segment C and its physical parent, if we declare C to have a pointer to its physical parent. In the logical database, this combined segment is a child of the logical parent of C.

A logical database consists of a collection of segments arranged in a hierarchy, just as a physical database does. The sources of these segments may range over several physical databases, and as we mentioned, one segment in the logical database can be composed of a segment and its physical or logical parent. In the logical database, a segment C can be the child of segment P if there is some pointer to follow from a source of P to a source of C. This pointer can be the usual pointer from a physical parent to child. Or it could be a pointer from logical child to logical parent or from physical child to physical parent, provided these pointers are declared in a SEGM statement. Thus, in the logical database the parent-child relationship could be a child-parent relationship in one of the underlying physical databases.

There are two additional rules regarding the construction of logical databases that we must remember.

---

† There is a middle parameter, often omitted, that causes two commas to appear in (8.1). We shall not discuss this matter here.

1.   The root segment of a logical database must be a root segment in
     some physical database.

2.   When the parent-child relationship in the logical database is a parent-
     child relationship in a physical database, we cannot use the physical
     parent in the logical database again. That is, suppose P is the parent
     of C in both a physical and a logical database. Then P cannot be a
     child of C in the logical database, even if there is a parent pointer in
     C segments.

     Thus, the two physical databases of Fig. 8.15(a), with the logical
parent pointer indicated by a dashed line, could give rise to the logical databases of Fig. 8.15(b) or (c). In Fig. 8.15(b), the segment C has been combined with G, its logical parent, while in Fig. 8.15(c), segment C has been
combined with its physical parent A.

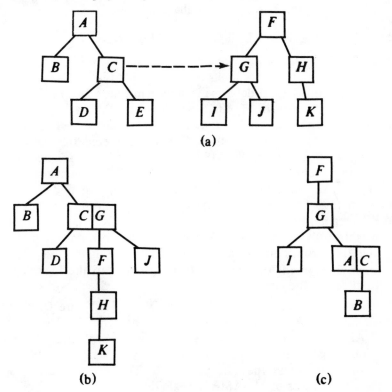

(a)

(b)   (c)

Fig. 8.15. Physical databases and some logical databases
constructed from these.

Let us now consider an example of how logical databases are declared.

```
DBD    NAME=LOG_ITEM, ACCESS=LOGICAL
SEGM   NAME=ITEMS, SOURCE=(INAME,ITEM_DB)
SEGM   NAME=ORDMEM, PARENT=ITEMS,
       SOURCE=((ORDERS,ITEM_DB), (MEMBERS,MEM_DB))
```

(a) Definition sketch for a logical database.

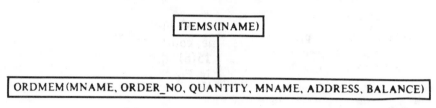

(b) The logical database scheme.

Fig. 8.16. Defining a logical database.

Example 8.10: Given the two physical databases shown in Fig. 8.13, we can construct a logical database that looks essentially like Fig. 8.12. A sketch of the declaration of this logical database is shown in Fig. 8.16(a). The logical database defined is shown in Fig. 8.16(b). The ORDMEM segment is the combination of ORDERS from the physical database ITEM_DB and MEMBERS from MEM_DB. It should be remembered that ORDMEM segments do not exist as such. If IMS is asked to retrieve a segment of this type, it finds the underlying ORDERS and MEMBERS segment occurrences (the assembled version of Fig. 8.16(a) tells IMS how to find them) and retrieves six fields. The first, MNAME, is the fully concatenated key of the MEMBERS segment occurrence. Since MEMBERS is the root of MEM_DB, this fully concatenated key consists of only one field, but in general, the fully concatenated key would have one field (the sequence field) from each segment on the path from the root to the logical parent segment involved in the combination.

The next two fields, ORDER_NO and QUANTITY, are from ORDERS; these fields form the intersection data. The remaining three fields, MNAME, ADDRESS, and BALANCE, are from MEMBERS. Note that MNAME thus appears twice. No real redundancy exists, since ORDMEM segments only exist when they are retrieved. The extra time and space used to make two copies of MNAME is negligible. □

Representing Many-Many Relationships

The power of logical databases in IMS is illustrated by the fact that we can use them to represent a many-many relationship between two entity sets *A* and *B*. The general idea is shown in Fig. 8.17, where we see two physical databases. One consists of a segment *A*, whose fields are the attributes for entity set *A*. It has a child segment PTB, consisting only of a logical parent pointer to segment *B*. In turn, segment *B*, which represents entity set *B*, has a child segment with a pointer to *A*. For example, if the relationship consists of the pairs (a_1,b_1), (a_1,b_2), (a_2,b_1), and (a_3,b_1), the actual physical databases would be as shown in Fig. 8.18.

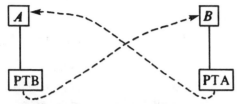

8.17. Representing a many-many mapping.

From these physical databases we can construct, using the methods just described, either of the two logical databases shown in Fig. 8.19. An application program can work on views identical to both these logical databases, using Fig. 8.19(a) to determine the *B*'s associated with an *A* and Fig. 8.19(b) to find the *A*'s associated with a *B*. Note that because of the hierarchical nature of IMS, neither logical database by itself is sufficient to represent the relationship in both directions efficiently.

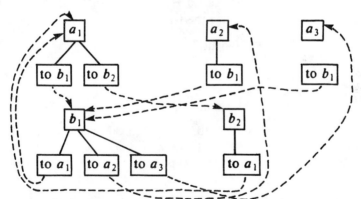

Fig. 8.18. The actual physical database.

Representing DBTG Sets

A DBTG set, representing a many-one mapping, is a special case of a many-many mapping. Thus it should be no surprise that if we have a DBTG set *S* with owner type *A* and member type *B*, we can represent *S* by the pair of logical databases of Fig. 8.19. Since for each *B* segment there is at most one owner segment of type *A*, in the actual database of which Fig. 8.19 is the scheme, each *B* occurrence will have at most one child. However, a program may still need both (a) and (b), since with (a) alone it

(a)   (b)

Fig. 8.19. Two logical databases constructable from Fig. 8.18.

cannot find the owner of a *B* occurrence conveniently.

As a consequence of the above, it should be clear that any network can be represented by a collection of IMS logical databases with little loss of efficiency. Conversely, as a hierarchy is a special case of a network, an IMS database could be converted to a database using a DBTG-oriented database system without losing much efficiency. Thus the network and hierarchical models are equivalent in this strong sense, at least when the hierarchically oriented system has the capabilities of IMS.

8.4 Storage Organizations

As we have mentioned, there are four storage organizations available for physical database. These are called HSAM, HISAM, HIDAM, and HDAM. To decode these acronyms, use the following key.

> AM = access method
> H   = hierarchical
> I   = indexed
> S   = sequential
> D   = direct (i.e., via pointers)

For example, HISAM stands for "hierarchical indexed sequential access method." The purpose of this choice of storage organizations, as for location or set modes in the DBTG proposal, is to give the database designer the flexibility to obtain efficiency of operation for a particular mix of database manipulations. For example, we shall see that there are opportunities to obtain faster performance if we use more space, and there are opportunities to favor sequential search of the database or to favor search for "randomly" specified segments.

Basic Terminology

Each of these four storage methods at least tries to keep a root segment occurrence and all its descendant segment occurrences together. Such a collection of segments is called a *database record.* Storage is divided into fixed length blocks of memory, which IMS calls "records," but for which we retain the term "block" to be consistent with Chapter 2. Database records often cover several blocks, but no one segment may overlap two blocks. The blocks are grouped into one or more areas of memory called data sets. All pointers, both logical parent pointers used in physical databases and pointers introduced by the access methods, are actually offsets from the beginning of a data set.

The HSAM Organization

If HSAM is used as the storage organization, the database records appear in sorted order, according to the value in the sequence field of each root segment. Within a database record, segments appear in preorder. To implement a GET command, the entire database must be searched, either from the beginning or from the current segment moving right, if a GET NEXT is called for. Insertions, deletions, and replacements are not permitted.

The HSAM organization is well suited to a database stored on tape, which is read sequentially. Perhaps a new copy of the database will be made, and updates gathered over a long period of time are reflected in the new version. It is also useful to give backup copies of a database the HSAM organization, even if the original uses some other organization, as HSAM uses the minimum possible space.

The HISAM Organization

The HISAM organization stores database records in chains of blocks, as usually the segments of one database record do not fit on one block. As a matter of efficiency it is wise to choose the block size small enough that database records usually exceed the block length, or there will be much wasted space at the end of the average block.

With HISAM, there is a sparse index on the sequence field of the root segment type, similar to that described in Section 2.3. However, unlike in that section, the index does not contain a pointer for every block, but rather contains one pointer for every k database records. The parameter k, like the block length, is selected when the storage structure for the physical database is defined, and $k=1$ is, of course, a possible choice.

The blocks used to hold the data are grouped into *primary* and *overflow* areas. Each database record begins in one primary block, and any other blocks it needs are taken from the overflow area. Initially the database is created from raw data presented in preorder; an IMS utility routine is available for this purpose. As each database record is presented, it is given the next available primary block and as many overflow blocks as it needs. Thus the primary blocks are filled in order of the sequence field values of the root segments, and it is a simple matter to create an index consisting of a pointer to every k^{th} primary block, along with the root's sequence field value for that block.

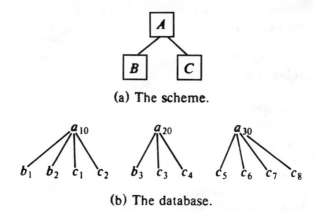

(a) The scheme.

(b) The database.

Fig. 8.20. Example database and its scheme.

Example 8.11: Suppose we have a database with the simple scheme shown in Fig. 8.20(a); Fig. 8.20(b) shows an actual database having this scheme. In Fig. 8.21 we see how the database records of Fig. 8.20(b) would be spread across primary and overflow blocks, using some unstated assumptions about the relative sizes of segments of various types. We also show an index, assuming that $k=1$ and that the sequence field value of segment a_i is i itself. If $k>1$ were chosen, the index pointers would go to the first of a group of k primary blocks, while the key value would be for the last root segment in the group. Note that primary blocks are found in consecutive storage, so the entire group is easily accessible from the first of the group. Also note that pointers chaining the blocks for one database record are shown at the end, and space for a pointer at the beginning has been left empty. We shall discuss the latter pointer shortly. □

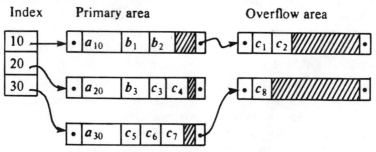

Fig. 8.21. A HISAM organization.

Insertions and Deletions Using HISAM

The way in which insertions and deletions of segments are handled differs in minor respects, depending on which of two underlying *basic storage organizations* are used. These basic organizations are referred to as ISAM/OSAM and VSAM. Acronym fans will enjoy knowing that O = overflow and V = virtual. In what follows we shall assume ISAM/OSAM for specificity. To insert a segment other than a root segment, we simply place the segment in the proper (preorder) position in its database record. Segments following in the same database record are shifted to the right; they are moved to the next block in the chain if necessary, and we may add blocks to the chain if needed.†

The insertion of a new root segment is similar to the strategy discussed in Section 2.3 for pinned records. Inserted roots are given a block in the overflow area, and from each block of the primary area, the pointer at the head begins a chain of overflow blocks used for inserted roots. All inserted roots in the chain have sequence field values that precede the sequence field value of the root segment in the primary area,‡ and inserted roots on the chain appear in ascending sequence. While odd at first glance, this arrangement makes sense, since to scan roots in ascending order of sequence field values, one visits each primary block in turn, first scanning its chain of inserted root segments, in order down the chain, then scanning the root segment in the primary block.

Deletions of any segment are effected by setting a "deletion bit" in the deleted segment; the deleted segment stays where it is. The only way to get rid of the segment is to make a copy of the database and then reinitialize it, using IMS utility routines available for the purpose.

Example 8.12: Suppose that in the database of Fig. 8.21, we insert b_4 as a child of a_{30}. Using our relative segment size assumptions, it will be necessary to move c_7 to the block now occupied by c_8, while shifting c_5, c_6, and c_8 to the right. If we then delete c_6, we simply set a deletion bit in that segment. No motion of the segments is made.

Now imagine we add root segment a_{12} with children b_5 and c_9, then add root segment a_{15} with children b_6, b_7, and b_8. We use three overflow blocks. The first holds (a_{12}, b_5, c_9), the second holds (a_{15}, b_6, b_7), and

---

† One may wonder how movement of segments, such as occurs when a nonroot segment is inserted, can be safe, since the database being implemented may have pointers, such as logical parent pointers, as discussed in Section 8.3. The answer is that when HISAM is the organization, pointers are represented by the fully concatenated key, while in HIDAM and HDAM, to be discussed next, true pointers are used for this and other purposes, and no motion of segments is allowed.

‡ This is opposite to the organization in Section 2.3, where the first key value on the chain preceded all others on the chain.

the last holds only b_8. The blocks with a_{12} and a_{15} are chained in that order from the head of the primary block for a_{20}. The block with b_8 is chained from the tail of the block with a_{15}. Figure 8.22 illustrates all these changes. □

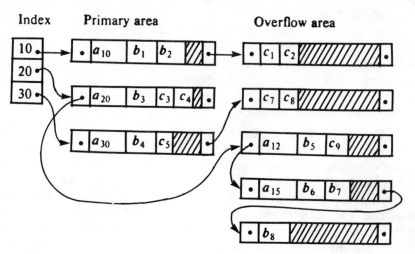

Fig. 8.22. A HISAM database after some insertions and deletions.

The HIDAM Organization

To build a HIDAM database, we start with the initial database stored in preorder, filling a sequence of blocks, just as in the HSAM organization. We then add two features to speed access. First, there is a dense index, in the sense of Section 2.5, consisting of pairs of the form (v, p), where v is the sequence field value of a root segment occurrence, and p is a pointer to that segment. This index is organized like a HISAM database consisting only of root segment occurrences, these occurrences being the pairs (v, p) mentioned above, with the first field serving as the sequence field of the index segments (as well as of the HIDAM database's root segments).

The second feature is a collection of pointers linking the segments of a database record. Here, two options are available.

1. *Preorder threads* (called *hierarchical pointers* in IMS terminology). Each segment has a pointer to the next segment in the preorder sequence of segment occurrences.†

---

† While this is exactly the sequence in which segments are placed in the initial database, segments inserted later can be scattered over various blocks in no particular order.

2. *Leftmost child/right sibling pointers* (IMS jargon is *child/twin)* Each segment occurrence has a (leftmost child) pointer to its leftmost (that is, first in preorder sequence) child segment occurrence, if one exists, and it also has a (right sibling) pointer to the next segment occurrence with the same parent, if one exists. Note that the right sibling may be of a different segment type. Also, there is one leftmost child pointer per segment occurrence, no matter how many different types of segments are found among its children.

Example 8.13: Recall Fig. 8.3, which included an example of a complete database record for our example real estate agency database. Figure 8.23(a) shows that database record with hierarchical pointers, and Fig. 8.23(b) shows it with child/twin pointers; pointers to the leftmost child are solid, while pointers to the right sibling are dashed. □

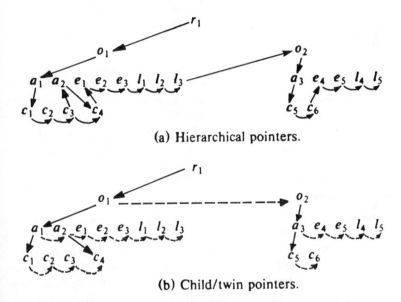

(a) Hierarchical pointers.

(b) Child/twin pointers.

Fig. 8.23. Hierarchical and child/twin pointers.

As an option, either hierarchical or child/twin pointers can be made two-way. It is also an option to link root segment occurrences with two way pointers in the order of their sequence field values. Whether or not these pointers are present, the index allows us to scan the root segments in order of their sequence field values efficiently. Finally, it is also an option to use hierarchical pointers for some segments and child/twin pointers for others.

Example 8.14: To tie the HIDAM concepts together, we show in Fig. 8.24 the database of Fig. 8.21 organized as a HIDAM database with hierarchical pointers. We have not, however, shown the HISAM organization of the index database. □

Index

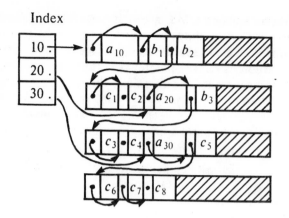

Fig. 8.24. A HIDAM database.

Insertions and Deletions in HIDAM

Deleted segments have their space made available for reuse. The hierarchical or child/twin pointers are updated to reflect the deletion of the segment; we leave as an exercise the algorithm for manipulating these pointers. Inserted segments, including new root segments, are placed as close to their predecessor in preorder as possible† and pointers are updated appropriately. An insertion into the index database occurs when a root segment is inserted.

The HDAM Organization

The hierarchical direct organization connects segments of a database record by the user's choice of hierarchical or child/twin pointers, just as in HIDAM. The essential difference between HIDAM and HDAM is that in HDAM, the index accessing root segments is replaced by a hash function. Storage for an HDAM database is divided into primary and overflow areas; there is one primary block for each possible value to be returned by the hash function and as many overflow blocks as the designer calls for. Overflow blocks are available to the buckets corresponding to any hash value.

Segments are initially loaded into a HDAM database in any order, unlike HSAM, HISAM, or HIDAM databases, where initial loading must be in the correct preorder sequence. Root segments are placed in the primary block that corresponds to the value of the hash function, applied to

---

† This requirement is motivated by the assumption that it is easier to access a block having just accessed a nearby block than otherwise. For example, nearby blocks may be on the same cylinder of a disk, thus obviating the need for head motion.

the sequence field value of the segment. If no room exists in this block, HDAM chooses a primary block that is as close physically as is currently possible. This strategy minimizes the amount of search time necessary to find a given root segment. For example, if we cannot arrange that all root segments with a given hash value reside in the same block, we would like them to be on the same cylinder of a disk. All root segments with the same hash value are chained together in ascending order of sequence field values, so if these segments are all physically close, the entire chain can be scanned relatively efficiently. Root segments are not, in general, chained in order of their sequence field values, and, in fact, GET NEXT applied to root segments will not necessarily return the segments in proper order if HDAM is the organization used.

Nonroot segments are loaded into the same primary block as their root segment, provided there is space, or into a physically closest nonfull primary block if not. However, as a parameter of the HDAM organization, we can limit the amount of primary space devoted to the segments of any one database record. When this limit is exceeded, additional segments are placed in the overflow area. Note that the hierarchical or child/twin pointers used with HDAM prevent segments from getting lost wherever they are put. Limiting the use of the primary area helps guarantee that at least the root segments will tend to appear in the block to which they are hashed.

Insertions and Deletions in HDAM

When segments are deleted, their space may be reused later. Insertions are done essentially as during the initial loading of the database, with the space of deleted segments used where possible. If the entire primary area is filled, even root segments may be inserted into the overflow area. Of course, the hierarchical or child/twin pointers must be adjusted with each insertion and deletion.

Secondary Indices

We can supplement a database using the HISAM, HIDAM, or HDAM organization by one or more secondary indices, which are themselves databases with a HISAM-like organization. While we shall not go into the details here, suffice it to say that we can create a secondary index on any list of up to five fields from a single segment type. The secondary index can be made to associate with values for these fields, either the segment occurrences having these values in designated fields, or the ancestor of a specified segment type, for each of these occurrences. For example, in the database scheme of Fig. 8.2, we could create a secondary index on PRICE that would associate with each price the listings at that price. Or, we could instead associate with a price the offices having listings at that price.

Comparison of the IMS Storage Organizations

To begin, we should remark on the relative advantages of hierarchical and child/twin pointers, as used in HIDAM and HDAM. First, hierarchical pointers take less space, since each segment requires exactly one pointer, while for child/twin pointers, space for one pointer to the leftmost child and one to the right sibling must be made available. Interestingly, at any time, a given database record has the same number of nonnull pointers whether hierarchical or child/twin pointers are used. However, in the latter case, about half the space for pointers will be unused (null). Yet there is no way to avoid leaving space for two pointers per segment, since pointers can switch from null to nonnull, as segments are inserted and deleted.

It might thus seem that hierarchical pointers are always to be preferred. Such is not the case. It is true that in a tree with only a root and its children, hierarchical and child/twin pointers are essentially the same, so we would prefer the former on space considerations. However, in trees of depth greater than two, where each segment has many children, the execution of a GET command that specifies a path to a leaf far to the right in the tree is greatly speeded up if we use child/twin pointers.

Example 8.15: In Figure 8.25 we see a database tree in which each segment occurrence has ten child occurrences. If we specify a path by giving field values that identify a, b_{10}, and $c_{10,10}$, using the right sibling pointers shown, we can go from a to b_1 to b_{10} by following one child and nine sibling pointers, then from $c_{10,1}$ to $c_{10,10}$ following another child and nine sibling pointers. Thus only 20 pointers are followed. If hierarchical pointers are used instead, we would have to visit $c_{1,1}, \ldots, c_{1,10}$ to get from b_1 to b_2, and so on, thus following 110 pointers to get to $c_{10,10}$. $\square$

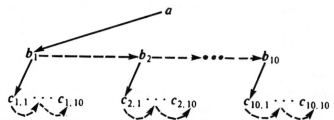

Fig. 8.25. A tree showing the advantage of child/twin pointers.

Now let us compare the four access methods, HSAM, HISAM, HIDAM, and HDAM themselves. There are a variety of criteria that can be used, and it is required of the database designer that he consider the factors most important for the database at hand when selecting a method.

1. *Space utilization.* HSAM uses the minimum possible amount of space. This is probably the only justification for using HSAM, as it is generally far too limiting a method, not even permitting insertions or deletions to the database. Next most compact is HISAM, since it requires only space for an index and no pointer space as do HIDAM and HDAM. Of the direct methods, HIDAM requires space for an index database, which HDAM does not. HISAM does not permit the reuse of the space for deleted segments (except when VSAM is used) as the direct methods do, so the space used by a typical HISAM database will increase more rapidly than for HIDAM and HDAM. However, if the database is copied and reloaded frequently, or little deletion is done, this factor may not be important.

2. *Lookup speed.* Lookup of a random segment in a HSAM database requires, on the average, scanning half the database. Thus HSAM is impractical if segments are to be accessed in an order that is not very close to the preorder sequence. Since database records are kept together in HISAM and HIDAM, these methods may be somewhat faster than HDAM when large database records must be searched. However, HDAM, because it provides hashed access to root segments, is better for finding root segments than are the indexed methods. As mentioned in Example 8.15, for database records of at least three levels, the direct methods using child/twin pointers may be superior to HISAM, which requires a preorder search of the database record.

3. *Insertion speed.* Insertion in HISAM requires shifting of other segments, so it is slower than the direct methods. Insertion is not even possible in HSAM, of course.

4. *Pointer following.* HIDAM and HDAM use true pointers, so accesses to logical databases can be done efficiently when one of the direct methods is used for the underlying physical database. In HISAM, pointers are simulated by the fully concatenated key, so it takes extra time to follow them.

Exercises

8.1: Give an IMS database description for the baseball database used as a running example in Chapter 3.

*8.2: The beer drinkers' database, first introduced in Exercise 4.6, presents problems when we try to implement it as a hierarchy. We need the three logical databases shown in Fig. 8.26, so that we can find conveniently, given a drinker, the bars frequented and the beers liked, and so we can also find the significant information regarding bars and beers conveniently. Give database descriptions for appropriate underlying physical databases and for the logical databases of Fig. 8.26.

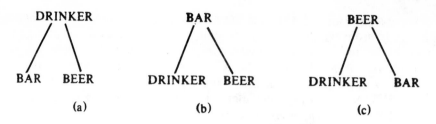

Fig. 8.26. Three logical databases.

*8.3: Suppose we wish to write a program that reads a drinker and deter-
mines the bars that serve a beer that he likes, whether or not he frequents the bar. (Note that BAR segments in Fig. 8.26(a) do not provide this information, since they represent bars frequented.)

a) Select the views needed by this program, and write the view
definitions (program communication blocks) in terms of the logical databases of Fig. 8.26.

b) Write the program in "Pidgin DL/I."

8.4: In Fig. 8.27 we see an IMS database (either physical or logical)
representing the navies of the world. Give the definition of a view of
this database that indicates only the submarines owned by each country, and in which we are allowed only to read COUNTRIES segments,
but may perform any operation on SUBMARINES segments.

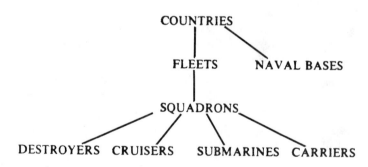

Fig. 8.27. Naval database.

8.5: Figure 8.28 shows a database record. Indicate the (a) hierarchical (b)
child-twin pointers for this database record.

*8.6: Give algorithms to update (a) hierarchical (b) child-twin pointers
when a segment is inserted or deleted.

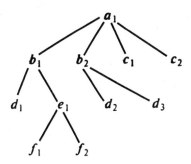

Fig. 8.28. A database record.

8.7: Suppose we have a HISAM database in which blocks hold 1000 bytes of data, and the three segment types (*A*, *B*, and *C*) are 300, 200, and 400 bytes long, respectively. In Fig. 8.29(a) we see the initial database records, where the sequence field of *A* (root) segments is assumed to be the subscript i in the symbol a_i representing a segment occurrence.

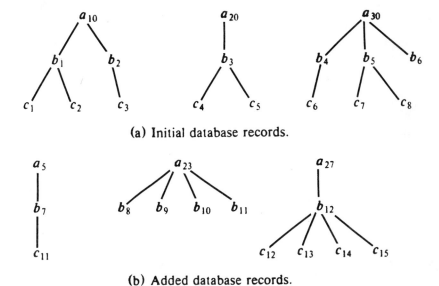

(a) Initial database records.

(b) Added database records.

Fig. 8.29. Creation of a HISAM database.

a) Show the initial distribution of segment occurrences in primary and overflow blocks.

b)   Suppose we add c_9 as the first child of b_1 and c_{10} as the first child of b_4. Show the revised placement of segment occurrences.

c)   Suppose we add the database records of Fig. 8.29(b). Show the resulting placement of segment occurrences.

Bibliographic Notes

There are a number of versions of IMS available. This chapter is based on IMS/VS version 1, as described in the set of manuals IBM [1978b]. An extensive treatment of IMS can be found in Date [1977].

MRI's System 2000 (MRI [1978]) is another important hierarchical system. Descriptions of this system can also be found in Tsichritzis and Lochovsky [1977] and Cardenas [1979].

9

Protecting the Database Against Misuse

In any complete DBMS we find facilities to prevent incorrect data from being stored in a database and to prevent the reading of data that should not be disclosed to the person reading. There are two sources of incorrect data: accidents, such as mistyping of input or programming errors, and malicious use of the database. We can divide the problem of protecting the database into two subproblems:

. *Integrity preservation.* This aspect concerns nonmalicious errors and their prevention. For example, it is reasonable to expect a DBMS to provide facilities for declaring that the value of a field AGE should be less than 150. The DBMS can also help detect some programming bugs, such as a procedure that inserts a record with the same values in the key fields as a record that already exists in the database (assuming we tell the system we do not want such an insertion to be made). In this case, the program should be rewritten to check first whether such a record is present.

2. *Security* (or *access control*). Here we are concerned primarily with restricting certain users to access and/or modify only a subset of the database. It might appear that any attempt on the part of a user to access a restricted portion of the database would be malicious, but in fact a programming error could as well cause the attempted access to restricted data.

Both integrity and security aspects of a DBMS will be considered in this chapter. We devote considerable attention to some of the subtle problems of security for *statistical databases,* such as census data, where the problem is not to restrict the user from accessing any part of the database in particular, but rather to prevent his deducing detailed data, such as the income of one particular individual, from statistical information such as the average salaries of several large classes of individuals.

9.1 Integrity

There are two essentially different kinds of constraints we would like a DBMS to enforce. As discussed at the beginning of Chapter 5, one type is structural, concerning only equalities among values in the database. By far the most prevalent instances of such constraints are what we there called functional dependencies. Many, but not all, functional dependencies can be expressed if the DBMS allows the user to declare that a set of fields or attributes forms a key for a record type or relation. The need to express functional dependencies is not restricted to relational systems, nor do all relational systems have such a facility, explicitly. For example, we noted in Chapter 8 that IMS permits us to declare a sequence field to be "unique." Thus the sequence field of the root can be made to function as a key for that segment type, although for nonroot segment types the sequence field will only be unique among children of a single segment of the parent type. Note, however, that if the sequence fields for all segment types are declared unique, then the fully concatenated key serves as a "key" for segments of any type, although technically, some fields of the fully concatenated key may not be part of the segment itself.

The second kind of integrity constraint concerns the actual values stored in the database. Typically these constraints restrict the value of a field to some range or express some arithmetic relationship among various fields. For example, a credit union might expect that the sum of the BAL-ANCE field, taken over all members of the credit union, equals the net assets of the union. As another example, if the record for a course contained fields E%, H%, and L%, indicating the percentage of the grade devoted to exams, homework, and labs, we would expect that in each such record the sum of the values in these fields is 100.

Query Languages as Integrity Constraint Languages

A fundamental idea concerning integrity constraints is that the data manipulation language can be used as the language in which integrity constraints are expressed. The declaration of an integrity constraint has two parts. First, we must express the constraint itself; for this part the data manipulation language is generally quite suitable. The second part is a description of when the constraint is to be checked. The general idea is that the integrity constraints are allowed to function as high-level "interrupts," like ON conditions in PL/I.

For example, the DBTG proposal allows any number of ON clauses of the form

ON < command list > CALL < procedure >

in the declaration of DBTG sets and record types. For a DBTG set, the < command list > may include any of INSERT, REMOVE, and FIND. The

<procedure> is an arbitrary routine written in the DBTG data manipulation language, which, we recall, is an extension of COBOL, and thus has full computing capability as well as the ability to access any part of the database. For example, if we declare for DBTG set S:

ON INSERT CALL P1

The procedure P1 could check that certain fields of the current of run-unit, the record being inserted, are not already present in the selected set occurrence, thus assuring that these fields are functionally dependent on the fields of the owner record type for S.

The <command list> for an ON clause in a record type declaration can include any of the above three commands and also the remaining four: STORE, DELETE, MODIFY, and GET. Such an ON clause is triggered whenever a command in the list is executed and the current of run-unit is of the relevant record type.

9.2 Integrity Constraints in Query-by-Example

To demonstrate how the ideas of the previous section can be put into practice, we shall discuss integrity in the Query-by-Example system in depth. First, if we review Section 4.7, we note that when a relation is declared, we are allowed to specify whether each field is key or nonkey. The system then enforces the functional dependency of each nonkey field on the set of key fields taken together. This integrity check is triggered on each insertion or modification of a tuple in the relation, and operations that would cause a violation of the dependency are not done; a warning is printed. We shall discuss later how to set up functional dependency constraints that are not of the form key → nonkey.

The QBE system maintains a constraint table for each relation. To create a constraint on relation R, we call for a table skeleton for R. We enter one or more rows representing the constraints into the skeleton. Below the relation name we enter

I.CONSTR(<condition list>). I.

As always, the first I. refers to the entry itself and the second I. to the constraint in the portion of the row that follows. The <condition list> can consist of any or all of I.(insert), D.(delete), U.(update), and identifiers that represent user defined conditions, to be described subsequently. The terms in the <condition list> indicate when the integrity constraint is to be tested; for example, CONSTR(I.,U.). tells us to test the constraint whenever an insertion or modification occurs in the relevant relation. CONSTR. is short for CONSTR(I.,U.,D.).

What follows in the rows are entries for some or all of the attributes. An entry may be a constant, which says the tuple being inserted, deleted, or modified must have that constant value for that attribute. An entry can be of the form θc, where c is a constant and θ an arithmetic comparison which says that the tuple must stand in relation θ to c in that attribute. It can be blank or have a variable name beginning with underscore, which means the tuple can be arbitrary in that attribute. Moreover, there can be additional rows entered in the skeleton for R or in another skeleton; these rows place additional constraints on the values that may appear in the tuple being inserted, deleted, or modified, according to the semantics of the QBE language.

Example 9.1: Let us once more resurrect the HVFC database of Example 4.12. To place the constraint on balances that no one owe more than 100 dollars, we could call for a MEMBERS skeleton and enter

MEMBERS	NAME	ADDR	BALANCE
I.CONSTR (I.,U.). I.			> = -100

To guarantee that no order be accepted for an item for which no supplier exists, we can call for ORDERS and SUPPLIERS skeletons and enter the information shown in Fig. 9.1. This constraint says that the inserted tuple, which defines a value for _hotdog equal to the value of the ITEM attribute in the inserted tuple, must be such that some tuple in the SUPPLIERS relation has that value for its ITEM attribute. □

ORDERS	NAME	ITEM	QUANTITY
I.CONSTR (I.). I.		_hotdog	

SUPPLIERS	SNAME	SADDR	ITEM	PRICE
			_hotdog	

Fig. 9.1. Constraint that orders may only be placed for supplied items.

Defined Triggers for Integrity Checks

There is, in QBE, the capability to define a condition that, when satisfied by an inserted or modified tuple, causes an associated integrity check or checks to be made on that tuple. As we mentioned, in the phrase CONSTR(<condition list>)., the <condition list> can include arbitrary character strings as well as I., D., and U. These character strings, called *defined triggers,* are the names of conditions expressed as rows in the QBE language.

Example 9.2: Suppose we wish to constrain Brooks so that he cannot owe as much as 100 dollars. We could write

MEMBERS	NAME	ADDR	BALANCE
BL I.CONSTR(BL) .I.	Brooks,B.		>−100

The first row indicates that there is a defined trigger called BL that is "triggered" whenever we modify or insert a tuple for Brooks. The second row says that if the MEMBERS tuple for Brooks is inserted or modified, check that his new balance is not lower than −99.99. The tuples for other members are not affected by this constraint. □

Old-New Constraints

Sometimes one wishes to constrain updates in such a way that there is a relationship between the old and new values for certain attributes. We include in the constraint specification a line representing the old tuple as well as the constraint tuple itself. Often the QBE language allows the relationship between the old and new tuples to be expressed in the tuples themselves, but if not, a condition box can be used.

Example 9.3: To create a constraint that a supplier cannot raise the price of granola we enter:

SUPPLIERS	SNAME	SADDR	ITEM	PRICE
I.CONSTR(U.). I.	_supl		Granola	< =_p
I.	_supl		Granola	_p

The row with the keyword CONSTR. represents the new value, and the other row represents the old value. The presence of I. in the latter row distinguishes the old-new type of constraints from a general constraint requiring more than one row to express, as in the second part of Example 9.1. The presence of variable _supl in both rows is necessary, or else we would only check that the new price for the supplier involved in the change is greater than the price charged for granola by at least one other supplier. □

Timing of Constraint Enforcement

The QBE system allows one to enter an entire screenful of commands at once, and this collection of commands may include several insertions, deletions, or updates. It is important to note that integrity constraints are not checked as each command in the collection is executed, but only after all the commands in the collection are executed. This feature allows us certain freedoms in the order in which we specify commands, as long as the commands are entered together.

Thus, in Example 9.1 we constrained our HVFC database in such a way that we could not place an order for an item not supplied. If we enter as one "screenload" several orders for rolled oats and the fact that Tasti Supply now sells rolled oats, we would not violate the constraint. However, if the system entered the orders and checked the integrity constraints before entering the new supply information, we would have had an integrity violation.

The Constraint Table

All integrity constraints declared are available to the user. We can print the constraints pertaining to a relation R if we enter

P. CONSTR. P.

under the relation name in a skeleton for R. Alternatively, we could print only the constraints of specified type; for example

P. CONSTR (I.) P.

prints only the insertion constraints.

We can delete a constraint on R by entering under R in a skeleton for this relation

D. CONSTR (<condition list>).

followed, in the columns for the attributes, by a description of the constraint. Note that a trailing D. is not needed the way a second I. is needed when we insert or print a constraint.

9.3 Security

The subject of database security, the protection of the database against unauthorized use, has many different aspects and approaches. First, we need to protect against both undesired modification or destruction of data and against unauthorized reading of data. Many of the problems associated with security are not unique to database systems, but must be faced by the designer of an operating system, for example. Therefore, let us touch on some of the techniques common to security for database systems and more general systems, and then turn to some of the specialized problems and techniques germane to existing database systems.

1. *User identification.* Generally, different users are accorded different rights to different databases or different portions of the database, such as relations or attributes. These rights may include the reading of portions of the database, and the insertion, deletion, or modification of data. The most common scheme to identify users is a password known only to the system and the individual. Presumably, the passwords are protected by the system at least as well as the data, although to be realistic, guarantees or proofs of security are nonexistent.

2.   *Physical Protection.* A completely reliable protection scheme must take
into account the possibility of physical attacks on the database, ranging from forced disclosure of a password to theft of the physical
storage devices. We can protect against theft fairly well by encrypting
the data. A high security system needs better identification than a
password, such as personal recognition of the user by a guard. It
should not surprise the reader if we rule this topic outside the scope
of the book.

3.   *Maintenance and Transmittal of Rights.* The system needs to maintain
a list of rights enjoyed by each user on each protected portion of the
database. One of these rights may be the right to confer rights on
others. For example, as we mentioned in Section 7.4, the DBTG proposal calls for DBTG sets, record types, and areas to be protected; the
mechanism could be a password for each protected object. The proposal does not call for a table of user rights to protected objects, and
transmission of rights can be handled outside the system, by inform-
ing users of passwords, for example. Both System R† and the
Query-by-Example System (to be discussed further in Section 9.4)
maintain a table of rights and permit the granting of rights to others.

Now let us turn to the consideration of two mechanisms of protection
that are specially designed for use in database systems.

Views as Protection Mechanisms

The view, in addition to making the writing of application programs easier
by allowing some redefinition of the conceptual database and promoting
logical data independence, serves as a convenient protection facility in
many cases. There are two distinct kinds of view facilities. The first, which
we discussed in connection with ISBL and Query-by-Example (Sections 4.4
and 4.7), allows no modification to the view. We call such a view facility
read-only. There are many situations in which the owner of a database (or
of any protectable object for that matter) wishes to give the public the
privilege of reading his data but wishes to reserve the privilege of modifying the database to himself or to a limited set of associates. The read-only
view is ideal for this purpose.

For example, in ISBL or QBE, we may define a view equal to the
current value of a given relation and allow public (read-only) access to this
view. There is also the option of creating a view containing only part of the
information of a relation, or parts of several relations, thus shielding certain
attributes or tuples from public view.

---

† The DBMS discussed in Section 4.5 in connection with SEQUEL.

The other type of view permits both reading and writing of the objects that are part of the view, and modifications to the view are reflected in the conceptual scheme. IMS, System R, and the DBTG proposal permit this sort of view, for example. Clearly this facility is more versatile than the read-only view, as far as the design of application programs is concerned. In IMS, at least, the PROCOPT parameter associated with each segment of the view can permit or forbid insertions, deletions, or modifications, so in a sense the IMS view facility provides more general protection than a read-only view.†

The Use of Query Languages to Define Rights

The second important idea concerning security as it pertains to database systems is that the data manipulation language can be used to define the privileges each user has for accessing the database, in much the same way that this language can be used to define integrity constraints. Each of the four relational systems discussed in Chapter 4 follow this general approach; we shall discuss Query-by-Example's security mechanism in detail in the next section. The DBTG proposal allows the "privacy lock" for a protectable object to be an arbitrary procedure, so here too we could expect arbitrary checks, expressed in the DBTG data manipulation language, for granting or denying a request to access a protected object.

9.4 Security in Query-by-Example

The QBE system recognizes the four rights: insert (I.), delete (D.), update (U.), and read (P., for "print"). To confer one or more rights to a relation R upon a person or group of people, the owner of relation R enters a tuple in an R skeleton. Under the relation name R appears the entry

    I.AUTR(<list>). <name> I.

where <list> is a list of one or more of the four rights, I., D., U., and P.; <name> is either the name of the person being given the rights or a variable, representing an arbitrary person. We may omit (<list>) if we intend to grant all four rights, and we may omit <name> if we wish to grant a set of rights to all users.

To complete the row with the AUTR. keyword, we enter variables or constants in some or all of the columns for the attributes. A variable indicates that the right applies to the column. A constant indicates the right applies only to tuples with that constant value in that column. A blank indicates that the column cannot be accessed. Note that this rule differs from the general QBE policy that blanks are synonymous with variables

---

† There is a problem in IMS that deletion of a segment, where permitted, also deletes all descendant segments, even if they are not part of the view and thus ineligible even for reading.

nentioned only once. The full power of the QBE language can be brought o bear to refine the set of tuples in the relation R to which the right is ranted. For example, we can use condition boxes to constrain the values f variables, and we can add additional rows that restrict values of variables.

Example 9.4: Let us again use the HVFC database as an example. To give ser Brooks the right to read the ORDERS relation we say

ORDERS	NAME	ITEM	QUANTITY
I.AUTR(P.). Brooks I.	_n	_i	_q

o grant Brooks all four access rights to the ORDERS relation we can write

ORDERS	NAME	ITEM	QUANTITY
I.AUTR. Brooks I.	_n	_i	_q

o give anyone the right to read names and balances (but not addresses) rom the MEMBERS relation, provided the balance is nonnegative, we say

MEMBERS	NAME	ADDR	BALANCE
I.AUTR(P.). Lark I.	_n		>0

As a final example, to allow anyone access to read orders for items upplied by Sunshine Produce, we may write the command shown in Fig. .2. □

ORDERS	NAME	ITEM	QUANTITY
I.AUTR(P.). _Lark I.	_n	_i	_q

SUPPLIERS	SNAME	SADDR	ITEM	PRICE
	Sunshine Produce		_i	

Fig. 9.2. Anyone may read orders for items supplied by Sunshine Produce.

Constraints on the Name of the Grantee

We have so far shown two kinds of grants: to anyone or to one specific peron. We can use the QBE language to express subsets of the set of users, nd we can even allow the set of accessible tuples to be different for lifferent users. The technique is to use a variable for <name> in the AUTR. entry, and to use the same name in the tuple or tuples describing he right granted to each individual user. The system provides a facility to elate the name of the user to the representation of his name as it appears n the database.

Example 9.5: We can give everyone authorization to read only his own balnce by:

MEMBERS	NAME	ADDR	BALANCE
I.AUTR(P.) _Lark I.	_Lark		_b

□

The Authorization Table

As for integrity constraints, all AUTR. statements are placed in a table From this table we can print the rights granted to an individual concernin a relation, or all grants concerning a relation, in much the same manner a we print integrity constraints. Similarly, the owner of a relation can delet rights from the table concerning that relation.

9.5 Security in Statistical Databases

A *statistical database* is a database from which aggregate information abou large subsets of entities of an entity set is to be obtained, such as a databas of census data, or for certain applications, a file of employees, tax returns or hospital patients. In addition to the usual problems of forbidding unau thorized access to or modification of the database, there is, in a statistica database, the rather subtle problem of permitting queries such as "Print th average income of all persons in the state of New Jersey" while forbiddin access to the income of an individual, John Jones.

It is not sufficient simply to forbid queries that ask for information pertaining to a single record. For example, Fred Smith could ask for th average income of the set {Fred Smith, John Jones}, from which, knowin his own income, Smith could deduce Jones' income. Nor can one simpl insist that queries ask for aggregate information about a set of at least n individuals, for a suitably large m fixed by the security mechanism of th database. For then Smith could take a set S of $m-1$ or more individuals whose incomes he need not know, and obtain the average income of thes individuals plus Jones. Then, Smith obtains the average income of the se consisting of himself and the individuals in set S, from which, knowing hi own income, he can deduce Jones', by subtracting the two answers.

The problem with the above example was not that we allowed querie about small sets; m can be as large as we wish. Rather, the problem lies i the interrogator's ability to ask two queries that are almost the same. Thi possibility suggests that we put a limit not only on the size of sets abou which statistics can be taken, but also that we limit the size of the intersec tion of two sets that are queried. We shall see that this restriction helps we cannot prevent the disclosure of individual data, but we can prove tha it becomes arbitrarily difficult.

A Model of a Statistical Database

Let us assume for simplicity that a statistical database consists of a single file of records. Each record consists of several fields. A query specifies values for certain fields, and produces some aggregate information, such as a sum or average, of the values in one field, taken over all records that satisfy the conditions of the query. For example, if the records consist of name, occupation, and salary, a query might ask for the average salary of all persons named Smith or for the sum of the salaries of all lawyers.

We assume there is a protection mechanism that, in addition to performing the normal security functions discussed in Section 9.3, monitors all queries made by each user, remembering some large number of previous queries he has made. The protection mechanism can enforce a protection strategy, such as refusing to answer queries involving fewer than a predetermined minimum number of records, or refusing to answer a query that has too large an intersection with a previous query.

In general the latter rule may require that the system record a bit vector representing each set of records queried by anyone, over a long period of time, and therefore may not be practical to implement. Some limits regarding what is remembered must be imposed. For example, we could choose to remember only a limited number of queries, or we could partition the records into groups and only remember which groups had records that satisfied a given query. The first of these methods may answer queries it should not answer, while the second method may forbid answering a query that it could safely answer.

Linear Queries

Let us consider a database of n records, and let $\mathbf{v} = (v_1, v_2, \ldots, v_n)$ be the vector of values of these records in a particular nonkey field. A *linear query* is a linear sum $\sum_{i=1}^{n} c_i v_i$, where the c_i's are arbitrary real numbers. The most important cases are sums over set S, where $c_i = 1$ if record i is in S and 0 if not, and averages, where $c_i = 1/p$ if record i is in S and 0 if not; p is the number of records in S. However, what we say about our ability to *compromise* a database (deduce the value of an individual v_i) will generally depend on the number of nonzero c_i's we allow, not on their exact values, or on whether the nonzero c_i's are equal.

Suppose we have a set of q queries, where the ith query extracts from the database $r_i = \sum_{j=1}^{n} c_{ij} v_j$. The results of these queries can be expressed in matrix formulation as

$$\mathbf{r}^T = M\mathbf{v}^T$$

where M is a q by n matrix whose entry in row i and column j is c_{ij}, and $\mathbf{v}$ and $\mathbf{r}$ are the vectors $(v_1, \ldots, v_n)$ and $(r_1, \ldots, r_q)$, respectively. Superscript T stands for the transpose, making a column vector out of a row vector such as $\mathbf{r}$ or $\mathbf{v}$. If we are to compromise the database, we need to compute some function $f(r_1, \ldots, r_q)$ that is equal to one of the v_j's, say v_1 without loss of generality. A fundamental fact is stated in the following lemma.

Lemma 9.1: If, in the notation used above, there is some function f such that $f(r_1, \ldots, r_q) = v_1$, then there is a linear such function f.

Proof: The proof requires some linear algebra and multivariable calculus. We omit the proof, giving hints in the exercises for those willing to tackle it. □

Suppose now that f is linear. Then there is some vector $\mathbf{d} = (d_1, \ldots, d_q)$ such that $f(r_1, \ldots, r_q) = \sum_{i=1}^{q} d_i r_i = v_1$. Then substituting $M\mathbf{v}^T$ for $\mathbf{r}$, we have

$$\mathbf{d}\mathbf{r}^T = \mathbf{d}M\mathbf{v}^T = v_1$$

It follows that $\mathbf{d}M$ must be the vector $(1, 0, \ldots, 0)$ of length n. In terms of statistical databases, to compromise the database, which we without loss of generality take to mean computation of the element v_1, we must find a collection of q queries forming a matrix M such that there is some vector $\mathbf{d}$ for which $\mathbf{d}M = (1, 0, \ldots, 0)$. If we put constraints on the queries, which means constraining the rows of M, we may be able to prove that M must have many rows i.e., many queries are necessary, if such a $\mathbf{d}$ exists. In particular, we shall consider two constraints on M.

1.   Each row has at least m nonzero elements. That is, queries must each involve at least m values.

2.   No two rows have more than k columns in which both have nonzero elements. In database terms, the intersection of the sets of elements involved in two queries has size at most k.

Example 9.6: Let us consider a database of seven elements $v_1, \ldots, v_7$, and use the following five queries.

$$r_1 = v_2 + v_3 + v_4$$
$$r_2 = v_5 + v_6 + v_7$$
$$r_3 = v_1 + v_2 + v_5$$
$$r_4 = v_1 + v_3 + v_6$$
$$r_5 = v_1 + v_4 + v_7$$

Then $v_1 = (r_3 + r_4 + r_5 - r_1 - r_2)/3$. Note that each query involves at least three values, and no two queries have an intersection of size greater than one. That is, $m=3$, and $k=1$. In matrix terms the queries compute the matrix-vector product of Fig. 9.3. The vector d is $(-1/3, -1/3, 1/3, 1/3, 1/3)$. Note that d times the matrix in Fig. 9.3 is $(1, 0, 0, 0, 0, 0, 0)$. $\square$

$$\begin{bmatrix} r_1 \\ r_2 \\ r_3 \\ r_4 \\ r_5 \end{bmatrix} = \begin{bmatrix} 0 & 1 & 1 & 1 & 0 & 0 & 0 \\ 0 & 0 & 0 & 0 & 1 & 1 & 1 \\ 1 & 1 & 0 & 0 & 1 & 0 & 0 \\ 1 & 0 & 1 & 0 & 0 & 1 & 0 \\ 1 & 0 & 0 & 1 & 0 & 0 & 1 \end{bmatrix} \begin{bmatrix} v_1 \\ v_2 \\ v_3 \\ v_4 \\ v_5 \\ v_6 \\ v_7 \end{bmatrix}$$

Fig. 9.3. Query expressed as matrix-vector product.

We shall now derive upper and lower bounds on the number of queries needed to compromise a database, assuming each query involves at least m elements, and no two queries involve more than k elements in common. We can also assume that p values are already known, and that to compromise the database, we must determine an element not already known.

Theorem 9.1: Suppose we are allowed only to make queries that produce a linear function of at least m elements, and no two queries may involve more than k elements in common. Further suppose that p elements are already known. Then to compute some element not already known, we must make at least $1+(m-1-p)/k$ queries.

Proof: Consider the first query, which produces a linear sum over a set S of at least m elements. Let v_i be a member of S. If v_i is not among the p elements already known, and v_i is not the element computed by the matrix-vector product dM (using the same notation as previously), then there must be some other query that involves v_i. For we may assume M has the smallest possible number of rows, that is, we make no more queries than necessary to compromise the database. Put another way, we assume the vector d has no zero components. In this circumstance, if only one query involves v_i, then the product dM must have a nonzero i^{th} component. Since no query may intersect the set S in more than k places, and altogether, at least $m-p-1$ members of S must appear in another query, there must be at least $(m-p-1)/k$ queries in addition to the first, from which the theorem follows. $\square$

Theorem 9.1 has an important consequence. Assuming p, the number of previously known elements, is small compared with m, it takes approximately m/k queries to compromise the database. As m and k are parameters of the protection strategy, we have only to choose them so their ratio is large, say 1000, and we shall be assured that great effort will be required to compromise the database. However, note that a large m and small k may put a burden on the user interested in legitimate statistical information. Also, remembering the last 1000 queries by each user may easily tax the storage capacity of the system, so we question whether limiting the size and intersection of queries is a practical way to proceed in general.

One might wonder if Theorem 9.1 is too pessimistic; perhaps it really takes many more than m/k queries to compromise the database. Unfortunately, this is not the case. Suppose $p=0$, $k=1$, and $n=1+m(m+1)/2$. Consider an $(m+1)$ by $(1+m(m+1)/2)$ matrix M, where the first column has a single 1 and the rest 0's. Each of the remaining columns has two nonzero entries, and no two columns have the same two nonzero rows. This is possible because the number of choices of two rows out of $m+1$ is $m(m+1)/2$. In each of columns 2 through $1+m(m+1)/2$ there is a single 1 and a single -1. Then the sum of all the rows of M is $(1, 0, 0, \ldots, 0)$, allowing us to compromise the database by computing v_1. Since no two columns are identical, and each column has at most two nonzero entries, it follows that no two rows can be zero simultaneously in more than one column. Figure 9.4 shows M for $m=3$.

$$\begin{bmatrix} 0 & 1 & 1 & 1 & 0 & 0 & 0 \\ 0 & -1 & 0 & 0 & 1 & 1 & 0 \\ 0 & 0 & -1 & 0 & -1 & 0 & 1 \\ 1 & 0 & 0 & -1 & 0 & -1 & -1 \end{bmatrix}$$

Fig. 9.4 A matrix M showing fast compromise.

By replacing each column but the leftmost by k identical columns, we can generalize the above strategy to compromise a database with $1+m/k$ queries, which is very close to the lower bound of Theorem 9.1. A proof is left as an exercise.

Perhaps general linear queries allow rapid compromise, but if we restrict ourselves to queries that ask for sums or averages, which is what we would expect a query language to provide, then we can improve on the lower bound of Theorem 9.1. The issue is somewhat in doubt, but we can show that for $k=1$, $2m-1$ queries asking for sums are sufficient to compromise the database. Suppose we have $n=1+m(m-1)$. The first query asks for the sum of elements 2 through $m+1$, the second for $m+2$ through $2m+1$, the third for $2m+2$ through $3m+1$, and so on. The last m queries each ask for a sum including the first element; query m also includes 2, $m+2$, $2m+2$, $\ldots$, query $m+1$ includes 3, $m+3$, $2m+3$, $\ldots$, and so on. The matrix for $m=3$ was shown in Fig. 9.3. The argument given with that figure generalizes to show that $2m/k - 1$ queries suffice for arbitrary m and k.

Limits on the Structure of Queries

So far we have assumed queries specify arbitrary subsets of the records in the database, with only a lower limit on the size of subsets. We found that compromising a database using such queries is not impossible, but it is time consuming if we limit the overlap of the sets defined by two queries. Perhaps if we did not allow all "big" queries, we could actually guarantee noncompromisability.

One approach that has been studied is to assume that the key for records consists of k bits, and that for each key value, or for almost every key value, a record is actually present. Queries are allowed to specify values for up to s of the bits in a key and retrieve the sum of the data items associated with all records whose key values agree with the query in the s specified bits. For example, if $k=3$ and $s=2$, we might specify that bit 1 has value 1 and bit 3 has value 0. Then the result of the query would be the sum of the data in the records with keys 100 and 110.

Note that we are in effect performing a partial match retrieval, as discussed in Section 4.8. As in that section, we are not actually limited to binary key values; we could assume a key consisting of some number of fields, each of which takes values from a particular "small" set of values. Unlike Section 4.8, we are assuming that the result of a query is not the full set of matching records, but rather the sum of the contents of a particular field (the "data" in record) from each of those records.

Example 9.7: Suppose our statistical database consists of U.S. census data, with each record holding data that is the sum of the incomes of all persons whose "characteristics" match the bits of the key value for that record. The key consists of 6 bits representing the state in which the person lives, another 8 bits denoting a locality within the state (perhaps a county or city), 1 bit indicating the sex of the person, 6 bits indicating an occupation (divided arbitrarily into 64 categories), and 5 bits indicating the brand of automobile owned (we assume only one brand of car per person is recorded in the database). Thus $k=6+8+1+6+5=26$. As 2^k is about 67 million, each record represents the income of a few individuals, on the average.

We might let $s=15$, so we could ask in one query for the sum of the incomes of all males living in Washington County, Idaho (which specifies 15 bits), or for the sum of the incomes of all bricklayers owning Plymouths (which specifies 11 bits), but we could not ask for the sum of incomes of bricklayers in Idaho owning Plymouths (which specifies 20 bits). We could, in principle, specify up to 15 bits that included some, but not all, of the bits for a state, some from the occupation, and so on. □

It turns out that in the above model, no collection of legal queries can yield the data of an individual record, provided $s < k$, that is, provided we are not allowed to specify all the bits in a query. In fact we can prove considerably more than that. We cannot compute, from the answers to queries specifying up to s of the k bits of the key, any function involving fewer than 2^{k-s} of the records. The formal statement of the theorem follows.

Theorem 9.2: If queries produce the sum of the "data" in all records whose keys match up to s specified bits, and keys have k bits in all, then no rational function† of the result of such queries can be a function of the data values in more than zero, but fewer than 2^{k-s} of the records.

Proof: The proof is beyond the scope of this book but is found in A. Yao [1979]. □

Corollary: If $s < k$, then no rational function of the results of queries can be the value of the data item in one record, that is, the database cannot be compromised. □

Exercises

9.1: Suppose we have a Query-by-Example database consisting of relations

    EMPS(EMP_NO, NAME, ADDR, SALARY, DEPT_NO)
    DEPTS(DEPT_NO, DNAME, MANAGER)

Express the following integrity constraints.

a)   No employee earns more than 100,000.

b)   No employee in department 72 earns more than 50,000.

c)   No employee in the Toy Department ("Toy" is a value for attribute DNAME) earns more than 50,000.

*d)   No two departments have the same number. *Hint:* Use the CNT. (count) operator.

**9.2: Show that every functional and multivalued dependency can be expressed in the QBE constraint language.

9.3: Express in the QBE authorization language the following authorizations, which pertain to the database of Exercise 9.1.

a)   Anyone can read the EMPS relation, except for the SALARY attribute.

b)   Any employee can read his own salary.

c)   The manager of a department can read the salary of any employee in his department.

---

† That is, a function with addition, subtraction, multiplication, and division for operators.

d) Employee Warbucks can insert and delete EMPS tuples and can modify salaries.

9.4: In Fig. 9.5 we see the database of the West Side Mob. Naturally, the members wish to keep their incomes secret, and their database allows only queries asking for the sum of the incomes of m or more mob members. Moreover, no two queries can involve more than k members in common. For what values of m and k is this particular database secure, in the sense that no individual's income can be deduced? *Hint:* The analysis following Theorem 9.1, which implied that the lower bound of that theorem was attainable (i.e., databases were compromisable for all m and k, albeit slowly), actually assumes the database is sufficiently large. For databases with a small number of individuals, the construction following Theorem 9.1 may not work.

NAME	BOOKMAKING	SMUGGLING	NUMBERS	INCOME
Ralph the Rat	yes	yes	no	?
"Fingers"	yes	no	yes	?
"Scarface"	no	yes	yes	?
"Gouger"	yes	no	no	?
Sam the Snake	no	no	yes	?
"172039"	yes	yes	yes	?

Fig. 9.5. The West Side Mob database.

9.5: Suppose we restrict queries of the West Side Mob database to ask for the sum of incomes over categories, where a category is defined by specifying whether a person is or is not engaged in up to two particular activities of the mob. For example, we could ask for the sum of incomes of all persons engaged in smuggling but not numbers. This query would happen to give us the income of Ralph the Rat, so the database is compromisable. Show that using queries constrained as above, we can deduce the income of each member of the mob.

9.6: Why does Exercise 9.5 not contradict Theorem 9.2?

9.7: Prove Lemma 9.1, that if $f(r_1, \ldots, r_q) = v_1$, then we may assume f is linear. *Hint:* Note that

$$\frac{\partial f}{\partial v_i} = \sum_{j=1}^{q} \frac{\partial f}{\partial r_j} \frac{\partial r_j}{\partial v_i}$$

Also, $\dfrac{\partial r_j}{\partial v_i}$ is the constant c_{ij}, and $\dfrac{\partial f}{\partial v_i}$ is 1 if $i=1$ and 0 otherwise.

9.8:   Show that Theorem 9.1 is a tight lower bound, even for $k > 1$. *Hint*: Generalize the argument for $k=1$ given after Theorem 9.1.

**9.9:   Prove Theorem 9.2.

Bibliographic Notes

The books by Hoffman [1977] and DeMillo, Dobkin, Jones, and Lipton [1978] discuss the general problem of security in computer systems. The material in Sections 9.2 and 9.4 on security and integrity in Query-by-Example, is taken from Zloof [1978]. Note that these features are not currently available in the commercial version of QBE described in IBM [1978a]. Similar techniques in connection with the INGRES system, but including the idea of security and integrity checks by adding constraints to the where-clause of each query, are found in Stonebraker and Wong [1974], Stonebraker [1975], and Stonebraker and Rubinstein [1976].

The paper by Fagin [1978] studies and proves correct an algorithm for granting authorizations to a database with the possibility that the right to grant further authorizations can itself be granted. This idea was earlier studied by Griffiths and Wade [1976]. A brief survey of database security techniques is by Mresse [1978], and a more extensive one is by Hsiao, Kerr, and Madnick [1978].

The earliest formulations of the problem of security in statistical databases are in Hoffman and Miller [1970] and Haq [1974, 1975]. Formal study of the problem began with Dobkin, Jones, and Lipton [1979], who proved Theorem 9.1. Their model has been examined further by Reiss [1979] and VanLeeuwen [1979]. Theorem 9.2 is by A. Yao [1979], although Kam and Ullman [1977] had previously proved the theorem for the special case where the rational function is linear.

A variety of strategies for protecting statistical databases have been studied recently. Chin [1978] considers schemes that refuse to answer queries about small sets, and shows that even if values cannot be deduced, the presence of a record in the database can often be confirmed or refuted. DeMillo, Dobkin, and Lipton [1978] consider strategies where the database sometimes deliberately gives a false answer and show that even this mechanism is not secure. Denning, Denning, and Schwartz [1977] consider a database in which there is a partitioning of the keys, with queries forbidden to ask about too many individuals from any one block of the partition. Generalizing ideas of Schlorer [1975, 1976], Denning, Denning, and Schwartz [1979] show how it is in general possible to construct a "tracker," that is, a query that will obtain information about records satisfying a set of characteristics, even when this set is smaller than the database security system allows.

Surveys of statistical database security and additional references can be found in Yu and Chin [1977] and Denning [1978].

10
Concurrent Operations on the Database

Until now, our concept of a database has been one in which programs accessing the database are run one at a time *(serially)*. Often this is indeed the case. However, there are also numerous applications in which more than one program, or different executions of the same program, run simultaneously *(concurrently)*. An example is an airline reservation system, where many sales agents may be selling tickets and therefore changing lists of passengers and counts of available seats. The canonical problem is that if we are not careful how we allow two or more programs to access the database, we could sell the same seat twice. Intuitively, two processes that read and change the value of the same object must not be allowed to run concurrently.

A second example is a statistical database, such as census data, where many people may be querying the database at once. Here, as long as no one is changing the data, we do not really care in what order the processes read data; we can let the operating system schedule simultaneous read requests as it wishes. In this sort of situation, where only reading is being done, we want to allow maximum concurrent operation, so time can be saved. For contrast, in the case of a reservation system, where both reading and writing are in progress, we need restrictions on when we allow two programs to execute concurrently.

In this chapter we shall consider models of concurrent processes as they pertain to database operation. The models are distinguished primarily by the detail in which they portray access to elements of the database. For each model we shall describe a reasonable way to allow those concurrent operations that preserve the integrity of the database while preventing concurrent operations that might, as far as a model of limited detail can tell, destroy its integrity. As a rule, the more detailed the model, the more concurrency we can allow safely.

10.1 Basic Concepts

A *transaction* is a single execution of a program. This program may be a simple query expressed in one of the query languages of Chapter 4 or an elaborate host language program with embedded calls to a query language such as QUEL, SEQUEL, the DBTG's data manipulation language or IMS's DL/I. Several independent executions of the same program may be in progress simultaneously; each is a transaction.

Items

We imagine that the database is partitioned into *items,* which are portions of the database that can be *locked.* That is, by locking an item, a transaction can prevent other transactions from accessing the item, until the transaction holding the lock unlocks the item. A part of a DBMS called the *lock manager* assigns and records locks, as well as arbitrating among two or more requests for a lock on the same item.

The nature and size of items are the subject of some debate. In the relational model of data, for example, we could choose large items, like relations, or small items like individual tuples or even components of tuples. We could pick an intermediate size for items; for example, items could be collections of 100 tuples from some relation. In the network model, an item could be the collection of all records of a single type, or what the DBTG proposal terms a set occurrence, for example.

Choosing large items cuts down on the system overhead due to maintaining locks, while choosing small items allows many transactions to operate in parallel. At the risk of oversimplifying the conclusions of a number of analyses mentioned in the bibliographic notes, let us suggest that the proper choice for the size of an item is such that the average transaction accesses a few items. Thus if the typical transaction (in a relational system) reads or modifies one tuple, which it finds via an index, it would be appropriate to treat tuples as items. If the typical transaction takes a join of two or more relations, and thereby requires access to all the tuples of these relations, then perhaps we should treat relations as items.

In what follows, we shall assume that when part of an item is modified, the whole item is modified and receives a value that is unique and unequal to the value that could be obtained by any other modification. We make this assumption not only to simplify the modeling of transactions. In practice, it requires too much work on the part of the system to deduce facts such as that the result of one modification of an item gives that item the same value as it had after some previous modification. Furthermore, if the system is to remember whether part of an item remains unchanged after the item is modified, it may as well divide the item into several smaller items. A consequence of our assumption of the indivisibility of items is that we shall not go wrong if we view items as simple variables as used in common programming languages.

Locks

Example 10.1: To see the need for locking items, let us consider two transactions T_1 and T_2. Each accesses an item A, which we assume has an integer value, and adds one to A. The two transactions are executions of the program P defined as

$$P: \text{READ } A;\ A := A+1;\ \text{WRITE } A$$

The value of A exists in the database. P reads A into its workspace, adds one to the value in the workspace, and writes the result into the database. In Fig. 10.1 we see the two transactions executing in an interleaved fashion[†], and we record the value of A as it appears in the database at each step.

A in database	5	5	5	5	6	6
T_1:	READ A		$A := A+1$			WRITE A
T_2:		READ A		$A := A+1$	WRITE A	
A in T_1's workspace	5	5	6	6	6	6
A in T_2's workspace		5	5	6	6	

Fig. 10.1. Transactions exhibiting a need to lock item A.

We notice that although two transactions have each added 1 to A, the value of A has only increased by 1. This is a serious problem if A represents seats sold on an airplane flight, for example. □

The solution to the problem represented by Example 10.1 is to provide a lock on A. Before reading A, a transaction T must lock A, which prevents another transaction from accessing A until T is finished with A. Furthermore, the need for T to set a lock on A prevents T from accessing A if some other transaction is already using A. T must wait until the other transaction unlocks A, which it should do only after finishing with A.

Let us now consider programs that interact with the database not only by reading and writing items but by locking and unlocking them. We assume that a lock must be placed on an item before reading or writing it.

[†] Note that we do not assume necessarily that two similar steps take the same time, so it is possible that T_2 finishes before T_1, even though both transactions execute the same steps. However, the point of the example is not lost if T_1 writes before T_2.

and that the operation of locking acts as a synchronization primitive. That is, if a transaction tries to lock an already locked item, it waits until the lock is released by an unlock command, which is executed by the transaction holding the lock. We assume that each program is written to unlock any item it locks, eventually. A schedule of the elementary steps of two or more transactions, such that the above rules regarding locks are obeyed, is termed *legal*.

Example 10.2: The program P of Example 10.1 could be written with locks as

$$P: \text{LOCK } A; \quad \text{READ } A; \quad A:=A+1; \quad \text{WRITE } A; \quad \text{UNLOCK } A$$

Suppose again that T_1 and T_2 are two executions of P. If T_1 begins first, it requests a lock on A. Assuming no other transaction has locked A, the system grants this lock. Now T_1, and only T_1 can access A. If T_2 begins before T_1 finishes, then when T_2 tries to execute LOCK A, the system causes T_2 to wait. Only when T_1 executes UNLOCK A will the system allow T_2 to proceed. As a result, the anomaly indicated in Example 10.1 cannot occur; either T_1 or T_2 executes completely before the other starts, and their combined effect is to add 2 to A. □

Livelock and Deadlock

We have postulated a part of a DBMS that grants and enforces locks on items. Such a system cannot behave capriciously, or certain undesirable phenomena occur. As an instance, we assumed in Example 10.2 that when T_1 released its lock on A, the lock was granted to T_2. What if while T_2 was waiting, a transaction T_3 also requested a lock on A, and T_3 was granted the lock before T_2. Then while T_3 had the lock on A, T_4 requested a lock, which was granted after T_3 unlocked A, and so on. Evidently, it is possible that T_2 could wait forever, while some other transaction always had a lock on A, even though there are an unlimited number of times at which T_2 might have been given a chance to lock A.

Such a condition is called *livelock*. It is a problem that occurs potentially in any environment where processes execute concurrently. A variety of solutions have been proposed by designers of operating systems, and we shall not discuss the subject here, as it does not pertain solely to database systems. A simple way to avoid livelock is for the system granting locks to record all requests that are not granted immediately, and when an item A is unlocked, grant a lock on A to the transaction that requested it first, among all those waiting to lock A. This first-come-first-served strategy eliminates livelocks,† and we shall assume from here on that livelock is not a

---

† Although it may cause "deadlock," to be discussed next.

problem.

There is a more serious problem of concurrent processing that can occur if we are not careful. This problem, called "deadlock," can best be illustrated by an example.

Example 10.3: Suppose we have two transactions T_1 and T_2 whose significant actions, as far as concurrent processing is concerned are:

T_1: LOCK A LOCK B UNLOCK A UNLOCK B
T_2: LOCK B LOCK A UNLOCK B UNLOCK A

Presumably T_1 and T_2 do something with A and B, but this is not important here. Suppose T_1 and T_2 begin execution at about the same time. T_1 requests and is granted a lock on A, and T_2 requests and is granted a lock on B. Then T_1 requests a lock on B, and is forced to wait because T_2 has a lock on that item. Similarly, T_2 requests a lock on A and must wait for T_1 to unlock A. Thus neither transaction can proceed; each is waiting for the other to unlock a needed item, so both T_1 and T_2 wait forever. □

A situation in which each of a set S of two or more transactions are waiting to lock an item currently locked by some other transaction in the set S is called a *deadlock*. Since each transaction in S is waiting, it cannot unlock the item some other transaction in S needs to proceed, so all wait forever. Like livelock, the prevention of deadlock is a subject much studied in the literature of operating systems and concurrent processing in general. Among the approaches to a solution are the following.

1.   Require each transaction to request all its locks at once, and let the system grant them all, if possible, or grant none and make the process wait, if one or more are held by another transaction. Notice how this rule would have prevented the deadlock in Example 10.3. The system would grant locks on both A and B to T_1 if it requested first; T_1 would complete, and then T_2 could have both locks.

2.   Assign an arbitrary linear ordering to the items, and require all transactions to request locks in this order.

The second approach also prevents deadlock. In Example 10.3, suppose A precedes B in the ordering (there could be other items between A and B in the ordering). Then T_2 would request a lock for A before B and would find A already locked by T_1. T_2 would not yet get to lock B, so a lock on B would be available to T_1 when requested. T_1 would complete, whereupon the locks on A and B would be released. T_2 could then proceed. To see that no deadlocks can occur in general, suppose we have a set S of deadlocked transactions, and each transaction R_i in S is waiting for some other transaction in S to unlock an item A_i. We may assume that each R_i in S holds at least one of the A_i's, else we could remove R_i from S and still have a deadlocked set. Let A_k be the first item among the A_i's in the assumed linear order. Then R_k, waiting for A_k, cannot hold any of the A_i's, for $i \neq k$, which is a contradiction.

Another approach to handling deadlocks is to do nothing to prevent them. Rather, periodically examine the lock requests and see if there is a deadlock. The algorithm of drawing a graph whose nodes are transactions and whose arcs $T_1 \rightarrow T_2$ signify that transaction T_1 is waiting to lock an item on which T_2 holds the lock, makes this test easy; every cycle indicates a deadlock, and if there are no cycles, neither are there any deadlocks. If a deadlock is discovered, at least one of the deadlocked transactions must be restarted, and its effects on the database must be cancelled. This process of restart can be complicated if we are not careful about the way transactions write into the database before they complete. The subject is taken up in Section 10.6.

In the future, we shall assume that neither livelocks nor deadlocks will occur when executing transactions.

Serializability

Now we come to a concurrency issue of concern primarily to database system designers. By way of introduction, let us review Example 10.1, where two transactions executing a program P each added 1 to A, yet A only increased by 1. Intuitively, we feel this situation is wrong, yet perhaps these transactions did exactly what the writer of P wanted. However, it is doubtful that the programmer had this behavior in mind, because if we run first T_1 and then T_2, we get a different result; 2 is added to A. Since it is always possible that transactions will execute one at a time *(serially)* it is reasonable to assume that the normal, or intended, result of a transaction is the result we obtain when we execute it with no other transactions executing concurrently. Thus the concurrent execution of several transactions is correct if and only if its effect is the same as that obtained by running the same transactions serially in some order.

Let us define a *schedule* for a set of transactions to be an order in which the elementary steps of the transactions (lock, read, and so on) are done. The steps of any given transaction must, naturally, appear in the schedule in the same order that they occur in the program of which the transaction is an execution. A schedule is *serial* if all the steps of each transaction occur consecutively. A schedule is *serializable* if its effect is equivalent to that of some serial schedule.

Example 10.4: Let us consider the following two transactions, which might be part of a bookkeeping operation that transfers funds from one account to another.

T_1: READ A; $A:=A-10$; WRITE A; READ B; $B:=B+10$; WRITE B
T_2: READ B; $B:=B-20$; WRITE B; READ C; $C:=C+20$; WRITE C

Clearly, any serial schedule has the property that the sum $A+B+C$ is preserved. In Fig. 10.2(a) we see a serial schedule, and in Fig. 10.2(b) is a serializable, but not serial, schedule. Figure 10.2(c) shows a nonserializable schedule. Note that Fig. 10.2(c) causes 10 to be added, rather than subtracted from B as a net effect, since T_1 reads B before T_2 writes the new value of B. It is possible to prevent the schedule of Fig. 10.2(c) from occurring by locking B. □

T_1	T_2	T_1	T_2	T_1	T_2
READ A		READ A		READ A	
$A:=A-10$			READ B	$A:=A-10$	
WRITE A		$A:=A-10$			READ B
READ B			$B:=B-20$	WRITE A	
$B:=B+10$		WRITE A		READ B	$B:=B-20$
WRITE B			WRITE B		
	READ B	READ B		$B:=B+10$	WRITE B
	$B:=B-20$		READ C	WRITE B	
	WRITE B	$B:=B+10$			READ C
	READ C		$C:=C+20$		
	$C:=C+20$	WRITE B			$C:=C+20$
	WRITE C		WRITE C		WRITE C
(a)		(b)		(c)	

Fig. 10.2. Some schedules.

Recall that we have defined a schedule to be serializable if its effect is equivalent to that of a serial schedule. In general, it is not possible to test whether two schedules have the same effect for all initial values of the items, if arbitrary operations on the items are allowed. In practice, we make some simplifying assumptions about what operations do to items. In particular, it is convenient to assume that values cannot be the same unless they are produced by exactly the same sequence of operations. Thus we do not regard $(A+10)-20$ and $(A+20)-30$ as producing the same values. Ignoring algebraic properties of arithmetic causes us to make only "nonfatal" errors, in the sense that we may disallow a schedule as nonserializable, when in fact it produces the same result as a serial schedule, but we shall never say a schedule is serializable when it in fact is not (a "fatal" error). Nonfatal errors may rule out some concurrent operations, and thereby cause the system to run more slowly than it theoretically could. However, these errors never cause an incorrect result to be computed, as a fatal error could. Succeeding sections will use progressively more detailed models that enable us to infer that wider classes of schedules are serializable, and therefore to achieve more concurrency while guaranteeing correctness.

Protocols and Schedules

We have seen that arbitrary transactions can, when executed concurrently, give rise to livelock, deadlock, and nonserializable behavior. To eliminate these problems we have two tools. The first is the *scheduler,* a portion of the database system that arbitrates between conflicting requests. We saw, for example, how a first-come, first-serve scheduler can eliminate livelock. A scheduler can also handle deadlocks and nonserializability by causing one or more transactions to restart, undoing all their actions so far. We shall consider restart of transactions in Section 10.6.

Another approach to handling deadlock and nonserializability is to use one or more protocols, that all transactions must follow. A *protocol,* in its most general sense, is simply a restriction on the sequences of steps that a transaction may perform. For example, the deadlock-avoiding strategy of requesting locks on items in some fixed order is a protocol. Much of what follows in this chapter concerns the development of protocols that guarantee serializability.

10.2 A Simple Transaction Model

Let us begin by introducing what is undoubtedly the simplest model of transactions that still enables us to talk about serializability. In this model, a transaction is viewed as a sequence of lock and unlock statements. Each item locked must subsequently be unlocked. Between a step LOCK A and the next UNLOCK A, a transaction is said to *hold a lock on A.* We assume a transaction does not try to lock an item if it currently holds a lock on that item, nor does it try to unlock an item on which it does not currently hold a lock.

We further assume that whenever a transaction locks on item A it changes the value of A, and the value that A has when unlocked is essentially unique, in the sense that if v_1 and v_2 are two values A may have before the LOCK A step, then the values held by A after UNLOCK A are always different in the two cases, provided $v_1 \neq v_2$.

A more formal way to look at the behavior of transactions is to associate with each pair LOCK A and its following UNLOCK A, a unique function f. Note that one transaction may have more than one such pair for a given A, since, although it is not generally a good idea, we may lock and unlock the same item more than once. Let A_0 be the initial value of A before any transactions are executed. *Values* that A may assume are formulas of the form $f_1 f_2 \cdots f_n(A_0)$, where the f_i's are functions associated with LOCK A–UNLOCK A pairs of the various transactions. No distinct values are equal. That is, values are regarded as uninterpreted formulas. This definition of "value" is a rigorous treatment of our informal statement in the previous section that we would assume no algebraic laws regarding the effects of transactions on items.

Example 10.5: In Fig. 10.3 we see three transactions and the functions associated with each LOCK-UNLOCK pair. Fig. 10.4 shows a possible schedule of these transactions and the resulting effect on items A, B, and C. We can observe that this schedule is not serializable. In proof, suppose it were. If T_1 precedes T_2, then the final value of B would be $f_3(f_2(B_0))$, not $f_2(f_3(B_0))$. If T_2 precedes T_1, then the final value of A would be $f_6(f_1(f_5(A_0)))$, $f_1(f_6(f_5(A_0)))$, or $f_1(f_5(f_6(A_0)))$, depending on whether the serial order was $T_2T_1T_3$, $T_2T_3T_1$, or $T_3T_2T_1$. As none of these formulas is the actual final value of A in Fig. 10.4, we see that T_2 can neither precede nor follow T_1 in an equivalent serial schedule, so a serial schedule does not exist.

Note how our assumption that functions produce unique values is essential in the proof. For example, if it were possible that $f_3f_2=f_2f_3$, then we could not rule out the possibility that T_1 precedes T_2. Let us reiterate that our assumption of unique values is not just for mathematical convenience. The work required to enable the database system to examine transactions and detect possibilities such as $f_3f_2=f_2f_3$, and thereby permit a wider class of schedules to be regarded as serializable, is not worth the effort in general. □

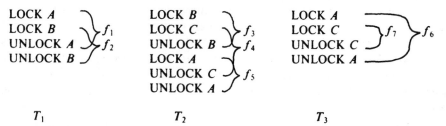

$$T_1 \qquad\qquad\qquad T_2 \qquad\qquad\qquad T_3$$

Fig. 10.3. Three transactions.

A Serializability Test

If we consider Example 10.5 and the proof that the schedule of Fig. 10.4 is not serializable, we see the key to a serializability test. We examine a schedule with regard to the order in which the various transactions lock a given item. This order must be consistent with the hypothetical equivalent serial schedule of the transactions. If the orders induced by two different items force two transactions to appear in different order, then we have a paradox, since both orders cannot be consistent with one serial schedule. We can express this test as a problem of finding cycles in a directed graph. The method is described formally in the next algorithm.

Algorithm 10.1: Testing Serializability of a Schedule.

Step		A	B	C
(1)	T_1: LOCK A	A_0	B_0	C_0
(2)	T_2: LOCK B	A_0	B_0	C_0
(3)	T_2: LOCK C	A_0	B_0	C_0
(4)	T_2: UNLOCK B	A_0	$f_3(B_0)$	C_0
(5)	T_1: LOCK B	A_0	$f_3(B_0)$	C_0
(6)	T_1: UNLOCK A	$f_1(A_0)$	$f_3(B_0)$	C_0
(7)	T_2: LOCK A	$f_1(A_0)$	$f_3(B_0)$	C_0
(8)	T_2: UNLOCK C	$f_1(A_0)$	$f_3(B_0)$	$f_4(C_0)$
(9)	T_2: UNLOCK A	$f_5(f_1(A_0))$	$f_3(B_0)$	$f_4(C_0)$
(10)	T_3: LOCK A	$f_5(f_1(A_0))$	$f_3(B_0)$	$f_4(C_0)$
(11)	T_3: LOCK C	$f_5(f_1(A_0))$	$f_3(B_0)$	$f_4(C_0)$
(12)	T_1: UNLOCK B	$f_5(f_1(A_0))$	$f_2(f_3(B_0))$	$f_4(C_0)$
(13)	T_3: UNLOCK C	$f_5(f_1(A_0))$	$f_2(f_3(B_0))$	$f_7(f_4(C_0))$
(14)	T_3: UNLOCK A	$f_6(f_5(f_1(A_0)))$	$f_2(f_3(B_0))$	$f_7(f_4(C_0))$

Fig. 10.4. A schedule.

Input: A schedule S for a set of transactions $T_1, \ldots, T_k$.

Output: A determination whether S is serializable, and if so, a serial schedule equivalent to S.

Method: Create a directed graph G (called a *precedence* graph), whose nodes correspond to the transactions. To determine the arcs in G, let S be $a_1; a_2; \cdots; a_n$, where each a_i is an action of the form

$$T_j: \text{LOCK } A_m \quad \text{or} \quad T_j: \text{UNLOCK } A_m$$

T_j indicates the transaction to which the step belongs. If a_i is

$$T_j: \text{UNLOCK } A_m$$

look for the next action a_p following a_i that is of the form $T_s: \text{LOCK } A_m$. If there is one, then draw an arc from T_j to T_s. The intuitive meaning of this arc is that in any serial schedule equivalent to S, T_j must precede T_s.

If G has a cycle, then S is not serializable. If G has no cycles, then find a linear order for the transactions such that T_i precedes T_j whenever there is an arc $T_i \rightarrow T_j$. This can always be done by the process known as *topological sorting,* defined as follows. There must be some node T_i with no entering arcs, else we can prove that G has a cycle. List T_i and remove T_i from G. Then repeat the process on the remaining graph until no nodes remain. The order in which the nodes are listed is a serial order for the transactions. □

Example 10.6: Consider the schedule of Fig. 10.4. The graph G, shown in Fig. 10.5 has nodes for T_1, T_2, and T_3. To find the arcs, we look at each UNLOCK step in Fig. 10.4. For example step (4), $T_2: \text{UNLOCK } B$, is followed by $T_1: \text{LOCK } B$; in this case, the lock occurs at the next step. We therefore draw an arc $T_2 \to T_1$. As another example, the action at step (8), T_2: UNLOCK C, is followed at step (11) by T_3: LOCK C, and no intervening step locks C. Therefore we draw an arc from T_2 to T_3. Steps (6) and (7) cause us to place an arc $T_1 \to T_2$. As there is a cycle, the schedule of Fig. 10.4 is not serializable. □

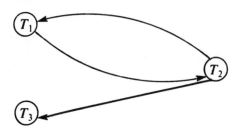

Fig. 10.5. Graph of precedences among transactions.

Example 10.7: In Fig. 10.6 we see a schedule for three transactions, and Fig. 10.7 shows its precedence graph. As there are no cycles, the schedule of Fig. 10.6 is serializable, and Algorithm 10.1 tells us that the serial order is T_1, T_2, T_3. It is interesting to note that in the serial order, T_1 precedes T_3, even though in Fig. 10.6, T_1 did not commence until T_3 had finished. □

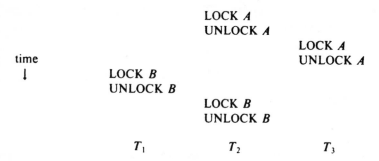

Fig. 10.6. A serializable schedule.

Theorem 10.1: Algorithm 10.1 correctly determines if a schedule is serializable.

Proof: Suppose the precedence graph G has no cycles. Consider the sequence of transactions $T_{i_1}, T_{i_2}, \ldots, T_{i_r}$ that in the schedule S lock and unlock item A, in that order. Then in G there are arcs $T_{i_1} \to T_{i_2} \to \cdots \to T_{i_r}$, so the transactions must appear in this order in the constructed serial schedule. As no other transaction locks A, it is easy to check that the value of A after executing S is the same as in the serial schedule constructed by Algorithm 10.1. Since the above holds for any item A, it follows that S is equivalent to the constructed serial schedule, so S is serializable.

Conversely, suppose G has a cycle $T_{j_1} \rightarrow T_{j_2} \rightarrow \cdots \rightarrow T_{j_t} \rightarrow T_{j_1}$. Let there be a serial schedule R equivalent to S, and suppose that in R, T_{j_p} appears first among the transactions in the cycle. Let the arc $T_{j_{p-1}} \rightarrow T_{j_p}$ (take j_{p-1} to be j_t if $p=1$) be in G because of item A. Then in R, since T_{j_p} appears before $T_{j_{p-1}}$, the final formula for A applies a function f associated with some LOCK A–UNLOCK A pair in T_{j_p} before applying some function g associated with a LOCK A–UNLOCK A pair in $T_{j_{p-1}}$. In S, however, $T_{j_{p-1}}$ precedes T_{j_p}, since there is an arc $T_{j_{p-1}} \rightarrow T_{j_p}$. Therefore, in S, g is applied before f. Thus the final value of A differs in R and S, in the sense that the two formulas are not the same, and we conclude that R and S are not equivalent. Thus S is equavalent to no serial schedule. □

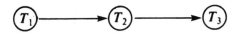

Fig. 10.7. Precedence graph for Fig. 10.6.

A Protocol that Guarantees Serializability

We shall give a simple protocol with the property that any collection of transactions obeying the protocol cannot have a legal nonserializable schedule. Moreover, this protocol is, in a sense to be discussed subsequently, the best that can be formulated. The protocol is, simply, to require that in any transaction, all locks precede all unlocks.† Transactions obeying this protocol are said to be *two-phase;* the first phase is the locking phase and the second the unlocking phase. For example, in Fig. 10.3, T_1 and T_3 are two-phase; T_2 is not.

Theorem 10.2: If S is any schedule of two-phase transactions, then S is serializable.

Proof: Suppose not. Then by Theorem 10.1, the precedence graph G for S has a cycle, $T_{i_1} \rightarrow T_{i_2} \rightarrow \cdots \rightarrow T_{i_p} \rightarrow T_{i_1}$. Then some lock by T_{i_2} follows an unlock by T_{i_1}; some lock by T_{i_3} follows an unlock by T_{i_2}, and so on. Finally, some lock by T_{i_1} follows an unlock by T_{i_p}. Therefore, a lock of T_{i_1} follows an unlock of T_{i_1}, contradicting the assumption that T_{i_1} is two-phase. □

---

† To avoid deadlock, the locks could be made according to a fixed linear order of the items. However, we do not deal with deadlock here, and some other method could also be used to avoid deadlock.

We mentioned that the two-phase protocol in is a sense the best that can be done. Precisely, what we can show is that if T_1 is any transaction that is not two phase, then there is some other transaction T_2 with which T_1 could be run in a nonserializable schedule. Suppose T_1 is not two phase. Then there is some step UNLOCK A of T_1 that precedes a step LOCK B. Let T_2 be:

T_2: LOCK A; LOCK B; UNLOCK A; UNLOCK B

Then the schedule of Fig. 10.8 is easily seen to be nonserializable, since the treatment of A requires that T_1 precede T_2, while the treatment of B requires the opposite.

Note that there are particular collections of transactions, not all two-phase, that yield only serial schedules. We shall consider an important example of such a collection in Section 10.5. However, since it is normal not to know the set of all transactions that could ever be executed concurrently with a given transaction, we are usually forced to require all transactions to be two-phase.

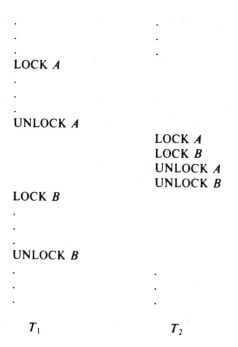

Fig. 10.8. A nonserializable schedule.

10.3 A Model with Read- and Write-Locks

In Section 10.2 we assumed that every time a transaction locked an item it changed that item. In practice, many times a transaction needs only to obtain the value of the item and is guaranteed not to change that value. If we distinguish between a read-only access and a read-write access, we can develop a more detailed model of transactions that will allow some concurrency forbidden in the model of the previous section.† Let us distinguish two kinds of locks.

1. *Read-locks.* A transaction T wishing only to read an item A executes RLOCK A, which prevents any other transaction from writing a new value of A while T is reading A. However, any number of transactions can hold a read-lock on A at the same time.

2. *Write-locks.* These are locks in the sense of the previous section. A transaction wishing to change the value of item A first obtains a write-lock by executing WLOCK A. When some transaction holds a write-lock on an item, no other transaction can obtain either a read- or write-lock on the item.

Both read- and write-locks are removed by an UNLOCK statement. As in Section 10.2, we assume no transaction tries to unlock an item on which it does not hold a read- or write-lock, and no transaction tries to read-lock an item on which it already holds any lock. Further, a transaction does not attempt to write-lock an item if it already holds a write-lock on that item, but under some circumstances, a write-lock may be issued for an item on which it holds a read-lock. The latter makes sense because a write-lock is more restrictive on the behavior of other transactions than a read-lock.

Two schedules are *equivalent* if

1. they produce the same value for each item, and

2. each read-lock applied by a given transaction occurs in both schedules at times when the item locked has the same value.

A Test of Serializability

As in the previous section, we assume that each time a write-lock is applied to an item, a unique function associated with that lock operates on the value of that item. However, a read-lock on an item does not change the value. Suppose we have a schedule S in which a write-lock is applied to A by transaction T_1, and let f be the function associated with that write-lock.

---

† Note that we still do not have write-only locks. The ability of transactions to write an item without reading it first will be seen in the next section to complicate greatly the question of serializability.

After T_1 unlocks A, let T_2 be one of the (perhaps many) transactions that subsequently read-lock A before any other transaction write-locks it. Then surely T_1 must precede T_2 in any serial schedule equivalent to S. Otherwise, T_2 reads a value of A that does not involve the function f, and no such value is identical to a value that does involve f. Similarly, if T_3 is the next transaction, after T_1, to write-lock A, then T_1 must precede T_3. The argument is essentially that of Theorem 10.1.

Now suppose T_4 is a transaction that read-locks A before T_1 write-locks it. If T_1 appears before T_4 in a serial schedule, then T_4 reads a value of A involving f, while in schedule S, the value read by T_4 does not involve f. Thus T_4 must precede T_1 in a serial schedule. The only inference we cannot make is that if in S two transactions read-lock the same item A in a particular order, then the transactions should appear in that order in a serial schedule. In fact, just the opposite is true. The relative order of read-locks makes no difference on the values produced by concurrently executing transactions. These observations suggest that an approach similar to that of Section 10.2 will allow us to tell whether a schedule is serializable.

Algorithm 10.2: Serializability test for schedules with read/write-locks.

Input: A schedule S for a set of transactions $T_1, \ldots, T_k$.

Output: A determination whether S is serializable, and if so, an equivalent serial schedule.

Method: We construct a precedence graph G as follows. The nodes correspond to the transactions as before. The arcs are determined by the following rules.

1. Suppose in S, transaction T_i read-locks item A, and T_j is the next transaction (if it exists) to write-lock A. Then place an arc from T_i to T_j.

2. Suppose in S, transaction T_i write-locks A, and T_j is the next transaction (if it exists) to write-lock A. Then draw an arc $T_i \rightarrow T_j$. Further, let T_m be any transaction that read-locks A after T_i unlocks its write-lock, but before T_j write-locks A (if there is no T_j, then T_m is any transaction to read-lock A after T_i unlocks A). Then draw an arc $T_i \rightarrow T_m$.

If G has a cycle, then S is not serializable. If G is acyclic, then any topological sort of G is a serial order for the transactions. □

Example 10.8: In Fig. 10.9 we see a schedule of four transactions, and in Fig. 10.10 is its precedence graph. The first UNLOCK is step (3), where T_3 removes its write-lock from A. Following step (3) are read-locks of A by T_1 and T_2 (steps 4 and 7) and a write-lock of A by T_4 at step (12). Thus T_1, T_2, and T_4 must follow T_3, and we draw arcs from T_3 to each of the other nodes. Notice that there is nothing wrong with both T_1 and T_2 holding read-locks on A after step (7). However, T_4 could not write-lock A until both T_1 and T_2 released their read-locks. As another example, T_4 releases a write-lock on B at step (5), and the next write-lock on B is by T_3, so we draw an arc from T_4 to T_3. We now have a cycle, so the schedule of Fig. 10.9 is not serializable. The complete set of arcs is shown in Fig. 10.10. □

	T_1	T_2	T_3	T_4
(1)			WLOCK A	
(2)				RLOCK B
(3)			UNLOCK A	
(4)	RLOCK A			
(5)				UNLOCK B
(6)			WLOCK B	
(7)		RLOCK A		
(8)			UNLOCK B	
(9)	WLOCK B			
(10)		UNLOCK A		
(11)	UNLOCK A			
(12)				WLOCK A
(13)	UNLOCK B			
(14)		RLOCK B		
(15)				UNLOCK A
(16)		UNLOCK B		

Fig. 10.9. A schedule.

Theorem 10.3: Algorithm 10.2 correctly determines if schedule S is serializable.

Proof: It is straightforward to argue, whenever we draw an arc from T_i to T_j, that in any equivalent serial schedule T_i must precede T_j. Thus if G has a cycle, we may prove as in Theorem 10.1 that no such serial schedule exists. Conversely, suppose G has no cycles. Then an argument like Theorem 10.1 shows that the final value of each item is the same in S as in the serial schedule R that is constructed from the topological sort of G. We must also show that corresponding read-locks on item A obtain the same value in R and S. But this proof is easy, since the arcs of G guarantee the write-locks on A that precede the given read-lock must be the same in R and S and that they must occur in the same order. □

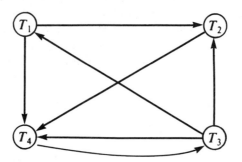

Fig. 10.10. Precedence graph of Fig. 10.9.

The Two-Phase Protocol

As with the model in the previous section, a two-phase protocol, in which all read- and write-locks precede all unlocking steps, is sufficient to guarantee serializability. Moreover, we have the same partial converse, that any transaction in which some UNLOCK precedes a read- or write-lock can be run in a nonserializable way with some other transaction. We leave these results as exercises.

10.4 A Read-Only, Write-Only Model

A subtle assumption with profound consequences that was made in Sections 10.2 and 10.3 is that whenever a transaction writes a new value for an item A, then it previously read the value of A, and more importantly, the new value of A depends on the old value. This assumption is built into the definition of "value" in the previous sections. A more realistic model would admit the possibility that a transaction reads a set of items (the *read-set*) and writes a set of items (the *write-set*), with the option that an item A could appear in either one of these sets or both.

For example, any transaction that queries a database but does not alter it has an empty write-set.† In the transaction

$$\text{READ } A; \text{ READ } B; \ C:=A+B; \ A:=A-1; \text{ WRITE } C; \text{ WRITE } A$$

the read-set is $\{A, B\}$ and the write-set is $\{A, C\}$.

---

† Alternatively, if the order in which query answers are produced is important, we could view the output device as an item in the write-set of a query.

Equivalence of Schedules

When we allow write-only items, we must revise our notion of when two schedules are equivalent. One important difference is the following. Suppose, in the model of Section 10.3, that the transaction T_1 wrote a value for item A, and later T_2 wrote a value for A. Then we assumed in Section 10.3 that T_2 write-locked A after T_1 unlocked A, and by implication, T_2 used the value of A in computing a new value, since the function associated with T_2's lock-unlock of A is assumed to produce a distinct new value of A for each old value of A. Therefore, when dealing with serializability, it was taken for granted that in a serial schedule, T_1 appears before T_2, and, incidentally, that no other transaction T write-locking A appears between T_1 and T_2. One gets the latter condition "for free" in Algorithm 10.2, since that algorithm forced T to appear either before T_1 or after T_2 in the serial schedule, whichever was the case in the given schedule S.

However, if we assume that T_2 has written its value for A without reading A, then the new value of A is independent of the old; it depends only on the values of items actually read by T_2. Thus, if between the times T_1 and T_2 write their values of A, no transaction reads A, we see that the value written by T_1 "gets lost" and has no effect on the database. As a consequence, in a serial schedule, we need not have T_1 appearing before T_2 (at least as far as A is concerned). In fact, the only requirement on T_1 is that it be done at a time when some other transaction T_3 will later write A, and between the times that T_1 and T_3 write A, no transaction reads A.

We can now formulate a new definition of serializability based on the concept that the values written by a transaction are functions only of the values read, and distinct values read produce distinct values written. These conditions are stated informally (and not completely accurately) as follows. If in schedule S, transaction T_2 reads the value of item A written by T_1, then

1. T_1 must precede T_2 in any serial schedule equivalent to S.
2. If T_3 is a transaction that writes A, then in any serial schedule equivalent to S, T_3 may either precede T_1 or follow T_2, but may not appear between T_1 and T_2.

There are also two details needed to make the above definition an accurate one. First, there are "edge effects" involving the reading of an item before any transaction has written it or writing an item that is never rewritten. These rules are best taken care of by postulating the existence of an *initial transaction* T_0 that writes every item, reading none, and a *final transaction* T_f that reads every item, writing none.

The second detail concerns transactions T whose output is "invisible" in the sense that no value T writes has any effect on the value read by T_f. Note that this effect need not be direct, but could result from some transaction T' reading a value written by T, another transaction T'' reading a value written by T', and so on, until we find a transaction in the chain that writes a value read by T_f. Call a transaction with no effect on T_f *useless*. Our second modification of the above rules is to rule out the possibility that T_2, in (1) and (2) above, is a useless transaction.†

Testing for Useless Transactions

It is easy, given a schedule S, to tell which transactions are useless. We create a graph whose nodes are the transactions, including the dummy transaction T_f assumed to exist at the end of S. If T_1 writes a value read by T_2, draw an arc from T_1 to T_2. Then the useless transactions are exactly those with no path to T_f. An example of this algorithm follows the discussion of a serializability test.

A Formal Model

Let us regard transactions as in Section 10.3, as a series of steps RLOCK A (read-lock item A), WLOCK A (write-lock A) and UNLOCK A. As before, we assume transactions do not unlock items on which they do not hold a read-or write lock, and they do not lock items on which they already hold a lock, except that a transaction may write-lock an item on which it holds a read-lock or vice versa. The only substantial difference between this model and the previous one lies in the semantics. Here we assume that when a transaction write-locks an item, it does not read its value (unless it also read-locks it), while previously we implied that a write-lock included reading privileges and in fact included the obligation to read and use the value read.

The Serializability Test

The simple precedence graph test of previous sections does not work here. Recall that there are in the current model two types of constraints on a potential serial schedule equivalent to a given schedule S. *Type 1* constraints are that if T_2 reads a value of A written by T_1 in S, then T_1 must precede T_2 in any serial schedule. This type of constraint can be expressed graphically by an arc from T_1 to T_2. The *type 2* constraints, that any T_3 writing A must appear either before T_1 or after T_2, cannot be expressed by a simple arc. Rather, we have a pair of arcs $T_3 \rightarrow T_1$ and $T_2 \rightarrow T_3$, one of which must be chosen. The schedule S is serializable if and only if after making some choice from each pair, we are left with an acyclic graph.

---

† We cannot simply remove useless transactions from S, since the portion of the system that schedules transactions cannot know that it is scheduling a transaction that will later prove to be useless.

A collection of nodes, arcs, and pairs of alternative arcs has been termed a *polygraph*. A polygraph is *acyclic* if there is some series of choices of one arc from each pair that results in an acyclic graph in the ordinary sense. The serializability test for the model presently under consideration is to construct a certain polygraph and determine if it is acyclic. Unfortunately, testing a polygraph for acyclicness is a hard problem; it has been shown NP-complete by Papadimitriou, Bernstein, and Rothnie [1977].

Algorithm 10.3: Serializability test for transactions with read-only and write-only locks.

Input: A schedule S for a set of transactions $T_1, T_2, \ldots, T_k$.

Output: A determination whether S is serializable, and if so, an equivalent serial schedule.

Method:

1. Augment S by appending to the beginning a sequence of steps in which a dummy transaction T_0 writes each item appearing in S and appending to the end steps in which dummy transaction T_f reads each such item.

2. Begin the creation of a polygraph P with one node for each transaction, including T_0 and T_f. Temporarily place an arc from T_i to T_j whenever T_j reads an item A that in the augmented S was last written by T_i.

3. Discover the useless transactions. A transaction T is useless if there is no path from T to T_f.

4. For each useless transaction T, remove all arcs entering T.

5. For each remaining arc $T_i \rightarrow T_j$, and for each item A such that T_j reads the value of A written by T_i, consider each other transaction $T \neq T_0$ that also writes A. If $T_i = T_0$ and $T_j = T_f$, add no arcs. If $T_i = T_0$ but $T_j \neq T_f$, add the arc $T_j \rightarrow T$. If $T_j = T_f$, but $T_i \neq T_0$, add the arc $T \rightarrow T_i$. If $T_i \neq T_0$ and $T_j \neq T_f$, then introduce the arc pair $(T \rightarrow T_i, T_j \rightarrow T)$.

6. Determine whether the resulting polygraph P is acyclic. For this step there is no substantially better method than the exhaustive one. If there are n arc pairs, try all 2^n choices of one arc from each pair to see if the result is an acyclic graph.† If P is acyclic, let G be an acyclic graph formed from P by choosing an arc from each pair. Then any topological sort of G, with T_0 and T_f removed, represents a serial

---

† Obviously one can think of some heuristics to make the job somewhat simpler than it appears at first glance. For example, if one of a pair of arcs causes a cycle with existing arcs, we must choose the other of the pair. However, there are cases where neither arc in a pair causes an immediate cycle, yet our choice influences what happens when we try to select arcs from other pairs.

schedule equivalent to S. If P is not acyclic, then no serial schedule equivalent to S exists. □

Example 10.9: Consider the schedule of Fig. 10.11. The arcs constructed by step (2) of Algorithm 10.3 are shown in Fig. 10.12; for clarity, the arcs are labeled with the item or items justifying their presence. In understanding how Fig. 10.12 was created it helps first to observe that the schedule of Fig. 10.11 is legal, in the sense that two transactions do not hold write-locks, or a read-and write-lock simultaneously. Thus, we may assume all reading and writing occurs at the time the lock is obtained, and we may ignore the UNLOCK steps.

Let us consider each read-lock step in turn. The read-locks on A at steps (1) and (2) read the value "written" by the dummy transaction T_0. Thus we draw arcs from T_0 to T_1 and T_2. At step (5) T_3 reads the value of C written by T_1 at step (3), so we have arc $T_1 \rightarrow T_3$. At step (8), T_4 reads what T_1 wrote at step (6), so we have arc $T_1 \rightarrow T_4$, and so on. Finally, at the end, T_f "reads" A, B, C, and D, whose values were last written by T_4, T_4, T_1, and T_2, respectively, explaining the three arcs into T_f.

	T_1	T_2	T_3	T_4
(1)		RLOCK A		
(2)	RLOCK A			
(3)	WLOCK C			
(4)	UNLOCK C			
(5)			RLOCK C	
(6)	WLOCK B			
(7)	UNLOCK B			
(8)				RLOCK B
(9)	UNLOCK A			
(10)		UNLOCK A		
(11)			WLOCK A	
(12)				RLOCK C
(13)		WLOCK D		
(14)				UNLOCK B
(15)			UNLOCK C	
(16)		RLOCK B		
(17)			UNLOCK A	
(18)				WLOCK A
(19)		UNLOCK B		
(20)				WLOCK B
(21)				UNLOCK B
(22)		UNLOCK D		
(23)				UNLOCK C
(24)				UNLOCK A

Fig. 10.11. A schedule.

Now we search for useless transactions, those with no path to T_f in Fig. 10.12; T_3 is the only such transaction. We therefore remove the arc

$T_1 \rightarrow T_3$ from Fig. 10.12.

In step (5) of Algorithm 10.3 we consider the arcs or arc pairs needed to prevent interference of one write operation with another. An item like C or D that is written by only one nondummy transaction does not figure into step (5). However, A is written by both T_3 and T_4, as well as dummy transaction T_0. The value written by T_3 is not read by any transaction, so T_4 need not appear in any particular position relative to T_3. The value written by T_4 is "read" by T_f. Therefore, as T_3 cannot appear after T_f, it must appear before T_4. In this case, no arc pair is needed; we simply add to P the arc $T_3 \rightarrow T_4$. The value of A written by T_0 is read by T_1 and T_2. As T_3 and T_4 cannot appear before T_0, we place arcs from T_1 and T_2 to T_3 and T_4; again no arc pair is necessary.

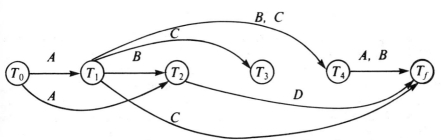

Fig. 10.12. First step in construction of a polygraph.

Item B is written by T_1 and T_4. The value of B written by T_4 is read only by T_f, so we need arc $T_1 \rightarrow T_4$. The value of B written by T_1 is read by T_2 and T_4. The writing of B by T_4 cannot interfere with the reading of B by T_4. Thus no requirement that "T_4 precedes T_1 or follows T_4" is needed. However, T_4 must not be interposed between T_1 and T_2, so we add the arc pair $(T_4 \rightarrow T_1, T_2 \rightarrow T_4)$. The resulting polygraph is shown in Fig. 10.13, with the one arc pair shown dashed. Note that arc $T_1 \rightarrow T_3$, removed in step (4), returns in step (5).

If we choose arc $T_4 \rightarrow T_1$ from the pair we get a cycle. However, choosing $T_2 \rightarrow T_4$ leaves an acyclic graph, from which we can take the serial order T_1, T_2, T_3, T_4. Thus the schedule of Fig. 10.11 is serializable. □

Theorem 10.4: Algorithm 10.3 correctly determines if a schedule is serializable.

Proof: We shall give a brief sketch of the proof. Suppose first that the resulting polygraph is acyclic. That is, there is some choice between arcs in each pair that results in an acyclic graph G. The construction of P in Algorithm 10.3 assures that each nonuseless transaction, including T_f, reads the same copy of each item in S as it does in the serial schedule resulting from a topological sort of G. Thus the corresponding values produced for each item are the same in both schedules.

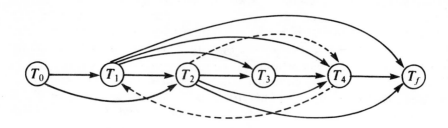

Fig. 10.13. Final polygraph.

Conversely, suppose there is a serial schedule S' equivalent to S. Then by the reasoning used in Theorem 10.1, if $T_i \rightarrow T_j$ is any arc introduced in step (2) and not removed in step (4), T_i must precede T_j in S'. Suppose the arc pair $(T_n \rightarrow T_i, T_j \rightarrow T_n)$ is introduced in step (5). Then T_n cannot appear between T_i and T_j in S'. Pick arc $T_n \rightarrow T_i$ from the pair if T_n precedes T_i in S', and pick $T_j \rightarrow T_n$ otherwise. The linear order implied by S' will be consistent with this choice from arc pairs. Similarly, a single arc added in step (5) must be consistent with this linear order, so we have a way of constructing, based on S', an acyclic graph from polygraph P. $\square$

The Two-phase Protocol, Again

As with the previous models, a two-phase protocol, requiring each transaction to do all locking before any unlocking, is successful in guaranteeing serializability of any legal schedule. To see why, let us suppose S is a legal schedule of transactions obeying the two phase protocol. Suppose $(T_3 \rightarrow T_1, T_2 \rightarrow T_3)$ is an arc pair in the polygraph P. Then there is some item A such that T_2 reads the copy of A written by T_1. If in S, T_3 unlocks A before T_1 read-locks A, then select $T_3 \rightarrow T_1$ from the pair. If T_3 write-locks A after T_2 unlocks it, select $T_2 \rightarrow T_3$. No other possibilities exist, since the arc pair was placed in P by Algorithm 10.5.

We now have a graph G constructed from P. Suppose G has a cycle $T_1 \rightarrow T_2 \rightarrow \cdots \rightarrow T_n \rightarrow T_1$. Surely, neither dummy transaction can be part of a cycle. Examination of Algorithm 10.5 and the above rules for constructing G from P indicates that for every arc $T_i \rightarrow T_{i+1}$ (with $T_{n+1} = T_1$) in the cycle, there is an item A_i such that in S, T_i unlocks A_i before T_{i+1} locks A_i. By the two phase protocol, T_{i+1} must unlock A_{i+1} after it locks A_i. Thus T_1 unlocks A_1 before T_{n+1} locks A_n. But T_{n+1} is T_1, and the two-phase protocol forbids T_1 from unlocking A_1 before it locks A_n. We have thus proved the following theorem.

Theorem 10.5: In the model of this section, if transactions obey the two-phase protocol, then any legal schedule is serializable. □

10.5 Concurrency for Hierarchically Structured Items

There are many instances where the set of items accessed by a transaction can be viewed naturally as a tree or forest. Some examples are:

1. Items are logical record occurrences (segment occurrences in Chapter 8) in a database structured according to the hierarchical model.

2. Items are nodes of a B-tree (see Section 2.4).

3. Items of various sizes are defined, with small items nested within larger ones. For example, a relational database could have items at four levels:

   i)   the entire database,

   ii)   each relation,

   iii)   each block in which the file corresponding to a relation is stored, and

   iv)   each tuple.

There are two different policies that could be followed when items are locked. First, a lock on an item could imply a lock on all its descendant items. This policy saves time, as locking many small items can be avoided. For example, in (3) above, a transaction that must read an entire relation can lock the relation as a whole, rather than locking each tuple individually. The second policy is to lock an item without implying anything about a lock on its descendants. For example, if we are searching a B-tree, we shall read a node and select one of its children to read next. We need not lock all descendants at the time we read a node. It turns out that an acceptable protocol for the policy of locking individual items is easier to explain than a protocol for the policy of locking subtrees, so we shall consider locking individual items first.

A Simple Protocol for Trees of Items

Let us revert to the model of Section 10.2 using only the LOCK and UNLOCK operations.† We assume that locking an item (node of a tree) does not automatically lock any descendants. As in Section 10.2, only one transaction can lock an item at a time. We say a transaction obeys the *tree protocol* if, except for the first item locked (which need not be the root), no item can be locked unless a lock is currently held on its parent.

---

† The protocol to be discussed also generalizes to the more complex models of Sections 10.3 and 10.4.

Observe that a transaction obeying the tree protocol need not be two-phase. For example, it might lock an item A, then lock its child B, unlock A and lock a child C of B. This situation is quite realistic, e.g., in the case that a transaction is performing an insert operation on a B-tree. If B is a node of the B-tree that has room for another pointer, then we know that no restructuring of the tree after insertion can involve the parent of B. Thus after examining B we can unlock the parent A, thereby allowing concurrent updates to the B-tree involving descendants of A that are not descendants of B.

Example 10.10: Figure 10.14 shows a tree of items, and Fig. 10.15 is the schedule of three transactions T_1, T_2, and T_3, obeying the tree protocol. Note that T_1 is not two-phase, since it locks C after unlocking B. $\square$

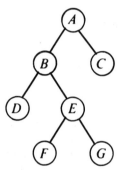

Fig. 10.14. A hierarchy of items.

While we shall not give a proof here (see Silberschatz and Kedem [1978]), all legal schedules of transactions that obey the tree protocol are serializable. The algorithm to construct a serial ordering of the transactions begins by creating a node for each transaction. Suppose T_i and T_j are two transactions that lock the same item (at different times, of course). Let FIRST(T) be the item first locked by transaction T. If FIRST(T_i) and FIRST(T_j) are independent (neither is a descendant of the other), then the tree protocol guarantees that T_i and T_j do not lock a node in common, and we need not draw an arc between them. Suppose therefore, without loss of generality, that FIRST(T_i) is an ancestor of FIRST(T_j). If T_i locks FIRST(T_j) before T_j does, then draw arc $T_i \rightarrow T_j$. Otherwise draw an arc $T_j \rightarrow T_i$.

It can be shown that the resulting graph has no cycles, and any topological sort of this graph is a serial order for the transactions. The intuition behind the proof is that at all times, each transaction has a frontier of lowest nodes in the tree on which it holds locks. The tree protocol guarantees that these frontiers do not pass over one another. Thus, if the frontier of T_i begins above the frontier of T_j, it must remain so, and every item locked by both T_i and T_j will be locked by T_j first.

	T_1	T_2	T_3
(1)	LOCK A		
(2)	LOCK B		
(3)	LOCK D		
(4)	UNLOCK B		
(5)		LOCK B	
(6)	LOCK C		
(7)			LOCK E
(8)	UNLOCK D		
(9)			LOCK F
(10)	UNLOCK A		
(11)			LOCK G
(12)	UNLOCK C		
(13)			UNLOCK E
(14)		LOCK E	
(15)			UNLOCK F
(16)		UNLOCK B	
(17)			UNLOCK G
(18)		UNLOCK E	

Fig. 10.15. A schedule of transactions obeying the tree protocol.

Example 10.11. Let us reconsider the schedule of Fig. 10.15.

$\text{FIRST}(T_1) = A$, $\text{FIRST}(T_2) = B$, and $\text{FIRST}(T_3) = E$.

T_1 and T_2 both lock B, and T_1 does so first, so we have arc $T_1 \rightarrow T_2$. Also, T_2 and T_3 each lock E, but T_3 precedes T_2 in doing so. Thus we have arc $T_3 \rightarrow T_2$. The precedence graph for this schedule is shown in Fig. 10.16, and there are two possible serial schedules, T_1, T_3, T_2 and T_3, T_1, T_2. □

Fig. 10.16. Precedence graph for Fig. 10.15.

A Protocol Allowing Locks on Subtrees

It is convenient, when the hierarchy of items includes items that are subsets of other items, as in our earlier example (3) of a hierarchy: database-relations-blocks-tuples, to allow a lock on an item to imply a lock on all its descendants. For example, if a transaction must lock most or all the tuples of a relation, it may as well lock the relation itself. At a cost of possibly excluding some concurrent operations on the relation, the system does far less work locking and unlocking items if we lock the relation as a whole.

However, indiscriminant locking can result in illegal schedules, where two transactions effectively hold a lock on the same item at the same time. For example, suppose transaction T_1 locks E (and therefore, by our new assumptions, F and G) in Fig. 10.14. Then let T_2 lock B, thereby acquiring a conflicting lock on E, F and G. To avoid this conflict, a protocol has been devised in which a transaction cannot place a lock on an item unless it first places a "warning" at all its ancestors. A warning on item A prevents any other transaction from locking A, but it does not prevent it from also placing a warning at A or locking some descendant of A that does not have a warning.

We shall here consider transactions to consist of operations

1. LOCK, which locks an item and all its descendants. No two transactions may hold a lock on an item at the same time.

2. WARN, which places a "warning" on an item. No transaction may lock an item on which some other transaction has placed a warning.

3. UNLOCK, which removes either a lock or a warning or both from an item.

A transaction obeys the *warning protocol* on a hierarchy of items if

1. It begins by placing a lock or warning at the root.

2. It dos not place a lock or warning on an item unless it holds a warning on its parent.†

3. It does not remove a lock or warning unless it holds no locks or warnings on its children.

4. It obeys the two-phase protocol, in the sense that all unlocks follow all warnings and locks.

Example 10.12: Figure 10.17 shows a hierarchy, and Fig. 10.18 is a schedule of three transactions obeying the warning protocol. Notice, for example that at step (4) T_1 places a warning on B. Therefore T_3 was not able to lock B until T_1 unlocked its warning on B at step (10). However, at steps (1)−(3) all three transactions place warnings on A, which is legal.

The lock of C by T_2 at step (5) implicitly locks C, F, and G. We assume that any or all of these items are changed by T_2 before the lock is removed at step (7). □

---

† Note that there is no need to place a lock on an item if a lock on its parent is already held.

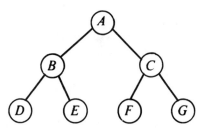

Fig. 10.17. A hierarchy.

Theorem 10.6: Schedules obeying the warning protocol are serializable.

Proof: Parts (1)–(3) of the warning protocol guarantee that no transaction can place a lock on an item unless it holds warnings on all its ancestors. It follows that at no time can two transactions hold locks on two ancestors of the same item. We can now show that a schedule obeying the warning protocol is equivalent to a schedule using the model of Section 10.2, in which all items are locked explicitly (not implicitly, by locking an ancestor). Given a schedule S satisfying the warning protocol, construct a schedule S' in the model of Section 10.2 as follows.

1.   Remove all warning steps, and their matching unlock steps.

2.   Replace all locks by locks on the item and all its descendants. Do the same for the corresponding unlocks.

The resulting schedule S' is legal because of parts (1)–(3) of the warning protocol, and its transactions are two-phase because those of S are two-phase, by part (4) of the warning protocol. □

10.6 Protecting Against Crashes

Until now we have assumed that each transaction runs happily to completion. In practice, several things might happen to prevent a transaction from completing.

1.   The system could fail from a variety of hardware or software causes. In this case, all active transactions are prevented from completing, and it is even possible that some completed transactions must be "cancelled," because they read values written by transactions that have not yet completed. System crashes cause serious problems, since we must not only find a set of transactions to "cancel" that will bring us back to a consistent state, but we must make sure that some way of reconstructing that state exists.

2.   A single transaction could be forced to stop before completion for a variety of reasons. If deadlock detection is done by the system, the transaction could be found to be a partial cause of a deadlock and be selected for cancellation by the system. A bug in the transaction, e.g.,

	T_1	T_2	T_3
(1)	WARN A		
(2)		WARN A	
(3)			WARN A
(4)	WARN B		
(5)		LOCK C	
(6)	LOCK D		
(7)		UNLOCK C	
(8)	UNLOCK D		
(9)		UNLOCK A	
(10)	UNLOCK B		
(11)			LOCK B
(12)			WARN C
(13)			LOCK F
(14)	UNLOCK A		
(15)			UNLOCK B
(16)			UNLOCK F
(17)			UNLOCK C
(18)			UNLOCK A

$$T_1 \qquad T_2 \qquad T_3$$

Fig. 10.18. A schedule of transactions satisfying the warning protocol.

a division by zero, could cause an interrupt and cancellation of the transaction. Similarly, the user could cause an interrupt at his terminal for the express purpose of cancelling a transaction.

Backup Copies

It should be evident that we cannot rely on the indefinite preservation of the data in a database. Data in the machine's registers or solid state memory cannot be presumed to survive a power outage, for example. Magnetic devices such as tapes, disks, or magnetic core memory will usually be preserved even if the machine has to be shut down, but even this data is vulnerable to physical problems such as disk "head crashes" or a small child with a large magnet running amok in the computer room. Further, no data is completely safe from being obliterated by system software errors.

For these reasons, it is essential that backup copies of the database be made periodically, at least once a day if possible, although enormous databases, for which the copying process could take hours, must be copied less frequently. The copy, once made on tape on disk, should be removed from the vicinity of the computer (in case of fire, for example), and stored in a safe place. For extra security, several of the most recent copies could be stored in different places.

When making a copy, it is important that the copied data represent a consistent state. Therefore, the copying utility routine must itself be a transaction that read-locks all items in the database.

The Journal

We must also be prepared to restore the database to a consistent state that reflects the situation after some number, perhaps a large number, of transactions were completed following the creation of the last backup copy.[†] For this reason, we need to preserve in a relatively safe place, e.g., on a tape or disk, a history, called a *journal* or *log*, of all changes to the database since the last backup copy was made. In the most general case, journal entries consist of

1. A unique identifier for the transaction causing the change,
2. The old value of the item, and
3. The new value of the item.

We also expect the journal to record key times in the progress of a transaction, such as its beginning, end, and what we shall later call its "commit point."

The need for old and new values will become evident when we consider that it may not only be necessary to redo transactions, but to undo them, that is to erase completely the effect of certain transactions. If items are large, if they are relations for example, then it is wise to represent the changes only, rather than listing the complete old and new values. For example, we could list the inserted and deleted tuples and give the old and new values for the modified tuples.

Committed Transactions

When dealing with transactions that may have to be redone or undone, it helps to think in terms of "committed" and "uncommitted" transactions. There is a point during the execution of any transaction at which we regard it as completed. All calculations done by the transaction in its workspace must have been finished, and a copy of the results of the transaction must have been written in a secure place, presumably in the journal. At this time we may regard the transaction as *committed;* if a system crash occurs subsequently, its effects will survive the crash, even though the values produced by the transaction may not yet have appeared in the database itself. The

---

[†] This consistent state may never have existed during the history of the database, since other uncompleted, or even completed, transactions may have been running concurrently with the selected set of transactions on which the state is based.

action of committing the transaction may itself be written in the journal, so if we have to recover from a crash by examining the journal, we know which transactions are committed. We define the *two-phase commit* † policy as follows.

1.   A transaction cannot write into the database until it has committed.

2.   A transaction cannot commit until it has recorded all its changes to items in the journal.

Note that phase one is the writing of data in the journal and phase two is writing the same data in the database.

If in addition, transactions follow the two-phase locking protocol, and unlocking occurs after commitment, then we know that no transaction can read from the database a value written by an uncommitted transaction. In the case of a system crash, it is then possible to examine the log and redo all the committed transactions that did not have a chance to write their values in the database. If the crash is of a nature that destroys data in the database, we shall have to redo all committed transactions since the last backup copy was made, which is generally far more time consuming. It is not necessary to undo any transactions that did not reach their commit point before the system crash, since these have no effect on the database. It would be a good idea to print a message to the user warning him that his transaction did not complete. To be able to do so after a crash, it is necessary routinely to enter into the journal the fact that a transaction has begun. Also note that a crash may cause locks to be left on items, either from committed or uncommitted transactions, and these must be removed by the recovery routine.

Failure of Individual Transactions

Less serious than a system crash is the failure of a single transaction, when, for example, it causes deadlock or is interrupted for some reason. If we follow the two-phase commit policy, we know that there is no effect on the database, provided no interruption of a transaction can occur after commitment. If we are following the two-phase protocol, then no locks or calculation can occur after commitment, so it is not possible that a deadlock is created after commitment, or that an arithmetic error causes an interrupt. Thus, failed transactions leave no trace on the database. A notation indicating that a transaction was cancelled should be placed in the journal, so if restart occurs after a system crash, we know to ignore any journal entries for that transaction.

---

† There is no connection between the "two-phase protocol" and "two-phase commitment," except that they are both sensible ideas.

Transactions That do not Obey the Two-Phase Commit Policy

Let us briefly consider what happens if transactions are not required to reach their commit point before writing into the database. By relaxing this requirement, we may allow transactions to unlock items earlier, and thereby allow other transactions to execute concurrently instead of waiting. However, this potential increase in concurrency is paid for by making recovery after a crash more difficult, as we shall see.

We still assume that each item has its changes entered in the journal before the database itself is actually changed, and we assume transactions obey the two-phase protocol with regard to locking. We also assume a transaction does not commit until it has completed writing into the journal whatever items it changes. Under our new assumptions it is not impossible to recover from system crashes or failures of individual transactions, but it becomes more difficult for two reasons.

1. A transaction that is uncommitted when the crash occurs must have the changes that it made to the database undone.

2. A transaction that has read a value written by some transaction that must be undone, must itself be undone. This effect can propagate indefinitely.

Example 10.13: Consider the two transactions of Fig. 10.19. Fundamentally these transactions follow the model of Section 10.2, although to make clear certain details of timing, we have explicitly shown commitment, reads, writes, and the arithmetic done in the workspace of each transaction. The WRITE steps are presumed to write the old and new values in the journal and then in the database. Suppose that after step (14) there is a crash. Since T_1 is the only active transaction, it doesn't matter whether it was a system crash or a failure of T_1, say because division by 0 occurred at step (14).

We must undo T_1 because it is uncommitted. Since it holds a lock on B, that lock must be removed. Then we must restore to A its value prior to step (1). We must also undo T_2, even though it is committed, and in fact completed. If some other transaction T_3 had read A between steps (13) and (14), then T_3 would have to be redone as well, even if T_3 were completed, and so on.

To undo transactions that must be undone, we consider each item C written by one or more of the transactions that must be undone. Examine the journal for the earliest write of C by one of the undone transactions. This journal entry will have the old value of C, which can be placed in the database. Note that since we assume all transactions are two-phase, and we are using the model of Section 10.2, where all items locked are assumed to be read as well as written, it is not possible that some transaction T, which does not have to be redone, wrote a value for C later than the earliest

(1)	LOCK A	
(2)	READ A	
(3)	$A := A - 1$	
(4)	WRITE A	
(5)	LOCK B	
(6)	UNLOCK A	
(7)		LOCK A
(8)		READ A
(9)		$A := A*2$
(10)	READ B	
(11)		WRITE A
(12)		COMMIT
(13)		UNLOCK A
(14)	$B := B/A$	
	T_1	T_2

Fig. 10.19. A schedule.

undone transaction wrote C. We leave as an exercise the correct algorithm for modifying the database to reflect the undoing of transactions when the model of Section 10.4, which permits writing without reading, is used.

In the case of our example in Fig. 10.19, only A was written by the transactions T_1 and T_2 prior to the crash. We find that the earliest write of A by either of these transactions was by T_1 at step (4). The journal entry for step (4) will include the old value of A, the value read at step (2). Replacing A by that value cancels all effects of T_1 and T_2 on the database. □

One might assume that having undone T_1 and T_2 in Example 10.13, it is now possible to redo T_2, since it was committed, simply by examining the journal, rather than by running it again. Such is not the case, since T_2 read the value of A written into the database by T_1, and that value is no longer there. To retrieve that value of A from the journal, without rerunning T_1, might lead to an inconsistency in the database.

Exercises

10.1: In Fig. 10.20 we see a schedule of four transactions. Assume that write-locks imply reading, as in Section 10.3. Draw the precedence graph and determine whether the schedule is serializable.

10.2: Repeat Exercise 10.1 under the assumptions of Section 10.4, where a write-lock does not imply that the value is read.

(1)		RLOCK A		
(2)			RLOCK A	
(3)		WLOCK B		
(4)		UNLOCK A		
(5)			WLOCK A	
(6)		UNLOCK B		
(7)	RLOCK B			
(8)			UNLOCK A	
(9)				RLOCK B
(10)	RLOCK A			
(11)				UNLOCK B
(12)	WLOCK C			
(13)	UNLOCK A			
(14)				WLOCK A
(15)				UNLOCK A
(16)	UNLOCK B			
(17)	UNLOCK C			
	T_1	T_2	T_3	T_4

Fig. 10.20. A schedule.

*10.3: In Fig. 10.21 are two transactions. In how many ways can they be scheduled legally? How many of these schedules are serializable?

LOCK A	LOCK B
LOCK B	UNLOCK B
UNLOCK A	LOCK A
UNLOCK B	UNLOCK A
T_1	T_2

Fig. 10.21. Two schedules.

10.4: Give an example of why the assumption of Section 10.2, that a unique function can be associated with each time that a transaction locks an item, is too strong. That is, give a schedule of transactions that Algorithm 10.1 says is not serializable, but that actually has the same effect as some serial schedule.

10.5: Prove that if a transaction on a tree of items does not obey the tree protocol, then there is some transaction (that, in fact, does obey the tree protocol) such that the two transactions have a legal schedule that is not serializable.

*10.6: Suppose we have three transactions that obey the tree protocol on the hierarchy of Fig. 10.17 in Section 10.5. The first transaction locks *A*, *B*, *C*, and *E*; the second locks *C* and *F*; the third locks *B* and *E*. In how many ways can these transactions be scheduled legally?

**10.7: A generalization of the warning protocol of Section 10.5 allows both read- and write-locks and warnings regarding these locks, with the obvious semantics. There are thus in principle sixteen "states" an item may be given by a transaction, corresponding to the sixteen subsets of two kinds of lock and two kinds of warning. However, some combinations are useless. For example, it is not necessary to place a read-warning and a write-warning on the same item, since a write-warning forbids any action that a read-warning does. In how many different states might a transaction wish to place an item? Give a table indicating which combinations of states can be placed on any item by two different transactions. For example, two transactions can each place a read-warning on an item, but one cannot place a read-lock when the other has a write-warning.

**10.8: Suppose a set of items forms a directed, acyclic graph *(DAG)*. Show that the following protocol assures serializability.

i) The first lock can be on any node.

ii) Subsequently, a node *n* can be locked only if the transaction holds a lock on at least one predecessor of *n*, and the transaction has locked each predecessor of *n* at some time in the past.

**10.9: Show that the following protocol is also safe for DAG's.

i) The first lock can be on any node.

ii) Subsequently, a transaction can lock a node only if it holds locks on a majority of its predecessors.

Bibliographic Notes

The concurrency model of Sections 10.2 and 10.3, the two phase protocol and its necessity for serializability are all from Eswaran et al. [1976]. The model of Section 10.4 (allowing write-only locks) and the polygraph-based serializability test are from Papadimitriou, Bernstein, and Rothnie [1977] and Papadimitriou [1978]. See also Lein and Weinberger [1978] concerning protocols with read- and write-locks.

  The tree protocol for hierarchically structured databases is from Silberschatz and Kedem [1978]. Bayer and Shkolnick [1977], and Ellis [1978] develop algorithms for the special case of concurrent access to B-trees. Also, Kedem and Silberschatz [1979a] explore the limits of what we call the "tree protocol" for use on collections of items structured in more general ways.

The "warning protocol" is a simplification of ideas (sketched in Exercise 10.7) described in Gray, Putzolo, and Traiger [1976] and Gray [1978]. The latter article also discusses the two-phase commit policy and is a good survey of locking, concurrency, and crash recovery in general. Menasce, Popek, and Muntz [1978] is a careful analysis of a strategy for crash recovery, including what happens when a crash occurs during recovery.

There are a number of other directions concerning concurrency that have been explored. Rosenkrantz et al. [1978] and Stearns et al. [1976] model "system-wide scheduling," where transactions do not lock items, but a central lock manager records locks and decides whether a request to read or write an item should be granted. The papers by Bernstein et al. [1977], Bernstein et al. [1978], Epstein et al. [1978], Thomas [1975, 1979], and Garcia-Molina [1979] evaluate algorithms for the maintenance of widely separated copies of a database. In this situation, one encounters problems when different transactions at different sites execute concurrently and then broadcast to the other sites the changes they have made.

Kung and Papadimitriou [1979] develop the theory of how the information one uses in scheduling transactions influences the protocol one can use to assure serializability. Yannakakis [1979] investigates the relationship between the structure of items (such as the tree structure discussed in Section 10.5) and the protocols that guarantee serializability. The DAG protocol of Exercise 10.8 is from there, and the protocol of Exercise 10.9 is from Kedem and Silberschatz [1979b].

Gray, Lorie, and Putzolo [1975], and Reis and Stonebraker [1977, 1978] discuss the issue of "locking granularity," that is, how large individually lockable items should be.

Coffman and Denning [1973] is a source for general material on concurrent systems. Rothnie and Goodman [1978] survey concurrency techniques for distributed database systems.

Bibliography

Aho, A. V., C. Beeri, and J. D. Ullman [1978]. "The theory of joins in relational databases," submitted to *TODS*. A preliminary version appeared in *Proc. Eighteenth Annual IEEE Symposium on Foundations of Computer Science*, pp. 107-113.

Aho, A. V., J. E. Hopcroft, and J. D. Ullman [1974]. *The Design and Analysis of Computer Algorithms*, Addison Wesley, Reading, Mass.

Aho, A. V., B. W. Kernighan, and P. J. Weinberger [1979]. "Awk – a pattern scanning and processing language," *Software Practice and Experience* 9, pp. 267-279.

Aho, A. V., Y. Sagiv, and J. D. Ullman [1979]. "Equivalence of relational expressions," *SIAM J. Computing* 8:2, pp. 218-246.

Aho, A. V. and J. D. Ullman [1979a]. "Optimal partial match retrieval when fields are independently specified," *ACM Trans. on Database Systems* 4:2, pp. 168-179.

Aho, A. V. and J. D. Ullman [1979b]. "Universality of data retrieval languages," *Proc. Sixth ACM Symposium on Principles of Programming Languages*, pp. 110-120.

ANSI [1975]. "Study group on data base management systems: interim report," *FDT* 7:2, ACM, New York.

Armstrong, W. W. [1974]. "Dependency structures of data base relationships," *Proc. 1974 IFIP Congress*, pp. 580-583, North Holland, Amsterdam.

Arora, A. K. and C. R. Carlson [1978]. "The information preserving properties of certain relational database transformations," *Proc. ACM Intl. Conf. on Very Large Data Bases*, pp. 352-359.

Astrahan, M. M. and D. D. Chamberlin [1975]. "Implementation of a structured English query language," *Comm. ACM* 18:10, pp. 580-587.

Astrahan, M. M., et al. [1976]. "System R: a relational approach to data management," *ACM Trans. on Database Systems* 1:2, pp. 97-137.

Bachman, C. W. [1969]. "Data structure diagrams," *Data Base* 1:2, pp. 4-10.

Bancilhon, F. [1978]. "On the completeness of query languages for relational databases," *Proc. Seventh Symp. on Mathematical Foundations of Computer Science*, Springer-Verlag.

Bayer, R. and E. M. McCreight [1972]. "Organization and maintenance of large ordered indices," *Acta Informatica* **1:3**, pp. 173-189.

Bayer, R. and M. Shkolnick [1977]. "Concurrency of operating on B-trees," *Acta Informatica* **9:1**, pp. 1-21.

Beck, L. L. [1978]. "On minimal sets of operations for relational data sublanguages," TR CS-7802, SMU, Dallas.

Beeri, C. [1977]. "On the membership problem for multivalued dependencies in relational databases," TR229, Dept. of EECS, Princeton Univ., Princeton, N. J.

Beeri, C. and P. A. Bernstein [1979]. "Computational problems related to the design of normal form relation schemes," *ACM Trans. on Database Systems* **4:1**, pp. 30-59.

Beeri, C., P. A. Bernstein, and N. Goodman [1978]. "A sophisticate's introduction to database normalization theory," *Proc. ACM Intl. Conf. on Very Large Data Bases*, pp. 113-124.

Beeri, C., R. Fagin, and J. H. Howard [1977]. "A complete axiomatization for functional and multivalued dependencies," *ACM/SIGMOD International Symposium on Management of Data*, pp. 47-61.

Beeri, C., A. O. Mendelzon, Y. Sagiv, and J. D. Ullman [1979]. "Equivalence of relational database schemes," *Proc. Eleventh Annual ACM Symposium on the Theory of Computing*, pp. 319-329.

Bernstein, P. A. [1976]. "Synthesizing third normal form relations from functional dependencies," *ACM Trans. on Database Systems* **1:4**, pp. 277-298.

Bernstein, P. A., N. Goodman, J. B. Rothnie, and C. H. Papadimitriou [1978]. "Analysis of serializability of SDD-1: a system of distributed databases (the fully redundant case)," to appear in *IEEE Trans. Software Engg.*

Bernstein, P. A., D. W. Shipman, J. B. Rothnie, and N. Goodman [1977]. "The concurrency control mechanism of SDD-1: a system for distributed databases (the general case)," TR CCA-77-09, Computer Corp. of America, Cambridge, Mass.

Biskup, J. [1978]. "Inferences of multivalued dependencies in fixed and undetermined universes." Unpublished manuscript, to appear in *Theor. Computer Science*.

Biskup, J., U. Dayal, and P. A. Bernstein [1979]. "Synthesizing independent database schemas," *ACM/SIGMOD International Symposium on Management of Data*, pp. 143-152.

Bolour, A. [1979]. "Optimality properties of multiple key hashing functions," *J. ACM* **26:2**, pp. 196-210.

Boyce, R. F., D .D. Chamberlin, W. F. King, and M. M. Hammer [1975]. "Specifying queries as relational expressions: the SQUARE data sublanguage," *Comm. ACM* **18:11**, pp. 621-628.

Burkhard, W. A. [1976]. "Hashing and trie algorithms for partial match retrieval," *ACM Trans. on Database Systems* **1:2**, pp. 175-187.

Cardenas, A. F. [1979]. *Data Base Management Systems*, Allyn and Bacon, Boston, Mass.

Carlson, C. R. and R. S. Kaplan [1976]. "A generalized access path model and its application to a relational database system," *ACM/SIGMOD International Symposium on Management of Data*, pp. 143-156.

Chamberlin, D. D., et al. [1976]. "SEQUEL 2: a unified approach to data definition, manipulation, and control," *IBM J. Res.* **20:6**, pp. 560-575.

Chandra, A. K., and D. Harel [1979]. "Computable queries for relational databases," *Proc. Eleventh Annual ACM Symposium on the Theory of Computing*, pp. 309-319.

Chandra, A. K. and P. M. Merlin [1976]. "Optimal implementation of conjunctive queries in relational databases," *Proc. Ninth Annual ACM Symposium on the Theory of Computing*, pp. 77-90.

Chen, P. P. [1976]. "The entity-relationship model: toward a unified view of data," *ACM Trans. on Database Systems* **1:1**, pp. 9-36.

Childs, D. L. [1968]. "Feasibility of a set-theoretical data structure - a general structure based on a reconstituted definition of relation," *Proc. 1968 IFIP Congress*, pp. 162-172, North Holland, Amsterdam.

Chin, F. Y. [1978]. "Security in statistical databases for queries with small counts," *ACM Trans. on Database Systems* **3:1**, pp. 92-104.

Cincom [1978]. *OS TOTAL Reference Manual*, Cincom Systems, Cincinnati, Ohio.

CODASYL [1971]. *CODASYL Data Base Task Group April 71 Report*, ACM, New York.

CODASYL [1978]. *COBOL J. Development*, Materiel Data Management Center, Quebec, Que. Earlier editions appeared in 1973 and 1968.

Codd, E. F. [1970]. "A relational model for large shared data banks," *Comm. ACM* **13:6**, pp. 377-387.

Codd, E. F. [1972a]. "Further normalization of the data base relational model," in *Data Base Systems* (R. Rustin, ed.) Prentice Hall, Englewood Cliffs, N. J. pp. 33-64.

Codd, E. F. [1972b]. "Relational completeness of data base sublanguages," *ibid.* pp. 65-98.

Codd, E. F. [1975]. "Understanding relations," *FDT* **7:3-4**, pp. 23-28, ACM, New York.

Codd, E. F. [1978]. "How about recently," in Shneiderman [1978], pp. 3-28.

Codd, E. F. [1979]. "Extending the data base relational model," *ACM/SIGMOD International Symposium on Management of Data*, pp. 161. To appear in a special issue of *TODS*.

Codd, E. F., R. S. Arnold, J. M. Cadiou, C. L. Chang, and N. Roussopoulos [1978]. "Rendezvous version I: an experimental English language query formulation system for casual users of relational databases," RJ2144, IBM, San Jose.

Coffman, E. G. and P. J. Denning [1973]. *Operating Systems Theory*, Prentice Hall, Englewood Cliffs, N. J.

Comer, D. [1978]. "The difficulty of optimum index selection," *ACM Trans. on Database Systems* **3:4**, pp. 440-445.

Cullinane [1978]. *IDMS DML Programmer's Reference Guide*, Cullinane Corp., Wellesley, Mass.

Date, C. J. [1977]. *An Introduction to Database Systems*, Addison Wesley, Reading, Mass.

Dell'Orco, P., V. N. Spadavecchio, and M. King [1977]. "Using knowledge of a data base world in interpreting natural language queries," *Proc. 1977 IFIP Congress*, pp. 139-144, North Holland, Amsterdam.

Delobel, C. [1978]. "Normalization and hierarchical dependencies in the relational data model," *ACM Trans. on Database Systems* **3:3**, pp. 201-222. See also, "Contributions theoretiques a la conception d'un systeme d'informations," doctoral dissertation, Univ. of Grenoble, Oct., 1973.

Delobel, C. and R. C. Casey [1972]. "Decomposition of a database and the theory of Boolean switching functions," *IBM J. Res.* **17:5**, pp. 370-386.

DeMillo, R. A., D. P. Dobkin, A. K. Jones, and R. J. Lipton [1978]. *Foundations of Secure Computation*, Academic Press, New York.

DeMillo, R. A., D. P. Dobkin, and R. J. Lipton [1978]. "Even databases that lie can be compromised," *IEEE Trans. on Software Engineering* **SE4:1**, pp. 73-75.

Denning, D. E. [1978]. "A review of research on statistical database security," in DeMillo et al. [1978], pp. 15-26.

Denning, D. E., P. J. Denning, and M. D. Schwartz [1977]. "Securing databases under linear queries," *Proc. 1977 IFIP Congress*, pp. 395-398, North Holland, Amsterdam. Also see *ACM Trans. on Database Systems* **4:2**, pp. 156-167.

Denning, D. E., P. J. Denning, and M. D. Schwartz [1979]. "The tracker: a threat to statistical database security," *ACM Trans. on Database Systems* **4:1**, pp. 76-96.

Dobkin, D., A. K. Jones, and R. J. Lipton [1979]. "Secure databases: protection against user inference," *ACM Trans. on Database Systems* **4:1**, pp. 97-106.

Douque, B. C. M. and G. M. Nijssen [1976]. *Database Description*, North Holland, Amsterdam.

Ellis, C. S. [1978]. "Concurrent search and insertion in 2-3 trees," TR-78-05-01, Dept. of Computer Science, Univ. of Washington, Seattle.

Epstein, R., M. R. Stonebraker, and E. Wong [1978]. "Distributed query processing in a relational database system," *ACM/SIGMOD International Symposium on Management of Data*, pp. 169-180.

Eswaran, K. P., J. N. Gray, R. A. Lorie, and I. L. Traiger [1976]. "The notions of consistency and predicate locks in a database system," *Comm. ACM* **19:11**, pp. 624-633.

Fagin, R. [1977]. "Multivalued dependencies and a new normal form for relational databases," *ACM Trans. on Database Systems* **2:3**, pp. 262-278.

Fagin, R. [1978]. "On an authorization mechanism," *ACM Trans. on Database Systems* **3:3**, pp. 310-319.

Fagin, R. [1979a]. "Normal forms and relational database operators," *ACM/SIGMOD International Symposium on Management of Data*, pp. 153-160.

Fagin, R. [1979b]. "A normal form for relational databases that is based on domains and keys," RJ2520, IBM, San Jose.

Furtado, A. L. [1978]. "Formal aspects of the relational model," *Information systems* **3:2**, pp. 131-140.

Gallaire, H. and J. Minker [1978]. *Logic and Databases*, Plenum Press, New York.

Garcia-Molina, H. [1979]. "Performance comparison of update algorithms for distributed databases," Part I: Tech. Note 143, Part II: Tech. Note 146, Digital Systems Laboratory, Stanford Univ.

Garey, M. R. and D. S. Johnson [1979]. *Computers and Intractability: A Guide to the Theory of NP-Completeness*, Freeman, San Francisco.

Gotlieb, C. C. and L. R. Gotlieb [1978]. *Data Types and Structures*, Prentice Hall, Englewood Cliffs, N. J.

Gotlieb, C. C. and F. W. Tompa [1973]. "Choosing a storage schema," *Acta Informatica* **3**, pp. 297-319.

Gotlieb, L. R. [1975]. "Computing joins of relations," *ACM/SIGMOD International Symposium on Management of Data*, pp. 55-63.

Gray, J. N. [1978]. "Notes on data base operating systems," RJ2188, IBM, San Jose, Calif.

Gray, J. N., R. A. Lorie, and G. R. Putzolo [1975]. "Granularity of locks in a shared database," *Proc. ACM Intl. Conf. on Very Large Data Bases*, pp. 428-451.

Gray, J. N., F. Putzolo, and I. Traiger [1976]. "Granularity of locks and degrees of consistency in a shared data base," in Nijssen [1976].

Greenblatt, D. and J. Waxman [1978]. "A study of three database query languages," in Shneiderman [1978], pp. 77-98.

Griffiths, P. P., M. M. Astrahan, D. D. Chamberlin, R. A. Lorie, and T. G. Price [1979]. "Access path selection in a relational database management system," RJ2429, IBM, San Jose.

Griffiths, P. P. and B. W. Wade [1976]. "An authorization mechanism for a relational database system," *ACM Trans. on Database Systems* 1:3, pp. 242-255.

Hagihara, K., M. Ito, K. Taniguchi, and T. Kasami [1979]. "Decision problems for multivalued dependencies in relational databases," *SIAM J. Computing* 8:2, pp. 247-264.

Hall, P. A. V. [1976]. "Optimization of a single relational expression in a relational database," *IBM J. Res.* 20:3, pp. 244-257.

Haq, M. I. [1974]. "Security in a statistical database," *Proc. Amer. Soc. Inform. Science* 11:1, pp. 33-39.

Haq, M. I. [1975]. "Insuring individual's privacy from statistical database users," *Proc. 1975 National Computer Conference*, pp. 941-946, AFIPS Press, Montvale, N. J.

Held, G. and M. Stonebraker [1978]. "B-trees reexamined," *Comm. ACM* 21:2, pp. 139-143.

Hoffman, L. J. [1977]. *Modern Methods for Computer Security and Privacy*, Prentice Hall, Englewood Cliffs, N. J.

Hoffman, L. J. and W. F. Miller [1970]. "Getting a personal dossier from a statistical data bank," *Datamation* 16:5, pp. 74-75.

Horowitz, E. and S. Sahni [1976]. *Fundamentals of Data Structures*, Computer Science Press, Potomac, Md.

Hsiao, D. K., D. S. Kerr, and S. E. Madnick [1978]. "Privacy and security of data communications and data bases," *Proc. ACM Intl. Conf. on Very Large Data Bases*, pp. 55-67.

Hunt, H. B. III and D. J. Rosenkrantz [1979]. "The complexity of testing predicate locks," *ACM/SIGMOD International Symposium on Management of Data*, pp. 127-133.

IBM [1978a]. *Query-by Example terminal Users Guide*, SH20-2078-0, IBM, White Plains, N. Y.

IBM [1978b]. IMS/VS publications, especially GH20-1260 *(General Information)*, SH20-9025 *(System/Application Design Guide)*, SH20-9026 *(Application Programming Reference Manual)*, and SH20-9027 *(Systems Programming Reference Manual)*, IBM, White Plains, N. Y.

Jacobs, B. E. [1979]. On queries definable in database structures," TR 757, Dept. of Computer Science, Univ. of Maryland.

Kambayashi, Y. [1978]. "An efficient algorithm for processing multirelation queries in relational databases," ER78-01, Dept. of Information Science, Kyoto Univ., Kyoto, Japan.

Kam, J. B. and J. D. Ullman [1977]. "A model of statistical databases and their security," *ACM Trans. on Database Systems* **2:1**, pp. 1-10.

Kedem, Z. and A. Silberschatz [1979a]. "A characterization of database graphs admitting a simple locking protocol," TR 49, Dept. of Mathematical Sciences, Univ. of Texas, Dallas.

Kedem, Z. and A. Silberschatz [1979b]. "Controlling concurrency using locking protocols." To appear in *Proc. IEEE Twentieth Annl. Symp. on Foundations of Computer Science*.

Kerschberg, L., A. Klug, and D. C. Tsichritzis [1977]. "A taxonomy of data models," in *Systems for Large Data Bases* (Lockemann and Neuhold, eds.), North Holland, Amsterdam, pp. 43-64.

Knuth, D. E. [1968]. *The Art of Computer Programming*, Vol. 1, *Fundamental Algorithms*, Addison Wesley, Reading, Mass.

Knuth, D. E. [1973]. *The Art of Computer Programming*, Vol. 3, *Sorting and Searching*, Addison Wesley, Reading, Mass.

Kuhns, J. L. [1967]. "Answering questions by computer; a logical study," RM-5428-PR, Rand Corp., Santa Monica, Calif.

Kung, H. T. and C. H. Papadimitriou [1979]. "An optimality theory of concurrency control for databases," *ACM/SIGMOD International Symposium on Management of Data*, pp. 116-126.

Lacroix, M. and A. Pirotte [1976]. "Generalized joins," *SIGMOD Record* **8:3**, pp. 14-15.

Lien, Y. E. and P. J. Weinberger [1978]. "Consistency, concurrency and crash recovery," *ACM/SIGMOD International Symposium on Management of Data*, pp. 9-14.

Ling, T.-W. and F. Tompa [1978]. "Adequate definitions for third normal form," CS-78-34, Dept. of CS, Univ. of Waterloo, Waterloo, Ont.

Lipski, W. Jr. [1978]. "On databases with incomplete information," unpublished memorandum, Univ. of Illinois.

Liu, L. and A. Demers [1978]. "An efficient algorithm for testing lossless joins in relational databases," TR 78-351, Dept. of Computer Science, Cornell Univ.

Lucchesi, C. L. and S. L. Osborn [1978]. "Candidate keys for relations." J. Computer and Systems Sciences 17:2, pp. 270-279.

Lum, V. and H. Ling [1970]. "Multi-attribute retrieval with combined indices," Comm. ACM 13:11, pp. 660-665.

Maier, D. [1979]. "Minimum covers in the relational database model," Proc. Eleventh Annual ACM Symposium on the Theory of Computing, pp. 330-337.

Maier, D., A. O. Mendelzon, F. Sadri, and J. D. Ullman [1978]. "Notions of decomposability in relational database schemes," unpublished memorandum, Dept. of EECS, Princeton Univ., Princeton, N. J.

Maier, D., A. O. Mendelzon, and Y. Sagiv [1978]. "Testing implications of data dependencies," ACM/SIGMOD International Symposium on Management of Data, pp. 152. To appear in special issue of TODS.

Martin, J. [1977]. Computer Data Base Organization, Prentice Hall, Englewood Cliffs, N. J.

Maurer, W. D. and T. G. Lewis [1975]. "Hash table methods," Computing Surveys 7:1, pp. 5-20.

Menasce, D. A., G. J. Popek, and R. R. Muntz [1978]. "A locking protocol for resource coordination in distributed databases," to appear in TODS.

Mendelzon, A. O. [1979]. "On axiomatizing multivalued dependencies in relational databases," J. ACM 26:1, pp. 37-44.

Mendelzon, A. O. and D. Maier [1979]. "Generalized mutual dependencies and the decomposition of database relations," Unpublished memorandum, Princeton Univ., Princeton, N. J.

Minker, J. [1975]. "Performing inferences over relational databases," TR363, Dept. of C. S., Univ. of Maryland, March, 1975.

Morris, R. [1968]. "Scatter storage techniques," Comm. ACM 11:1, pp. 38-43.

Mresse, M. [1978]. "Identification and authorization in data base systems," RJ2161, IBM, San Jose.

MRI [1978]. System 2000 Reference manual, MRI Systems Corp., Austin, Tex.

Nicolas, J. M. [1978]. "Mutual dependencies and some results on undecomposable relations," *Proc. ACM Intl. Conf. on Very Large Data Bases*, pp. 360-367.

Nijssen, G. M. [1977]. "On the gross architecture for the next generation database management systems," *Proc. 1977 IFIP Congress*, pp. 327-335, North Holland, Amsterdam.

Nijssen, G. M. (ed.) [1976]. *Modeling in Data Base Management Systems*, North Holland, Amsterdam.

Olle, T. W. [1978]. *The Codasyl Approach to Data Base Management*, John Wiley and Sons, New York.

Osborn, S. L. [1977]. "Normal forms for relational databases," Ph. D. Thesis, Univ. of Waterloo.

Palermo, F. P. [1974]. "A database search problem," *Information Systems COINS IV* (J. T. Tou, ed.), Plenum Press, N. Y.

Papadimitriou, C. H. [1978]. "The serializability of concurrent database updates," unpublished memorandum, Harvard Univ., Cambridge, Mass.

Papadimitriou ,C. H., P. A. Bernstein, and J. B. Rothnie [1977]. "Computational problems related to database concurrency control," *Proc. Conf. on Theoretical Computer Science*, Univ. of Waterloo, Waterloo, Ont.

Paredaens, J. [1978]. "On the expressive power of relational algebra," *Information Processing Letters*, **7:2**, pp. 107-111.

Pecherer, R. M. [1975]. "Efficient evaluation of expressions in a relational algebra," *Proc. ACM Pacific Conf.*, pp. 44-49.

Perl, Y., A. Itai, and H. Avni [1978]. "Interpolation search — a log log n search," *Comm. ACM* **21:7**, pp. 550-553.

Pirotte, A. [1978]. "High level data base query languages," in Gallaire and Minker [1978], pp. 409-436.

Reis, D. R. and M. R. Stonebraker [1977]. "Effects of locking granularity in a database management system," *ACM Trans. on Database Systems* **2:3**, pp. 233-246.

Reis, D. R. and M. R. Stonebraker [1978]. "Locking granularity revisited," UCB/ERL M78/71, Univ. of Calif., Berkeley.

Reiss, S. P. [1979]. "Security in databses: a combinatorial study," *J. ACM* **26:1**, pp. 45-57.

Rissanen, J. [1977]. "Independent components of relations," *ACM Trans. on Database Systems* **2:4**, pp. 317-325.

Rissanen, J. [1978]. "Relations with functional and join dependencies and their representation by independent components," unpublished manuscript, IBM, San Jose, Calif.

Rivest, R. L. [1976]. "Partial match retrieval algorithms," *SIAM J. Computing* **5:1**, pp. 19-50.

Roberts, C. S. [1978]. "Partial match retrieval via the method of superimposed codes," unpublished manuscript, Bell Laboratories, Holmdel, N. J.

Rosenkrantz, D. J., R. E. Stearns, and P. M. Lewis II [1978]. "System level concurrency control for distributed data base systems," *ACM Trans. on Database Systems* **3:2**, pp. 178-198.

Rothnie, J. B. and N. Goodman [1977]. "A survey of research and development in distributed database management," *Proc. ACM Intl. Conf. on Very Large Data Bases*, pp. 48-62.

Rothnie, J. B. Jr. and T. Lozano [1974]. "Attribute based file organization in a paged memory environment," *Comm. ACM* **17:2**, pp. 63-69.

Rustin, R. (ed.) [1974]. *Proc. ACM/SIGMOD Conf. on Data Models: Data-Structure-Set vs. Relational*, ACM, New York.

Sagiv, Y. and M. Yannakakis [1978]. "Equivalence among relational expressions with the union and difference operators," *Proc. Intl. Symp. on Very Large Data Bases*.

Schenk, K. L. and J. R. Pinkert [1977]. "An algorithm for servicing multirelational queries," *ACM/SIGMOD International Symposium on Management of Data*, pp. 10-19.

Schlorer, J. [1975]. "Identification and retrieval of personal records from a statistical data bank," *Methods of Inform. in Medicine* **14:1**, pp. 7-13.

Schlorer, J. [1976]. "Confidentiality of statistical records: a threat monitoring scheme for on-line dialogue," *Methods of Inform. in Medicine* **15:1**, pp. 36-42.

Schmid, H. A. and J. R. Swenson [1976]. "On the semantics of the relational model," *ACM/SIGMOD International Symposium on Management of Data*, pp. 9-36.

Sciore, E. [1979]. "Improving semantic specification in the database relational model," *ACM/SIGMOD International Symposium on Management of Data*, pp. 170-178.

Shneiderman, B. (ed.) [1978]. *Database: Improving Usability and responsiveness*, Academic Press, New York.

Sibley, E. (ed.) [1976]. *Computer Surveys* **8:1**, March, 1976.

Silberschatz, A. and Z. Kedem [1978]. "Consistency in hierarchical database systems," unpublished memorandum, Univ. of Texas, Dallas.

Smith, J. M. and P. Y. Chang [1975]. "Optimizing the performance of a relational algebra database interface," *Comm. ACM* **18:10**, pp. 568-579.

Smith, J. M. and D. C. P. Smith [1977]. "Database abstractions: aggregation and generalization," *ACM Trans. on Database Systems* **2:2**, pp. 105-133.

Snyder, L. [1978]. "On B-trees reexamined," *Comm. ACM* **21:7**, pp. 594.

Software AG [1978]. *ADABAS Introduction,* Software AG of North America, Reston, Va.

Stearns, R. E., P. M. Lewis II, and D. J. Rosenkrantz [1976]. "Concurrency control for database systems," *Proc. Seventeenth Annual IEEE Symposium on Foundations of Computer Science,* pp. 19-32.

Stonebraker, M. [1975]. "Implementation of integrity constraints and views by query modification," *ACM/SIGMOD International Symposium on Management of Data,* pp. 65-78.

Stonebraker, M. and L. A. Rowe [1977]. "Observations on data manipulation languages and their embedding in general purpose programming languages," TR UCB/ERL M77-53, Univ. of California, Berkeley, July, 1977.

Stonebraker, M. and P. Rubinstein [1976]. "The INGRES protection system," *Proc. ACM National Conf.,* pp. 80-84.

Stonebraker, M. and E. Wong [1974]. "Access control in a relational database management system by query modification," *Proc. ACM National Conf.,* pp. 180-187.

Stonebraker, M., E. Wong, P. Kreps, and G. Held [1976]. "The design and implementation of INGRES," *ACM Trans. on Database Systems* **1:3**, pp. 189-222.

Sundgren, B. [1975]. *Theory of Databases,* Mason/Charter, New York.

Tanaka, K., Y. Kambayashi, and S. Yajima [1978]. "Properties of embedded multivalued dependencies in relational databases," to appear in *J. IECE,* Japan.

Thomas, R. H. [1975]. "A solution to the update problem for multiple copy databases which use distributed control," Rept. 3340, Bolt Beranek, and Newman, Cambridge, Mass.

Thomas, R. H. [1979]. "A majority consensus approach to concurrency control," *ACM Trans. on Database Systems* **4:2**, pp. 180-219.

Todd, S. J. P. [1976]. "The Peterlee relational test vehicle — a system overview," *IBM Systems J.* **15:4**, pp. 285-308.

Tsichritzis, D. C. and F. H. Lochovsky [1977]. *Data Base Management Systems,* Academic Press, New York.

Tsichritzis, D. C. and F. H. Lochovsky [1979]. *Data Models.* To appear, Prentice Hall, Englewood Cliffs, N. J.

Tsichritzis, D. and A. Klug (eds.) [1978]. *The ANSI/X3/SPARC Framework,* AFIPS Press, Montvale, N. J.

VanLeeuwen, J. [1979]. "On compromising statistical databases with a few known elements," *Information Processing Letters,* **8**:3, pp. 149-153.

Vassiliou, Y. [1979]. "Null values in database management — a denotational semantics approach," *ACM/SIGMOD International Symposium on Management of Data,* pp. 162-169.

Weiderhold, G. [1977]. *Database Design,* McGraw Hill, New York.

Wong, E. and K. Youssefi [1976]. "Decomposition — a strategy for query processing," *ACM Trans. on Database Systems* **1**:3, pp. 223-241.

Yannakakis, M. [1979]. "Locking policies: safety and freedom from deadlock." To appear in *Proc. IEEE Twentieth Annl. Symp. on Foundations of Computer Science.*

Yao, A. C. [1978]. "On random 2-3 trees," *Acta Informatica* **9**:2, pp. 159-170.

Yao, A. C. [1979]. "A note on a conjecture of Kam and Ullman concerning statistical databases." To appear in *Inf. Proccessing Letters.*

Yao, A. C. and F. F. Yao [1976]. "The complexity of searching an ordered random table," *Proc. Seventeenth Annual IEEE Symposium on Foundations of Computer Science,* pp. 173-177.

Yao, S. B. [1979]. "Optimization of query evaluation algorithms," *ACM Trans. on Database Systems* **4**:2, pp. 133-155.

Yu, C. T. and F. Y. Chin [1977]. "A study on the protection of statistical databases," *ACM/SIGMOD International Symposium on Management of Data,* pp. 169-181.

Zaniolo, C. [1976]. "Analysis and design of relational schemata for database systems," doctoral dissertation, UCLA, July, 1976.

Zaniolo, C. [1977]. "Relational views in a database system support for queries," *Proc. IEEE COMPSAC 77.*

Zloof, M. M. [1975]. "Query-by-Example: operations on the transitive closure," IBM RC 5526, Yorktown Hts., N. Y.

Zloof, M. M. [1977]. "Query-by-Example: a data base language," *IBM Systems J.* **16**:4, pp. 324-343.

Zloof, M. M. [1978]. "Security and integrity within the Query-by-Example data base management language," IBM RC 6982, Yorktown Hts., N. Y.

Zook, W., K. Youssefi, N. Whyte, P. Rubinstein, P. Kreps, G. Held, J. Ford, R. Berman, and E. Allman [1977]. *INGRES Reference Manual,* Dept. of EECS, Univ. of California, Berkeley.

Index

A

ADABAS 270
Address 21
Address calculation search 33
Aggregate function 135, 147-148, 156
Aho, A. V. 72, 164, 208-209, 240
Allman, E. 164
Anomaly 167, 188
ANSI/SPARC report 18
APL 1, 99-100
Area 266
Arity 74
Armstrong, W. W. 208
Armstrong's axioms
        See Axioms
Arnold, R. S. 165
Arora, A. K. 209
Assembly language 277
Associative law 216
Astrahan, M. M. 164, 240
Atom 110, 116
Attribute 11, 74
Augmentation 172, 198
Authorization table 314
Avni, H. 72
Axioms 172-174, 198-199

B

Bachman, C. W. 18
Backup 352
Bancilhon, F. 164
Basic storage organization 295
Bayer, R. 72, 358
Beck, L. L. 165
Beeri, C. 200-202, 208-210
Berman, R. 164
Bernstein, P. A. 208, 210, 343, 358-359
Binary search 32

Biskup, J. 208-209
Block 21
Block access 21
Block header 22
Bolour, A. 65, 72
Bound occurrence of a variable 110-111, 116
Boyce, R. F. 164
Boyce-Codd normal form 189-193, 210
B-tree 42-49, 51, 140, 347
Bucket 24
Bucket directory 24
Burkhard, W. A. 72

C

Cadiou, J. M. 165
Calc-key 247, 251-252, 264
Cancelling, of a transaction 351-352
Candidate key 171
Cardenas, A. F. 270, 304
Carlson, C. R. 209
Cartesian product 73, 105, 112, 138, 211-217, 224-226
Casey, R. C. 208
Chaining 37, 41-42, 90
Chamberlin, D. D. 164, 240
Chandra, A. K. 164, 240
Chang, C. L. 165
Chang, P. Y. 240
Chen, P. P. 18
Childs, D. L. 103
Child/twin pointer 297-300
Chin, F. Y. 322-323
Closure, of a set of attributes 173, 175-177
Closure, of a set of dependencies 170
COBOL 241, 277
CODASYL 18, 241, 270
Codd, E. F. 103-104, 122, 164-165,

208
Coffman, E. G. 359
Comer, D. 72
Command code 278, 284
Committed transaction 353-356
Commutative law 215-216
Complementation 198
Complete query language 122, 127, 138-139, 145-147, 159-160
Complete set of axioms 172
Component 74
Compromise 315
Concatenation 154
Conceptual database 2-4
Conceptual scheme 3-4, 6-8
Concurrency 324-359
Condition box 158
Conjunctive query 233-238
Connection graph 226-232
Consistency constraint 2
    See also Integrity
Constraint table 310
Containment, of queries 234
Cover, of a set of dependencies 177-179
Crash protection 2, 351-356
Currency pointer 248-249, 257, 278
Current parent 280-281

D

DAG protocol 358-359
Dangling pointer 21
Database administrator 7
Database description 271-275, 287-290
Database key 247, 251-252
Database management system 1
Database record 273, 292
Database scheme 75
Data Base Task Group
    See DBTG proposal
Data definition language 4, 6-8, 243-244, 272
Data dependency 166-168
Data independence 9
Data item 241
Data manipulation language 8-9, 99-100, 104-165, 251-263, 306
    See also DL/I, ISBL, QUEL, Query-by-Example, SEQUEL, SQUARE
Data model 17
    See also Entity-relationship model, Hierarchical model, Network model, Relational model
Date, C. J. 304
Dayal, U. 208
DBD
    See Database definition
DBMS
    See Database management system
DBTG proposal 241-270, 312
DBTG set 242-243, 247, 249, 253-256, 258-260, 265-266, 291-292
DDL
    See Data definition language
Deadlock 328-329
Decomposition, of queries 223-232
Decomposition, of relation schemes 180-196, 203-205
Decomposition rule 173, 200
Defined trigger 308-309
Deletion 26-27, 35-36, 39, 46, 58, 81, 89-90, 134, 143, 156, 260-261, 263, 282-283, 295-296, 298
Deletion anomaly
    See Anomaly
Deletion bit 23, 25, 295
Dell'Orco, P. 165
Delobel, C. 208-209
Demers, A. 209
DeMillo, R. A. 322
DeMorgan's laws 159-160
Denning, D. E. 322-323
Denning, P. J. 322, 359
Dense index 49-51, 140
Dependency basis 201-202
Dependency preservation 185-186, 193-196
Dissection 228-232
DL/I 277-285
DML
    See Data manipulation language
Dobkin, D. P. 322
Domain 11, 73, 159

Domain calculus 116-122, 149, 151
Domain variable 116
Douque, B. C. M. 19
Duplicate tuples 135, 144

E

Ellis, C. S. 358
Embedded dependency 205-206
Entity 11
Entity-relationship diagram 16-17, 83-84
Entity-relationship model 10-17, 22, 75-76
Epstein, R. 359
Equijoin 108
Equivalence, of dependencies 177
Equivalence, of expressions 215
Equivalence, of queries 234
Equivalence, of schedules 330, 337, 340-341
Error-status word 253
Eswaran, K. P. 358

F

Fagin, R. 200, 208-209, 322
False drop 62
File 20
Final transaction 341
FIND 251-257
First normal form 187
Folding 235-238
Ford, J. 164
Forest 91
Fourth normal form 203-205
Free occurrence of a variable 110-111, 116
Free variable 132
    See also Free occurrence of a variable
Full family of dependencies 170
Fully concatenated key 277
Functional dependency 167-196, 198-199, 201-202, 205
Furtado, A. L. 165

G

Gallaire, H. 164
Garbage collection 23
Garcia-Molina, H. 359
Garey, M. R. 72
Generalization 165
GET 278-281
Goodman, N. 210, 359
Gotlieb, C. C. 71-72
Gotlieb, L. R. 71, 240
Gray, J. N. 358-359
Greenblatt, D. 164
Griffiths, P. 240, 322

H

Hagihara, K. 209
Hall, P. A. V. 240
Hammer, M. M. 164
Haq. M. I. 322
Harel, D. 164
Hash function 24
    See also Partitioned hash function
Hashing 24-30, 51, 149, 298
HDAM 298-299
Heap 23, 149
Held, G. 72, 164
HIDAM 296-298
Hierarchical model 5, 91-100, 271, 347
Hierarchical pointer 296-300
Hierarchy 91
HISAM 293-296
Hoffman, L. J. 322
Hopcroft, J. E. 72
Horowitz, E. 71
Host language 8
Howard, J. H. 200, 208-209
HSAM 293
Hsiao, D. K. 322
Hyperedge 226

I

Identification, of user 310
IDMS 270
IMS 271-304, 306, 312
Independence of operators 163
Index

See Dense index, Secondary index, Sparse index
Information System Base language
See ISBL
INGRES 148-149, 322
Initial transaction 341
Insertion 26, 34-35, 39, 46, 58, 81, 89-90, 133-134, 156-157, 258-261, 281-282, 295-296, 298
Insertion anomaly
See Anomaly
Instantiation 228-232
Integrity 2, 168, 305-309, 322-323
Intepreter 1
Interrupt 306
Intersection 107
Intersection data 288
Inverted file 59
See also Secondary index
isa 12
Isam
See Sparse index
ISAM/OSAM 295
ISBL 125-130, 240, 311
Itai, A. 72
Item 325
Ito, M. 209

J

Jacobs, B. E. 164
Johnson, D. S. 72
Join 108-109, 138, 213, 215-216, 225-226
Jones, A. K. 322
Journal 353-356

K

Kam, J. B. 322
Kambayashi, Y. 209
Kasami, T. 209
Kedem, Z. 358-359
Kernighan, B. W. 164
Kerr, D. S. 322
Kerschberg, L. 19
Key 11, 22, 24, 57, 157, 159, 171, 189, 307
King, M. 165

King, W. F. 164
Klug, A. 18-19
Knuth, D. E. 23, 71-72
Kreps, P. 164
Kuhns, J. L. 164
Kung, H. T. 359

L

Lacroix, M. 165
Lewis, P. M. 359
Lewis, T. G. 72
Lexicographic order 30
Lien, Y. E. 358
Linear query 315-320
Linear search 32
Ling, H. 72
Ling, T. W. 208
Link 83-84, 87-88, 141
Lipski, W. 165
Lipton, R. J. 322
LISP 100
Liu, L. 209
Livelock 327
Location mode 247, 264-265
Lochovsky, F. H. 19, 270, 304
Lock 325-327, 331
Lock manager 325
Log
See Journal
Logical child 286
Logical database 272, 285-292
Logical data independence 10
Logical file 52
Logical implication of dependencies 170, 173-174, 199-200
Logical parent 286
Logical record format 83
Logical record type 83, 91, 241, 253, 271
Lookup 20, 25-26, 34, 39, 44, 81
Lorie, R. A. 240, 358-359
Lossless join 180-185, 195-196, 202-203
Lozano, T. 72
Lucchesi, C. L. 210
Lum, V. 72

M

Madnick, S. E. 322
Maier, D. 209
Many-many relationship 13, 92-93, 290-291
Many-one relationship 13, 83
    See also Link
Mapping 131, 136, 233
Martin, J. 71
Maurer, W. D. 72
McCreight, E. M. 72
Member, of a DBTG set 242
Menasce, D. A. 359
Mendelzon, A. O. 208-209
Merlin, P. M. 240
Miller, W. F. 322
Minimal cover 178-179
Minker, J. 164, 240
Modification 26, 34, 39, 45, 81, 89, 134-135, 157, 262, 283
Morris, R. 72
Mresse, M. 322
Multilevel index 42-43
Multilist 87, 90
Multivalued dependency 196-206
Muntz, R. R. 359
Mutual dependency 209

N

Natural join 108-109, 180
Natural language query 165
Navigation 82, 250-251
Network 83, 91
Network model 4-5, 83-91, 241
Nicolas, J. M. 209
Nijssen, G. M. 18-19
Nonprime attribute 187
Normal form
    See Boyce-Codd normal form, Fourth normal form, Third normal form
NP-completeness 72, 208, 210, 238, 343
Null pointer 24
Null value 133, 165

O

Offset 21
Olle, T. W. 270
ON condition 268, 306
One-one relationship 13
Optimization 211-240
Osborn, S. L. 208, 210
Overflow block 293, 298
Owner, of a DBTG set 242

P

Palermo, F. P. 240
Papadimitriou, C. H. 343, 358-359
Paredaens, J. 164
Partial dependency 187
Partial match retrieval 60-69
Partitioned hash function 62-69
Password 310
PCB
    See Program communication block
Pecherer, R. M. 240
Perl, Y. 72
Peterlee relational Test Vehicle
    See PRTV
Physical block 20-21
    See also Block
Physical database 2-4, 271
Physical data independence 9
Physical scheme 3-4, 7-8
Pinkert, J. R. 209
Pinned record 23, 38-42, 51
Pirotte, A. 164-165
PL/I 100, 130, 139, 277, 284
Pointer 21-23, 286, 293
Polygraph 343
Popek, G. J. 359
Precedence graph 333
Preorder 96-97
Preorder thread 296
    See also Hierarchical pointer
Price, T. G. 240
Primary block 293, 298
Prime attribute 187
Processing option 275-276
Program communication block 274-277
Program specification block 275

Projection 105-106, 112, 214, 216-219
Project-join mapping 181
Protection
    See Security
Protocol 331
PRTV 125, 130
Pseudotransitivity 173, 200
Putzolo, F. 359

Q

QBE
    See Query-by-Example
Quantifier 111
QUEL 141-149, 223-233
Query 81-82, 90
Query-by-Example 149-161, 307-310, 312-314
Query language
    See Data manipulation language
Quotient 107-108

R

Rational function 320
Read-lock 337, 340
Read-only view 311-312
Record 20
Record format 20
Redundancy 167
Reflexivity 172, 198
Regular expression 53
Reis, D. R. 359
Reiss, S. P. 322
Relation 73-75
Relational algebra 104-109, 114-116, 118-125, 163, 214-223
Relational calculus 110
    See also Domain calculus, Tuple calculus
Relational database 75
Relational model 5, 73-82, 98-100, 104-240
Relational read/write file 130
Relation scheme 75, 83, 168-169
Relationship 12-13
Relationship set 12
Reserved space 55
Retention class 265-266

Rights, of access 311
Rissanen, J. 208-209
Rivest, R. L. 72
Roberts, C. S. 72
Rosenkrantz, D. J. 359
Rothnie, J. B. 72, 343, 358-359
Roussopoulos, N. 165
Rubinstein, P. 164, 322
Run-unit 249
Rustin, R. 103

S

Sadri, F. 209
Safe expression 112-114, 116-117
Safe formula 143
Sagiv, Y. 208-209, 240
Sahni, S. 71
Schedule 329
Scheduler 331
Schenk, K. L. 209
Schlorer, J. 322
Schmidt, H. A. 165
Schwartz, M. D. 322
Sciore, E. 165
Search key 268
Secondary index 58-62, 149, 159, 212-213, 268, 299
Secondary storage 20-21
Second normal form 187
Security 2, 7, 268, 305, 310-323, 352
Segment 271
Segment search argument 284
Selection 106, 112, 213-214, 217, 219
Select-project-join expression 124
Semantics 165
Sensitive segment 275
SEQUEL 136-139, 233, 240
Serializability 251, 329-330, 332-339, 342-346, 348, 358
Serial schedule 329
Set
    See DBTG set
Set difference 105, 112, 143, 217-218
SETL 100
Set mode 265
Set occurrence 242, 253-256, 266-267
Set selection 247-248, 258-260
Shipman, D. W. 359

Shkolnick, M. 72, 358
Sibley, E. 103
Silberschatz, A. 358-359
Singular set 255
Smith, D. C. P. 165
Smith, J. M. 165, 240
SNOBOL 100
Snyder, L. 72
Sorting 30, 213, 267
Sound inference rule 172
Spadavecchio, V. N. 165
Sparse index 30-42, 51, 149, 293
Speed
    See Time complexity
SQUARE 131-136, 233
Statistical database 305, 314-323
Stearns, R. E. 359
Stonebraker, M. 72, 164, 322, 359
STORE 258
Subblock 25
Subscheme
    See View
Subscheme data definition language 7-8
Superkey 171
Swenson, J. R. 165
Synchronization 2
    See also Concurrency
System 2000 304
System R 139-141, 312

T

Table directory 158
Table skeleton 149-150
Tanaka, K. 209
Taniguchi, K. 209
Third normal form 187-188, 193-196
Thomas, R. H. 359
Time complexity 29-30, 48-49, 51, 225, 301
    See also 21
Todd, S. J. P. 164
Tompa, F. 208
Tompa, F. W. 72
TOTAL 270
Traiger, I. L. 358-359
Transaction 325
Transitive closure 163-164

Transitive dependency 187
Transitivity 172, 198
Tree protocol 347
Tsichritzis, D. C. 18-19, 270, 304
Tuple 74, 83
Tuple calculus 110-118, 132, 141
Tuple identifier 140
Tuple variable 110
Two-phase commit 354
Two-phase protocol 335-336, 340, 346-347

U

Ullman, J. D. 72, 164, 208-209, 240, 322
Union 105, 111, 143-144, 217-218
Union rule 173, 200
Unpinned record 23, 33-37
Update anomaly
    See Anomaly
Useless transaction 342
User working area 248

V

VanLeeuwen, J. 322
Variable length record 20, 52-60, 96
Variable length record format 53
Vassilou, Y. 165
View 5-9, 126, 160-161, 248, 311-312
Virtual logical record type 91-92
VSAM 295

W

Wade, B. W. 322
Warning protocol 350
Waxman, J. 164
Weiderhold, G. 270
Weinberger, P. J. 164, 358
Whyte, N. 164
Wong, E. 164, 240, 322, 359
Write-lock 337, 340

Y

Yajima, S. 209
Yannakakis, M. 240, 359
Yao, A. C. 72, 322
Yao, F. F. 72

Yao, S. B. 240
Youssefi, K. 164, 240
Yu, C. T. 323

Z

Zaniolo, C. 165, 209
Zloof, M. M. 164, 322
Zook, W. 164